D0838972

JÉRÔME LEJEUNE

AUDE DUGAST

Jérôme Lejeune

A Man of Science and Conscience

Translated by Michael J. Miller

IGNATIUS PRESS SAN FRANCISCO

Original French edition:
Jérôme Lejeune: La liberté du savant

Cover photograph of Jérôme Lejeune courtesy of Aude Dugast

Cover design by Enrique J. Aguilar

ISBN 978-1-62164-411-8 (PB)
ISBN 978-1-64229-173-5 (eBook)
Library of Congress Control Number 2021936845
Printed in the United States of America ♾

Dedicated to the seven hopes of Mary.

To Pedro, whose angelic smile is a reflection of heaven, and to all the patients of Jérôme Lejeune and their families.

To those who love truth.

No one can be a friend of mankind
unless he is first a friend of truth.

—*Augustine of Hippo*

CONTENTS

AUTHOR'S NOTE

In this book, most of the words of Jérôme Lejeune are quotations.

All sentences printed as indented block citations are quotations; in each case, the author is indicated in a reference.

The short quotations included in the narrative or in a dialogue are referenced simply by a footnote.

When there is a series of excerpts from the same text, the reference is given for the final quotation.

Dialogues without a reference still come from real situations.

CHAPTER 1

THE WINGS OF FRIENDSHIP

1997

The treetops get closer; the pilot reduces his speed again and turns gently to face the wind and to prepare for the landing.

"This grassy quadrangle is large enough to accommodate our four helicopters easily", he observes. "There is no question of taking the slightest risk."

A shiver runs through him as he thinks of what would happen if he made a wrong maneuver.

In the back of the aircraft, its hull gleaming beneath the August sun, the Holy Father, John Paul II, is delighted. He has finally arrived here, in this little village of Chalo-Saint-Mars, for a moment of meditation at the tomb of his "brother Jérôme". All has not been easy. The program of those magnificent 1997 World Youth Days in Paris left him without a moment of respite. What a joy, nevertheless, to see those hundreds of thousands of young people gathered. Those beautiful, luminous faces, those young hearts and their thirst for challenging demands, beauty, and greatness. After that intense spiritual week, the hardest thing for them will be to keep living in a heart-to-heart dialogue with Jesus, not to give in to the pressures of the world, to continue "to be in the world without being of the world", but now they know that they are not alone. They are the new generation of Christians from France and from all over the world. The young universal Church.

The helicopter lands gently. The pope remembers with emotion his sadness three years earlier, at the announcement of the death of his friend Jérôme on April 3, 1994. Easter morning. With his head in his hands, he had exclaimed then: "My God, I needed him so much!" The next day, he sent to Cardinal Lustiger, archbishop of Paris, a letter of tribute in which he expressed his gratitude for the charism of Professor Jérôme Lejeune. Each one of the words that he carefully chose that day remains engraved on his heart:

> "I am the resurrection and the life; he who believes in me, though he die, yet shall he live" (Jn 11:25).
>
> These words of Christ come to mind when we find ourselves faced with the death of Professor Jérôme Lejeune. If the Father who is in heaven called him from this earth on the very day of Christ's Resurrection, it is difficult not to see in this coincidence a sign. The Resurrection of Christ stands as a great testimonial to the fact that life is stronger than death. Enlightened by these words of the Lord, we see the death of every human person as a participation in the death of Christ and in his Resurrection, especially when a death occurs on the very day of the Resurrection. Such a death gives an even stronger testimony to the life to which man is called in Jesus Christ. Throughout the life of our brother Jérôme, this call was a guiding force. In his capacity as a learned biologist, he was passionately interested in life. In his field, he was one of the greatest authorities in the world. Various organizations invited him to give lectures and consulted him for his advice. He was respected even by those who did not share his deepest convictions.
>
> We wish today to thank the Creator, "of whom all paternity in heaven and earth is named" [Eph 3:15 (Douay-Rheims)], for the particular charism of the deceased. One must speak here of a charism, because Professor Lejeune was always able to employ his profound knowledge of life and of its secrets for the true good of man and of humanity, and only for that purpose. He became one of the ardent defenders of life, especially of the life of preborn children, which, in our contemporary civilization, is often endangered to such an extent that one could think the danger to be by design. Today, this danger extends equally to elderly and sick persons. Human tribunals and democratically elected parliaments usurp the right to determine who has the right to live and, conversely, who could find that this right has been denied him through no fault of his own. In different ways, our century has experimented with such an attitude, above all during the Second World War, yet also after the end of the war. Professor Jérôme Lejeune assumed the full responsibility that was his as a scientist, and he was ready to become a "sign of contradiction", regardless of the pressures exerted by a permissive society or of the ostracism that he underwent.

We are faced today with the death of a great Christian of the twentieth century, of a man for whom the defense of life became an apostolate. It is clear that, in the present world situation, this form of lay apostolate is particularly necessary. We want to thank God today—He who is the Author of life—for everything that Professor Lejeune has been for us, for everything that he did to defend and to promote the dignity of human life. In particular, I would like to thank him for having taken the initiative in the creation of the Pontifical Academy pro Vita [for Life]. A longtime member of the Pontifical Academy of Sciences, Professor Lejeune made all the necessary preparations for this new foundation, and he became its first president. We are sure that henceforth he will pray to the Divine Wisdom for this institution, which is so important and which in large measure owes him its existence.

Christ said, "I am the resurrection and the life. He who believes in me, though he die, yet shall he live." We believe that these words have been accomplished in the life and in the death of our brother Jérôme. May the truth about life be also a source of spiritual strength for the family of the deceased, for the Church in France, and for all of us, to whom Professor Lejeune has left the truly brilliant witness of his life as a man and as a Christian.

In prayer, I unite myself with all those who participate in the funeral, and I impart to all, through the mediation of the cardinal-archbishop of Paris, my apostolic blessing.[1]

The helicopter blades stop. Escorted by his close collaborators and by several bishops, the Holy Father is soon walking at a slow, determined pace through the woods that border the cemetery where Jérôme's family is waiting for him. Overhanging the pretty valley of the Chalouette River, the cemetery of Chalot is at the gates of heaven. From the hollow of the valley, the steeple of the parish church rises to the height of the tombs clinging to that shining hill, showing them Paradise within arm's reach. From the moment you enter, the peace of that space hovering between earth and heaven captivates you.

The Holy Father notices the professor's wife, surrounded by her many children and grandchildren. They all crowd respectfully to welcome him. The civil authorities insisted that this be a very private visit. Only the family, the aged pastor of the village, a nun with Down syndrome, Marie-Ange, a young patient of Jérôme, Clément,

[1] John Paul II, letter to Cardinal Lustiger, April 4, 1994.

and a friend from the Center for Hope,[2] Roland, were authorized to come pray here with him. And so many gendarmes and policemen.... There are more of them than there are trees encircling the cemetery! In the distance, the crowd of friends who would have liked to pray with the Holy Father at the grave of Jérôme is held back by security barriers and cordons. All that they would see of the pope that day would be his helicopter.

John Paul II kneels before his friend's grave, which is decorated with yellow and white flowers, the colors of the Vatican—a thoughtful touch by Madame Lejeune—and contemplates, at the foot of the cross, this block of semi-polished pink granite, planted in a bed of flowers and shrubs. Death gives way to flowering life. From the stone springs living water. This is the victory of life, the victory engraved in four gilded Greek letters, N.I.K.E. Everyone feels an indescribable sensation of peace. And of joy.

The Holy Father remains recollected in silence for a long time, then intones the *Salve Regina*: "Hail, Holy Queen, Mother of mercy! Our life, our sweetness and our hope!"

Grown-ups and little ones emotionally join their voices with that of John Paul II. For a moment of eternity. The grandchildren are incredibly well-behaved.

John Paul II stands up. With a radiant smile, he invites each one to approach, happy to meet Jérôme's family, which he knew was so dear to his heart. One by one, the parents and then the children introduce themselves, bow, embrace him, and say a few words to him. In all the emotion, the sentences that were prepared days ago jostle each other. It is necessary to improvise. The warmth of the Holy Father's expression encourages them. Finally, the little ones have their turn. Vianney, with the candor of his three years, then raises his head toward the beautiful smile in a halo of white, impatient for the opportunity to ask the question that has occupied him all morning:

"Where is your helicopter?"

[2] Centre d'aide par le travail (CAT) de l'Espérance [Hope Center for aid through work, a medical-social establishment that offers jobs for the handicapped], which is very close to the Lejeune family.

CHAPTER 2

THE ROOTS OF HEAVEN

1926–1950

On that day, June 19, 1926, the bells of the Church of Saint James the Greater in Montrouge tolled cheerfully. Saint James, with his bronze voice, announced good news to the peaceful town. From roof to roof, the notes flew away and fell like a light, joyful rain on the gardens and the houses, slipped from one street to another to invite the inhabitants of the district to the same rejoicing.

"It is Pierre Lejeune who just had his second son", a woman proudly announced to a group of men who were calmly ensconced on the chairs that they had brought out onto the pavement to take advantage of the fine summer days together.

"Pierre, the son of Louis Lejeune, our former mayor?"

"Yes, he is the one", she confirmed, before adding a bit of gossip: "He had so much difficulty having a child, and look at him now with two sons!"

"The grandfather Lermat is the one who must be very pleased", exclaimed a man with a very thick mustache that was already white.

"Yes. By the way," the woman replied, "he, Hector Lermat, is the godfather. I think that the baby's name is Jérôme."

"And who is the godmother?"

"Ah! That I do not know", the woman said as she walked on.

A few steps away, at 51 route d'Orléans, the Lejeune family was bubbling with enthusiasm. Massa, her heavy, chestnut-brown tresses framing her pretty oval face, carefully put Jérôme into his baby carriage. Philippe, all of eighteen months old, toddled along beside her. He did not yet know that this tiny brother, whose deep-blue eyes he liked to look at, would be his playmate, confidant, and lifelong friend.

On the doorstep, Pierre-Ulysse, slender in his three-piece suit, waited patiently until his young family was finally ready. The living picture before his eyes filled him with new joy that managed to soothe his heart, which had been wounded by the very recent death of his dear father. Despite the fatigue of the childbirth, his pretty Massa—nickname for Marguerite Marcelle, who was very musical, cultured, and also quite competent—seemed so happy today. Pierre savored this moment all the more since they had experienced many trials since their engagement. First the war, which forced them a few months after their marriage to endure a long separation while he did military service. Then ten long years of sterility. Until the day when, finally, Massa had announced the wonderful news to him: God had answered their prayers; she was expecting a child! And now this second son.

"A week already since Jérôme was born", Pierre thought, counting the days since that beautiful June 13. "How good God is!"

Although Pierre was a Third Order Franciscan, attracted by a simple life with few possessions and eager to help the poor people in the parish, Massa and he did not choose the name of the little friar of Assisi for their boys. The name of their second son was Jean-Louis-Marie-Jérôme, and, according to an old tradition, they put the usual first name, Jérôme, in last place. Between John, Christ's favorite disciple, Mary, the tender Mother of the Child Jesus, and Jerome, the Doctor of the Church, their son would be well protected and advised.

On the church steps, the priest performed the last ritual gestures of the exorcism and of the invocation of the Spirit of God upon the child in a respectful silence. Even Philippe held his breath. Then the main door of the church opened wide, and, following the priest, who had placed a corner of his stole on the infant as a sign of fatherly protection, everyone entered into the subdued light that bathed the baptistry. Delicately holding her little godson in her arms, Aunt Charlotte Lejeune, née Clacquesin, proudly presented him to the celebrant. The priest then poured the baptismal water on the infant's forehead:

"Jean-Louis-Marie-Jérôme, I baptize you in the name of the Father, and of the Son, and of the Holy Spirit."

Cleansed of original sin, Jérôme became a child of God. He was now a priest, prophet, and king. "May he remain faithful to this extraordinary grace throughout his life." This was the intense prayer of Pierre and Massa at that moving moment.

With brown, curly hair and rosy cheeks from living in the fresh air, Jérôme took his first steps in the house in Montrouge, at the gates of Paris. Fox hunting was no longer a sport there, and the urbanization of the suburbs nibbled away at the extent of the produce farms each year, but the little town remained pastoral, and every morning the Lejeunes went to buy milk and fresh butter in the neighboring cowsheds, the last vestiges of country life. Jérôme, together with his brother, Philippe, whom he never left for a second, developed a fertile imagination while playing with the many backyard animals and the teams of horses used for business deliveries. Finally, the two boys had to take only a few steps to 84 route d'Orléans in order to dive into a world of noises, smells, and fire, where incandescent metal was bent and twisted, then rounded in regular lines under the hammer blows of their grandfather Hector, a magician with fire. A veterinarian and blacksmith, Hector Lermat was for his grandsons an unconventional, funny grandfather, and his inexhaustible inventions fascinated them. Massa no doubt got from her father this original, nimble cast of mind that had charmed Pierre, and Jérôme, whom everyone called Néno, adored his grandfather.

Often on Sunday, after Mass, they ate brunch at the home of Massa's parents, then went for a walk at the Jardin des Plantes [the Paris botanical gardens]. There the children could run around and admire the exotic animals. Jérôme, endowed with a curious mind, was thrilled to watch the monkeys, and his big blue eyes, round as saucers, would grow even bigger at that enchanting spectacle:

"Oh, look! What funny faces they make! It seems that they are imitating us."

He would always have a very lively interest in zoological gardens, which he would visit as often as possible in his travels around the world, and in that strange animal species that was so close and yet so far.

Another walk that Néno loved to take was the one that led to the carrefour d'Alésia [a marketplace]; reigning there as undisputed master was a big pink pig, whose chubby appearance delighted him. Néno never tired of asking his mother to tell him what the little girl in the red dress and scarf was saying to the attentive pig. And Massa, laughing, reread the sign over Noblet's butcher shop: "Don't cry, big beast, you are going to Noblet's!" Truly a title of nobility in return for a fine career as a pig; the sales promotion announced quality meat. People came from far and wide to buy their pig from Noblet. This consoling advertisement was also the subject of a thousand philosophical thoughts for the regular customers at the Café Biard and the Rouet Inn across the street from the shop, who looked with compassion at the little boy rooted to the spot in front of the sign.

Pierre had many obligations connected with the distillery inherited from his father and with the Industrial and Commercial Bank of the region south of Paris, created in 1922 for the needs of local businesses; when they left him some leisure time, he would gladly take his sons for a walk, discovering that he had an unsuspected paternal instinct. In the spring of 1931, Paris hosted the International Colonial Exposition, and he saw in this a good opportunity to travel far, to the gates of the capital.

"Boys, tomorrow, after school, at four-thirty, your mother and I will come to collect you with the car, and we will go to the Vincennes Wood to see the Colonial Exposition. It takes just a moment to climb into the Ford, and twenty minutes later, we will be there!" Pierre added, delighted in advance with the rapidity of the trip by automobile.

As soon as they entered the exposition grounds, the variety of the pavilions enchanted the family. A fascinating temple from Angkor (Cambodia) stood a few strides away from a lacy palace dreamed up by a Maharaja. Pierre almost expected to see a Bandar-Log [a monkey from Rudyard Kipling's *The Jungle Book*] leap out of one building or another and then to flee screaming from tree to tree toward the Porte Dorée. The Orient bewitched them again with the refinement of the Japanese pavilion, a masterpiece of delicacy, whereas the boys shouted for joy at the ochre-colored battlements of a Mandinka [West African] defending wall.

"Come on, Néno, let's go!" exclaimed Philippe, enchanted. "Let's try to get into the fort!" he proposed, already running toward the great wooden gate, with Néno at his heels.

On weekdays, the children went to Saint Joan of Arc School, a small institution for girls near their house, run by religious Sisters, which accepted boys until the age of six years. There Néno displayed an easy-going character, under the protective eye of his big brother. He was bright, cheerful, and rather well-behaved, but he was also stubborn, and, while his mother complained about it sometimes, his father saw in this the mark of a well-tempered soul and understood that it was up to him to direct this tenacity toward positive objectives. Deeply religious, Jérôme's parents taught him to love God and the Church, and every day, until they entered the *collège* [in this case, a primary school], the children said evening prayer with their father or their mother, kneeling in front of the crucifix. Massa taught them to say with faith, "I am Roman Catholic", and this identity seemed to them as natural as being French.

Every year, at the beginning of summer, the boys would wait impatiently for the great pandemonium of leaving for the seaside. Whether it was to Normandy, Brittany, or Royan, where their maternal grandparents, the Lermats, had a summer house, the family would go to a place where the children could breathe fresh, salty air. The suitcases piled up, packed by Massa, the boss lady, while the boys ran all around:

"My hat, I forgot my hat!"

"And I forgot my ball! But where is my ball? Mama?!"

Those vacations at the beach were a waking dream. They spent hours playing in the waves or building sand castles, alone or with the countless children from the neighboring houses.

At the start of the new school year in the autumn of 1932, since Montrouge was becoming increasingly urban, Pierre decided to buy a house with a garden in Étampes, which elicited shouts of enthusiasm from the children and delighted Massa. No more need to wait to summer to enjoy the games offered by nature. The garden would serve as a tremendous place for adventures and inventions. That year, while the children were taking possession of their kingdom by exploring every thicket, Massa sat peacefully on a bench to sun her face in the light of the beautiful September days. She felt weary because she was expecting a child and was in her ninth month. Several days later, on October 7, 1932, she brought into the world a handsome boy, Rémy, their third son. Alas, the childbirth went very badly, and Pierre feared that his wife was going to lose her life. Several long, crucial hours passed, and a blood transfusion was what saved the woman in labor. Tragedy was avoided, but Pierre realized that happiness in a family is very fragile and that each day must be savored.

With the arrival of a little brother, Néno became one of the big boys. But he had to wait for the start of the school year in 1933 and his seventh birthday to leave the school of the Sisters in Montrouge and to embark on his studies at the Collège Stanislas in Paris, with his brother Philippe. His heart filled with pride mixed with apprehension, Néno was leaving the security of the family cocoon for the first time. "Fortunately, Philippe is there", he thought with relief along the journey that led him to his new life. Every morning, while driving his sons to school, Pierre would teach them Latin and Greek and recited for them *The Odyssey* and Aesop's fables. These contained many lessons about human nature; "The Wolf and the Lamb", for example:

> Once upon a time a Wolf was lapping at a spring on a hillside when, looking up, what should he see but a Lamb just beginning to drink a little lower down. "There's my supper," thought he, "if only I can find some excuse to seize it." Then he called out to the Lamb, "How dare you muddle the water from which I am drinking?"
>
> "Nay, master, nay," said Lambikin; "if the water be muddy up there, I cannot be the cause of it, for it runs down from you to me."
>
> "Well, then," said the Wolf, "why did you call me bad names this time last year?"
>
> "That cannot be," said the Lamb; "I am only six months old."
>
> "I don't care," snarled the Wolf; "if it was not you it was your father." And with that he rushed upon the poor little Lamb and ate her all up.[1]

Jérôme listened, slightly disturbed. "But Papa, that is unfair! The lamb is innocent!"

"Yes, that is true", Pierre replied. "But be assured, in human society there is a system of justice that protects the weak from the strong."

At Stanislas, where the discipline was firm, the academic standard high, and the piety conventional, Jérôme settled into the mold without too much difficulty. Unlike his brother, whose grades were very good, at least at the start, he was not a distinguished scholar and gave the impression of being slow, which earned him a reputation for laziness. However, despite these modest appearances, he was always in

[1] Aesop, "The Wolf and the Lamb", in *Fables*, Harvard Classics, vol. 17, pt. 1, retold by Joseph Jacobs (New York: Collier, 1909–1914).

the top third of his class in all subjects. Massa, who had eyes only for her older son, Philippe, was surprised, therefore, when the instructors congratulated her on the grades of her son Jérôme. Poor Massa was all the more disappointed about her older son because another Philippe Lejeune wore out his trousers on the benches in Jérôme's class, and he was the one who took all the prizes each year. This Philippe Lejeune would become Vice Admiral of the French fleet and a man of great merit, and, although not a member of Jérôme's family, would remain a close and faithful friend.[2]

Pierre, for his part, assigned little value to grades and scholarly awards, but was interested in the quality of the teaching received and wanted his sons to nourish their intellect with the beauty of truth and the search for it, in all its variations. Therefore, he made sure that the teaching that they were receiving allowed them to discover classical culture: French, Latin, and Greek literature and philosophy, with its wealth of teachings.

"You know, Philippe, Greek myths are perpetually being played out again by men. You think that you are learning a story from the past, but you will soon discover that nothing is more relevant today than the quest of these heroes of antiquity. The heart of man has not changed over the centuries. He still dreams of being Icarus or Prometheus. And the same causes are followed by the same effects."

Loved by his family and backed up by his big brother, Jérôme quickly made friends with his schoolmates and liked the good Fathers who taught at Stanislas. He was very impressed by one of them, Father Balsan, who taught him to relish Latin to the point of achieving fluency in it. Years later, when he took his baccalaureate exams, this earned him an admiring comment from the examiner: "You read Cicero the way people read the newspaper."

Jérôme was impressed above all by Father Balsan's love for God. His clear views, always well-grounded but open toward heaven, left a mark on his spiritual life.

> "The important thing, boys, is to learn to love God!" "Love God!"
> "Don't give up anything, the Blessed Virgin, the rosary, that is what

[2] Admiral Philippe Lejeune would become the first president of the Medical Center created by the Jérôme Lejeune Foundation upon Jérôme's death in order to continue his work of caring for mentally handicapped persons and conducting research on their behalf.

will make a man of you. Set Marxism aside: small beer that has no depth; it sees only tomorrow but not eternity. It is too narrow-minded for people to keep talking about it."[3]

In 1936, Jérôme pursued his studies diligently at the Collège Stanislas, a thousand miles away from the worries of adults, and did not see that the political situation in France was deteriorating and that social tensions were becoming more pronounced. The elections in May 1936, which brought the Popular Front into power, created agitation in the Lejeune family. Although Pierre and Massa thought that the political rise of the Reds portended major troubles, they hoped that the staff of the family distillery would escape the new wind of union demands. But on the morning of June 9, when Pierre was getting ready to go take breakfast with his children, an employee appeared in his office and told him:

"Monsieur Lejeune, my comrades are waiting for you in the courtyard. They are not dressed for work, because they refuse to report to their posts."

After eating a quick bowl of "soup",[4] Pierre discovered all his employees in the courtyard and observed them. He noticed that not one of them seemed upset or disturbed, because they seemed to be obeying an order from somewhere else. Pierre made no speech but asked: "What do you want?"

"We want a raise of 10 to 15 percent", the boldest or the most demanding of them replied.

"Let each one, individually, tell me what he wants", Pierre replied, taking up his pen.

One by one, the employees called out a number, which Pierre wrote down meticulously. Then he told them:

"The Employers' Association of the distillers meets this afternoon at five o'clock. I will convey your demand to my colleagues. If we want to keep up with the competition, it is absolutely necessary for my colleagues to pay the same salaries. Do you understand?"

"Yes."

"Will you go to work while waiting for the decision?"

[3] J. Lejeune, *Hommage à l'abbé Balsan*, December 26, 1967.

[4] Pierre Lejeune in fact speaks about *potage* [soup] when he describes this scene in his *Journal*.

"Yes, we are willing to go back to work", they answered.

Pierre left them then in order to drive his sons to school, before making a tour at the shop and in the storehouses. A female employee took the opportunity to ask to be appointed head of the shop with a corresponding increase in salary. Pierre pointed out to her that that was not possible because she was no one's boss, working alone in her area, without organizing the work of any other employee. The woman hastily beat a retreat, admitting without actually saying so that the demand was not her own idea.

At five o'clock that afternoon, Pierre met with his colleagues of the Employers' Association. Some of them had all their personnel on strike. The debates were turbulent, but they finally reached an agreement to raise the salaries by between 7 to 12 percent. In the days that followed, events calmed down and everyone went back to work. But Pierre was still worried about the future, because he clearly saw some union representatives admonish the recalcitrant workers severely, and he noted that the latter immediately obeyed submissively. What they would never take from any boss, they accepted in fear and trembling from their union representative, and Pierre had a foreboding that this revolutionary discipline heralded future days of disillusionment. As for the children, they were still astonished to see that their friends of yesterday, usually so nice, had turned into anti-establishmentarians, but even more than that, they were impressed by the firmness of their father, who looked for a fair solution while remaining calm and courteous. Jérôme, all of ten years old, understood from his father's example that firmness commands respect and that a policy is judged in action.

One year later, on May 6, 1937, Jérôme made his First Holy Communion and received the Sacrament of Confirmation in the school chapel. He was about to turn eleven and was preparing to enter the sixth class. His teachers liked his seriousness, and his classmates—his liveliness and cheerfulness. Although naturally kind, he could not be manipulated, because from his grandfather Lejeune, a shrewd politician and businessman, he had the perspicacity to thwart the traps that were set along his path. During his years at the school, Jérôme devoured the novels of Jules Verne, which immersed him in a fantastic, hitherto unknown scientific universe, and with Philippe he enthusiastically spent hours building scale models of airplanes, while adhering to the laws of aerodynamics.[5] He also liked to swim, walk, and tour the countryside by bicycle, always with Philippe, and to enjoy the beauty of nature that surrounded them. Those were the days when, like many children his age, he dreamed of becoming an admiral or a fireman.[6]

The 1938–1939 school year followed its normal course, despite the annexation of the Sudetenland by Hitler, but that summer the family prudently remained in Étampes, where on September 1 they heard the news that war had been declared. After a lightning-fast trip to Montrouge, where they discovered that their horses and delivery wagons had been requisitioned, they returned to Étampes, hoping to find more safety in the old, humid house than at the gates of Paris, where night-time air raids repeatedly sent the frightened populace into makeshift shelters.

When the war began, Pierre made an important decision, which he announced to Philippe and Jérôme a few days before the start of the new school year: "My boys, you will not go to the Collège Stanislas this year; it is too dangerous. Nor to the school in Étampes, which is totally disorganized because of the war."

Philippe and Jérôme looked at each other, dumbfounded; then Philippe asked incredulously, "Do you mean that we will not go to school? Not at all? For the whole year?"

With a smile, Pierre answered: "Indeed, you will not go to school, but that does not mean that you are going to twiddle your thumbs. You will study at home. For you, Jérôme, who are going into the fourth class, and for you, Philippe, in the third class, a year of reading the classics will ensure a good formation: Latin, Greek, and French literature, with complementary private courses in mathematics and science. You can have the run of the library. You will find treasures in it. Livy, Homer, Racine, Shakespeare, Bernanos, Bergson ... Just choose whatever you wish. And if you do not know where to begin, ask me."

Jérôme threw himself into a frenzy of reading, including authors that are usually considered difficult for his age group, and made two discoveries that would leave a lasting mark on him: Pascal and Balzac.

[5] Conversation of the author with Philippe Lejeune.

[6] J. Lejeune, interview in *Radioscopie* by Jacques Chancel, December 13, 1973.

The family tradition claims that the example of Balzac's hero, Doctor Benassis, a remarkable country physician, was what gave rise to his vocation as a physician. In any case, at that time,[7] between the ages of twelve and fifteen, he started to take a close interest in biology, and this interest quickly led him to the field of medicine. Besides the unexpected freedom that Philippe and Jérôme relished during that period, they discovered an unsuspected joy in reading great authors, who broadened the horizons of their hearts and minds. Despite the war, that year would remain one of the most pleasant in their lives.

And yet they saw the war up close. In the spring of 1940, perched on the garden wall, Philippe and Jérôme, trembling with emotion, witnessed the entry of the Germans into Étampes. It was humiliating for the two young Frenchmen to see the occupying force arrive calmly, on bicycles ...[8] A few days later, there was a knock at the door. Massa went to open it, and the boys were surprised to hear a thick German accent: "*Guten Abend.* We have orders to requisition two rooms in your house. To quarter the senior medical officer. Can we come in?"

Without a word, after a moment of hesitation, Massa turned on her heels and gave them a sign to follow her. Did she have any choice?

The war went on, and at the start of the next school year, Pierre enrolled his children in the *lycée* in Étampes. Although it was difficult for the boys to go back to a compulsory curriculum and grading system after the extraordinary freedom of their home schooling, they had the joy of making good friends. Those were also the days when Jérôme and Philippe devoted themselves enthusiastically to the theater and formed a troupe, the Companions of Saint Genest, offering in their repertoire *The Bourgeois Gentleman, The Imaginary Invalid* [both by Molière], *Fantasio* [by Offenbach], *The Taming of the Shrew, The Barber of Seville* ... Jérôme excelled in the role of [the Countess] Almaviva [from *The Marriage of Figaro*],[9] Philippe valiantly built and decorated the sets, and, becoming more confident with their growing success, they soon courageously explored the tragedies of Corneille and Racine:

[7] Ibid.

[8] A. Bernet, *Jérôme Lejeune* (Paris: Presses de la Renaissance, 2004).

[9] Conversation of the author with Philippe Lejeune.

> Does God not fight for us, and show His zeal,
> who in the orphan cares for innocence,
> and at our weakness shows His strong defence?...
> Josabeth, your tears are not amiss
> though God would have us trust His care in this.
> Nor does He wrathfully oppress
> a son with his own father's sinfulness.[10]

The quality of the courses in theater and public speaking that they had taken at Stanislas, the wealth of their father's repertoire, Philip's artistic imagination for the costumes and the sets, and Jérôme's poise produced their effect. Soon the theater in Étampes welcomed a large audience, and the troupe crisscrossed the surrounding region of Beauce for performances in the little village theaters, hauling the sets and costumes in a makeshift cart.

Philippe often devoted himself to painting, and when he was seated in front of his easel, Jérôme sometimes asked him whether he could stay beside him: "I would like to see how a painting comes about."

When Philippe set down his brush a few hours later, Jérôme's response was always the same: "I didn't see anything!"[11]

There are mysterious things in the birth of a painting, and this gradual and sudden creation, which hides even from the most attentive observer the decisive moment of its conception, fascinated Jérôme. At first there are brush strokes, and then, all of a sudden, the painting is alive.

Sensing that he had no aptitude for painting, Jérôme joyfully devoted himself to tinkering, which could occupy him for an entire afternoon. Under Philippe's direction, he set out to build the simple Platonic solids, among them the dodecahedron, made out of twelve pentagons, and showed a lot of interest in manual demonstrations of theoretical scientific facts. And when the exercise was too difficult, such as the construction of the dihedral angle, the two boys did not hesitate to turn to the mathematics professor.[12] You kept busy any way you could during the war ...

[10] Jean Racine, *Athalie*, act 1, scene 2, Joad's speech. English translation by C. John Holcombe, *Athaliah* (Ocasio Press, 2011).

[11] Conversation of the author with Philippe Lejeune.

[12] Ibid.

Like all French families during those war years, the Lejeunes lived in difficult conditions. They suffered from the cold in their large, dank house, and the boys, who were growing quickly, often did not eat their fill. Massa, who before the war had complained about little everyday annoyances, bravely rose to the occasion and enthusiastically turned the flower beds into a vegetable garden. But that was not enough to make up for the meager portions allotted by the ration tickets. To make matters worse, Pierre had had to go into liquidation and sell the distillery in 1940, and the sale at a loss, in the middle of the war, aggravated their financial situation. Deep down, Pierre was not unhappy to be rid of the job of managing the distillery. He had never been interested in that work, which he performed only out of faithfulness to his father and in order to feed his family, while regretfully abandoning a legal career that was much more in keeping with his character and his study of the law. Fortunately, his duty as presiding judge at the Commercial Court in Paris allowed him to resume his professional activity, but it was meager satisfaction because—you have to face facts—this position did not occupy him full-time and did not provide a living for his family. After selling the distillery, Pierre worried and confided in Massa about it: "Now what can I do?"

He did not have much time to dwell on the question, though, because very soon, and to his great surprise, he received an invitation to take on new obligations. Since the municipal authorities of Étampes had fled, and many of the inhabitants with them, the town was looking for a capable man to assume the office of mayor, which was now vacant. The task was difficult and involved risk during the Occupation, and no one wanted to take it on—starting with Pierre, who had always been extremely cautious about politics and had no stomach for its sometimes dangerous games. Nevertheless, he was the one they came looking for. One morning, while he was discussing something with Massa, someone knocked at the door. One of the townspeople of Étampes whom the Lejeunes knew well and liked, accompanied by several men whose faces were not unknown to them, stood in front of them, hat in hand. Pierre told them to come in, and the conversation began:

"Monsieur Lejeune, everyone has gone; there is no one left at the town hall. We need you: Are you willing to assume the responsibility of mayor? It will not be easy, but no one else but you can take this job. Otherwise, we would not be here asking you to do so."

Pierre felt a vague shiver run down his spine. He did not dare to believe his ears: "But, my friends, you cannot be serious! I have always kept my distance from politics, unlike my father, who was mayor, and I am not going to start today!"

"Monsieur, reconsider, I beg of you. We are sure that you will do what is best for the people of Étampes. And that you will be able to keep the occupying forces at bay. Who else would do it?"

Pierre remained silent for a long interval, then answered: "I promise you that I will think about it. I will let you know my decision in a week."

And in fact, a few days later Pierre gave them his answer: he agreed, in order to serve his country and his town, well aware that he was not choosing an easy job during that time of the Occupation ...

1944, and still no end to the war. Jérôme was attending his final year at the *lycée* and preparing for the baccalaureate exams, intent on enrolling in medical school in the fall. His godmother, Aunt Charlotte, made a commitment to finance his studies, and so, despite the economic difficulties of his family, he was all set for the near future. As for Philippe, whose artistic talent was becoming brilliant while his grades at school were disappointing, he had only one idea in mind: to devote himself to painting and to enter the studio of Maurice Denis. Pierre gave him the green light.

On June 6, 1944, when the Allied bombardments that accompanied their landing cut off the road to Paris and sowed panic in Étampes, Philippe and Jérôme got on their bicycles to travel the fifty-five kilometers [34 miles] that separated them from Paris and the Maison des examens, where they had to take their written baccalaureate examinations. After arriving on time at the "House of Exams", they took their tests, then returned by bike to Étampes that same evening. One hundred ten kilometers [68 miles] by bicycle in one day, and the baccalaureate en route, then a good night's sleep before starting to prepare for their orals, which were scheduled for a few days later. But the orals were ultimately cancelled because the danger was too great, with a series of bombardments over the whole region of Paris. Étampes was soon being bombed, and, while the Lejeune family was spared in their neighborhood, Pierre walked through fields of ruins, saving the injured whenever he could. Then came long weeks of uneasy waiting as the Allies recaptured France.

On August 20, Pierre, perched on the roof of the town hall,[13] discovered with inexpressible joy that the Germans were bailing out before the Allied advance, without defending the town. Therefore, there would be neither bombs nor street combat; the inhabitants and their houses would be preserved. But his happiness was very short-lived. A few moments later, a young man with a gun across his shoulder knocked on his office door and said to Pierre Lejeune, "Don't touch anything; you are dismissed from your duties. Others will come to replace you. Follow me."

Pierre did not even try to discuss it; he understood that France had just entered a period during which arbitrary force might replace the law, and petty individuals, improvisational Robin Hoods, would cater to their own basest motivations.

On that day, Jérôme learned at the same time about the liberation of Étampes and the incarceration of his father. Through some rare relatives who had not turned their back on the family, Massa managed to learn, after a few days, that her husband was charged with undermining State security and collaborating with the enemy. This general proceeding against mayors who were in office during the Occupation was aggravated in Pierre's case by the vindictiveness of some political opponents who had always considered him a class enemy.

In late August, Massa took her two older sons to visit their father in prison. That moment of family communion was a great comfort for Pierre, who admitted that evening in his *Journal*:

> In those short moments, we were united with one another more than ever. Nothing crept in between our souls; they interpenetrated like the waters of a river, they called for each other like the notes of a melody, they blended like the perfumes of the evening.... My little Rémy was missing. His mother does not want him to see the sadness of a prison. He wrote a few words to me.[14]

The days dropped like leaves for Pierre, sad, gray, and gloomy in the cell that was furnished only with his thoughts, his books, and his

[13] A. Bernet, *Jérôme Lejeune.*

[14] Pierre Lejeune, *Journal,* quoted in *Ulysse en prison,* by Pierre Lejeune.

prayers. He tried to while away the hours by walking with his unsure steps in the exercise yard, but the conversations with the other prisoners very quickly brought his mind back to the annoyances of this life in a cage, and then he preferred to return to a solitude that had become familiar.

Massa, for her part, was living in anguish. She feared the worst, because during those days of the Purge, there was no lack of maltreatment and firing squads after summary judgments. Many of their former friends had disappeared: Massa had to face the crisis alone. Fortunately, in that desert, a friend came to visit when she called: André Gueury. Massa welcomed him gratefully.

"André, believe me: I am sure that Pierre is innocent. They ..."

André Gueury interrupted her calmly. "No explanation is necessary; Pierre is an honest man."[15]

This friendship calmed and strengthened the battered hearts of the family, and the children welcomed this comfort with relief. They had seen their father behind bars, they had seen him in handcuffs, but they were not altogether alone in their turmoil.

Several days later, several disreputable individuals called on the Lejeunes and tried to terrify and blackmail Massa, right in front of Jérôme and his brothers. "If you do not leave Étampes and your house immediately, we will not be responsible for your husband's fate. If you do not leave the party, Pierre Lejeune will never be set free."

Massa, pale with indignation, disdainfully showed them the door: "Get out. We will never leave!"

Jérôme and Philippe suffered, on behalf of their father, a helpless rage, but discovered that they had new strength to protect their mother, who was so proud and courageous. Standing by her, they became men.

On Christmas Eve, the family fervently hoped that the prison administration, in keeping with tradition, would set some of the detainees free, including Pierre. Her heart pounding with joy and anxiety, Massa left to meet him at the exit from the prison, while the boys waited for his return on the platform in the train station. There was a lump in Jérôme's throat when he saw his battered father painfully climb down from the train, and the immense happiness of their

[15] P. Lejeune, *Ulysse en prison*.

reunion did not manage to dispel the sadness that gripped him at that sight. A middle-aged man had been taken from them, and an old man was returned to them.

Pierre did not complain.[16] His sons asked him: "Papa, in prison, and seeing so much injustice, did you come to doubt? To doubt God?"

"No, my dear sons, I never doubted God. On the contrary, my faith in Him is what kept me alive. But yes, I did have doubts about men."

And Pierre fell silent. How could he explain to his sons that he was starting to doubt the feeling of security and self-assurance that a blameless conscience gives and to question the justice system about which he had taught them? He felt that something was broken.

"And what about hatred, Papa? You must hate all those despicable men who were ready to sacrifice you to hide their own crimes!"

Pierre regained his composure. He was able to answer that question calmly, because hatred had never taken hold of him. In a weary but firm voice, he replied, "No, I never hated anyone. Lucky for me, too, because hatred would have crushed me. And besides, I think that all those despicable men, as you call them, do not know what they are doing."

After four months of unjustified imprisonment, the judge dismissed the case for lack of any formal indictment, but in Étampes, political enemies continued to exert pressure on the family, and Pierre, weakened and frightened, no longer dared to walk in the streets.

Several weeks after their father was released from prison, in October 1944, Jérôme started his courses in medicine in Paris, in the old buildings of the School of Medicine that are still a part of the Sorbonne. The mere need to travel to Paris every morning was an obstacle course, but soon these daily trips turned into joyful spins for the students. On May 8, 1945, Germany capitulated, and a few days later Jérôme successfully passed his first-year exams. He continued to devote his leisure hours to theater, and the two brothers made so bold as to perform Shakespeare and Aeschylus. With some success. That was also the time when they became members of the Jeunesse étudiante chrétienne [Young Christian students' association]. Temporarily.

In the following months, Jérôme pursued his studies without difficulty and began internships at hospitals, which he chose then

[16] Judging from the account by Pierre Lejeune, *Ulysse en prison*.

essentially for their proximity to the train stations along the line to Étampes: la Salpêtrière (Austerlitz Station), l'Hôtel-Dieu (Saint-Michel Station), and Laënnec (Orsay Station).[17] His first experience at a hospital, in Salpêtrière, filled him with enthusiasm. Won over by the liveliness, drive, and brilliant intellect of Professor Léger, Jérôme became passionately interested in surgery.

Another internship led him to pediatrics, in the service of Professor Raymond Turpin, where he discovered the mysteries of human genetics, and he very quickly became fascinated by this discipline, whose Sibylline language signifies so many things in so few syllables. Professor Turpin noticed the interest and aptitude of this young student and, during the fourth year of his studies, offered to appoint him an extern for his consultation. Jérôme enthusiastically agreed, and Turpin soon assigned him to serve the mongoloid children [as they used to be called]. From then on, as he came to have great affection for them and following the example of his mentor, who gave them his full attention, Jérôme got to know them, learned how to examine them, and began to decipher skillfully the message inscribed in the lines on their palms.

The following year, Jérôme had to leave Turpin's service to pursue his education, and he joined the hospital in Étampes as a certified intern. With Doctors Thierry and Touzé, who welcomed him with friendly benevolence, Jérôme learned clinical methods and the rudiments of surgery. He worked a lot, acted as a substitute during his vacations from university, and provided occasional care in the evening and on the weekend.

Pressed to earn a living so as to give financial relief to his father, who had had to go back to work despite his extreme fatigue, Jérôme decided to compete for a position in the externship[18] of the Paris hospitals one year before his classmates, while he was still making the rounds as an intern. He failed and blamed himself for being lazy and slow. There was no reason for shame, though, because the competition was very selective in the 1950s: only one student out of four was accepted. He immediately prepared for the future sessions, because

[17] J. Lejeune, inaugural lecture, March 10, 1965.

[18] Until 1968, externship was the first step in the formation of medical students who wished to pursue a hospital career. The competition was not necessary in order to be a physician.

he had to succeed in order to follow the specialized curriculum that he was considering: surgery. But Jérôme failed two more times. A fourth and final chance for him remained, and he tried again a few months later. Alas, on the morning of the examination, exhausted and absentminded, he took the subway in the wrong direction and, when he finally arrived at Wagram Hall where the tests take place, the doors were closed.[19] Too late! Jérôme had to give up the idea of being a surgeon. He was very disappointed.

In the train that took him back to Étampes, Jérôme was discouraged. During dinner, his brothers and parents tried to console him by reminding him that surgery did not figure in his initial enthusiasm for medicine. "Don't worry. It won't prevent you from being a physician, and that is what matters."

"That is true", Jérôme replied. "I embarked on the study of medicine in order to be a country doctor. Might this be a way of rediscovering my initial first fervor? Could I perhaps work with Professor Turpin for the mongoloid children? While waiting, I have to defend my thesis in medicine and do my military service. After that, I will see. Tomorrow is another day."

On April 30, 1951, Jérôme appeared at the barracks in Clignancourt before joining the center in Vincennes, where he made two important discoveries: Lucien Israël and Jean de Grouchy. He quickly struck up a friendship with these two young physicians, and one evening, while he was discussing things with Lucien, a good-natured man whose gentleness elicited confidences, Jérôme indulged in some daydreaming:

"Since my internship with Turpin, I have thought a lot about those mongoloid children. In recent years I have been passionately interested in surgery and genetics, and since surgery is not possible for me now, it is an easy choice: I would like to continue in genetics. In fact, . . . those children . . . I wish I could find the causes for their condition . . ."

Then, after a moment of silence, he went on: "You will see: I will find out what the matter is with them and maybe how to cure them!"

Lucien looked at him in amusement and replied: "Terrific! When you do, I will not forget to remind you of what you just told me.[20]

[19] J. Lejeune, inaugural lecture, March 10, 1965. Jérôme relates his four failures.

[20] Lucien Israël reminded Jérôme about this incident when they met again at a conference on genetics in Tokyo in 1966. J. Lejeune, letter to Birthe, October 25, 1966.

As for me, I choose oncology. And I hope that we will meet again in a few years, when we have swapped our military doctor's uniforms for our white coats."

Jérôme was then assigned to the Rhine Valley to take four months of classes at the French military base in Boppard, with the guarantee that he could go back to Paris in early June to complete his thesis in medicine. On June 15, in the presence of his father and his godmother, Aunt Charlotte, who were both very moved, Jérôme defended his thesis[21] successfully and received high honors. On June 19, the very young Doctor Lejeune went back to Germany, this time to Freiburg, the French air base where he was to assist the Commandant Doctor. Jérôme showed little enthusiasm for military life, but he was not unhappy with that medical experience and liked the spirit of camaraderie that prevailed in the regiment. Nevertheless, little by little he became bored, because his heart remained in Paris. The festive outings with his comrades from the regiment in the city bars could no longer make him forget the delightful smile of a beautiful Danish girl.

[21] J. Lejeune, Thesis in medicine published under the title *Contribution à l'étude de la régression de l'indice de la masculinité dans les grossesses multiples* [A contribution to the study of the declining proportion of male children in multiple pregnancies], 1951.

CHAPTER 3

WITH LOVE AS THE ONLY BAGGAGE

1950–1952

The meeting between Jérôme and Birthe Bringsted in Paris in 1950 was straight from a novel. Sainte-Geneviève Library witnessed their first exchange of words. She, a young Danish Lutheran, an only daughter, had come to Paris to learn French; he was the product of a French Catholic family.

"Do you happen to have a pen, Monsieur?"

"Of course, Mademoiselle."

It was love at first sight. Jérôme was captivated by those dark eyes shining with a wild and tenderly timid gleam. Her high cheekbones, tanned complexion, the narrow slit of her eyes and her long, dark hair revealed Eskimo ancestry.

"She is so beautiful, so different!" he thought with emotion.

The thick medical textbook set out on his table became as dull as a winter evening. His mind looked for a way to prolong the conversation.

"Would you like to get some coffee, Mademoiselle?"

That led to long, amorous walks at the foot of Notre-Dame, accompanied by the romantic lullaby of the murmuring Seine and the eternal dreams of the Latin Quarter. Jérôme soon left for Denmark, since he had been invited to spend the August vacation at the house of Birthe's mother. However, a few months later, doubts set in, and the relationship ended. They were so different ...

Those were trying months for Birthe and Jérôme. Fortunately, one of Birthe's interests was cinema, and someone offered her a small part. She asked for advice from her Danish girlfriends in Paris, whose presence was invaluable in difficult moments. She also liked journalism very much and thought that she could be a good investigative journalist. What should she do? During that time, Jérôme tried to forget their love by having a good time with his friends in the regiment and by playing the eligible doctor who likes the finer things in life. Until the day when he made use of a leave to go to Paris and they met again in January 1952. They understood then that they could no longer live without each other. Despite their great differences and the misgivings of Jérôme's parents, they decided to get married, so as to love one another as they were, with all the richness of that complementarity. Jérôme left again for Freiburg, freed of his fears, revitalized, radiant. Birthe rediscovered the joy of living.

His friends in the regiment quickly noticed the change. Lejeune no longer went with them to drink beer in the taverns of Freiburg but shut himself up in the evening to write long letters to his fiancée, whom he had left so far away, down in Paris. Jérôme was transformed and told her so:

> My darling Birthe, I no longer have the slightest fear now; I have made a commitment, we are truly meant for each other, and our bond frees me more than you could know.... My orderlies claim that I am becoming a flag-waving chauvinist just because I am discovering what remarkable people the Danes are! It is plain to see that they don't know you! For I admit that your smile is not altogether unrelated to my admiration for [the Danish-American painter] Carlsen.[1]

He was filled with a new, confident joy and drew from his fiancée the strength to overcome the worries and the melancholy that too often besieged him. He made use of these long daily letters to open his soul to Birthe, to admit to her his weaknesses and his faults, and to tell her how much she was making him improve by her qualities and her love:

> I now admit all my weaknesses because I am starting to feel a new strength within me. Be assured that I am not letting myself be carried away by juvenile enthusiasm; I am speaking with the utmost sincerity: we have decided to be joined in God's sight, and this union will be total, despite all the difficulties that we will encounter or that will arise from us. You are the one who taught me this extraordinary secret, which everyone suspects but no one dares to put into practice and

[1] J. Lejeune, letter to Birthe, January 20, 1952.

which you alone will be able to help me utilize. The first days of our marriage will probably be rather difficult, because to tame me, you will have to have incredible dedication. You did more than bring me love; you made me understand hope. I love you, my Darling. More than I can say.[2]

He was overjoyed to see that Birthe understood him profoundly:

Everything that you write to me is so beautiful and so true only because you love me so—so—so much! I am amazed at each one of your letters; I would never have believed that such a thing was possible. Love gives you deep insight and a serene confidence that no knowledge in the world could have given you.[3]

While experiencing this beautiful human love, Jérôme understood that God was its source, and the engagement became an important stage in his spiritual journey. He had received his faith in childhood and had kept it alive by force of habit until he completed secondary school; now, at the dawn of his adult life, he discovered in it a new joy in recognizing the prevenient love of his Heavenly Father. A powerful, liberating love. And Jérôme confided this brand new happiness to his fiancée:

This morning I received Holy Communion for the two of us at eight o'clock in the cathedral. I have never been so happy, at peace, and in love with God.[4]

It was necessary for him to set free this source of joy, which he had received at Baptism, in order for it to gush forth and to irrigate their love, and Jérôme, feeling a new need to found his life on God, invited Birthe to do the same. Soon, with the approval of the chaplain, he asked her to share his Catholic faith:

It is necessary, my Darling, for you to love the Catholic religion; do it first out of love for me, and later on you will see that this same religion will help us to love each other better.[5]

[2] Ibid., February 24, 1952.
[3] Ibid.
[4] Ibid., March 9, 1952.
[5] Ibid., February 8, 1952.

She willingly agreed and, without wasting any time, went to take a catechism course with Canon Muller at the Church of Saint-Philippe-du-Roule in Paris, which she supplemented, at Jérôme's advice, with conversations about religious instruction with her future father-in-law, whose faith was so contagious. These long hours spent together conversing about God brought Pierre and Birthe to the point where great affection soon sprang up between these two human beings so dear to Jérôme's heart. Pierre discovered the valiant heart of his future daughter-in-law, and Birthe—the kindness of her fiancé's father.

And Jérôme, who was following all these developments at a distance, soon had only one worry left: that he did not love his Birthe enough.

> I love you, little Birthe; you will be the only woman for me, and I will not be fully happy or alive until we have been united definitively in God's sight. When you pray, do not forget to ask the Lord to help me to be able to love you well. This is the only thing in the world that I desire now.[6]

The wedding date was set for the end of Jérôme's military service, May 1, in the Catholic Church of Saint Alban in Odense, Denmark. It was to be very simple. Jérôme's parents and his brother Rémy could not come because Pierre did not have the strength for the journey and they could not afford to rent a car. Massa feared that her son Jérôme might take offense at their absence, and she admitted this to him a few days before the wedding. Jérôme hastened to reassure her and wrote to Birthe, who had left for Denmark to prepare for the ceremony:

> Birthe, my Darling, I returned in haste to Étampes because Rémy, who came to help me this afternoon, had told me that Mama was ill. [It was] not very serious, but the worst thing was that she was fretting terribly, thinking that I was mad at her for not coming to our wedding! Poor Mama, I did console her, and she was very pleased that I will be coming right back. She has almost recovered already.[7]

[6] Ibid., February 10, 1952.
[7] Ibid., April 24, 1952.

Philippe and his young wife, Geneviève Dormann, were not afraid of the distance and planned to travel by motorcycle! Pierre expressed to Philippe his concern about the length and the dangers of the trip, but he replied:

"There's no way I'd let Jérôme get married without me or even a single member of the family!"

Pierre was not unhappy with that vigorous response.

Now it was a matter of Jérôme quickly finding a position in which he could make a living for the family that he was getting ready to start. There was no lack of ideas: someone had suggested a post in Yemen and Afghanistan, but that adventure did not tempt either of the two fiancés. Could he become a country doctor to follow his original dream? Or else accept Doctor Raymond Turpin's offer of a position in his department working with his many mongoloid patients, whom most people ignored? Turpin had conducted research into the origin of mongolism some twenty-five years earlier, and he had proposed some interesting hypotheses on the subject, but to date nothing had been proved. Well, maybe this young doctor, whose inquisitive mind and sensitive attention he had noticed during his internship, could resume the research and find the solution....

Jérôme could not wait to meet with Turpin to discuss the plan more specifically, but as of mid-April Turpin was still away from Paris, and Jérôme wrote to Birthe about his impatience:

> My darling, how it bothers me not to be able to say to you, "I am doing this and that", but no, I pace back and forth, and as long as Turpin hasn't returned from Trouville, I cannot make any decision.[8]

Now the wedding was scheduled for two weeks later.... Finally, Turpin returned and proposed that Jérôme join his practice. Jérôme immediately informed his fiancée,

> This is it, tomorrow I will know a little more! [And he added:] Turpin is always charming; he wants me to write a book about mongoloids for him. If I manage to start, he will do everything he can to help me.[9]

[8] Ibid., April 12, 1952.
[9] Ibid., April 24, 1952.

This new encounter, on April 25, 1952, between Jérôme and those whom he would soon call *my little patients*, would turn his life upside down. That same evening, he wrote to Birthe:

> Turpin offered me a one- or two-year job working with the mongoloids. You know, the little retarded children. I am convinced that there is something to find and that it may be possible to better the lives of thousands of human beings (there are around 10,000 of them in France alone) if we manage to discover why they are like that. It is an exciting goal that will require great sacrifices of us, my Darling, but if you agree to accept a life that is rather precarious but honest and healthy, based on this hope, I am sure that we will reach it. (I say "we" because I will succeed at something only if you walk this path, too, if you help me.)[10]

And Birthe said "yes". A few days before their wedding, they decided together that they would devote their lives and combine their efforts to try "to better the lives of thousands of human beings". How? By finding the causes of this handicap, then treating it. To what point? "To the point of accepting great sacrifices, a life that is precarious but honest and healthy, based on this hope." A Yes directed toward others, by the grace of love. The Yes of Birthe to her fiancé, the Yes of Jérôme to the silent plea of these children who are "deprived of the freedom of the mind". Jérôme's work took root in this commitment of love, and his career as a physician would unfold within it.

With his professional prospects clear, Jérôme now had to find decent lodgings for his future wife. Because the wedding was rapidly approaching! Between the end of his military service and his departure for his wedding, he had only a few days to prepare the rooms his father had reserved for them in the old house on the rue Galande, a few steps away from Notre-Dame and the Sorbonne. This house, which Pierre had bought for a song because it was so dilapidated, and which had been spared *in extremis* in eminent domain proceedings, had been built before the discovery of America, and its venerable age did not make it very comfortable. Everything was dirty, dusty, and the building had no sanitation. It urgently needed repairs, but Jérôme was not wealthy. He had to carefully prioritize his options

[10] Ibid., April 25, 1952.

and make the right choices about the most necessary work. Jérôme confided to Birthe about it:

> My darling, . . . Alas, an unpleasant observation: the estimate offered to me to run the plumbing for the rue Galande is not 30,000 but 70,000 francs. I redid the calculations myself and, accounting for everything, buying the pipes from Creusy, the sink at the Bon Marché, etc., I end up at a minimum of 55 or 60,000! It is still way too much. This is our balance sheet in short. We still have 44,000 francs. If from this 44,000 francs, I dedicate 10 to 15 for the rue Galande (painting with Philippe, etc.) and another 3,295 for your dryer, I don't think that it will be possible to get to the 60,000 for the plumbing. What do you think, my dear?
>
> I don't know for certain yet how I am going to earn our daily bread. Do not think, though, that I am desperate; now that we are fiancés, I am dedicated, and we will get through this because I have you, so confident, so active, and so courageous. You see, these difficult beginnings—and they will be terribly difficult—will bind us together more strongly. That is why I speak to you so frankly and why I do not want to get us into any major repairs before we are a little more certain about tomorrow. Besides, in any case, we will not stay long on the rue Galande, because it is not that nice. So, is it worth the trouble to spend all our savings there?
>
> My little darling, how I bore you with all these calculations! Of course I would much rather tell you: look, everything will be ready on time, with every convenience, and you will be a little queen. My little Birthe, we are poor, you see, but not for long; one or two years maybe, but at the beginning we will have to fight hard. Fortunately, I know that I can count on you, . . . and God will help us a lot.[11]

With the help of his brothers, Philippe and Rémy, Jérôme attacked the essential issues: filling the cracks in the walls, which had shifted over time, painting the two little rooms in a bright color to make them look bigger and to try to make a kitchenette for Birthe. He finally managed to install a sink and a water tank and made cupboards and an ironing board by hand. The sink would double as the bathroom for the first few months. Jérôme hastened to describe to his fiancée how the work was progressing:

[11] Ibid., April 10, 1952.

> Tonight, I declare total victory: the plumbing is installed, the sink is splendid, the frame is sturdy, and the water flows perfectly. *Tra là là* (as you say) I have never seen such a lovely fixture. Philippe was a tremendous help to me and was the most charming and skillful of all brother-plumbers.... Thus everything will be in order upon your arrival, the kitchen (I won't describe it to you, you are in for a surprise), the ironing board (it is so solid that I use it as a workbench)....[12]

He would have liked to offer Birthe more, but after the purchase of a pair of shoes, his wedding suit, and the train ticket to Denmark, he truly had nothing left:

> Tomorrow I will look for my suit and my passport. I will not buy shoes until last because prices are falling noticeably right now. While I am at it, if I could save even 500 francs, that would already be something.[13]

This poverty dampened neither Jérôme's nor Birthe's enthusiasm, and they were preparing for their joyous reunion in Denmark. Jérôme anticipated arriving the day before the ceremony.

Massa, for her part, had made use of those last days to write a tactful letter to Birthe. It seemed that her initial misgivings, when she and Pierre were not yet acquainted with Birthe and were dreaming about a more prestigious marriage for their son, had given way to genuine affection:

> My dear little daughter, your charming letter gave us great pleasure.... I assure you, we deeply regret that we are unable to make this journey to Denmark to be with both of you on your beautiful wedding day, but our thoughts will be with you, and we will be delighted, knowing that you are happy. At least you will have Philippe and Geneviève in our place.
>
> Your apartment is ready. Philippe and Rémy went there to help Jérôme. They all worked like angels! (Angels who would be willing to lay pipes to ensure the comfort of a young couple with whom you are well acquainted!) All is well!

[12] Ibid., April 17, 1952.

[13] Ibid.

Your question, my dear daughter, gave me the greatest pleasure. Call me by whatever name you like. Whether you call me Mom or Mother, be assured that I already consider you my daughter.

Thank you again for writing. I send you my best thoughts and embrace you very affectionately. Your mother.

N.B. Sophie's doll is beautiful! You are a little fairy![14]

Another letter from Massa, several weeks earlier, while Jérôme was still in Germany, had already given Birthe the assurance that she was warmly welcomed into Jérôme's family:

> You have certainly brought happiness to our Jérôme, my little pixie, and I am sure that the Lord will bless both your efforts. Of course I expect you on Sunday! And you can stay with us as long as you like. I had already intended to ask you to come, but I feared that the house might seem to you a little bleak without Jérôme, but be assured that you will be very welcome always and at any time. Until Sunday! Thank you for everything you have said, and your words have filled my heart. Me too, I already love you dearly. And I embrace you. Your mother.[15]

The wedding took place on May 1 with the utmost simplicity. For her witnesses, Birthe had her mother, Magdalene Bringsted, and a longtime friend and girl scout leader, Aase Norup, who came with her husband. And on Jérôme's side, there was his brother Philippe with his wife, Geneviève. After the Mass, the little group met for the wedding feast. According to the Danish tradition, the young couple, sitting side-by-side, ate with spoons linked by a chain, symbolizing their married life. Two pearls, black as volcanic stones, and two sapphires, blue as heavenly bliss, sparkled on their faces. Birthe was radiant in her black dress, very demure, with her veil lifted. Accented by his thin moustache, Jérôme's smile was bursting with joy.

[14] Madame Pierre Lejeune, letter to Birthe, April 18, 1952.
[15] Ibid., March 1952.

CHAPTER 4

THE TAKEOFF

1952–1959

"Here you are, then, a research intern for the CNRS [French National Center for Scientific Research], Lejeune. I wish you a fine career. We will do great things together."

"Thank you, sir. I will do my best to find the cause of the mental retardation in these children you are entrusting to me."

That was how Turpin welcomed Doctor Lejeune, in the summer of 1952, into his department at Saint-Louis Hospital in Paris. Jérôme immediately plunged into his new professional life, a good part of which consisted of studying dermatoglyphs—fingerprints and hand folds of mongoloid children—with a magnifying glass. Turpin explained to him that the palm folds are a map containing a wealth of teachings for those who know how to decipher them.

The laboratory resources were more frugal than anyone could have imagined. As for the staff, they were few. Jérôme often asked Birthe for help, and she gave of her time unstintingly and assisted him in the study of the dermatoglyphs. She even coauthored a publication on the subject, alongside her husband. Her work had become so valuable to the department that Jérôme returned one day to rue Galande with very good news:

"My Bibi! Turpin understood that you helped me a lot and is offering to employ you at the laboratory! Isn't that wonderful news?"

Her eyes shining with a new glow, Birthe replied:

"Dear, that's terrific. But there's something better...."

And without giving Jérôme time to react, she went on, with a smile on her lips:

"We are going to have a baby in a few months."

A few days later, in the mid-afternoon, the bell rang at the door of rue Galande. Caught in the middle of a siesta, Birthe rubbed her eyes, then rose quickly to go to the door. A young woman, more or less the same age as Birthe, her brown hair trimmed in an urchin cut and her eyes framed by thick glasses, stood in the doorway.

"Hello. My name is Marie-Odile Rethoré, and I would like to see Doctor Lejeune, please. I am a medical student, and Father Ponsar, the parish priest of Saint-Séverin whom you know well, suggests that I go visit the sick poor people in the neighborhood. He told me that your husband used to do it regularly. Can I speak with him?"

Birthe answered: "A very good idea. Come back at eight o'clock this evening; he will be here."

At eight o'clock punctually, Jérôme greeted the visitor and, after inquiring about her level of education, suggested that she join the small team that provided care to the neediest in the neighborhood. They then met almost every week to tour the neighborhood. Birthe, who continued to work with Jérôme, thought about her successor as her due date approached. One evening she said to Jérôme:

"Why don't you ask Marie-Odile Rethoré to work with you as my replacement? I think she will do very well."

Jérôme, who had seen Marie-Odile at work and thought that she would make a good physician, agreed: "Why not, yes, good idea. I will suggest it to her."

The next day, when he met Marie-Odile Rethoré with the parish team, he made her an offer:

"Mademoiselle, my wife, who was helping me with research, will have to quit because of the impending birth of our baby. I need someone to help me with studies of ionizing radiations. There is a lot of work, and it is impossible to accomplish it alone. My wife strongly encouraged me to offer you this job. If you agree, I shall speak to Professor Turpin about it."

Marie-Odile Rethoré accepted enthusiastically—although she still felt not very qualified to embark on the adventure—and Turpin gave his approval. The matter was quickly settled, and a few days later she joined Professor Turpin's team and worked alongside Jérôme.

Since their marriage in the month of May, Jérôme and Birthe had been settled at rue Galande. During the summer, before the start of the academic year in September, Jérôme had had just enough time to make a little money working as a replacement in Cher [a department in central France], where Birthe had accompanied him. The disagreeable reception given to him by one of the doctors and the strange attitude of one family made Jérôme rather uncomfortable. At the end of his replacement work, he returned to Paris with relief. His old dream of becoming a country doctor had vanished.

Part of the money earned during that stay was used to buy treatises on mathematics, geometry, optics, and astronomy and to complete a scientific training that he considered too brief. On evenings and weekends, Jérôme plunged in and assimilated these materials with disconcerting ease. Mathematics especially seemed to him a wildly amusing game, and astronomy gave him great pleasure. He treated himself to a telescope and was very happy with this Christmas gift for 1952. He also began to learn English, a language widely used in the scientific publications that he read methodically to keep abreast of current research. With perseverance, he got up every morning earlier than usual to study English using the Assimil method and, in a few months, learned enough vocabulary and grammar to hold a conversation and to enchant the audience with his delightful British humor tinged with his very charming French accent! But despite this mastery of the English language, Jérôme intended to speak in French at international conferences; he was convinced that by speaking with simplicity and clarity, the English- and Spanish-speaking listeners would manage to understand without an interpreter.

On January 27, 1953, at the clinic of the Saint-Louis Hospital, Birthe brought into the world a pretty baby with slanted eyes and black hair. A real little Eskimo whom they named Anouk, because Birthe and Jérôme had chosen to give Danish names to their girls and French names to their boys. The baby's arrival filled the parents with joy; they delighted in this new happiness while discovering the fatigue of nights that were shortened to feed the little one. Jérôme was worried about his young wife:

"My poor little Bibi, how do you feel? You did not sleep much."

"Oh, don't worry about me! You know how easily I fall asleep and go back to sleep", Birthe replied with a beaming smile and rings under her eyes. "So, we are not going to complain about being awakened like this: we are so happy!"

But two months later, the death of his grandfather, Hector Lermat, cast a veil of sadness over their happiness. Now that his maternal grandfather had been called back to God, Jérôme's childhood in Montrouge lost one of its wonderful witnesses. Little Néno, now a doctor of medicine, gratefully remembered his first outings with his veterinarian grandfather and the hours spent in the workshop observing his powerful, clever hands when they nailed the iron shoes to the horses' hooves. What a smell and what noise! And what pride when his grandfather asked him:

"Néno, will you help me calm the horse?"

"Yes, of course!"

"Then come near me and gently caress his neck while speaking to him softly."

"You know," Jérôme confided to Birthe, who was sitting beside him with Anouk in her arms, "to some extent it is thanks to him that I chose medicine. With him I discovered the pleasure of caregiving, while accompanying him on his rounds as a veterinarian to visit the horses and cows of Montrouge. But I chose medicine because the suffering of mankind seems so great to me! I would be so happy if I can do something for them!"

Those days passed simply and happily for the family. While Jérôme studied the genetic effects of ionizing radiation—these powerful rays that can cause chemical recombinations in some poor children born to irradiated parents—Birthe put her whole heart into housekeeping, made their apartment a warm, welcoming home, and surrounded their little Anouk with her care. The child, who found this quite natural, would see this balance modified a few months later, though, by the arrival of a little brother. On April 27, 1955, Birthe was admitted to the Port Royal maternity hospital and brought their first son into the world. They called him Damien in honor of the saint, physician, and martyr. The two modest rooms of their apartment became too small to accommodate four people, but such considerations did not cloud their happiness. Birthe efficiently organized their new family life. Every day Jérôme was happy to come back to rue Galande for lunch in order to be with Birthe and his two little ones. And soon his three little ones, for less than two years later, the family circle grew again: on February 23, 1957, another little girl made her appearance.

They called her Karin, and, like her two elder siblings, she was a pretty Eskimo baby. Birthe teased Jérôme:

"Not one of them got your blue eyes!"

"I am spoiled to have four copies of you at home!" he replied with a laugh. "It's true that they seem to have gotten everything from your side! I will have to see whether that is genetically possible, by a natural phenomenon still unknown in the human race!"

Alas, the family was soon shaken by two tragedies. In the summer of 1957, Philippe's wife, Geneviève, asked for a divorce and left her husband and their three daughters. Philippe was devastated. Then, in January of 1958, Jérôme experienced a great trial, the death of his dear father. This period was for Jérôme one of the most painful in his life.

After an initial pulmonary alert the preceding year, Pierre had visibly become weaker, but not until the beginning of the year 1958 did Jérôme observe with alarm, for the first time, his father's domed fingernails, a sign of irremediable asphyxiation of the lungs.

"At that moment I would have given anything not to know or to have seen those poor nails", wrote Jérôme in his journal, which he started exactly one year after the death of his father, collecting those painful memories.

> Oh, it was still very discreet; nobody would notice it, but I could not deny the evidence: instead of the familiar flat shape that I knew so well, this terrible arching, which meant death! Papa told me that he was really at the end of his rope and that we doctors did not see what he had, that everything left him short of breath, that he felt life slipping away from him. And I said no, and again no, laughing affectionately and teasing him slightly, as we used to do when we two were alone and he told me about some little discomfort. And then my throat was tight, and it hurt.[1]

Jérôme immediately made an appointment for his father with his friend Lafourcade. The visit was scheduled for Saturday. The day before the appointment, his father came to stay over at rue Galande, and Jérôme and Birthe tried to give him a really good evening, surrounding him with affection. After dinner, Jérôme played the guitar.

[1] J. Lejeune, *Journal intime*, January 11, 1959.

Gently. He had a foreboding that this was one of his father's last happy evenings. The next day, in the corridors of the Trousseau Hospital, Jérôme was cut to the heart when he saw the extreme weakness of his father, who had difficulty walking. That evening he confided to Birthe, "It broke my heart, even more than anything I had feared; it is so unbearable to see our loved ones suffering."[2]

From then on, it all went very quickly. The following Wednesday, sensing the urgency of the situation, Jérôme hurried to Étampes. His presence was plainly a great joy for his father. When Pierre saw Jérôme enter his room, he stood up, embraced him affectionately, and said to him, "How good you are to have come!"

Jérôme's heart reeled at these words. They spoke softly, in a low voice, and Jérôme kidded a little to reassure him, but his throat hurt more and more, and his eyes misted in spite of himself. During the night, Jérôme heard in his sleep a loud voice shouting: "Bon Pa is going to die, Bon Pa is going to die." He turned over in bed, weeping, and said:

"I know, but don't shout it so loud!"[3]

Early the next morning, Jérôme hurried to Trousseau to show his father's X-rays, which were considered very bad, and returned to Étampes with Birthe and Rémy. Jérôme drove fast, very fast, thinking only:

"We must get there in time, Papa must receive Extreme Unction in time. I promised him; it has to be done." With Philippe already there, the family was now reunited.

In the late afternoon, when his three sons were near him, Pierre said to them: "How happy I am that all three of you are near me! But I cannot say that to you all the time."

The priest arrived, and Pierre received the last rites peacefully. When everyone had left, Jérôme remained alone with his father. The latter took his hand and said, "Son, it's up to you to fight now."

At these words, in spite of the grief that overcame him, Jérôme simply said, "I will do all that is humanly possible. God will decide."

While they exchanged a few words, Jérôme held the oxygen inhaler. At one point, Pierre remarked, between two breaths:

[2] In fact, Jérôme recorded these words in ibid.

[3] Ibid.

"Do you know that it has been more than thirty years now that we have lived together without ever a word between us?"

Then, after an asphyxiation attack stronger than the others, Pierre held Jérôme's hand and said to him gently: "*You* know how to love!"

And when Jérôme replied that everyone loved him, he corrected himself: "Yes, you are right, these are things that we do not say. We think them."[4]

When Philippe came to relieve Jérôme, his father quickly called him back: "Where is Jérôme?"

And suddenly, under Jérôme's fingers, the pulse stopped. Jérôme called his mother and brothers in a wail. Then the heart started again, while the family recited the rosary around the dying man. During those long hours, Jérôme held his father's hand and caught his last words. He heard him murmur "Jesus", then leaned over to his father's ear and said:

"Adieu, Papa, and thank you."

In his journal, Jérôme recalled:

> That was all I could think of to say to my dear father, whom I loved with all my soul but could not save. I thanked him for our whole life, for his goodness, our friendship and his kindness right up to these last moments....
>
> Then, with his hand in mine ... as he had done for his father, he gave up his spirit.[5]

Jérôme closed his father's eyes and received his wedding ring, with emotion, from his mother's hands. Jérôme's pain was immense, equal to the love that he had for his father:

> My dear Papa, whom I loved with all my heart, whom I loved and understood for many good years, who was for me a counselor and a friend—my dear Papa is no more.[6]

Pierre had died of lung cancer.

The months that followed were painful for Jérôme, but little by little life returned to normal. On July 1, in the early hours of the day,

[4] Ibid.

[5] This dialogue between Jerome and his father, in its entirety, repeats the narrative and the quotations in ibid.

[6] Ibid.

he bustled around with Birthe in the middle of suitcases and bags, going up and down the narrow stairs of the house on rue Galande, so that the family caravan could set out on time.

"I prepared the water bottles and the sandwiches. They're all in the cooler. Don't forget it", Birthe told her husband, who was standing in front of the already full trunk.

Jérôme could not help having a fit of ill humor. "The cooler! The only thing that was missing! I'm going to have to redo the entire load!" he exclaimed with annoyance.

It was the big summer departure for Kerteminde, Birthe's Danish village, and it took all of Jérôme's ingenuity to load and stow, in and on the rickety car, the luggage and the equipment necessary for a two-month stay by the family; not to mention the countless gifts for Danish friends. They were everywhere, in the trunk, on the roof, underfoot, on knees. Only the driver had a minimum of living space available, to ensure safety during the trip. They crossed Belgium, the Netherlands, and Germany—five countries, four borders, and three days—taking over from each other at the wheel every two hours so as not to waste time. The repeated expedition with one, then two, then three young children—unruly and carsick in turn—put the parents through the whole gamut of emotions; it was one of those human adventures that allowed them to test their limits, while the children, unaware of so much parental virtue, alternated laughter, screaming, tears, candy, and games, only to indulge finally in sleep a few kilometers away from the finish line. All revived in Kerteminde on the evening of the third day, when the brave little car finally parked in front of Birthe's childhood home.

In Kerteminde, Jérôme discovered a seaside life very different from that of his childhood in Normandy or Royan. He tipped over into a universe that he could not have imagined. Happiness for his wife was to settle on the beach at dawn and not to budge from it until evening, sheltered from frequent bad weather by a tent where her former classmates came to visit her. In all sorts of weather, rarely mild, they drank liters of black coffee and ate sandwiches spread with salmon cream cheese, all accompanied by jokes and discussions in Danish, which Jérôme obviously did not understand at all.... When it rained, they would play with the kids in the car or pile them into the tent and stuff them with cookies to keep them occupied. Fortunately, the beach was full of pebbles, and Jérôme—after having participated as nicely as possible in the conversation by exhausting his two words of Danish—had fun cutting prehistoric flints or carving bits of driftwood that had been polished by the waves with the small knife that he always kept in his pocket, while waiting for the opportunity to teach the art of navigation to his children. That was also when he read and reread his little book for the summer, *Rôle de plaisance*,[7] enchanted by its humor, which was fine and pungent like sea salt. Or Chesterton, whose free and flamboyant tone happily dusted off ancestral truths. In spite of these Spartan conditions, Jérôme valued this annual holiday in Kerteminde for the happiness it gave to Birthe, his children, and his mother-in-law, who was so delighted to be with her daughter and the little ones.

Over the years, this caravan set out according to an unchanging ritual: each year the family departed on July 1, at dawn, for Kerteminde, where it settled until the first days of September. Jérôme returned to Paris alone in mid-July, taking advantage of the quiet Parisian summer to work actively before returning to pick up the whole family in Kerteminde at the end of the summer and seeing Germany, the Netherlands, and Belgium again on the way back. The suitcases secured with ropes and bungee cords on the roof were as heavy as on the trip to Denmark, but slightly different. The gifts brought by Birthe to her Danish friends were replaced by Danish provisions that would assure Birthe's culinary fame in Paris and the joy of her guests: her renowned roast pig and her famous brown sauce. Jérôme was happy to return to Paris with all his little people. When he went back alone in mid-summer, he then had to face the silence of the empty apartment, listening in spite of himself for Birthe's footsteps and the children's voices, and he strove with a heavy heart to tame those imaginary noises and their absence. God knows he did not like those long, lonely summer nights. Only the daily letters that he and Birthe wrote to each other whenever they were far apart softened the absence a little.

Upon arriving at the hospital, Jérôme immersed himself in the study of mongoloid patients, about whom little was known. These children, wounded in their intelligence and marked in their bodies, suffered from a complete misunderstanding that aggravated their

[7] Jacques Perret, *Rôle de plaisance*.

sickness and affected their hearts. They were the underprivileged of science. Their peculiar physical appearance, first described by Doctor Seguin in 1844 as "furfuraceous idiocy", probably in reference to the softness of rag dolls, then led people to think that they had some kinship with the inhabitants of Mongolia, hence the term mongolism due to Sir Langdon Down, who in 1866 described "Mongolian idiocy". This classification is based on a serious scientific error that Jérôme then described to Birthe:

"Do you know that, at the moment, the only pseudo-scientific explanation we have for mongolism is totally racist? They say that this mental disability stems from the regression of certain characteristics typical of the white race toward another race.[8] Frankly, it is urgent to find the true cause of mongolism, because one thing that is absolutely certain: that is not the right one!"

Since the beginning of the twentieth century, the disease had been a subject of scientific controversy, and hypotheses had followed one after another without ever being confirmed. In 1937, Turpin and Caratzali considered the possibility of chromosomal aberration, and in 1939, two other well-known researchers, Penrose and Fanconi, came up with the same suggestion.[9] These theoretical considerations about a possible chromosomal origin of mongolism were then abandoned, so that, from 1940 on, no more publications mention this etiological possibility. Scientists looked elsewhere. In all, more than sixty different hypotheses have been proposed.[10]

"What do you think, Lejeune?" Turpin asked his young collaborator.

"Sir, I think that too many hypotheses kill the hypothesis. I would like to start over from clinical observation."

"Very well", Turpin replied. "I was going to suggest it to you."

In 1952, Lejeune resumed the clinical study and incorporated recent advances in science to try to find the solution.

[8] Jérôme mentions this racist explanation in his thesis on science, *Le mongolisme, trisomie dégressive*, 1960, 1.

[9] J. Lejeune, *Le mongolisme, trisomie dégressive*, thèse ès Sciences, 1960. In it, Jerome states that Waardenburg, in 1932, and Bleyer, in 1934, envisaged the possibility of a case of trisomy, but these studies were ignored by Turpin's department at the time of their research. Their publication in 1959 thus confirmed without knowing it, a quarter of a century later, the reasoning of these two authors.

[10] In his historical survey published in 1960, Warkany would list more than sixty hypotheses. Cited by Jérôme Lejeune in his science thesis.

From 1953 on, Turpin and he thus highlighted the relations between dermatoglyphs (hand lines and fingerprints) and the patient's physical and psychological characteristics. They showed that the structure of these lines, which are specific to each person and do not change over the course of life, is determined at the beginning of the embryo's development, very early, even before the first month *in utero*. Now an in-depth statistical study showed that a classification of fingerprints according to four criteria makes it possible to diagnose mongolism effectively,[11] in particular the fusion of two folds of palm flexion. Another original observation aroused Jérôme's curiosity. One evening, before leaving the hospital, he discussed it with a young doctor on the team, his friend Jacques Lafourcade.

"It's strange. The white blood cells of mongoloid children have a particular quality, and the frequency of acute leukemia is twenty times higher in them than in normal children. It would therefore seem logical to assume that these two characteristics could result from one and the same mechanism: an abnormal and possibly imbalanced chromosomal constitution."[12]

"You must be right", replied his friend, with interest.

Jérôme stopped for a brief moment to light his cigarette and went on:

"And I noticed that the influence of the mother's age in the occurrence of mongolism is the only point on which the authors have seemed to agree for fifty years."[13]

"Unbelievable", replied Lafourcade, more and more interested.

"Observing twin pregnancies was also instructive", Jérôme continued between two puffs. "From these studies it seems legitimate to conclude that mongolism is a constitutional malady.[14] Mongolism is therefore a constitutional disease, determined before the fifteenth day of life *in utero*, which does not appear entirely random, is

[11]Jerome's explanation in his science thesis. In it, he cites the studies: R. Turpin and J. Lejeune, "Étude dermatoglyphique de la paume des mongoliens et de leurs parents et germains", in *Semaine des Hôpitaux* (Paris, 1953), 176, and J. Lejeune, "Le diagnostic palmoscopique du mongolisme", in *Anthrop. Diff. et Sc. Types. Const.*, vol. 3 (Geneva, 1955).

[12]J. Lejeune, *Mongolisme, trisomie dégressive*, 9.

[13]Ibid.

[14]Ibid., 10.

influenced by non-hereditary traits, and concerns a large number of genes",[15] he concluded.

"Terrific! But what you are saying is very important!" cried Lafourcade.

"In any case," said Jérôme, "this methodical reasoning reinforces the initial hypothesis."

"And what is that?" his friend asked.

After a short moment of silence, Jérôme replied: "The only hypothesis that can reconcile these apparently contradictory conclusions is that of a chromosomal accident, as Turpin and Caratzali had suggested as early as 1937."[16]

Then, looking at his friend with a slight smile on his lips, Jérôme added: "All we have left is to prove it."

At the age of twenty-seven, the very young Doctor Lejeune coauthored with Turpin four articles on this subject in 1953 and 1954, then in 1955 signed six others, alone, and three with Turpin. He worked enthusiastically and published fourteen new articles in 1956 and 1957. The publications show the evolution of Jérôme's research, as his training, his experience, and the advances in science progressed. The CNRS "Research Intern" became "Research Associate" in 1954 and, then, "Head of Research" in 1956. Meanwhile, he successfully passed examinations for his certificate in genetics in 1954 and the following year for his certificate in biochemistry.

Jérôme was working at the same time on a subject that made its appearance on the international scene after the bombings of Hiroshima and Nagasaki and which continued his reflections: the effects of atomic radiation on the human hereditary patrimony. In 1955, he coauthored with Turpin their first publication on the subject, which would be followed by so many others that Jérôme was quickly recognized internationally as a specialist in atomic radiation. One of these publications had a great national impact and saved the lives of several hundred shoe salespersons:[17] After a survey and an analysis of

[15] Ibid., 12–13. This sentence is not an exact quotation from Jérôme Lejeune but a repetition of the four points of his conclusion.

[16] Ibid., 13.

[17] R. Turpin, J. Lejeune, "Influence possible sur la stabilité du patrimoine héréditaire humain de l'utilisation industrielle de l'énergie atomique", *Bulletin de l'Académie nationale de médecine*, February 8, 1955: 104.

thousands of questionnaires, Jérôme demonstrated that repeated use of X-ray machines—then a very fashionable method of measuring customers' size—is dangerous for the salesperson. In 1957, at the age of thirty-one, his work on atomic radiation had become so extensive that he was appointed French expert on the United Nations Scientific Committee on the effects of radiation, in the section on genetics. This appointment would be renewed for more than twenty years, and in this capacity he departed on his first trip across the Atlantic, in June 1957, to New York.

Jérôme's first flight to the United States delighted Birthe:

"My Jérôme, I am sure that you will be very brilliant, as always, and that everyone will applaud you", she said with conviction, beaming with admiration. "When I think that my husband is invited to New York, to the U.N.! I am very proud!" she added tenderly.

Jérôme smiled at her: "If my audience is as impartial as you, I have no need to worry!"

Then, reassuring her: "Don't worry, everything will be fine, I am well prepared. And then we'll write to each other every day, and you'll know everything. I just hope these long days, when you take care of the three little ones alone, won't be too tiring for you. Not that I help you much in the kitchen," he added, laughing, "but at least when I'm around, you know you can count on me if you need me."

Turpin, for his part, expected a lot from this trip. He sent his young collaborator confidently, hoping that he would brilliantly defend the banner of French genetics. A few days after Jérôme arrived in New York, he wrote to him and gave him some news about the department:

> Dear friend, you are performing a hard duty rather than a pleasure trip. However, if we stay in the spotlight during these U.N. deliberations, you will be well rewarded. Mademoiselle Rethoré defended her thesis yesterday. The ceremony at the hall (*foyer*) gave me the opportunity to tell her publicly what I thought of her dedication and diligence. The creation of the Institut de Progénèse is becoming increasingly necessary. Mademoiselle Gautier started an initial culture of heart tissue. I got the microscope Bocquet asked for. In short, everything continues to progress little by little. Do not tire yourself too much, but defend our colors well. We are at a turning point (I mean the country)

that is of capital importance for our future. Activity remains very high. There is no lack of energy. Very truly yours.[18]

The small team of researchers had grown over the months. In addition to Turpin and Lejeune, it was made up of Doctors Jacques Lafourcade, Henri Jérôme, Marie-Odile Rethoré, and recently included Marthe Gautier, who had completed her internship and successfully defended her thesis in 1955, and Madame Macé, the technician. In 1956, Professor Turpin's entire department left Saint-Louis Hospital for Trousseau Hospital, but the equipment was still not very satisfactory, and resourcefulness was the order of the day. To Birthe, who asked him whether they had settled in, Jérôme replied, "The room where we work is superb."

Then he added, "It has two large bays, opening onto the sky, but there is no water, no gas, no lab bench."

"Huh?!" Birthe was surprised. "But the equipment is more modern than what you had at Saint-Louis!" she worried.

"Our microscope, which was the pride of the hospital around the 1920s, still behaves rather valiantly, especially when I pad the worn teeth of its rack with a bit of the tinfoil wrapper from a chocolate bar, carefully inserted between the gears."

"With you there, that does not surprise me at all!" said Birthe, amused.

"This optical wonder sits on a gurney that stands in as a bench, and a high chair, rather similar to the ones still seen in rural churches behind the old harmonium, completes the layout", Jérôme continued, pantomiming the installation, before adding with a laugh: "It is truly a makeshift installation that will bring us luck, I am sure of it!"[19]

Since Jérôme had developed the hypothesis of chromosomal accident as the cause of mongolism, he sought to demonstrate it, and the major discovery of Levan and Tjio, in 1956, proving that human cells contain forty-six chromosomes, offered him new possibilities. Now he had to check whether this was the case with mongoloid children. To do this, he improved the technique of growing tissue culture[20]

[18] R. Turpin, letter to J. Lejeune, June 29, 1957.

[19] Jérôme Lejeune, cited by P. Debray-Ritzen, *Éloge pour l'élection à l'Académie des sciences morales et politiques de Jérôme Lejeune*, November 28, 1983.

[20] Lejeune, Turpin, and Gautier, "Étude des chromosomes somatiques humains", *Revue française d'études cliniques et biologiques* 5 (1960).

that had been imported very helpfully from the United States by Marthe Gautier, who came to work in the afternoons at Trousseau, and he perfected an original technique for staining chromosomes.[21] After weeks of trial and error, he found a novel method that he described that evening to his wife:

"I finally managed to find how to stain the chromosomes a deep purple to bring them out against an absolutely colorless background. This makes it easier to observe them and to take pictures. And these improvements will allow us to avoid the frequent errors in counting chromosomes."

"And then, how do you count them?" asked Birthe, always showing great interest in her husband's work.

"One important step is then to enlarge the images on which the counts will be carried out, because some small chromosomes are very difficult, if not impossible, to identify without quality photos. Imagine a bit, it is like counting forty-six little vermicelli of different sizes, vaguely X-shaped and softened, swimming in disarray on the bottom of a plate."

"And you manage to count them on the picture?" Birthe asked.

"On the photograph, the chromosomes are scattered, so I cut them out, and then I group them, side by side, and I paste them in descending order of size into twenty-two pairs plus the twenty-third pair of sex chromosomes (Y and/or X)."

"Do you have any special instruments to make this montage?" his attentive wife asked.

"Yes, of course. We have scissors and pots of glue, just like in school", he replied mischievously. "And what's more, it's true", he added, amused at Birthe's incredulity.

After having verified in his turn, in 1958, the constant presence of forty-six chromosomes in normal individuals, Jérôme could finally get down to looking for chromosomal abnormalities in the mongoloid child. After many trials and tribulations in establishing and reading karyotypes, a process that he refined with Marthe Gautier in the spring of 1958 by observing the chromosomes of a tissue cell of one of his mongoloid patients, he managed, for the first time in the history of medicine, to identify an extra chromosome. In this case, the

[21] Lejeune, Turpin, and Gautier, "Le mongolisme, 1er exemple d'aberration autosomique humaine", *Annales de génétique* 1 (1959).

chromosome was added to the smallest pair.[22] In his logbook of analysis, which Jérôme began on July 10, 1957,[23] in which he recorded meticulously by hand the karyotypes obtained, that is to say, the map of chromosomes classified by pair, he wrote in the ninth line:

> May 22, 1958: Jean-François R. (three months), mongoloid, one extra chromosome.

While he noted on line 10:

> Ellyet D., June 13, 1958, intersex syndrome, reportedly 47 chromosomes.

Not only did Jérôme manage to count an extra chromosome, but he also knew how to identify the one that is responsible for mongolism and the one that causes an intersex syndrome.

That same week, a young American geneticist, Kurt Hirschhorn, who had been sent across the Atlantic for a tour of the noteworthy European geneticists, came to Paris to meet young Doctor Lejeune. After a visit to Sweden's Karolinska University to the people who awarded the Nobel Prize, he was amazed to see the antiquated laboratory and equipment at the disposal of Professor Turpin's team. Yet he was not at the end of his surprises.

Returning to the room where a monocular microscope from the 1930s reigned, he saw Jérôme literally jumping with enthusiasm.

"I am very happy that you came. I have to show you this!" he said, quite excited.

And taking Kurt Hirschhorn by the arm, he brought him over to the microscope and signaled for him to look. The American could not get over it.

"But that's an extra chromosome! A forty-seventh chromosome!"

Then, lifting his eyes from the luminous circle to look Jérôme in the face:

"And, according to you, this would be the explanation for mongolism?! I admit that it is extremely exciting to look into the microscope and see what produces this congenital pathology."[24]

[22] J. Lejeune, *Mongolisme, trisomie dégressive.*

[23] J. Lejeune, *Carnet d'analyse, Laboratoire d'études nucléaires*, started on July 10, 1957.

[24] K. Hirschhorn, *Oral History of Human Genetics Project*, UCL, Johns Hopkins University, August 7, 2002, and his interview in *Jérôme Lejeune: Au plus petit d'entre les miens*, documentary film by F. Lespés, April 2015.

Jérôme was delighted with what he saw, but he did not get carried away because he had to confirm this result with other similar observations.

"Yes, it is fantastic. But it intrigues me. I thought it was one less chromosome and not an extra chromosome that would cause this mental handicap. But it is apparently an extra chromosome, on the smallest pair. What a surprise! I have to check this observation with other cases. Until it is confirmed, we cannot be sure of anything. It could be, for example, a split of a chromosome in two, and not two chromosomes as it appears to us under the microscope."

'That's true", replied Kurt, nodding his head.

"Unfortunately," said Jérôme, "I cannot check all these things now because I have to be away from the laboratory for several months. I am leaving for Canada and then the United States. I will not be back until December."

"Ah, too bad! And what are your plans during these four months?" the American asked.

"First, I will go to the genetics conference in Montreal, August 18–31, followed by a seminar at the genetics lab at McGill University in Montreal; then I will go to Quebec, Ottawa, Toronto, Saskatoon, Vancouver, Seattle. I will stay in Canada the whole month of September. Then I am off to California, to Pasadena. Professor Beadle, whom you surely know, the head of the laboratory of the Department of Biology and Genetics of the [California] Institute of Technology, invited me to give a course on human genetics to his students. I will be there from October 1 to November 19. Then Denver, where I will visit the laboratories of Professors Puck and Tjio, whose technique I just used to observe chromosomes, and I will finish my tour with a few lectures in Ann Arbor, Michigan, then in Baltimore, at Johns Hopkins Hospital.

"What an itinerary!" Kurt Hirschhorn exclaimed.

"Yes. This is the first time that I have so many lectures and courses to give", Jérôme added simply, "and I admit that the stakes of all this frighten me a little."

Jérôme did not tell his American colleague that, in addition, Turpin had given him orders to "defend the position of French genetics."[25]

[25] R. Turpin, letter to J. Lejeune, September 5, 1958.

Turpin was very happy about this trip; he was convinced that his young collaborator would be able to demonstrate the quality of the French studies and that he would develop their network while collecting useful information. After Jérôme had left, Turpin wrote to him regularly to encourage him. For example, on October 12:

> My dear friend, the pangs you felt at the prospect of the perilous lectures must now be dispelled, at least in part, since your course is no doubt well under way. You will certainly make an excellent impression. Be sure to take any information about the equipment that you will need. Have you seen any electronic tests? Some tests have certainly been done. What were the results?[26]

He also gave him important news about the laboratory.

> Two visitors who came to see me; Cordero Ferreira (a pediatrician from Lisbon) and J. Mohr from Oslo were amazed by your chromosomal preparations. Mlle. Gautier and Mme. Macé are still at forty-six [in their repeated count].

Then again some instructions:

> When this letter reaches you, you will have only one month "to shoot". I think that this rather difficult trip will have been very profitable. Because of the value of the men that you met, the documentation that you collected (apparatus necessary for chromosomal studies, do they have electronic tests?), and your conferences, some of which will certainly be usable in writing your prospective book.[27]

Jérôme, plainly, left a great void in the department, for his colleagues also wrote to him on several occasions. For instance Marthe Gautier, on October 20, 1958:

> Dear friend, I recently received your letters after some delay because they sat for a while in a supervisor's drawer. Put on the address:

[26] Ibid., October 12, 1958.

[27] Ibid., October 27, 1958. (In this letter, Turpin writes the name Macé with a misspelling that we have deliberately not reproduced here.)

Parrot Lab or my address. I do not know whether this letter will reach you, because you may have left the enchanting places in California. Recently we had some very fine cells to count, but still at the developmental stage in a case of achondroplasia [dwarfism]. Still enormous difficulties in getting new tissue cultures. Nothing since June 15. Your return, I hope, will facilitate this wait for tissues, which is becoming intolerable. I obtain some from normal patients in other hospitals. Nothing worse than the force of inertia. Apart from that, the blow-ups look better since we started using benzododecinium (genus tween). So, some nice pictures in perspective. Grab all the tips you can about tissue cultures and all the other off-prints that are given out on your visits. Regards.[28]

Or Henri Jérôme:

I look forward to your return to enhance my intellectual environment.[29]

Another good friend, Jean de Grouchy, whom he had met during his military service and whom he encountered again in the corridors of the hospital, also wrote to him:

Dear Jérôme, thanks for your gracious letter full of spicy news. However, I am surprised by a certain apathy that emerges between the lines. Do not despair, you will see your homeland again; instead, take advantage of this wonderful opportunity [two words written in English in the original] that you have to spend these few months in the U.S. This is an opportunity that may not come again soon. Note that I do not envy you for having to teach genetics to Beadle and to your eminent colleagues. Personally, I would have been in the situation of someone who wished he were buried very deep in the ground. I'm sure you got away with all the honors and glory. The rocket left yesterday, and I am following it passionately. I think that in the U.S. you must all be very excited. That is really something. My little father, I look forward impatiently to your return. Goodbye, my man, have fun and don't be sorry: your loneliness is golden and is worth the trouble, believe me.[30]

[28] M. Gautier, letter to J. Lejeune, October 20, 1958.
[29] H. Jérôme, letter to J. Lejeune, November 11, 1958.
[30] J. de Grouchy, letter to J. Lejeune, October 1958.

Although Jérôme was languishing, far from his family, he was also very happy with the important and enriching encounters that he had throughout those four months. A few days after his arrival in Montreal, on August 26, he gave his lecture on the variations of masculinity in the descendants of irradiated parents. And that evening, satisfied with the assignment and relieved, he told Birthe, in his daily letter to her, all the details for which she was waiting:

> My paper was considered very interesting, and I gave it in French, without reading the text, and the Americans told me that they had understood almost everything. In fact, they all agreed on finding the observed effect very curious, hardly believable. It is indeed my opinion, and I was very careful in my demonstration.[31]

Like all congresses, it offered the participants the opportunity to compare their studies, and Jérôme counted on taking the opportunity to confirm or invalidate his hypothesis on the causes of mongolism. The day after his arrival, he visited the genetic exhibition, where the world's best photos of human chromosomes were displayed, and the comparison of these photos with his own was not at all to his disadvantage. He hastened to write to Birthe:

> Mine are just as good, but I kept them in my pocket.[32]

Then to some geneticists whom he knew and appreciated, like Schultz, Neel, or Kodani, he showed his photo of forty-seven chromosomes, and they acknowledged its extraordinary quality. He was pleased to note their interest and refined his own hypothesis by discussing with them "the hypothesis of an extra chromosome or of a preferential rupture at a 'weak' point."[33] Jérôme also showed some naïveté, because he did not hesitate to report on his studies at the McGill University seminar—hoping for a fruitful exchange of ideas—at the risk of being overtaken by another copycat team, which did not escape Turpin. The latter urged him to have the utmost

[31] J. Lejeune, letter to Birthe, August 26, 1958.

[32] Ibid., August 22, 1958.

[33] J. Lejeune and R. Turpin, *Deux exemples de maladies chromosomiques humaines*, 1959.

discretion, oscillating between the fear of appearing ridiculous with a worthless "observation" and the fear of others getting credit first if, on the contrary, it really was a major discovery.

Jérôme, more and more convinced that an additional chromosome was the cause of mongolism, ardently resumed his research projects as soon as he returned to Paris. And a few days later, in December, his efforts were crowned with success: he managed to find two new cases of an extra chromosome in two mongoloid children. That evening, at the house on rue Galande, he did not wait for dinner to announce the good news to Birthe. He had scarcely taken off his coat when he very happily called to her, "I have two new cases! It's fantastic! These two additional photos confirm the first observation last May. It seems that the hypothesis of a forty-seventh chromosome that is responsible for mongolism is really becoming clear."

"Bravo!" Birthe exclaimed. "Have you told Turpin?" she asked with her usual practical sense.

"No, not yet. Tomorrow I will do it as soon as he arrives, and I will ask him whether we can prepare a note for the Academy of Sciences. I hope that he is willing."

After some hesitations, always divided between fear of an error of observation or analysis and fear of someone else publishing first, Turpin let Jérôme convince him and agreed to present a note to the Académie des Sciences. On the evening of January 16, 1959, Jérôme wrote in his journal:

> The mongoloids definitely do seem to have 47 chromosomes. Yesterday, new photos finally convinced me. The note for the Academy was written, carefully.[34]

The very simple note mentions three cases of mongolism associated with the presence of forty-seven chromosomes, under the title: "Human Chromosomes in Tissue Culture".[35] It is signed Lejeune, Gauthier, and Turpin, in the usual order: signed first by the principal author, last by the head of the department, and in the middle by the one or by those who participated in the work.

[34] J. Lejeune, *Journal intime*, January 16, 1959.

[35] J. Lejeune, M. Gauthier, and R. Turpin, "Les chromosomes humains en culture de tissus", in *Comptes rendus de l'Académie des sciences*, 248:602–3, session of January 26, 1959. In this note, Gautier is mistakenly written with an "h".

Comfortably seated on the sofa, which was covered with a Danish plaid to protect them in winter from the cold that the stove in the apartment just managed to dispel—Jérôme and Birthe indulged in a moment of quiet. The three little ones were taking a nap, the house was silent. Jérôme, with his wife at his side, was as happy as Ulysses after his long journey.

"My Birthe, the year 1959 opens up before us, promising work and happiness. The three children are well, our little family is well united, and we have no worries about money, although we are not rich. Maybe for that very reason, by the way. The Institut de Progenèse has just been officially established by the minister's decision, and its research into chromosomes is almost up and running. Already I can correctly diagnose sex based on chromosomal garniture, and maybe an anomaly of one of the smallest chromosomes (a disjunction at ovular chromatic reduction) is the cause of mongolism."[36]

"That's true, darling. We are very fortunate. And your research is progressing well. But," Birthe added, "I see that you are a little worried all the same."

Jérôme looked at her tenderly. "My Birthe certainly reads me like an open book", he thought before answering, reassured to be able to confide his concern:

"Since my return from America, the idea of the book I am supposed to write with Turpin has been tormenting me. It is a very heavy task, which I accepted very lightly. I am almost sure that I can do it, but such a performance is at the very limit of my capabilities, so that every day I try to push back the deadline and avoid such a severe confrontation. I have not yet had the courage to apply myself to it, and yet, it is high time now! Alas, I am lazier and more negligent than you can imagine. Everything takes me a lot of effort, and apart from a good read in an armchair, the rest of the everyday commotion hardly tempts me."

And while Birthe was finding words to encourage him, Jérôme said to himself silently:

"This is a fine confession, at which I am the first to blush. But should we not try sometimes to look a little more closely at our own shortcomings?"[37]

[36] J. Lejeune, *Journal intime*, January 13, 1959.

[37] Paragraph composed of quotations from the *Journal intime*, by Jérôme Lejeune, of January 27 and February 1, 1959.

More than with writing the book, Jérôme's time was taken up by his research projects. The January note to the Académie des Sciences, so cautious and without a photo, had had little impact, and he was eager to confirm this first publication with new observations. He himself still hesitated about the importance of this work. In early February, he wrote in his journal:

> Of course, I always hesitate before stating that we have "discovered" the secret of mongolism, but even if it were true, what good would that do us! Ah, if it were a treatment I might think otherwise, but that would be a very different situation.[38]

The months of January and February brought him the confirmations he was looking for, and Jérôme thought that the hour had come to publish a second note, more complete than the first.

In early March, Jérôme took advantage of one of his usual late-afternoon discussions with Turpin to propose to him a second publication: "The chromosomes of mongoloids still seem to be stabilizing at forty-seven. Already three girls have come to be added to the four previous boys! Another girl and a couple of twins, one of them mongoloid, will probably be ready to analyze on Friday or Saturday. If everything goes as we hope, a new note could be issued next Monday."[39]

While saying this, Jérôme observed his boss. He seemed impatient to know more about it. Confident, Jérôme continued:

"Besides, I have already mentioned this in Barsinghausen."

Suddenly taken aback by this announcement, which he considered premature, Turpin replied, "But Lejeune, it is not yet absolutely certain."

"But that is precisely what I told them, sir", Jérôme answered.

"But why talk about it so soon? Penrose will find out!" said Turpin, unhappy and worried.

"But if he reads the reports of the Académie des Sciences, he already knows it, sir", Jérôme said, defending himself.[40]

Turpin remained silent for a moment, then let it go. "All right, we will publish. When can you bring me the note, Lejeune?"

[38] Lejeune, *Journal intime*, February 10, 1959.

[39] Ibid., March 4, 1959.

[40] Ibid.

"I expect the latest results on Saturday, and if they confirm the previous work, I will bring them to you on Monday, sir."

"Perfect", replied Turpin, with an indefinable air.

Jérôme went home, all excited. To Birthe, who asked him her usual question: "Whom did you see, who told you what?" he answered enthusiastically:

"I just spoke with Turpin."

"About what?" Birthe inquired while putting a plate of potatoes and a little green salad on the table.

"About a second publication on the link between an extra chromosome and mongolism", Jérôme said.

Then he exclaimed,

> How difficult it is to know whether or not we have found something solid! Neither Turpin nor I doubt it, and yet we cannot quite believe it. For him, I understand, because I am the only one who counted and recounted the chromosomes in question. But for me, my mind is made up: the normal ones are forty-six, I counted two new cases this morning, and the mongoloids have forty-seven.[41]

"You have to publish very quickly, so that someone else doesn't do it first", his wife interrupted.

Jérôme continued, thinking:

> I wonder what Tjio, the promoter of the method, will say about our next article, which will be decisive, with supporting photos. Enough! As long as we don't "doctor" the photos, I don't see what would prevent us from publishing our results. It "fits nicely" and all the better, and if it happens later that it does not "fit nicely" in all cases, well, another hypothesis more refined than the current one will come to replace it. Really, I would not be ashamed at all to make a mistake, since I do it in good faith, and I do not risk harming anyone. Besides, by the end of this week, I will most likely be sure![42]

Since the latest observations confirmed all the previous ones, Jérôme got down to work on the meticulous writing of the note. Every word counted. But all this work exhausted him, and he confided to his journal:

[41] Ibid., March 15, 1959.

[42] Ibid.

Over the past few days, I have been very worried about the final version of the note on the mongoloids' extra chromosome. The note will be presented to the Academy tomorrow by the dean, and then I can finally breathe. But the work and the haste have tired me out, and several boils have just indicated that this overwork does me no good.[43]

The second note was published at the Académie des Sciences on March 16, 1959. Cautiously, it states:

In nine mongoloid children, the study ... enabled us to observe regularly the presence of 47 chromosomes.[44]

But not until April 1959 and their third publication, this one in the *Bulletin de l'Académie de médecine*, did they write:

In conclusion, we think that we can say that mongolism is a chromosomal disease, the first to be definitively demonstrated in our species.[45]

For the first time, in this long and detailed publication, Lejeune presented photos of karyotypes in support of the demonstration. Thus, from the simple observation mentioned in the publication in January 1959 to the observation in March 1959, they arrived in April 1959 at the affirmation ... eleven months after Jérôme first observed forty-seven chromosomes in a mongoloid child.

These results were also confirmed by the Anglo-Scottish team of Brown and Jacobs. Upon discovering their publication, sitting in front of his desk, Jérôme was delighted to see his conclusions cross-checked by another team. However, his face revealed a slight sign of annoyance that did not escape his friend, Jacques Lafourcade, who was standing beside him:

"What is it, Jérôme? Is something wrong?"

"No, nothing serious," he replied, "but I notice that they cite only our first publication and not the second. However," he went on, "I sent to Court Brown, at his request, the second note to the Academy

[43] Ibid.

[44] J. Lejeune, M. Gautier, and R. Turpin, "Étude des chromosomes somatiques de neuf enfants mongoliens", in *Comptes rendus de l'Académie des sciences* 248 (March 16, 1959): 1721–22.

[45] J. Lejeune, M. Gautier, and R. Turpin, "Le mongolisme, maladie chromosomique", *Bulletin de l'Académie nationale de médecine*, 2nd trimester, 1959: 143.

concerning nine mongoloids and describing the mechanism of the malady. He was very careful not to mention it; he only has six cases, and he was content to cite the first note, which mentioned only three cases. After all, that is his right, strictly speaking, but a few more scruples and accuracy would not have dishonored him."[46]

"That's obvious", replied Lafourcade, before adding in a bantering tone: "Well, old man, don't worry, it doesn't change the anteriority of the first publication, which is French! And not English!"

"You are right," replied Jérôme, whose outburst of bad humor had already faded, "this little business of the chromosome is a closed case.[47] Besides, it doesn't matter much, as long as we figure out now how to cure these children."

A few days later, in May 1959, a Swedish team in turn published its results on the cause of mongolism. The discovery was confirmed again. It opened a new chapter in human genetics: cytogenetics.

The interest in this novel discovery was immense. On the one hand, it demonstrated, for the first time in the history of medicine, the chromosomal origin of a human disease, and, on the other hand, it proved the existence of a totally unknown mechanism in human beings, namely, the transmission of a chromosomal aberration. This opened up extraordinary prospects for research. But most important of all was the change that it made for the patients, those for whom Jérôme worked. This discovery freed parents from the overwhelming view of [French] society that regarded mongoloid children as a punishment for their misconduct. A condemning, lethal view that led parents to hide their child, who had become an object of shame for the family. Before the discovery, the parents were alone in confronting their fate, without hope of treatment. Now, by demonstrating that it was a disease caused by the chance presence of an extra chromosome that was not diseased and not hereditary, much less a punishment for ancestral sins, and by launching the search for a cure, Jérôme delivered the parents from this feeling of guilt. For the first time, it broke the isolation of families and gave them a little hope. The French would no longer speak of mongolism but about trisomy. It was the dawn of a revolution.

[46] J. Lejeune, *Journal intime*, April 1, 1959.
[47] Ibid.

CHAPTER 5

"THE DREAM OF MY LIFE"

1959–1962

> Delicious beer, German sausages and cigars—nothing was missing. The friendship of Carter, and especially of Lewis, made the first part of this stay a pleasant rest. Then two days of work at the I.C.R.F. [Imperial Cancer Research Fund], of which I was elected a member. Then two days to compose the note, a solemn lecture, and roaming about for a day with Théo. A delicious saddle of venison went on the expense account for our farewell meal, and we two parted emotionally.[1]

While folding up her husband's letter, postmarked Munich, Birthe remarked to her mother with satisfaction: "At least success is not going to his head. He tells me more about the joy of meeting his friends than about his election or his conference!"

Then, sitting down across from her mother in front of a big mug of black coffee: "I am glad to see that he is getting a little rest. This is his second conference this summer, and the program of the next few months is very busy. It is not stealing to take a few moments of relaxation. After Italy and Germany, he has to go to London, too, and then to the United States!"

While Birthe listed these countries as so many victories of her husband, Magdalene looked affectionately at her daughter: it was touching that her little *Bittenur* was so happy about her husband's successes. "These two are truly made for each other", she said to herself again joyfully.

Then she added out loud, smiling at her daughter: "I am sure that your Jérôme has not finished making people talk about him."

[1] This account is in fact an excerpt from the *Journal intime* of J. Lejeune, August 1959.

Indeed, ever since the discovery of the cause of mongolism, Jérôme found that his invitations to international conferences were proliferating. His career, which had already started well, took flight again. In 1959, by secret ballot, he was unanimously elected head of research projects at the CNRS [Centre national de la recherche scientifique, French national center for scientific research],[2] and abroad his success was spreading like a wave. Many had spotted this young physician who was presenting high-quality, original studies and defending the colors of French genetics tactfully and brilliantly at international conferences, and without delay they celebrated this discovery and opened their doors to him. He was immediately identified by the international community as the principal discoverer of trisomy 21. Several awards, countless letters, and a few interviews rained down on him.

In June 1959, he gave a conference in Venice to a symposium on radiation. It was an opportunity for Jérôme to discover that enchanting city whose magic and beauty overwhelmed the greatest poets. Although prepared to be disappointed by those mazes of canals unceasingly described in such emphatic terms, Jérôme in turn was smitten. He would come back, though, with an unhappy memory. At the opera house La Fenice, he lost his wallet and his father's wedding ring, which he had devoutly placed in it. This loss grieved him deeply. After Venice, he finally visited his family in Denmark, where he spent two weeks on vacation, then flew to Munich for the conference on radiology before returning in late August to meet with the whole family in Kerteminde.

The return trip to Paris was noisy. The old boat, loaded down to the waterline with children and packages, was behaving well despite the 115,000 kilometers [71,300 miles] on the odometer, and for this southbound excursion it was launched with a full gas tank. With the result that the tailpipe broke between Hamburg and Bienne.

"Do you think that we should stop and see a mechanic in Bienne, Darling?" Jérôme asked Birthe, who was dozing beside him despite the terrible din.

"No. We are going back to Paris. Better to go to our mechanic than to a stranger. We would not even have German money to pay for it!"

[2] Ibid., June 6, 1959.

"Quite right", Jérôme acknowledged. "Nothing left for us to do but to hum *Eine Kleine Nachtmusik* to harmonize with that racket which, I hope, will not be the swan song of our faithful torpedo!"

After several exhausting hours, the Lejeune crew made a triumphal entry on the rue Galande. No neighbor could be unaware of the family's arrival!

Jérôme made use of the few days in Paris to finish improving the technique for dyeing chromosomes by replacing the acidic solution recommended in the manuals with an alkaline solution. This work was quickly interrupted by his departure for the symposium on human chromosomes that was being held at King's College in London on September 18 and 19. Jérôme was aware that this meeting was important for him and for French genetics because, being the only Frenchman invited, he was going to present to the participants his team's pioneering studies on mongolism.

Several weeks later, Jérôme found that an important scientific prize was being offered to him, but this good news was accompanied by an unpleasant surprise, which the envoy from the jury announced to him at the same time: "You will receive the N. Prize and the 100,000 francs that go with it, but I must tell you that it is on one condition: you must oust your boss from the project."

Jérôme was staggered. "How is such a proposal possible?" he silently asked himself. "I am very naïve, no doubt! But it is out of the question." Jérôme flatly refused the deal, aware that he was losing the award and the 100,000 francs that went with it, but his decision was irrevocable. He frankly told the envoy from the jury: "Then I will not receive it; don't rely on me to oust my boss."

That evening, when Birthe had already fallen asleep, Jérôme wrote what he was thinking deep down:

> I prefer not winning to having a dirty trick on my conscience.
>
> But [he added] I cannot help feeling a kind of bitterness when I remember the conduct of the person concerned during the last competitive exam. To have been sold out for F. and to continue to play the game is obviously the only honorable position, but it is a bitter pill to take![3]

[3] Ibid., October 29, 1959.

Jérôme quickly forgot these annoyances in his preparations for his next trip to New York, where American psychiatrists were inviting him to explain to them the chromosomal constitution of mongoloids.

While Birthe was helping her husband to pack his suitcase to brave a snow-covered New York, she told him, while handing him a large sweater: "Just one year ago, you were returning from your first trip to the United States! You have made such progress since then!"

"Yes, that is true", Jérôme replied. "What a year! But the most wonderful thing of all is our little well-united family. And this time I am leaving for only a few days. Fortunately."

"Yes, fortunately", Birthe answered. "The little ones will be asking for you. We will count the nights while waiting for you to return. Try to remember to bring them some souvenirs. If you can."

Jérôme was awaited at the Roosevelt Institute and at prestigious Columbia University, where his conferences met with an enthusiastic reception. On the evening of his first speech, he described to his wife the American frenzy for chromosomes:

> There you have it, the long speech is over, and as for having success, I did have some: they applauded for a minute by the clock (or almost). Everyone adored the chromosomes; that is all they talk about, and everyone is doing research on it. It is a true passion.[4]

Jérôme was astonished at this infatuation, and even more at the warmth of the reception that was given to him. They took him to the best restaurants, pampered him, and surrounded him with care. One evening, during a very private dinner, Jérôme discovered what was really at stake in these invitations.

"Do you know", one of the organizers of the conference asked him, "that next year Columbia is supposed to endow a chair of human genetics?"

"No, I did not know that. It is a very good idea", Jérôme replied.

"And do you know whom we have chosen for that?"

Jérôme reflected quickly. Several names came to his mind, but he was not well enough acquainted with his American colleagues to

[4] J. Lejeune, letter to Birthe, December 11, 1959.

venture onto that terrain. Shaking his head, he replied in the negative: "No, I have no idea."

"I'm not surprised. It is difficult to find the right person", his host agreed. Then he continued with a big smile: "Therefore we thought of you. You are the one whom we chose."[5]

Suddenly Jérôme understood. This invitation, these receptions, this incredible welcome! And before he could say a word, his interlocutor explained: "The faculty council elected you three months ago. You see that I am not making this proposal to you lightly. Obviously, your salary will be in keeping with your responsibilities. If my information is correct, I think that it will be three times as much as you are earning in Paris."

"What an honor", Jérôme answered, struggling to recover from his surprise. "Your proposal is an honor, and I thank you for it. You will understand that I must reflect on it before giving you my answer."

Back in Paris, Jérôme reported this proposal to Turpin. The latter took the blow courageously and wanted to appeal to the Dean of the University in order to find a solution. But Columbia, in order to be sure of catching him, renewed its proposal eight months later, in September 1960, and increased its offer.[6] The promised sums seemed colossal to Jérôme, far beyond anything that he could have imagined, not to speak of the fringe benefits in kind: a house, a car ...

In April 1960, Jérôme left for Denver, where they were waiting for him to participate in a restricted committee that was going to decide on the classification of chromosomes. Once again, he was the only Frenchman in this international group of around fifteen persons. The debates were fierce, and Jérôme understood rather quickly that he would not succeed in having his classification accepted. He found himself compelled to accept the classification and the numbering of chromosomes in descending order of size, from one to twenty-three. Mongolism would henceforth be called trisomy 21, the extra chromosome of mongoloids being one of the smallest. He came round to this decision, which after all is of no importance, but noted in passing the unusual tension among the participants. One of his colleagues explained it.

"There is some feverishness in the air, don't you think?"

[5] J. Lejeune, *Journal intime*, December 19, 1959.

[6] J. Lejeune, letter to Birthe, September 2, 1960, and *Journal intime*, September 5–9, 1960.

"Indeed", Jérôme replied. "And I wonder why. The final decision about the classification is not that important; it is only a convention!"

"Hah, you don't get it at all!" his interlocutor said with a laugh. "It is not about that! The stakes are much higher: a rumor is going around that the Nobel Prize might be awarded to a specialist in chromosomes. Just think: it is a race!"

"Ah, I understand," Jérôme said, a bit surprised nevertheless, "but I think it is really a shame that this tension complicated the discussions."

He added, laughing, "Unless the Nobel Prize will be awarded to the promoter of the classification of chromosomes?"

But Jérôme still had some surprises left. He soon learned that the organizers would no longer reimburse traveling expenses, as had initially been expected, and he found himself compelled to deduct 400,000 francs from the family budget.

"That is an enormous sum! And for what? Just to have my classification rejected!"[7] he thought on the plane that brought him back to Orly. "Fortunately, my trips are usually better organized and more efficient! Well, no reason to worry: if my next conferences in Sweden, Switzerland, the USSR, and the United States are at my expense, I will go by bike!"

In June, one month after his return from Denver, Jérôme successfully defended his thesis on natural science. So he was a doctor twice over. His research naturally concerned *Mongolism, degressive trisomy*,[8] but during the argumentation, his poor mother thought that "they" would refuse to give him the title of *dignus intrare* ["worthy to enter"]. It must be said that the suspense was well managed and that the deliberation of the jury, with Professors Lamotte and L'Héritier, seemed imposing for the uninitiated. The ceremony was followed by a small, very pleasant reception in the laboratory. L'Héritier, Lamotte, and Turpin, who postponed his departure for Trouville, were warm and friendly as they attended alongside Jérôme's relatives: his mother, Philippe, Rémy, and Aunt Charlotte. Birthe, beautiful in a pretty summer dress, was radiant, and Jérôme, quite joyful, skillfully proposed a toast for everyone, without forgetting to mention his two dear relatives who were absent.

[7] J. Lejeune, *Journal intime*, May 2, 1960.

[8] J. Lejeune, *Le mongolisme, trisomie dégressive*, thesis in science, 1960.

> To my dear Papa who urged me to write this thesis. Dear God, may he be able to rejoice with us this evening, because his wish has been fulfilled. And to my dear grandfather. As Philippe pointed out to me, both of them were the reason for my present career, each in his own way. My memory of them seems to me too pale and discolored to satisfy my affection, but certainly I do not forget them.[9]

And Jérôme added: "To my patients, finally, and to all persons with trisomy, to whom this study is dedicated. They are its inspiration and guidance."

His happiness made their appeal even more urgent, and that same evening he recorded these feelings in his *Journal*:

> When we see every day these poor children whom we cannot help at all, I want to work, to "do something" in order to avoid the sort of reproach that I hear from them: "Oh, sure, you complete your thesis with our extra chromosome, but what are you doing for us?" I could not admit that to the jury today, but this feeling is not just a literary amusement for me. It is true.[10]

In the days that followed his thesis, Jérôme remarked with a smile that those who had shown little interest in mongolism several months before suddenly proved to be enthralled by the topic and hastened to congratulate him. But he had already learned that these congratulations on the lips do not always come from the heart. For several months, Jérôme had observed sadly the effects of success on some of his acquaintances.

> Maybe my character is souring, but I get the impression that success, as well as adversity, shows who your true friends are; the false friends become jealous and show it despite themselves. Ugh![11]

In September 1960, Jérôme was the delegate of the International Atomic Agency to a colloquium of the World Health Organization (WHO) in Geneva. When he arrived, they took the opportunity to offer him the position of geneticist of the WHO. Jérôme was aware

[9] J. Lejeune, *Journal intime*, June 24, 1960.

[10] Ibid.

[11] Ibid., November 30, 1959.

that this position was a "golden sinecure",[12] but he prepared to reject it. For he had a dream. A dream that he had carried inside secretly since the first publication about the discovery of trisomy and that guided his research:

> To make a mongoloid capable of being appointed a professor on the faculty of medicine in Paris! That is the dream of my life.[13]

His growing fame did not cause him to forget his initial impulse, when he met those children while assisting Professor Turpin eight years earlier. Their silent appeal transformed the physician that he was by vocation into a passionate researcher so as to find some way to cure them. And this passion was not extinguished with success. On the contrary, the appeal was all the more urgent.

That evening, in his hotel room, standing beside the window and looking out at the passersby going down toward Lake Léman without seeing them, Jérôme reflected: "We made this discovery for my patients and thanks to them; there is no question of abandoning them now." Still, the choice was not an obvious one. For Jérôme was interested in everything and had talent. He loved mathematics, physics, astronomy, and his ingenuity and his distinctions offered him numerous opportunities for research in a wide variety of areas far from mongolism. So there were many temptations.

Slowly moving away from the window, Jérôme went back to the table and sat down to start his evening letter. He mechanically took his letter paper and a pen, but before he wrote a single word, his thoughts jostled one another.

> Always the same haunting problem: What can be done for these children? I remember last summer Birthe forwarded to me in Munich a moving letter from a mother who had heard about the discovery of the chromosome and wanted to know all about it. Every time I try to escape from mongolism to study mutations, polytene chromosomes, or forms of leukemia, a mother or a child is there to call me back to order and to tell me: Us first, your petty scientific ideas afterward![14]

[12] Ibid., September 5–9, 1960.
[13] Ibid., January 16, 1959.
[14] Ibid., August 1959.

Jérôme had not forgotten the sense of urgency that had gripped him then. As on that evening:

> In fact I am almost ashamed of the petty celebrity that surrounds a discovery that leads us to no treatment! It is necessary to do something![15]

The compassion that he felt for his patients was stronger than his intellectual enthusiasm for promising subjects. His decision was made: "The offer from WHO, which would take me away from this research, is not for me. I will decline it as I did the offer from Columbia. I will speak about it to Birthe, but I already know that this will be her choice!" And soon his pen was gliding over the thin paper.

"Papa, Papa!"

Jérôme did not have time to remove his coat when two little bulldozers charged up to him and clung to his legs, nearly causing him to stumble. Giving in to this priceless welcome, Jérôme leaned over and caught Karin up in his arms; being all of three years old, she was a lighter load for his poor back, while with his free left hand he tousled the black hair of Damien, who at age five still looked like a little Eskimo, and caressed the cheek of Anouk, his older daughter, who came to embrace him, her eyes shining. She was already seven, and Jérôme observed that she had in fact reached that fine age of reason that sometimes makes children wiser than adults. On the sofa, Birthe welcomed him with a happy smile. "*Bonjour*, my Darling. The baby is feeding."

The delicate blond head, snuggled in the crook of Birthe's arm, was swallowing nourishment in big gulps. While Birthe made a hand gesture to her husband, a cry that escaped from little lips beaded with milk told Jérôme that their youngest daughter had a sense of priorities: a feeding cannot wait, whereas her father ... When he approached, Jérôme saw two blue marbles staring at him, and he gently caressed the chubby hands gripping the baby bottle.

"Our little Clara already seems to be very determined", he noted with pleasure. "I wonder who she gets that from", he added, while glancing cheerfully at Birthe.

[15] Ibid., August 3, 1959.

"Surely from you, since she has your eyes!" she replied in amusement.

"However that may be, I hope that she will have your health and not mine", Jérôme said, who marveled daily at his wife's resistance and gauged the energy that she spent each day caring for the four children.

Clara's birth in January had been a true blessing for the whole family, but Jérôme was a bit uneasy about the lack of space in their apartment, which made the daily routine more difficult. The family was living in three rooms, which for six persons is a little tight. He wished he could offer something better to his wife and children. He confided in Birthe:

"Poor little Clara, she sleeps in a crib on wheels that we move from one room to another in order to avoid traffic jams.[16] If only we could take back two rooms of the house that are occupied by tenants!"

"Don't worry, my dear," she reassured him, "sooner or later that will happen. Very soon would be best, but while waiting we will manage very well."

In fact, a few months later, they got the two additional rooms and could expand. To them this sudden comfort seemed very luxurious. Birthe bustled around with more leeway, and Jérôme had some breathing space. He could now work in peace, even though that domestic calm was entirely relative, just a few meters away from the resounding commotion of the four little ones. On Saturday afternoon, Birthe sometimes asked him to take care of the big kids while she went shopping, bringing Clara along. Jérôme enjoyed this assignment and, while helping Anouk to prepare her dictation, would answer a question from Damien about the existence of angels and console Karin, whose doll had lost her shoe. One evening, however, after he had said prayers with the children and Birthe had put them to bed, he admitted to her:

> How difficult happiness itself is to endure! Three charming children for two hours, and here I am about to have a temper tantrum. Learned books praise patience, and I bet that the father of a family worthy of that name ought to make it his main virtue, not to mention the

[16] Ibid., January 28, 1960.

> essential one. Moreover, life sets out to prove to me a little more each day that this cliché is a pivotal truth![17]

Sitting beside him on the sofa, Birthe answered him affectionately: "Contrary to what you say, you are always very patient with them and available. The children love to play with you, and I admire you because they can bother you incessantly, and you always answer them with a smile. Sometimes I wonder how you do it."

And while Jérôme thanked her with a big smile, she continued softly, "But as for patience, yes, I need that. When you don't take out the trash."

Jérôme looked at her in astonishment. "My darling, I am very sorry; don't hesitate to ask me. You know how I am, if you don't tell me things plainly, I don't know what it is you need. And then," he added, "don't hesitate to tell me again, because you know how absentminded I am!"

Laughing, Birthe replied: "Very well, then, my dear. When I put the trash can in front of the door, it is so that you will take it out, not so that you can kick it aside before leaving."

"Did I do that?" Jérôme asked sheepishly.

Seeing her husband's crestfallen expression, Birthe concluded half-seriously, half-teasingly: "We agree then. I promise that I will tell you to take out the trash as often as necessary. You can count on me!"

However she had few illusions, because although Jérôme's good will was real, his absentmindedness was obvious. His mind, in perpetual motion, was focused more on his research than on everyday chores.

The year 1961 started on the other side of the Atlantic. Jérôme departed again for the United States in January to give a series of conferences in Boston for the 150th anniversary of Massachusetts General Hospital and in Philadelphia, at the Cancer Institute. He passed through New York, too, where he met with his excellent friend Bearn, whose warm welcome he appreciated, and he hastened to write to Birthe about it:

> It should be noted that at his house they drink a Vosne-Romanée wine that would make a Geiger counter poetic.[18]

[17] Ibid., February 8, 1959.
[18] Ibid., January 30, 1961.

In New York, Jérôme had to give his answer to Columbia University, which was still patiently awaiting it. Before leaving Paris, a final discussion with Birthe had confirmed their decision. "Darling, you do agree with me, then, that I should refuse their offer?"

"Of course", she answered. "You love your patients too much to abandon them, and you love France too much to go work in another country. The answer is very simple."

Jérôme admired his wife's tranquility and her ability to make quick, sound decisions. To tease her, nevertheless, he bantered: "Are you quite sure that you will not regret the great life, American style: A White House with columns lining the porch, a nice car with a chauffeur, and lots of pretty dresses?"

"Don't talk nonsense. Anyway, if I had lots of pretty dresses, I would have no time to put them on!" Birthe interrupted, laughing.

She knew very well that with the salary being offered to them over there, they could live in a kind of luxury far removed from their current situation, but what did that matter?

"What would we do with all that money? We have enough to be happy", Jérôme concluded, as though reading her thoughts.

In New York, Jérôme also met with Cournand, their official supporter for the Nobel Prize. Turpin had ordered him, several months earlier, to prepare a dossier for his candidacy, and he had done so, with some muttering about that waste of time. In the evening, upon returning to the hotel, Jérôme related to Birthe how impressed he had been by the quality of Cournand's analysis.

> He "grilled" me with the greatest possible good will but with an analytical severity that surprised me.
>
> Everything was included: the exact role played by Turpin, the extent to which he participates in the research, etc....
>
> This man does not act lightly at all and knows how to evaluate people. He wrote a very detailed report based on letters, testimonies obtained from England and America, producing a plea that is so convincing that finally it almost gave me the impression not only that this candidacy was well-founded but that there was no doubt at all about its success.[19]

[19] Ibid.

Upon returning to Paris, Jérôme finally had six months in which to work, interrupted only by a short trip to Geneva and then to Brussels, and he made use of this time to see the patients who came to his office in ever greater numbers to consult with him. Jérôme was deeply moved by the immense distress that he perceived in the constant stream of families from all over the world. Confronting that reality, and knowing that good feelings are not enough, Jérôme devoted all his mornings to consultations with patients and concentrated on his research in the afternoon. But when there was a long line, or in an emergency, it was not uncommon for Jérôme to see patients in the afternoon, too, in his laboratory. To a colleague who was surprised at this, Jérôme said:

> When parents are upset about a sick child, we do not have the right to make them wait, not even one night, if we can do otherwise.[20]

For the parents, who often experienced their child's birth as a painful trial, it would all start the moment they entered the modest office of Doctor Lejeune.

"Good morning, Madame, good morning, Monsieur. Have a seat, please."

Instead of the haughty old professor whom they were afraid of meeting in that Parisian hospital, they found a young physician with eyes as round and blue as the sky, who welcomed them with a warm smile, enhanced by a thin, well-trimmed moustache. Jérôme went up to the mother, who was carrying the child in her arms, and asked her gently whether she would be so kind as to entrust the child to him. He would take him delicately and place him on the apron that he had arranged on his knees and then, as he examined him with a stethoscope, looking kindly and constantly at the child, he asked the parents, "What is your son's name?"

"His name is Paul, Doctor", the mother replied, with tears welling up in her eyes.

She thought: "This is the first time that I have realized that I have a son, Paul, and not just a handicapped child. I finally feel that I am my little Paul's mom." Then, looking at Doctor Lejeune, she understood:

[20] J. Lejeune, *Symphonie de la Vie* (Fondation Lejeune, 2000), 21.

> This is the first time that I have seen someone look at my son with so much love. Thanks to that look, I have come to understand that my son's life has value and that my Paul needs me.[21]

Something had just changed in her heart. She looked at her husband, and he, too, looked like a new father. Time was suspended while Doctor Lejeune delicately observed the palms of his son's little hands and played with his fingers. When he started to untie his shoelaces, the mother stepped up: "I will do that, Doctor; please don't bother."

"No, no. Let me do it", he replied.

And while he was untying the boy's shoes, the looks that he exchanged with the child betrayed their complicity. Little Paul, happy and relaxed, smiled from ear to ear at his new friend in the white coat, who looked at him as an equal.[22] When he stood up and looked at the parents, Jérôme was unaware of what had just played out in their hearts. He told them simply:

"Your little Paul is well. We cannot take away his trisomy, but together we can help him. Not everything will be easy, but do not worry. Come back and see me next year, or in six months if you prefer."

The parents then asked a few questions, which Jérôme answered simply and soberly. The consultation lasted less than thirty minutes, and the parents found themselves outside, with Paul in his mother's arms.

"It was incredible. He didn't say anything in particular, but for me everything changed. I no longer see Paul as I did before. Most of my questions, which were connected with my fears, are gone."

"Me, too", her husband said, slightly taken aback by this new strength that he felt within himself. "I sense that I'm stronger to confront this handicap. We are no longer alone; we have this physician with us. I admit that I was very impressed by his way of looking at Paul. He looked at him as though he were in the presence of a prince. It is quite plain that Paul has an immense value in his eyes."[23]

His wife listened to him in astonishment: "This doctor has performed his first miracle: this long tirade by my husband! It is the first

[21] Conversation of the author with the mother of a patient of Jérôme Lejeune.
[22] Conversation of the author with the father of a patient of Jérôme Lejeune.
[23] Conversation of the author with the father of a trisomic child treated by Jérôme Lejeune.

time that he has confided even a little since Paul's birth. This is definitely a great day", she thought, lightheartedly, while hugging her son a little tighter.

In August, Jérôme departed for Argentina, where for two weeks he gave a course on chromosomal analysis and set up a tissue culture laboratory for the faculty of sciences in Buenos Aires. He made use of these courses to show the students the clinical interest of these research projects and took trisomy 21 as an example:

> With their slightly slanted eyes, their little nose in a round face, and their incompletely chiseled features, children with trisomy 21 are children more than others are. Every child has short hands and short fingers; theirs are shorter. Their whole anatomy seems to be rounded off, without ruggedness or firmness. Their ligaments and muscles have a suppleness that gives a tender languor to their manner. And this sweetness extends to their character: they are expansive and affectionate, with a special charm that is easier to cherish than to describe. This is not to say that trisomy 21 is a desirable condition. It is an implacable disease that deprives the child of the most precious quality that our genetic heritage confers on us: the full faculty of rational thought. This combination of a tragic chromosomal error and a truly attractive nature reveals at a glance what medicine really is: hatred of the disease and love of the patient.[24]

Jérôme then flew to Peru, where he was to give a series of conferences on trisomy. After the unforgettable flight over the Andes, he arrived in the middle of a university strike in Lima and learned that, given the circumstances, his course on genetics had been canceled. Having only two conferences left to give in a week, he let himself be tempted by an excursion to Machu Picchu. "By economizing on the costs of the hotel and meals, I should be able to come up with the money necessary to make the voyage possible for me", he calculated, while he went to get information about the schedule of trains. After making his decision, he departed for Cuzco, where he took the little train, something right out of *The Adventures of Tintin* [a Belgian

[24] J. Lejeune, working document "Research and Trisomy", reprinted many times, particularly for a conference in Beirut in May 1987, and published in J. Lejeune, *Symphonie de la Vie*, 15.

comic-book character], which carried him off to the clouds and set him down, after three hours of a dizzying ascent, at the entrance to Machu Picchu, at an altitude of 2,500 meters [82,000 feet]. Poised like a precious stone on a case of green velour, between the valley that encircles it and the surrounding mountains, Machu Picchu seemed to Jérôme to be one of the most extraordinary sites in the world, floating in the light air of a perpetual springtime.

Jérôme was as though in a dream: the site was so beautiful and the trip so unexpected! Alas, his joy was short-lived.

"Cuidado! Señora, cuidado! Es peligroso!" [Careful! Ma'am, be careful! It is dangerous!]

The guard shouted himself hoarse while running toward an American tourist who was gamboling about in a dangerous zone and remained deaf to his calls.

"Cuidado, Señora!"

Alas, the imprudent woman slipped on some fallen rocks and collapsed to the ground, senseless. And while the guard shouted all the louder, this time out of fear, Jérôme rushed over. Although the young woman quickly regained consciousness, Jérôme feared a head injury and decided to accompany her to Cuzco; it was necessary to travel back down without delay to take X-rays there. "Obviously, it will be impossible for me to come back up in time to see the sunset", he thought with regret and a touch of irritation against the careless tourist. "I will have passed only a half hour at the Inca site. Well, that was already marvelously beautiful."

From Lima, Jérôme departed for New York, where he participated in a meeting on chromosomes from August 28–30. The atmosphere there was heavy. On the evening of his arrival, he wrote to Birthe the reasons for this particular tension:

> Everyone is staggered by the Russians' decision to resume their atomic tests with a super-super bomb![25]

During this colloquium, Jérôme was impressed by the position of a Russian geneticist, Arseniova, a sixty-five-year-old woman, who

[25] J. Lejeune, letter to Birthe, August 31, 1961.

was snubbed by some of the delegates. She befriended Jérôme and in veiled terms confided in him. Jérôme understood that Lysenko, the famous Soviet geneticist who subjected the laws of genetics to the requirements of Marxism, had returned to power at the Academy of Sciences in Moscow. Under orders from the Party, Lysenko wiped clean the slate of classical genetics, denying that genes and chromosomes had any role in hereditary transmission, and clung to the outdated but proletarianly correct dogma of "the inheritance of acquired characteristics". Arseniova feared that modern genetics might be forbidden once again in the U.S.S.R.

"They have started hunting down geneticists, the institutes of classical genetics are closed, and Soviet science is making a leap backward", she confided sadly. It struck Jérôme that he sensed fear in the murmur of that renowned geneticist. He saw in it an extraordinary sign of Communist power. And he understood that that woman might be participating for the last time in an international meeting. Then, thinking about his next trip to Moscow, scheduled for a few days later, he discreetly questioned Arseniova:

"I have been invited to give a conference on genetics in Moscow in two weeks. With this recent promotion of Lysenko to the Academy of Sciences, there is a danger of complications.... Do you think that my trip will be canceled?"

Jérôme did not dare to admit to her that Lysenko's return and the resumption of the atomic tests made him earnestly wish for a cancellation.

After spending a few days in Paris to attend to the immediate needs of the lab, Jérôme departed again for Rome, in mid-September, for a congress on genetics. He was happy to revisit the majestic beauty of Saint Peter's Basilica; its immensity does not crush the visitor but lifts him toward heaven, in a subdued light that trembles with beauty. He was pleased to discover there the tomb of Pius XII, and he meditated with great emotion near the tomb of Saint Peter, which he saw for the first time. Thanks to Pius XII, who had ordered the excavations of the *scavi* during World War II, they had managed to find that tomb, at the place where Christian tradition had pointed it out for two thousand years. It is situated directly beneath the altar, the baldachin, and the cupola of the Basilica, aligned in a perfect vertical axis, thus confirming the Christian tradition that reported that Emperor

Constantine had erected Saint Peter's Basilica precisely over the tomb of the Prince of the Apostles, a few meters from the place of his martyrdom. Jérôme described his joy to Birthe:

> In the underground gallery of the tombs of the popes, there is a place where you see the tomb of Saint Peter, ten meters [33 feet] below the level of the crypt. You have to kneel down to see anything, and it is extremely moving. I said a prayer for you and the children and also for Marie-Odile [Rethoré], who had expressly recommended it to me.

And Jérôme, tactfully, did not fail to explain to Birthe:

> I am ashamed to see such beautiful things all alone when I think of the pleasure that you would have in being there and of the happiness that would be mine to have you at my side. It is so good to be able to share everything with you.[26]

After those blessed hours in the Eternal City, Jérôme had to depart, finally, for Moscow. He flew there on September 13 for a short, three-day stay. This trip, which he had wanted to cancel, started badly. Upon his arrival in Moscow, it was painful to note the contrast between "the marvelous Christian city, the cradle of civilization, and the enormous, ugly metropolis of Communism".[27] He observed with displeasure the insincerely warm reception of the authorities, who confiscated his passport when he arrived, and the relative but shameless luxury of the official hotels, while crowds of needy people were sleeping in the train stations. At the hotel, Jérôme revised his conference, having in mind the information that Arseniova had conveyed to him in New York. "You never know", he reflected. "Lysenko could send one of his henchmen or come personally to contradict me. It is necessary to make use of the opportunity to show that the inheritance of acquired characteristics, as he has described it, plainly contradicts modern genetics." Satisfied with his last-minute modifications, he went down to the hotel auditorium and met his personal attaché dispatched by the organizers. The latter greeted him with a fixed smile and announced to him in almost-perfect French:

[26] Ibid., September 7, 1961.
[27] J. Lejeune, *Journal intime*, March 12, 1963.

"Monsieur, there has been a change of program. Because of unexpected work being done in the room that was reserved for you in the Academy of Sciences, your conference has been cancelled. You see how sorry we are about it."

The man recited his script without his Asiatic face showing the slightest emotion, then fell silent, impassible. Jérôme did not ask him whether the Academy of Sciences might have another space available. "What good would it do?" he asked himself. "They will tell me No, of course. I may as well play along and appear as little surprised as possible. And with a bit of luck, the French ambassador, whom I have to meet this afternoon, will be able to find a solution."

The ambassador agreed very gladly to help him and proposed a hall at the French pavilion of the Universal Exposition. On neutral territory. Having understood very well that his conference had been cancelled in order to prevent him from telling Russian scholars about the latest advances in modern genetics, Jérôme prepared to adapt his conference for an uninformed French audience. "This will be for them quite a unique visit to the Universal Exposition", he noted with amusement as he saw the French listeners taking their seats in the auditorium. But a few moments after his conference started, he noted in the back of the room the discreet arrival of a strange person, dressed in a heavy winter coat with the collar up and his hat down to his eyes. But it was not that cold in the month of September! Then, while he was setting out the main idea of his conference, Jérôme noticed other individuals, just like the first one, who wandered around in the back, wrapped up as though in the dead of winter, their faces hidden by their *shapka* and their collars up. "Well, well, this is strange", Jérôme said to himself. "Could these be our friends, the members of the Academy? I admit that I wouldn't be unhappy about that!" Without losing the thread of his speech, he observed that these shadowy figures grew more and more numerous and were looking at one another. They exchanged little nods. One removed his cap, and the others followed. They were, indeed, the members of the Academy of Sciences. Not all of them, but the majority were there. Jérôme was happy. With such brave scientists, Lysenko's obscurantism could not last.[28] Finally satisfied with his trip, which had enabled him to bring

[28] Several months later, Lysenko would be rejected by a vote of the Academy members.

points for reflection to the Russian scientific community, Jérôme left Moscow with pleasure to join his family in Denmark and then bring them back to Paris in time for the new school year.

In mid-September, Jérôme was happy to go back to his little patients and his laboratory because he was eager to implement the plans that he had mulled over during the summer and to continue his research. His travels were important, because they allowed for important exchanges of scientific facts, but each trip added to his fatigue and interrupted his work. An entry in his journal shows how much Jérôme preferred to remain in Paris to devote himself wholeheartedly to research and care:

> Little Pierre[29] seems to be making continued progress. After a setback, he has started speaking again imperfectly and has learned to tie his shoelaces. It may mean nothing but seems encouraging. At the faculty, the dosages look like they are trying to reveal something, although it is the opposite of what we were expecting. We will have to clear this up next week. I have very little time left, alas, until my departure for Oak Ridge, and as usual I am starting to curse these trips that prevent me from working. But I make sure to say nothing about it; my friends would think that I was preening and fishing for compliments.[30]

Since the discovery of trisomy 21, research on chromosomes was expanding quickly in France and in the world, and new anomalies were being described by foreign teams: Turner's syndrome, trisomy 13, trisomy 18. As for Jérôme, he stayed on his course and identified a translocation of chromosomes. He was the first to demonstrate this genetic mutation due to the mixing of fragments of chromosomes. With the help of a great number of biopsies performed with Marie-Odile Rethoré—Jérôme, incidentally, gave a little party for the hundredth biopsy—he was able to study different kinds of chromosomal rearrangements. Among the effects observed, he was researching in particular a possible chromosomal origin for Fanconi anemia. As for trisomy 21, Jérôme, together with Jacques Lafourcade and Henri Jérôme, launched the first therapeutic test on mongoloids, and he was conducting biochemical studies, trying to observe the reactions of cells

[29] First name changed.

[30] J. Lejeune, *Journal intime*, March 19, 1960.

to certain molecules. After testing the saliva of drosophila flies—those little fruit flies with a short life-span that reproduce abundantly—to slow down cellular development, and seeing that it was useless, he discovered that trisomic patients suffer from troubles with an important molecule, tryptophan. This observation was confirmed for him by an American geneticist from Philadelphia. During their discussion, the latter told him that he had just published a paper on the subject. Although Jérôme was disappointed to see that another scientist had made the discovery first, he was glad to find confirmation of the approach. But these results were soon contradicted by other experiments! The approach was therefore very uncertain.... Jérôme noticed during international meetings that their laboratory was two years ahead of the foreign teams in biochemistry, but instead of being content with that, he was seething because he had not yet found the solution to mongolism. He had devoted himself for two years, with his friend Henri Jérôme, to finding a treatment after the discovery of trisomy 21. Alas, despite the sometimes encouraging results, which offered hope that the solution was near, everything collapsed, and it was necessary to find another point of departure.

During those two years, 1960 and 1961, Jérôme authored twenty-one publications and welcomed many scientists visiting from Europe and North and South America who wanted to observe the research projects in the laboratory. His growing renown also attracted young medical interns, and this was the beginning of a continuous stream of geneticists who came from all over the world to train with him, some of whom would remain faithful friends. Jérôme also won several prizes: the silver medal for scientific research (CNRS) and, with Turpin, the prestigious Jean-Toy Prize from the Academy of Sciences in Paris.

All this activity did not escape the notice of the Kennedy Foundation, founded by Joseph, the father of the very young president of the United States, in memory of his son who had died in the war and probably, although without publicity, for his daughter Rosemary, who was mentally handicapped. This foundation, which was intended to develop research on mental retardation by subsidizing promising researchers, sent to Paris in the summer of 1962, while Jérôme was on vacation in Denmark, two emissaries to investigate the circumstances of the discovery of trisomy 21. Jérôme knew nothing about it and first heard of it when he returned to Paris.

"It is astonishing", he told Birthe when she in turn came back from Kerteminde. "Two men came to the lab this summer from the Kennedy Foundation. They questioned Turpin and the coworkers who were present, then left. We will see whether this summer visit has any result."

The answer arrived a few weeks later, through an invitation from the Kennedy Foundation for Jérôme. He was expected in Washington in December for an official dinner with the president of the United States, at the White House.

"At the White House! With John Kennedy!" exclaimed Birthe, who was so surprised that she forgot to light the cigarette already at her lips.

And seeing that Jérôme was hesitant, she went on: "You will go, certainly! This is a terrific opportunity to meet them, and who knows, this may be able to help you in your research."

Who knows, indeed?

CHAPTER 6

INTELLECT AT THE SERVICE OF THE POOR

1962–1967

Washington, December 5, 1962. A knock at the door of the hotel room. The voice of the floor housekeeper called: "Mister Lejeune?"

"Yes", Jérôme answered in English as he opened the door.

"This is for you", the young man said, offering him a letter.

Jérôme thanked him, took the large envelope, and noticed that it bore the acronym of the Kennedy Foundation. "No doubt some instructions for the dinner at the White House", he thought. He opened it quickly and read:

> Dear Doctor Lejeune,
>
> In the name of the Joseph P. Kennedy, Jr. Foundation, I have the pleasure of informing you that you have been selected to receive one of our first international awards for scientific research on mental handicaps. Your extraordinary work and your exceptional contribution in this field, and to science in general, represent the utmost degree of effort and of success and set the bar so high that it will be difficult for the future award winners to reach. You have our deepest respect and admiration. The international award will be given to you by President Kennedy on Thursday, December 6, 1962, in the evening during the dinner. Until then, we respectfully ask you to be so kind as to keep this information confidential. The other winners of the personal award, selected by the committee, are Doctor Murray Barr and Mister Joe Hin Tjio.[1]

[1] The discovery of the 46 human chromosomes by Tjio was published (co-signed by Levan) in the Scandinavian journal *Hereditas* dated January 26, 1956.

While still reeling from this excellent surprise, Jérôme checked the date of the letter signed by Robert Sargent Shriver, Jr., the executive director of the Kennedy Foundation: "December 4! It was written yesterday, for tomorrow! The least that you can say is that this is short notice." Amused, Jérôme finally understood why the Kennedy Foundation had invited him long ago to this party on December 6, telling him that it was an official dinner at the White House. Now it was too late for him to tell Birthe. "What a shame that she cannot come! She would have been so happy, and so would I! All the more so since my winning this prize is thanks to her, too, because without her unfailing support and her patience with my carelessness, I could not be as immersed in my research as I am." Jérôme immediately wrote to Birthe about the good news, well aware that his letter would not arrive, alas, until after the ceremony. And he already smiled at the thought of what she would say in response: "This is why the Kennedy Foundation sent investigators to Turpin's practice last summer, when you were on vacation in Denmark, to study your work on trisomy 21! And they saw all that you have done! I am proud of you!" Obviously she would not complain about herself, caring only about the joy that she shared with her husband, but Jérôme promised himself that he would make up for her absence. Maybe she would be able to come next year, when the former prizewinner (which he would be then) would attend the new award ceremony!

The next day, Jérôme was expected, along with the other recipients, for a visit at the White House, followed by a photo session with President John Kennedy. Then it was time to go back to the hotel to change, and Jérôme left again for the gala banquet, culminating in the presentation of the Kennedy Award by the president personally. Amid the crackling of the flash bulbs in the Oval Office, Jérôme received, with justifiable pleasure and pride, the crystal trophy that symbolized the value and brilliance of his research. Back at the hotel, knowing how impatiently Birthe was awaiting all the details, he hurried to write her a letter about them.

> There were six recipients, and since there were only three statues ready, the same one was used for all of us. We gave it back to the president, each one in turn. After all that commotion, well ordered

> but very good-natured and typically American, with a concert by Judy Garland and a film on the award winners, I spoke for a few moments to Mrs. Kennedy, the president's mother. As this elderly woman spoke to me about her sons, who have had such great success, and about her poor daughter, who is mentally disabled, she was no longer a great lady on display but a mother talking about her children. I found this quite touching, and the courage of the Kennedys, who do not hide their disgrace but try to help other sick people with their money, seemed to me noble and worthy of respect.[2]

Jérôme was rewarded "for his exceptional contribution to the research on mental retardation" and for "his scientific work as a whole" and, along with Tjio and Barr, he received two checks made out in his name, one for $8,000 for his personal use, which seemed to him a colossal sum [ca. $68,000 in 2020 dollars], and the other for $25,000 [ca. $215,000 today] for his research in the laboratory. This $25,000, which he made over to the Institut de Progénèse, established the team definitively, and the $8,000 allowed the Lejeunes to plan the purchase of a country house—the subject of countless plans, speculations, and discussions by the whole family![3]

Birthe immediately started looking for the ideal house, one that was easy to maintain, close to Paris, and not too far away from Étampes, where they went regularly to visit Jérôme's mother. The older woman loved to see them but quickly became fatigued by the children's liveliness: it was time to find another house close enough to visit her, but where the children could run around without bothering her. These many good reasons helped Jérôme to abandon his dream of having a house in the forest, in Sologne, or on the seacoast. They had luck several months later in Saint-Hilaire, near Chalo-Saint-Mars, not far from Étampes. The little house, nestled in the hollow of the valley of the Chalouette River, was situated beside a yard that was as big as the world for the children and yet on a human scale for Jérôme, who would be saddled with the gardening. Humorously and enthusiastically, they named it *The Little White House*.

In the French scientific world, news of the Kennedy Award that Jérôme had received was welcomed with joy, because through

[2] J. Lejeune, *Journal intime*, March 12, 1963.

[3] Ibid.

him, the first French winner of the award, France was honored. He received many congratulations, among them from the director of the CNRS, Professor Jacquinot:

> Dear Sir,
>
> It is with very great pleasure that I was informed about the honor that you have just received: the Kennedy Award. I was anxious to express to you, on my own account and on behalf of the CNRS, my most sincere congratulations, on the occasion of this award, which has now crowned studies that honor French scientific research.[4]

Birthe, for her part, started preserving systematically all records of her husband's success and, before Jérôme had the time to deposit the two American checks in the bank, made precious copies of them, which she archived in a file cabinet. "You never know", she thought. "If someday they write Jérôme's biography, they will have all the documentation."

Though crowned by the Kennedy Award, the year 1962 was adorned for Jérôme with other important appointments: he was appointed expert in human genetics for the WHO and was admitted as a member of the prestigious American Society of Human Genetics. In 1963, the CNRS appointed him director of research, and he received the Cognacq-Jay Prize of the Institut de France and the Essec Prize as well. He was also elected a member of the International Commission for Radiological Protection.

Turpin was so frightened by the thought of the possible departure of Jérôme, who was receiving very interesting offers from all sides, that he decided to obtain for him the creation of a university chair of cytogenetics. In April 1963, the council of the faculty of medicine followed his recommendation and decided to create a chair of fundamental genetics, which would be conferred on Doctor Lejeune. It took long months to get everything in place, though, and during that time Jérôme, who had been promoted to the rank of senior professor, continued his daily work, which had become a crushing load. He divided his time between consultations with his patients in the

[4] P. Jacquinot, letter to J. Lejeune, December 17, 1962.

morning, at Necker Children's Hospital, where the team was now settled, and his research projects in the afternoon at Les Cordeliers laboratory of the faculty of medicine, in Odéon.[5] Not to mention the numerous invitations to international conferences. He was short of time on all fronts. "How can I respond to all these demands without doing an injustice to the patients and their parents?" he wondered incessantly. Of course, his research projects were useful to his patients, and when he participated in scientific conferences, it was again to promote research for the benefit of his little patients, but that could not and should not prevent him from giving them his time personally, too, in consultations. "How difficult it is to know how to do one's best to relieve bodies and hearts in distress", he sighed while pedaling between Necker Hospital and the Odéon faculty.

The people in the neighborhood soon became accustomed to seeing this famous doctor go by on his big black bike, lost in thought. It was a miracle that he was not run down in Parisian traffic! The only accident in his career occurred one summer on a country road. Between Étampes and Chalo-Saint-Mars, Jérôme was thrown into the ditch where, unable to budge, he was rescued by a passerby, who was quite astonished to find the illustrious Doctor Lejeune in that position. A broken clavicle and contusions, however, did not shake his love for his silent two-wheeler, which was ready to confront all sorts of bad weather. Those close to him even suspected that he took a mischievous pleasure in preferring his racing bike to the ostentatious automobiles of his colleagues....

The team, which had been enlarged with the arrival of a young, talented physician-turned-researcher, Doctor Roland Berger, and two devoted assistants, Madame Dallo and Madame Lenné, grew in potential and worked industriously. After his success in identifying a first case of translocation,[6] Jérôme showed the importance of this structural aberration and published new notes on a new translocation of chromosomes 13 and 15, a chromosomal aberration between monozygotic [identical] twins and a new variety of hermaphroditism.

[5] The Les Cordeliers faculty of medicine is today called the faculty of medicine at Paris-Descartes University.

[6] A translocation is a genetic anomaly due to an exchange of fragments between two chromosomes that do not belong to the same pair.

Finally, in 1963, these efforts culminated in an important discovery: with his collaborators, Jérôme identified a new anomaly, due to the deletion[7] of the short arm of chromosome 5,[8] and confirmed this observation several weeks later with five new cases. When someone suggested that he call this malady "Lejeune's Syndrome", Jérôme refused. He explained why to Birthe:

> Mc Intyre wrote me a very charming letter in which he asked my permission to call it Lejeune's Syndrome. I was quite touched by his tact, but I refused because an eponymous malady has no significance either for the students or for the families. I only asked that it be called *cri du chat* [cat's cry] syndrome. In French. Mc Intyre very gladly agreed.[9]

Jérôme gave it this name because those who suffer from it are unable to speak a word and only utter little cries that resemble those of kittens. At his request, this French name is kept in the international nomenclature. This was another major advance, five years after the discovery of trisomy 21.

But working at that pace was exhausting Jérôme, whose health was frail, and in the summer of 1963, he suffered from tachycardia [rapid heartbeat]. Birthe, whose ironclad constitution would bankrupt generations of physicians, was worried, writing from Denmark:

> We miss you terribly, and even though life in Kerteminde is not the ideal sort of rest, still it is less tiring than your life in Paris. It worries me so much to think that you do not get enough rest. How is your heart, are you still sick?? Jacques [Lafourcade] told me in his letter the other day that it was necessary for you to take a vacation, and I would be so happy if the air in Kerteminde could give you the same health and well-being as it does to the children. They are magnificent, very tan and quite plump; they have all grown. I miss you terribly, my darling.[10]

[7] A deletion is a genetic modification characterized by the loss of a fragment of a chromosome. The deletion described here is therefore the loss of a piece of chromosome 5, on its shorter arm (segment).

[8] J. Lejeune, J. Lafourcade, J. de Grouchy, R. Berger, M. Gautier, Ch. Salmon, and R. Turpin, "Délétion partielle du bras court du chromosome 5: Individualisation d'un nouvel état morbide", *Semaine des Hôpitaux de Paris* 40 (1964): 1069–79.

[9] J. Lejeune. This quotation is actually an excerpt from Jérôme's letter to Doctor Niebuhr, dated May 3, 1977.

[10] B. Lejeune, letter to Jérôme, July 30, 1963.

Jérôme was exhausted, but he still had to leave for Stockholm in a few weeks, because he had been appointed a member of the official delegation of French research. "I would gladly skip this trip", he thought, grumbling a bit interiorly. "But I cannot refuse. This delegation is too important." Although concerned about his health, Birthe encouraged him to participate in it because she had grasped the importance of this trip.

> I am writing to you while lying on the beach this afternoon. The weather is splendid, provided it lasts. Thank you for your 3 letters this morning. I think that it is absolutely necessary for you to go to Sweden. I read somewhere that the government is doing a lot of campaigning for a Frenchman to have the Nobel Prize soon, and to me this invitation seems to be organized to demonstrate the French hopes. Anyway, the trip lasts only 2–3 days, and Sweden is not so far that the trip could be tiring.[11]

Jérôme therefore left for Stockholm in October, and as soon as he arrived on site, he noticed that Birthe had seen things correctly. But the maneuver was so crude that it made him feel somewhat ill at ease.

> The all-too-clear purpose of this delegation was to go claim a Nobel Prize for a Frenchman, and this display of thinking heads: the rector, the dean of the faculty of sciences, the director of the CNRS (there were 10 of us, and I do not know who decided that I should be part of the group) looked a bit too much like they were grandstanding![12]

Despite that, he was happy about the opportunities for high-quality visits and meetings during that week and appreciated some particularly interesting discussions. One afternoon, he was invited to see Klein, one of the "kingmakers" of the Nobel Prize, who very kindly showed him his laboratory and innocuously presented to him three problems connected with his research, for which he said he could not find the solution. Out of the three, Jérôme showed that two were insoluble because there was a variable in the data, and he found the last problem so simple that he solved it on the spot. Klein proved to be very impressed. Jérôme did not know whether he was

[11] Ibid., July 29, 1963.
[12] J. Lejeune, *Journal intime*, November 15, 1963.

taking a test there or whether it really was a scientific discussion. In any case, he acquitted himself very respectably.

Alas, that same week Birthe had the sorrow of losing her mother, and Jérôme quickly left Sweden to meet her in Denmark and to stand by her in those difficult days. An only daughter, Birthe courageously endured that bereavement, which now deprived her of her last family tie to her native land. With great emotion, Jérôme helped her to clear out the house; its modesty, warmth, and simplicity matched his own. Back in Paris, Jérôme recorded in his journal this very sad memory.

> The sight of the empty house and of these humble witnesses to a simple life that was entirely devoted to her children and grandchildren upset me. The poor, dear old woman, living only for her "Bittenur". She fell asleep gently, without a crisis, and without alerting anyone, although she had a telephone at her bedside and the owners of the house, living on the upper floor, were willing to help her at any time. The funeral ceremonies in marvelous weather were touching in their simplicity. Beforehand, I had placed at her feet, in the coffin, the letters that she had kept. The ones from her husband and the ones from Birthe. This is an enormous trial for my poor Bibi, who is now the only one left from her family. Fortunately we are with her, but for her it is the end of her whole life before our marriage. She is brave, as always, but I know how she is suffering.[13]

It was necessary to wait a few more months until, in 1964, with the slowness that befits aged and venerable persons, the university administration finally managed to create the chair of fundamental genetics that had been decided on a year earlier. Jérôme had been chosen to hold that first chair of fundamental genetics in France, and one of the first in the world. But there was a major obstacle: according to the university rules, he could not be appointed a professor, because his failure at the externship closed the door to a career teaching at the university. But that did not take into account the administration's providential resources, requested by Jacques Lafourcade, his long-time friend and collaborator. He showed up one day in the laboratory, triumphantly waving a document that he held under Jérôme's nose.

"Just look, old man! I think that we will be able to put the champagne on ice!"

[13] Ibid.

Lafourcade was so excited that for a moment Jérôme dropped his tables of karyotypes, put out his Balto [cigarette], and took the paper that his friend was holding out to him.

But without allowing him time to read one line of it, Jacques continued enthusiastically: "Good Napoleon will come to our aid!"

"Napoleon?" Jérôme repeated incredulously. "What are you talking about? Have you already been hitting the champagne?"

"Wait a bit, you will see", Jacques answered while sitting down astride a chair, facing his friend, whose increasingly perplexed expression enchanted him. Finally, he let loose with the explanation.

"We found a very unusual provision going back to Napoleon that allows a personage of great merit to be appointed professor. It requires the favorable opinions of the Academy of Sciences and of the Academy of Medicine and, boom, it's all set! Napoleon used this provision once. You will be the second."

"Incredible!" Jérôme replied. "You seem, though, to be very sure of yourself. But we cannot prejudge the results of the votes by the Academies. It is up to them to decide."

"Yes, yes," Lafourcade said vehemently, "but I am sure that they will vote for you. You are, obviously, the one best positioned to teach fundamental genetics in France!"

This provision was quickly proposed and accepted at the highest level, and the two Academies, in two sessions, voted massively in favor of Jérôme. This historical appointment brought Jérôme countless letters of praise. From the time of his election by the faculty council in 1963 until the vote by the Academies in 1964, there was a constant shower of congratulations. Thus Doctor Justin-Besançon wrote to him:

> My dear friend,
>
> Not only will I vote for you next Tuesday and campaign for you, but I intend to say a few words to express my admiration for your work and to support your candidacy. I will say in particular that I just met with the highest American university authorities, and I will confide to the faculty council the pride I felt to see your work so unanimously admired across the Atlantic. I hope that you will have a fine election.[14]

[14] L. Justin-Besançon, letter to J. Lejeune, April 11, 1963, on the occasion of the vote by the faculty council deciding the creation of the chair of fundamental genetics and the appointment of Jérôme Lejeune.

So did Doctor Lafay, a member of the Academy of Medicine:

> I was very happy to join all my colleagues in the Academy when you were designated for the chair of genetics. No one could present better than our teacher, Professor Turpin, your titles and your achievements, the list of which is particularly rich and brilliant. But I was anxious to tell you the great esteem in which you are held by everyone who knows you.[15]

So it was that Jérôme became the first professor of fundamental genetics in France, and at the same time he was appointed department head at Necker Children's Hospital, with a laboratory and consultation for fundamental genetics. It was necessary to wait a few more months for the official inauguration of the chair, and, finally, on March 10, 1965, the new Professor Lejeune brilliantly gave his inaugural lecture to a gathering of his colleagues, family, and friends at the Odéon Faculty of Medicine. With talent and humor, he recounted the epic of cytogenetics and tactfully thanked his boss and his coworkers. Birthe was amused to see him turning the pages one after the other, as though he were reading his text, because she knew very well that he had learned it by heart. Standing in his long, black academic robe, his hands resting on the lectern, Jérôme intoned his speech in an inimitable, slightly raised tone of voice that immediately captured his audience. He first addressed the eminent deans and directors:

> Allow me, gentlemen, to assure you of my very deep gratitude. Not only were you so kind as to consider me worthy to be admitted to your council, but you even took your benevolence to the point of great audacity by entrusting to me a brand new chair and by investing me with your authority to carry out the teaching office that you decided to create.

Then he continued, as was the custom, by outlining his career; he recalled the familial and spiritual roots of it.

> My father was an admirable guide, to whom I owe everything I know that is really important. He taught me by his example that a man's life must be ruled by two imperatives: right judgment and enthusiasm

[15] B. Lafay, letter to J. Lejeune, January 9, 1964.

for the truth. His memory is dear to me, and it is an enormous sorrow that he is not here at all this evening. My mother taught me the greatness of devotion and the omnipotence of kindness. Of their three sons, I alone set out in search of what is verifiable; my two brothers chose a still nobler quest, the search for beauty.

Rarely were there occasions for Jérôme to confide to those close to him his immense gratitude and the admiration that he had for them, but today was the perfect occasion. He seized it and rejoiced to see Philippe's smile broaden, like a luminous parenthesis, on his emaciated face. Then he related in broad strokes, tinged with humor and emotion, his fourteen years of work with his boss, Professor Turpin, and emphasized:

He is the only boss that I have known personally, the only one with whom I have worked and still work.

And tilting his head slightly in his direction, Jérôme continued deferentially:

My dear Professor, you were able to do the work of an innovator and the work of a creator. As an innovator, you introduced the teaching of genetics in our faculty; as a creator, you formed around yourself a team of researchers. Twenty-five years ago ... you inaugurated the first course on human genetics in France. For five years you awoke interest in this discipline, which was almost unknown to physicians then. Twenty years later, the faculty is delegating one of your students to take up the torch. I think that this continuity should be seen as a genuine acknowledgment of your pioneering activity.

Finally, the coworkers had their turn as Jérôme described their friendship, ardor, and merit. First, his friend Jacques Lafourcade, emphasizing his extraordinary ability to make chromosomal diagnoses with the naked eye, equipped only with a magnifying glass. Taking his eyes off his friend for a moment to look at the assembly, Jérôme explained: "In order to achieve that mastery, it is necessary to combine a lot of laboriously gained knowledge with a subtle mind—something that cannot be learned." Looking back at Lafourcade, Jérôme continued: "As for the knowledge, you possess it, and as for the subtle mind, you never even suspected it; you received it at birth."

Then, addressing Henri Jérôme, he continued:

> You are the pragmatist on our team.... Our sometimes disheveled theories leave you cold and positive.... Like the laborer tilling his field from right to left and back again [*en boustrophédon*], you take up the problem from one end and then from the other.... And so when you admit that a link of the chain may be there, each one of us breathes a sigh of relief. If you agree to say it, there is nothing left to do but to record the fact.

After greeting in this way these two elders who, according to the custom, were designated to welcome him at the ceremony, Jérôme turned to his third colleague and went on:

> My dear Marthe Gautier, you were the only one of us who knew the techniques of cell culture. Together we started to read the human karyotype. The reason why I recall these first years of trial and error, in 1957 and 1958, is to say that those two years of failures and partial results were finally crowned with success only because of your skill and tenacity. As a renowned pediatric cardiologist, you did not abandon the team, despite all your duties, and we still meet every Monday to discuss the past week and to preview the week to come. It is with great pleasure that I express to you from the bottom of my heart my very affectionate gratitude.

Then came the turn of the two other younger but no less talented coworkers, whom Jérôme described warmly.

> Our two younger colleagues enliven the laboratory, one with the ardor of intellect and the other with the perspicacity of devotion.

And he continued, addressing Mademoiselle Rethoré:

> My dear Marie-Odile Rethoré, you have guessed it: the devotion is you and the perspicacity is yours. For almost twelve years, we have worked side by side. You have always accepted the most difficult tasks and the most delicate missions. As head of research projects, you combine scientific rigor with the knowledge of the heart. Thanks to you,

genetics is not a classification of anomalies but becomes a discovery of the patient that is renewed each day. This is the only possible way of humanizing science, and, instinctively, you were able to discover it.

Then, turning to the young physician seated beside Marie-Odile Rethoré, Jérôme continued:

My dear Roland Berger, the ardor of intellect is you.... Having in a way witnessed your conversion, I can say that you came back to research the way some people go back to their religion. You, too, are an accomplished physician, able to recognize the sick person beyond the sickness. But what characterizes you most, I think, is that passion for truth which thoroughly animates you. If I had to define you with one word, I would say, and very affectionately, that you are the "Saint-Just" [a French Revolutionary leader] of the chromosome, never compromising with ignorance or incompetence.

Finally, recalling that "a research laboratory is a sort of machine for seizing the opportunity, the efficiency of which is based on a permanent state of alert", Jérôme insisted on emphasizing the more discreet but indispensable role of the technicians, "the kingpins of the whole mechanism". Jérôme noticed the first of them all, Madame Macé, seated timidly in the back. And before the deans and directors ensconced in the first rows, Jérôme addressed to her his thanks:

Madame Macé, you have been hard at work since the very beginning; your devotion and your know-how have been decisive. A high-ranking technician, you have reached the point of training pupils. Does this remind you of one of the most famous, a professor of genetics from North America? Well, he learned his trade by imitating your gestures.

Then Jérôme extended this compliment to Madame Gavaïni and insisted on expressing his deep gratitude to Madame Besançon for her vigilance and availability and to Madame Dallo for her untiring threefold activity as secretary, archivist, and administrator. Finally, to Madame Lenné he addressed his last homage with a bit of humor:

You who with self-denial carry out the most obscure duties, since most of your time is spent in the darkroom.

Having finished the acknowledgments, Jérôme stopped for a brief moment for effect. Everyone in the audience settled down again comfortably on his seat and held his breath to hear the brand-new professor present his new discipline. Jérôme began:

> I would like to hang at the door of this auditorium a truthful notice that is encouraging for well-born minds: "In the present state of ignorance"....

Then he led his guests to observe and to contemplate fundamental genetics in its cradle, all trembling with life, and described for them this child of science with paternal admiration:

> An ardent, passionate quest for true knowledge, the kind that finally enables us to do something for those who suffer.[16]

From the day of his nomination, Jérôme had immersed himself in preparations for the course, and the exercise seemed difficult to him, although he had already provided much of this training in France or abroad. He loved to transmit to young physicians his passion for research and care. Because of this, he had trained more than 120 researchers in the laboratory since 1959, three quarters of them foreigners, but this time he had to set up a complete program of formation. A high-wire act!

In the department that he now directed, projects continued and discoveries followed one after another. Jérôme observed two cases of monosomy 13 and identified another new anomaly: the deletion of the long arm of chromosome 18. Then he described the notion of *type and countertype*. But he struggled to have it accepted by the scientific community. It must be said that his unique way of following an intuition that arises from observation disconcerted a good number of his peers, who were accustomed to more mechanical, demonstrable arguments. He had to find other conclusive cases in order to win them over. Several weeks later, he presented a countertype of trisomy 21, then of trisomy 18, and finally a countertype of *cri du chat* syndrome, and thus ended up convincing the scientific community.

[16] J. Lejeune, inaugural lecture, March 10, 1965.

Since then, this idea of *type and countertype* has become generally accepted as a basic notion in genetics.

In addition to these research activities, which would occupy Jérôme's mind night and day if life permitted it, colleagues sounded Jérôme out about joining the circle of the twelve "wise men", a name given to the Consultative Committee on Scientific and Technological Research that was tasked with advising the prime minister, Georges Pompidou, in scientific policy matters. He was appointed a member of this committee of wise men in 1965 and performed this important role with interest. However, after a series of meetings in the Hôtel Matignon [the French prime minister's residence], this responsibility very quickly became too demanding, and he confided in Birthe:

> The "wise men" take up an enormous amount of my time, and I feel that time is being whittled away![17]

In fact, Jérôme's days were becoming like scenes from Dante, because to his threefold activity of care, research, and formation were added the supplementary duties connected with his new functions as department head. One evening, during the family dinner, when Birthe asked him her ritual question, "Whom did you see, and what did they say to you?" Jérôme confided his uneasiness.

"Since my appointment as department head last year, the hospital administration has not given me any way of developing the department."

"And yet," Birthe interrupted, "you told me that Turpin was going to retire next year!"

"Yes, exactly, that is the problem", Jérôme replied. "It becomes urgent to reorganize the department. I am wasting a tremendous amount of time trying to get the necessary financial and human resources, and I admit that I don't need that to take up my days. How stupid it is to spend precious time on these things!"

Thanks to his efforts, however, he succeeded in obtaining new funding to employ several additional coworkers, and the team filled out with the arrival of two brilliant young researchers, Bernard

[17] J. Lejeune, *Journal intime*, July 19, 1966.

Dutrillaux and Sophie Carpentier, and a secretary, Madame Alice. Jérôme also welcomed Doctor Marguerite Prieur, who wished to be trained in genetics by participating in his consultations. Encouraging his coworkers and training them to assume responsibility took time, but Jérôme did it very gladly, because he enjoyed sharing and transmitting. His office door was always open, and his colleagues knew that they could come to talk with him about a professional or personal difficulty without ever getting the impression that they were disturbing him.

Several months later, Jean-Marcel Jeanneney, who had recently been appointed minister of social affairs, announced to Jérôme an extraordinary subsidy for his laboratory:

> The information that was furnished to me about the financial situation of your laboratory and about the great interest in the research projects that you are conducting prompt me to allocate to you ... a subsidy of 100,000 francs.... I call your attention to the very exceptional character of this funding. The increase of resources assigned to medical research foreseen by the budget plan for 1967 excludes in advance, for next year, the renewal of any similar measure.[18]

Jérôme welcomed this good news with relief and did not fail to reply to the minister immediately, showing him that this subsidy was arriving just in time.

> This exceptional financial aid will allow me to set up a unit to preserve cell lines containing an exceptional chromosomal anomaly. The WHO had asked me to serve as a reference laboratory for this fundamental work, but the moderate level of my funding until now had not allowed me to accept this offer.[19]

Jérôme was also much in demand to preside or to speak at scientific congresses worldwide. Sweden, England, Belgium, Switzerland, Italy, Brazil, Argentina, and the United States: all told, between 1962 and 1965, more than thirty conferences in eight foreign countries, about chromosomes, cancer, atomic radiation.... He shared

[18] J.-M. Jeanneney, letter to J. Lejeune, October 3, 1966.
[19] J. Lejeune, letter to Minister Jeanneney, October 10, 1966.

the congresses with his coworkers, including Roland Berger, whom he recommended for Madrid or Chicago depending on the subjects for the presentations. During one of his many trips to the United States, he was struck by the devotion and the extreme efficiency of the personnel at the Kennedy Center in New York, which admitted severely handicapped persons, and the dedication of President Kennedy's sister, Eunice Shriver, to persons with mental deficiencies elicited his admiration, which was soon shared by Birthe.

The pace of his conferences persisted in 1966 and 1967, and during those two years Jérôme made thirteen trips, including one to Israel, four to the United States, where he gave conferences at Rockefeller University, Harvard, the University of Chicago, in Los Angeles, and to the United Nations committee, a trip to Japan for conferences on atomic radiation in Tokyo and Hiroshima, two speeches in Italy, then in England, Belgium, Spain, and Denmark. However, Jérôme declined many invitations—not only for the stability of his department, but also for the good of his family—and refused any new responsibilities. He accepted only one new nomination, as expert for the National Institute of Health in Bethesda, Maryland.

Jérôme's immense fame also brought him a great deal of correspondence. Every week he received letters from scientific teams in France and throughout the world: they wrote to him from Tokyo, Bombay, Buenos Aires, Chicago, Ottawa. Jérôme was at the heart of an international network of rare scope, and the tone of the letters that were addressed to him and his way of responding reveal his authority within the scientific community. People asked him for genetic advice, scientific information, and requested that he write, proofread, or co-sign articles. For example, this letter from Doctor Simone Gilgenkrantz, from the Regional Center for Blood Transfusions in Nancy, dated November 17, 1966:

> Dear Sir, I would like to submit to you this article about forms of trisomy 18 that I wrote in collaboration with the pediatric department of Professor Pierson. Among the four cases presented, the most interesting no doubt is the one about A., whose fibroblasts you studied and which appears to you to be a trisomy 16. Any comments that you may have on this study would be welcome. You might find these cases too dissimilar and too uncertain to warrant a publication. If, on the other

hand, you like this study, it goes without saying that I would be happy if you agreed to share in its publication. I am embarrassed to take up your time this way, but I am very anxious to have your opinion. Therefore I thank you in advance, dear Monsieur. Sincerely yours.[20]

It was quite an extraordinary thing that, despite the quantity of letters that he received each day, Jérôme did not let mail pile up on his desk and would respond within a week, with remarkable regularity! He used to write his response by hand, with beautiful calligraphic script, on the back side of the letter; then he gave it to his secretary, who typed it and submitted it to him for his signature. Thus as early as November 21 he responded to Doctor Gilgenkrantz:

> Dear Madame, I have just read through your text and made some notes on it. An analysis of the parents' chromosomes in case 2 is indispensable, it seems to me; likewise the sexual chromatin.... For the last case, I think that the cytological impression can be summarized thus (see attached paper). The citation of this little text would seem to me to be quite sufficient, accompanied at the end of the text by the classic lines of acknowledgments. Indeed, by no means do I want to co-sign with you this article as a whole, because it is a long study that is entirely yours, dear Madame. Kind regards.[21]

As always, Jérôme was very glad to collaborate, and despite the time that was slipping away, he managed to provide a document about a study that could improve his colleague's article, but, on the other hand, he quite spontaneously refused to co-sign this publication, so as not to diminish the author's merits. Yet Jérôme did not hesitate to have the publications on which he had worked a lot signed by several young coworkers who participated very little in it, but would thereby have a chance to become better known.

In order to cope with this avalanche of mail, Jérôme was flanked, thank God, by an orderly wife and a secretary who kept him from losing important documents among the sheets piled up on his desk and filed everything meticulously. And Birthe did the same for the personal mail received on rue Galande.

[20] S. Gilgenkrantz, letter to J. Lejeune, November 17, 1966.
[21] J. Lejeune, letter to S. Gilgenkrantz, November 21, 1966.

One morning Jérôme received an unexpected letter from Portugal. It was from Professor Tavarès, a member of the faculty of medicine in Porto, who announced to him:

> Dear Professor Lejeune, I have the pleasure of informing you of my response to a question from the Nobel Committee proposing your name for the Nobel Prize in medicine for 1966. Be assured of my great respect, and I hope that a movement will be organized in support of your candidacy.[22]

"This letter", Jérôme thought with a smile, "will surely be archived by my Bibi. As for the Nobel Prize, we will see."

"You know, Professor Tavarès from Porto has recommended me for the Nobel Prize. He just wrote to tell me."

"Terrific!" Jacques exclaimed.

"Yes, but don't get carried away. I'm not the only one on the list. I have few illusions", Jérôme replied calmly.

"Listen, Jérôme, that's true. You are not the only one to make important discoveries", his friend retorted. "But, to my knowledge, you are the only French physician today who has become a researcher in order to find a treatment for his patients and who, moreover, has had the nerve to find one. And not only trisomy 21, which was already revolutionary, but also *cri du chat* syndrome. There are many researchers who seek, but few who find. You are one of them. And you were 'only a physician', without an externship to boot! I may as well tell you that this is going to earn you not only friendships.... Jealousy will show you who your true friends are.... But you know that already."

Jérôme looked at his friend and was content to nod without replying. "God knows, Jacques is right!" he thought. Ever since he had started navigating in the upper stratosphere of the university, he had observed there, with dread, a back side of the stage set that he would have preferred to keep ignoring. But he did not want to say that to him. "What good would it be to tell stories? That would oblige me to name names, and I do not want to damage the reputation of these people or those." But what he had seen he described one evening in his journal, certain that it would be kept quite confidential:

[22] Tavarès, letter to J. Lejeune, January 24, 1966.

> It was difficult at the start, and the first revelation of the faculty's base acts during the rigged election of S. as an associate professor left me in a sort of fright. Those intrigues—those hidden decisions that have ripened for a long time and that their authors do everything they can to implement despite all justice or simply naïve honesty—made me shiver in the true sense of the word. Someone had told me about it, but I did not know it firsthand. In a little while, I will be resigned to it, and the worst is already past: I know the value of men such as B., H., D., and that cardiologist whose name escapes me, although I'll never forget the evil eye with which he greeted me one day. Before having access to these secrets, I was a joyful child. Having skirted these abysses of treachery, among people who maybe, I want to think, can sometimes be devout individuals elsewhere, and even unselfish perhaps, I now know the men, and it takes a heart triply plated with brass to behold that spectacle![23]

Jérôme was horrified by those schemes; they were foreign to him. He knew that by refusing to play the game, he was provoking hostilities that would harm his career. "So what", he said to himself. "Then, too, not all of them are like that. Others are honest. They are the ones I want to work with." He wanted to ignore those shadowy battles and managed to do so all the more easily since he saw every morning during his consultations the faces of his patients, their smiles and tears, which reminded him of the essential thing.

At the age of forty, Jérôme was young, an award-winner, and highly respected, and he was aware of having reached an important milestone in his career. He was a titular professor, a "boss", but he did not flatter himself at all, because his mind was completely taken up by the search for a treatment for his patients, and he threw all his energy into the battle against disease. And when it happened that his strength failed him—so crushing had his workload become—he remembered a man whose exemplary life had imbued his childhood, a humble apostle of charity who left his mark on French history, Saint Vincent de Paul. To those who asked the saint, "What can we do to help the poor?" he used to answer: "More." Jérôme, too, wanted to do "more", for those whom he called the "poorest of the poor", those who are "wounded in their intellect", in "the freedom of their mind". His little patients.

[23] J. Lejeune, *Journal intime*, July 19, 1966.

Nevertheless, despite all that energy being expended, the flourishing studies, and the discoveries of his team, a sense of powerlessness gripped him, because he had the painful impression that he was stagnating. One evening in July 1966, when he finally managed to take up his journal again, he confided these thoughts to writing:

> Since 1963, we have made some progress but nothing mightily spectacular. The study of various forms of cancer is at a standstill. In November, I have to present the opening speech at the congress of oncologists, and I notice that the whole theory from 1963 is still valid; I will do little more than repeat the first long speech by Villejuif, supplemented by a few hundred publications. Maybe, after all, the logical model is acceptable. Nothing has come to modify it, and everything that I have been able to read or see in the last thirty years has only reinforced my conviction. With Berger we described the "common variant" of ovarian cancer, or at the very least ... what I think corresponds to it. But the definitive proof will take a long time to establish. A new disease, too, the deletion of the long arm of [chromosome] 18, which is just as nosological [concerned with the classification of diseases] as the *cri du chat* syndrome, which is now confirmed everywhere.... As for those with trisomy 21, the attempts to treat them follow one another patiently, but we have nothing certain, or even probable yet.... What upsets me in taking up this book again is to see that despite the problem that is posed daily, despite our repeated and untiring efforts, we are at the same point as in 1959. Not entirely, perhaps, but almost. I tried to let the audience share this impression of powerlessness during my inaugural lecture, and I think that I succeeded in doing so. The students who were there—and there were some—understood, I think, what sort of battle we have to wage and the need that presses us![24]

Jérôme's journal was the barometer of his activity, because he wrote in it so frequently. When Jérôme took advantage of that calm evening in July 1966, while Birthe and the children were in Denmark, to reawaken those slumbering pages, he was quite astonished to discover the last date noted on those pages covered with his fine handwriting:

[24] Ibid.

"1963. Almost three years already! I thought that I had reopened this notebook several times meanwhile!"

And sitting at his little wooden desk, in the halo of light projected by the architect's lamp clamped to the edge of it, he wrote:

> First, the most important thing of all: Thomas Pierre Ulysse Lejeune has made his appearance in our family. He is now three months old; everyone adores him, and I, who claimed not to be interested in children until they were around six months or a year old, I found him very nice the first day, very gifted the first week, and outstandingly intelligent ever since! It is true that he is a very charming child, but I do think that a quadragenarian is much less partial about this subject than a man of twenty-five or thirty. This must be the grandfatherly strand that is starting its patient development![25]

Jérôme proposed the name Thomas for their second son in order to commend him to two saints whom he greatly admired: Thomas Aquinas, for his extraordinary intellect, drawn to the truth and so skillful at deciphering the great book of creation, and Thomas More, for his upright conscience and his courage to follow it, even at the cost of his life. Then Jérôme wrote: "Damien and I do a half hour of the *Epitome [of Greek Mythology]*, just as Papa used to have me read Canto VI of *The Odyssey*."

In writing these words, Jérôme was happy to be able to hand down to his eleven-year-old son this ancestral treasure that he had received from his father at the same age. In thinking about those peaceful years of childhood, he restrained his hand and fixed his eyes on the photo of his father, who looked at him with a smile, wearing his big straw hat like a halo while standing in the garden in Étampes. Then he resumed writing.

"I have three years to catch up on, and no time to daydream."

And bending over his literary work, he now recorded the most important news about the laboratory.

That summer, Jérôme had to confront not only the solitude of the empty house but also his natural distraction, which was becoming legendary and took charge as soon as Birthe had left the premises. Sometimes things got complicated, to the great amusement of

[25] Ibid.

his friends. Thus, one summer Jérôme left his wife and children in Kerteminde to return to Paris, where he had an appointment with an enforcement agent, Monsieur Jeuniot. Since the meeting was to take place in the afternoon, he had time in the morning to stop by his laboratory to catch up on work that had accumulated during the vacation. There, immersed in his correspondence, he conscientiously remained in his office, and, when he lifted his head again at dinnertime, he realized in a flash: "My meeting!" Obviously, it was too late to run to it. "And too late to warn poor Jeuniot, who must have waited for me a long while without being able to meet with me!" That evening, after a frugal dinner, he admitted to his wife:

> I was quite annoyed all the same at my carelessness, but my good faith was so evident that Jeuniot himself consoled me.[26]

Birthe replied several days later:

> Everyone laughed when I told them that you forgot to go to the appointment; to do that, you really have to be distracted—but then I wasn't there to remind you about it![27]

Every summer, or almost, when he left Denmark, the family was also accustomed to running after him, from one station to the next, to retrieve there the car keys that he would forget and leave in his pocket with disconcerting regularity. Fortunately the understanding station masters would gladly forward the request and collect the set of keys, while Jérôme continued his trip to Paris. Another time, his distraction might have caused harm, if it had not been caught in time. It was in June 1966. Jérôme was in New York, where he was giving a conference, after which he planned a meeting that afternoon with several colleagues from the U.N. And suddenly he recalled, in a surge of memory, that at the hour set for that gathering he was expected to speak at a congress in Washington. He had just enough time to jump into a taxi, then a plane, and again a taxi, to arrive on time and to reassure the organizers, who were justly uneasy. Every time he told

[26] J. Lejeune, letter to Birthe, July 22, 1967.
[27] B. Lejeune, letter to Jérôme, July 28, 1967.

Birthe about his setbacks, she was amused, quite happy to see how necessary her presence at his side was.

Summer 1967 was a special moment for Jérôme. In August, he had the joy of being invited to Israel for an international scientific congress, and he hoped that between two sessions he could visit some of the holy places. "What a shame that my Bibi is not coming", he thought while boarding the airplane. "For once, spouses had been invited! But obviously, with five little ones and the heat in Jerusalem in the month of August, it was impossible!" Despite his wife's absence, Jérôme enthusiastically traveled through that Holy Land where Jesus had walked. Although the modern era had changed the places, Jérôme discovered with amazement the Dead Sea, gleaming like a green topaz, the Lake of Tiberias, which he described in his letters to Birthe as "one of the most beautiful landscapes in the world", preserving "all its Gospel beauty", and Jerusalem, "splendid and dramatic".[28] The contrast between the holiness of these places that witnessed salvation history and the vulgar disrespect of some members of the group, who went into the churches without taking off their hats and laughed uproariously there, was a trial for Jérôme. The height of this irreverence was when an old woman from the group told him that she almost burst out laughing when she saw him make the sign of the cross; then she declared in a brash yet uneasy tone of voice: "And, you know, it didn't frighten me!"

Jérôme was left gaping by such ignorance, but he wrote to Birthe that evening,

> I nevertheless have an unforgettable memory of that holy Galilee, and I prayed for you all.[29]

What Jérôme did not describe then, out of discretion concerning his interior life, was the spiritual experience that seized him on the shores of the Sea of Galilee, in the little chapel in Tiberias. Only after his return, when rue Galande was still deserted, did he take up his pen to confide to Philippe this spiritual experience that he himself found astonishing.

[28] J. Lejeune, letter to Birthe, July 1967.
[29] Ibid.

And in this little chapel furnished in poor taste, on this recent pavement that may not yet be thirty years old, I stretched out at full length to kiss the imaginary footprint of the One who was once there. This naïve or, I would almost say, instinctive gesture in itself seemed to me ridiculous, but certainly not the feeling that prompted me to make it.

It is always impossible to express the fact that one loves, and the classic declaration of love by putting one knee on the ground is probably much truer than the theatrical image leads us to suppose. Nevertheless, like a monk who arrives late at a chapter meeting, I kissed the pavement as a sign of affectionate deference, because I did not know what to say and could think of nothing else to do. Above all, my dear brother, do not think that I had a vision at that moment, that I was transported in spirit, rapt by an ineffable ecstasy. All that was within me was as reasonable as usual, judging my action ridiculous, and even so, it all resounded to an unknown and yet familiar vibration, trying by adoration to join a unison to which I could not aspire. A son finding a dearly beloved Father, a father finally known, a revered teacher, a very sacred heart being discovered—there was something of all of that in it and much more.

How could I tell about this tenderness, sweetness, affection, timid, and yet determined love? A need to make known how deeply my heart had been touched by so much kindness and goodness on His part: that He was willing to be there, that He had agreed that I should know Him and that He had welcomed me so simply and fraternally. How to tell about the most obvious and tender love?

When I stood up again, because my adoration had lasted only the time it took to make the move, I laughed a little at myself, recognizing that for all my knowledge I had been able to offer nothing better than an ancestral posture, and I told myself that like the soldier stiff at attention and discovering the pride of respect, I had discovered in the position of a suppliant slave the tender affection of the voluntary Devotee.

Outside the sun was shining, as bright and cheerful as when I entered. The dear Franciscan friar, wearied by age and the heat of the day, had gone off into his tiny convent. And I walked away once again toward the Sea of Galilee, carrying with me forever assurance about the reunion and the marvelous intimacy that Jesus has prepared for human beings, here or there, here below or there on high or down there and up here, very far away, very far, but perhaps very soon, and this real reverse side of everything that exists and that is finally discovered only when one can see it from the other side of time.[30]

[30] J. Lejeune, *Holy Land in Tiberias*, letter to his brother Philippe, July 1967. This letter, never sent, was found in his desk blotter the day after his death.

Jérôme put his pencil down. After a moment's hesitation, he finally decided not to send that letter to Philippe, and he carefully deposited it like a treasure in his brown leather desk blotter. Out of humility as much as out of modesty.

Jérôme's words describing this experience of God are very simple, almost naïve. He carefully notes that it was not a mystical ecstasy and that everything within him "was as reasonable as usual", but that he experienced the profound, vibrant joy of "a son finding a dearly beloved Father, a father finally known, a revered teacher". This sobriety, more than any Baroque exuberance, indirectly reveals the intensity of the encounter.

Why did Jérôme receive a grace like that in August 1967? Maybe by this anticipated reunion the Lord wanted to assure him of His presence and to strengthen him before the battle.

CHAPTER 7

HIS SOUL AT PEACE, HIS HEART POUNDING

1967–1969

In the limpid September sky, the sun kept climbing toward the zenith. On the horizon, a light white mist, which only a sharp eye could distinguish, stretched out slowly, heralding a change of weather. The heat, despite the lateness of the season, had overcome the men, who waited, prostrate in the shade of their old houses, for more clement hours, while under the apple tree in the garden of Saint-Hilaire, two straw hats, moving slightly, indicated that the torpor was not universal. Jérôme and his brother Philippe, comfortably seated in garden chairs, contemplated the world, a small glass of Amaretto in hand. The lawn, which Jérôme had just mown, did not yet give off any fragrance; they would have to wait until dusk to savor the scents of the earth and of the freshly cut grass.

"When the sun finishes its course this evening, the world will be much better!" Jérôme declared to his brother, laughing about their discussions.

Since dessert, they had already revisited the theory of relativity, compared the play of light (*chiaroscuro*) in Caravaggio and Rembrandt, and commented on the genius of Thomas Aquinas.

"You just have to read it to understand so many things!" remarked Philippe. "From the presence of evil in the world, which troubles many Christians, to the philosophical proofs for the existence of God, there are already so many answers."

"You're right", Jérôme answered. "And the most fascinating thing for me is his ability to present all the opposing arguments and to respond to them methodically in a genuine search for the truth. I have not found one argument defended in our twentieth century that was not already discussed in his works, whether they were written for his Catholic students or composed for the pagans. He refuted in advance all the contradictory theories of modern man. And he lived in the thirteenth century! There is definitely nothing new under the sun, despite the differences in language."

"Yes, this is one brilliant guy who got his intellect to work! And who was not afraid of confrontation, provided that it was constructive; that, no doubt, is the best bulwark against materialism", Philippe added. "But he was perhaps too methodical for me", he continued. "I prefer the genius of Saint Augustine. In the fourth century, he had already dealt with all the really important subjects: what troubles the heart of man and what heals it, the love of God. The rest, basically, doesn't matter."

A silence settled in between the two brothers, filled with their deep and lighthearted thoughts, like the air close by them that quivered in the sun. Then Jérôme, with his face suddenly serious, broke the silence:

"We could use both of them for what's coming."

Philippe, astonished by this unexpected change of tone, for a moment left off looking at the rays of light that played in the branches of the apple tree to observe his brother's face, and waited.

"For some time now, I have noticed in international scientific circles the emergence of ideas that I do not like. Last year, I received an official invitation to become a member of the International Federation of Scientific Societies in Helsinki. The introductory document enclosed with the letter was entitled 'Toward a New Humanity', and reading those pages pointed out to me a spine-chilling trend: it was the program of a Malthusian and eugenicist scientific policy."

"What did you do about it?" asked Philippe.

"I replied: 'Since I cannot subscribe to the theoretical solutions outlined, for scientific as well as ethical reasons, it is absolutely impossible for me to associate myself with the aims of your Federation.' "[1]

Philippe congratulated him: "There's an answer that has the merit of being clear."

"If I do not say what I believe to be true, then I let the others occupy the field, and I fear that they will end up making terrible

[1] J. Lejeune, letter to the president of the Federation of Scientific Societies, March 9, 1966.

decisions for the little patients", Jérôme replied. "I saw it last week in Washington. Eunice Shriver Kennedy, who has noticed these changes, is worried, too, and she asked me to take part in this symposium, to defend the medicine of all times, Hippocratic medicine. So, I went to it, and I was the only geneticist among the obstetricians, psychiatrists, lawyers, and churchmen."

"And how did the debates go? Did the others have any solid arguments?" his brother asked.

"To tell the truth," replied Jérôme, "the only logical position is that of the Catholics, and the others, Protestants and Jews, were unanimous in recognizing it. They reproach Catholics for being cut and dried, but when each of the proponents describes how far he is willing to go, he differs from his neighbor and cannot explain why he stops there and goes no farther! The most striking fact is that Catholic teaching is the most biological of all and, to tell the truth, the only consistent teaching.[2] I have noticed it. And", Jérôme continued calmly, "there is no contradiction between the Hippocratic Oath—written four hundred years before Christ, which says, 'First, do no harm,' and explains, 'I will not administer a poison to anybody when asked to do so, nor will I suggest such a course; similarly I will not give to a woman a pessary to cause abortion'—and my duty as a Christian, which tells me, 'Thou shalt not kill.' On the contrary, I see a twofold obligation to serve the children, whether they are sick or well."

Philippe looked at his brother, who had become pensive. Jérôme was a privileged witness to mental disabilities. He knew from experience that the "intellectual illnesses" of his patients, a term he used to describe the mental handicaps from which they suffered, were not diseases of the heart, because these patients had a great capacity for love that radiated widely around them. But he saw in the world another more serious form of intellectual illness, that of reason darkened by its refusal to receive the light of truth. And this illness affected him doubly, as a Catholic scientist and as a physician. As a Catholic scientist, because he nourished a preferential love for the truth, which he loved and sought. As a physician, because he understood that his patients would quickly become victims of the intellects

[2] J. Lejeune, letter to Birthe, September 6, 1967, recounting this colloquium in Washington.

that shape a world deprived of truth. History had taught him that when people no longer believe in God who is "the Way, the Truth and the Life", they end up no longer believing in man, and when there is no longer this unconditional respect for human brotherhood, the worst becomes possible. Following the thread of his thoughts, Jérôme continued, as if talking to himself:

> Chromosomal racism is horrible, like all forms of racism.[3]
>
> Compassion toward parents is a feeling that every physician must have. A man who could announce to parents that their child is suffering seriously yet would not feel his heart sinking at the thought of the pain that will overwhelm them—such a man would not be worthy of our profession. But we do not protect others from a misfortune by committing a crime; we do not relieve the pain of a human being by killing another human being.[4]

Impressed by this tragic accent that he heard for the first time in his brother's voice, Philippe asked: "Do you really think we've reached that point?"

"Not yet," Jérôme replied, "but I fear that it will happen sooner than we thought."

The following eight months passed quietly. While observing the increasing demands of a society that was losing its bearings, Jérôme prudently kept his distance from politics and gave all his time to his patients and his scientific meditations. Appointed Executive Director of the Institut de Progénèse and, for the second year in a row, a member of the Scientific Council of the Institut Pasteur, he tried as much as possible to concentrate on his work. The only escape that he allowed himself was to construct hypotheses on scientific topics as varied as the modeling of an airless hot-air balloon and the creation of man.

His scientific mind enjoyed trying to elucidate certain mysteries of the Bible, like the creation of Adam and Eve, which was of

[3] J. Lejeune, *Le Quotidien de Paris*, no. 3449 (December 29, 1990), quoted in *Tom Pouce*, no. 25 (March-April 1991).

[4] J. Lejeune, "Avant Hitler? Des psychiatres allemands liquidaient les schizophrènes qu'ils ne pouvaient guérir" [Before Hitler? German psychiatrists liquidated schizophrenics whom they could not cure], *Paris Match*, November 7, 1980.

particular interest to him, being a geneticist. He was not satisfied with the neo-Darwinian theory that, in an attempt to explain the appearance of man, proposed the hypothesis of a progressive humanization. However, although evolution proves to be accurate about variations within the same species, it cannot explain the passage from one species to another—from monkey to man. No paleontologist has ever found an intermediate species between animal and man. Jérôme suggested the Adamic hypothesis, that is, the sudden appearance of man by a restructuring (qualitative leap) of the chromosomes of the great apes, which contradicts neither genetics nor paleontology nor Genesis. He published his first article on the subject in the *Nouvelle revue théologique* of the University of Louvain in February 1968. Immediately, a neo-Darwinist responded to Jérôme in the same review and dismantled his arguments. The debate had begun. Jérôme did not claim to be right, but since neo-Darwinism was only a theory, he proposed another hypothesis, sticking more closely to scientific observation. This subject fascinated him and provided material for many conversations with his brother Philippe.

In the artist's studio in Étampes, a kingdom protected from the dullness of the world by large bay windows that captured the light of spring, Philippe listened with interest. Behind him the sometimes serious faces on the barely finished canvases scrutinized Jérôme without batting an eyelid. And the long silhouettes, pelted with color by the artist's brush, remained captured in their eternal movement. Standing in the middle of this attentive assembly, Philippe spoke up:

"The theory of evolution, often used as a weapon against the Church, is encountering a few detractors in the scientific world today.[5] What do you think of these debates?"

Jérôme answered:

> Don't mix things up. Although Darwin's theory is totally open to criticism, it is not on account of any difficulty with the Church's revelation. Darwin certainly used his theory to try to dismantle Christian anthropology. There is no disputing that, and he himself admitted it, and his wife wrote him some extraordinary letters on the subject to

[5] On this subject, see the book by Michael Denton: *Evolution: A Theory in Crisis* (Adler & Adler, 1985).

> try to dissuade him from such a project. That being true, we must not believe that the Bible is necessarily opposed to the concept of evolution. The Bible is even the first evolutionary book, since it gives the steps of creation. The most surprising thing is that, in the Bible, first the sea animals appear, then the flying animals, then the animals on earth, and then last of all man. In other words, the Bible, in an absolutely dazzling shortcut, lists the appearance of living beings in the order in which we find them in the geological layers. There is real reason here for astonishment, both for the scientist and for the believer, and there is by no means a quarrel between the Bible and geology.[6]

"You are right, I had never thought of that!" Philippe remarked, very surprised. "But in your opinion, are the arguments in favor of evolution credible?" he asked, as he sat down beside his easel and gestured to his brother to take a seat beside him.

Jérôme walked over to the chair and, after settling in comfortably, answered:

> Let's be clear about what you call evolution. If you call evolution the notion that species have succeeded each other on the surface of the earth during its history, I think that there is no scientist who rejects the notion of evolution, and I add that on this point it is in full agreement with biblical teaching.[7]

"Okay", Philippe replied. Then he added: "But for most people, evolution means that man descended from the monkey and that all life originally began starting with an initial cell from which the different life forms descended. What do you think?"

"That is the Theory of Evolution", Jérôme answered. "It is not fact. The fact is that in time, forms succeeded one another, and it is true that man was the last to arrive. About that no scientist disagrees. So much for the chronological order. In the order of causality: How did it happen? The precise answer is that we know nothing about it. There is a neo-Darwinian theory that assumes that everything was produced by random mutations sorted out by natural selection."[8]

[6] J. Lejeune, "La fin du darwinisme", interview in *La Nef*, no. 12 (December 1991).
[7] Ibid.
[8] Ibid.

After a short silence allowing Philippe to follow his brother's thought, he asked him:

"But how come there are species?"

"Bravo!" answered Jérôme.

Exactly, this is a question that evolutionists do not ask themselves. It is nevertheless very interesting, because: suppose that Darwin is right and that mutations occur that are selected by the need to survive and that eventually the life forms evolve in this way. Why wouldn't there be a kind of continuum from the amoeba to the elephant, and a continuum where you would see amoebas elephantizing (even very slowly!)? Why is there no such thing? Why does an elephant always reproduce strictly in the elephant species? There is a reason for this. And we are beginning to know this reason, at least for the higher species: it is because their genetic patrimony is organized in a structure, which are the chromosomes, and because chromosomes are in a way the volumes of the encyclopedia of life, the tables of the law of life engraved with these characters: in other words, because each species has its own tables of law that we know how to distinguish from each other. Generally speaking, each species has a specific karyotype (appearance and internal structure of chromosomes). We recognize the chimpanzee, orangutan, or gorilla by its karyotype, and in the same way, we recognize all human beings because they all have the same karyotype....

As far as the origin of life is concerned, we can only construct hypotheses. What we can say with certainty, on the other hand, is that if we took the neo-Darwinian mechanism (mutation selection), evolution between species would not have occurred because, given the quantity of successive favorable changes that you would have to imagine between the amoeba and man, it is absolutely impossible that man or other higher animals would have appeared. The absolute unlikelihood that information increases by the simple action of chance is such that writers keep returning to this image of the monkey who would type *The Odyssey* simply by striking typewriter keys at random. There is no way to escape from this difficulty. We are absolutely sure that it is not possible to explain the appearance of the species and the different forms of life by applying the neo-Darwinian theory.[9]

[9] Ibid.

"Do you mean that it has had its day, that it doesn't explain anything?" Philippe asked.

"Yes", Jérôme replied.

> But no one is able to provide another explanation and the truth, and this is the deep uneasiness, the fact that we have no explanation for evolution. No one knows how it was possible. It could not have happened by chance and by selection, because then it would not have taken place. It is absurd to imagine that chance is capable of building a machine much more complicated than the biggest computers. It is as absurd to suppose that the human brain was made by trial and error as it is to suppose that spare computer parts manufactured a small IBM by themselves. There has to be something else. And this other thing is called information or spirit. Now we are completely ignorant about how information or spirit entered into matter, to appropriate matter and control it.[10]

"And, in your opinion, can we call into question the principle of evolution that makes a species pass from one species to another?" Philippe asked.

"No, I don't think so. We cannot explain how one species can become another species. But that does not mean it cannot happen. And I think it would be a serious mistake to claim that this is surely impossible."[11]

Philip's observant eye perceived a gleam in his brother's eyes just after he uttered those words.

"Oh, so you have an idea on the subject!" he exclaimed with growing interest. "Tell me!"

Jérôme reflected for a brief moment and said to him:

"Yes, I have an idea, but it is only an idea, an hypothesis, to be discussed."

And Jérôme explained to him the Adamic hypothesis, which he had described in the *Nouvelle revue de Théologie* a few weeks earlier. Philippe listened in fascination and tried to put up some intellectual resistance before admitting defeat. Laughing, Jérôme concluded: "All this is only the product of my cogitations. Do not take it as proved!"

[10] Ibid.

[11] Ibid.

Anxious to confirm the solidity of this Adamic hypothesis, Jérôme wanted to take advantage of his next trip to New York, in the spring of 1968, to discuss it with one of the best specialists in the field. He made an appointment with Professor Theodosius Dobzhansky at the Rockefeller Institute in April. On that day, as he entered the famous building in Manhattan, Jérôme rejoiced because he was finally going to be able to confront this eminent geneticist and evolutionary theorist with his idea. "We'll see what's left of my proposals. The important thing is to try to move the debate forward", he said to himself enthusiastically. Dobzhansky warmly welcomed him and took him to the elevator, which soon led them to the fifteenth floor.

"What an incredible panorama!" Jérôme exclaimed as he entered the office of his host, where a bay window offered a breathtaking view of Central Park and the East River.

Then he added, with false modesty, "In Paris we have no building this tall, but we do have the towers of Notre-Dame to lift us toward the sky."

And, with a smirk, he added, sure of making an effect: "Do you know that the house where I live, near Notre-Dame, has a connection with your country?"

"No, what is it?" Dobzhansky asked with interest.

"My house was built in 1480, before the discovery of America."

"Incredible!" the American exclaimed, really surprised. Laughing, he then added: "I see that, in evolutionary terms, the Rockefeller Building descended from the house!"

After these introductory pleasantries, the two geneticists sat down to address at last the subject that had brought them together, and Jérôme explained his hypothesis in detail. Dobzhansky listened to him attentively and asked him the essential questions. At the end of their conversation, the American geneticist thought that the hypothesis developed by the Frenchman was rather unlikely but acknowledged that the theoretical argument was correct. Jérôme concluded that if even this evolutionary expert saw no error in it, the idea could make its way. And he left the Rockefeller Institute more passionate than ever about the subject.

Jérôme's research on the creation of the world showed the harmonious development of his intellect in the fields of faith and science. He was not a scientist on one side and a Christian on the other, he was a Christian researcher who saw with the eyes of the intellect and with the eyes of the heart, and this binocular vision gave him depth perception. Like many of his contemporaries, he might have declared that the fact of believing is opposed to the fact of seeking, that the light of faith is useless for modern man, who is an adult now, that it is only a "subjective light"[12] inaccessible to reason. Now, on the contrary, he, the great researcher, saw that faith and science are complementary in the search for truth, one clarifying the "why", the other seeking to know the "how" of things. Thus, he perfectly accepted this twofold conviction:

> It may seem inappropriate to reconcile the data of revelation with assumptions based on scientific findings. These two modes of knowledge are fundamentally different. One, given freely, is expressed in a poetic language that the heart understands with joy; the other, gained laboriously, is a difficult discourse that reason masters with difficulty. Through the variations of explanatory theories, these two paths have seemed sometimes to confirm, sometimes to contradict each other, whereas they both must lead us to the truth.[13]

Jérôme even regarded science as "an ally of faith in understanding the designs of God",[14] and he was not afraid to study the data revealed by the Bible in the light of scientific discoveries and to pass them through his critical mind. However, he rigorously distinguished the two levels: faith and science are complementary, but not interchangeable. As a result, he refuted both *discordisme*—the dogmatic separation of the two—that assigns the Bible to the category of tales and legends, and the concordism that shifts it to the department of the exact sciences. And to discuss his thought with his friends and to illustrate it, he liked to take the example of the creation of the world:

> Let us begin, if you will, with the Book of Genesis, which we will take on the first day. God said: *Fiat lux*, let there be light, and there was light.... Hubble had shown that galaxies move away faster, the farther they are from us: a puff of dust expanding into infinity: this was demonstrated by the shift of the spectrum toward red; Father Lemaître deduced from this that if this movement lasted for a long

[12] Pope Francis, encyclical *Lumen fidei*.

[13] J. Lejeune, "Biologie, conscience et foi", conference at Notre-Dame de Paris, October 10, 1982.

[14] Benedict XVI, address, November 21, 2012.

> time (astronomers count in billions of years), it was certainly necessary that at the previous moment everything was gathered in a smaller volume. He proposed that the entire universe came from a hyperdense matter: the primitive atom. The *discordisme* of pride rose up vigorously, then the tumult subsided, since no other hypothesis was able to resist the accumulation of facts.[15]

In 1968, when Jérôme was developing his Adamic theory, Father Georges Lemaître, a priest astronomer and physicist, had been dead for two years without his merits being recognized. Yet he was the one who described in 1927 the theory of an expanding universe that has a beginning and, in 1931, that of the primitive atom, against the opinion of most of his colleagues in cosmology, including Einstein, who did not adhere to this idea and maintained that the universe is static. Not until 1965, with the fortuitous discovery of "cosmological thermal radiation" by two young Americans, Ano Penzias and Robert Wilson, did the scientific community finally recognize that Father Lemaître had been right in laying the foundations of the Big Bang Theory. But this recognition was too late for him to win the Nobel Prize, and the two young Americans were the ones who received it in 1978. The Church had not waited so long to recognize the quality of this discovery and had appointed Father Lemaître president of the Pontifical Academy of Sciences in 1960.[16]

Father Lemaître, in describing the primitive atom at the origin of the universe, brilliantly showed how science and faith work in tandem and how the *discordisme* described by Jérôme can blind scientists. This example was so emblematic that years later another observer of this textbook case would write:

> Had he not been a priest, Georges Lemaître would have been vindicated more quickly. But no doubt he also had to be a priest in order to think about a beginning of the world.[17]

[15] J. Lejeune, "Biologie, conscience et foi".

[16] At the time of this writing, in October 2018, the International Astronomical Union officially recognized Father Lemaître's role in the discovery of the Big Bang. It recommended that the famous Hubble's Law be called from now on Hubble-Lemaître's Law.

[17] In an article dated August 7, 2018, "Georges Lemaître, prêtre et premier théoricien du Big Bang", signed by Yann Verdo, the online newspaper *Les Echos.fr*, discussed this late and precise recognition, quoting Laurent Lemire (*Ces savants qui ont eu raison trop tôt* [Tallandier, 2013]): "Had he not been a priest, Georges Lemaître would have been vindicated more quickly. But no doubt he also had to be a priest in order to think about a beginning of the world."

Jérôme liked to recall this example because it illustrated the relationships that he maintained with faith and science in the search for truth that guided his whole life:

> I have never found an irreducible contradiction between what I have learned through long scientific experience and what has been transmitted to me by the Catholic faith. I have seen difficulties, but not one that was insurmountable or presented absolute contradictions.[18]

His conclusion was simple:

> On no known point is there a divorce between the today's science and the religion of all time. Religion and science: How could there be a contradiction between the true and the verified? The second is always the one that lags.[19]

Jérôme's original contribution was to make faith an ally of science. Attentive to seeing the traces of God in the beauty of the world, he incorporated the order of creation in his reflection and researched using a method different from others. A method in which observation, the constant reference to a harmony, and the rejection of any transgression of the natural order have a decisive place. The quality of his work, like that of Father Lemaître, was a fruit of this method that reconciled the intellect with itself. His intellect enlightened by faith surpassed itself. His faith enlightened by intelligence flourished. And this intellectual and spiritual harmony gave him great joy and great freedom.

While Jérôme liked to look for the "why" and the "how" of the appearance of life on earth, French society was in the middle of mutating, and spring 1968 promised to be eventful. In May 1968, student demonstrations were in full swing, and what appeared to be a temporary protest turned out to be a revolution against the established order, whether moral or social. Although at the age of forty-one Jérôme did not feel like an old man, the twenty years that separated him from these young revolutionaries seemed to him like centuries. He was well situated to know that the academic world was not perfect, but he did not believe for a moment in the progress of

[18] J. Lejeune, "La fin du darwinisme".

[19] J. Lejeune, *Journal intime*, January 25, 1970.

anarchy or violent methods, and he preferred revolution by example, simplicity, and truth ... which he already put into practice, naturally, with his patients. Around him, many medical professors behaved like mandarins. Seldom present in their offices, they would arrive in a car driven by a chauffeur, pass by like comets, and hand down their opinions from the height of their arrogance. Jérôme did not share these methods, and, from the beginning of his career, his consideration and kindness struck the parents who brought their children to him. He did not lose this warm and soothing attitude when he became successful, and, at the height of his career, during that troubled period in 1968, Jérôme remained simple and accessible.

As the days passed in May 1968, the protest intensified. There were street fights in the Latin Quarter and barricades on the Boulevard Saint-Michel. In their house on rue Galande, a stone's throw from the Sorbonne, the Lejeunes had front-row seats. Jérôme—who remembered the events of May 1936, when employees of the family distillery threatened to strike, and the postwar turmoil that threw his father in prison—did not need to think very long to know how to behave. He did not like violence and feared it, but not more than cowardice. He continued his work firmly and calmly and tried as much as possible, within the limits of his abilities, to curb those young revolutionaries.

At the School of Medicine, there was total disorder. The premises were occupied and the entrances blocked by picket lines. When Jérôme approached, one of the students in the mass gathering in front of the porch told him with a swaggering air:

"You can't get through; the med school is blocked."

But Jérôme responded in a calm, determined tone, and the young people, impressed in spite of themselves, understood that nothing and nobody would prevent this man from working, and they let him enter. In this way, Jérôme crossed the barrier each day and went to his office, even at the height of the tension. They could insult him or go so far as to threaten him; Jérôme was not cowed.

In fact, he was not afraid. Sometimes he would walk in the corridors invaded by the activists and quietly give his opinion. One day, he made a tour of the faculty building in the company of one of his collaborators, and when they returned to his office, the colleague said to him:

"Sir, I must say I wasn't feeling very confident when you were making your comments to the students in the hallways. But you were so calm, as though it was perfectly natural to tell them what you thought. Your courage amazed me."

Another time, some students knocked on the door of his office, not to annoy him, but to ask for his cooperation. A young woman, escorted by three young men loaded down with big bags, stood in front of him and said, gesturing with her chin toward her henchmen:

"We've been taking some medications because we're going to need them soon. Yes, you understand", she added quickly in a tone more enthusiastic than provocative, "there may be a break-in tomorrow against the CRS [Compagnies républicaines de sécurité, French national police reserves]."

And before Jérôme had time to utter a word, the girl went on to say:

"Could you keep them? We wouldn't want them to be wasted. We'll come back for them tomorrow."

Jérôme, who understood that these medicines had been stolen from the hospital pharmacy, agreed very kindly, and the precious deposit was soon locked up in his office. The next day, when the students came back to get the medicines, Jérôme replied:

"Yes, of course, you want the medicines. Do you have the removal order?"

A stunned silence greeted this question. Faced with their insistence and their arguments, Jérôme responded with an imperturbable determination:

"I understand your request, but without a removal order I can't do anything; that's the rule."

The students were furious, but they did not dare to attack physically this Professor Lejeune who barred them from access to his office. Defeated, they gave up, but not without murmuring threats.

At the Necker Children's Hospital, things were relatively calm, and Jérôme managed to work almost normally, without being bothered by the demonstrators.

Soon he became involved once again because of his responsibility as professor of the Chair of Genetics, because with all these riots, there was talk about cancelling the September examinations. In early July, while the rioters continued to occupy the premises, the opposition was organized thanks to thirteen professors who shared a horror of the violence and disorder, among them Jérôme and his friend Jacques Lafourcade. They were going to set up the university defense. First, by establishing a counterforce, by creating a union that would make its voice heard and would break the monopoly of the leftist unions, which, in the student assemblies, terrorized their opponents with the methods of a revolutionary tribunal. Jacques Lafourcade worked on it successfully, and within a few days a new union came to light. Next, by announcing that the examinations would be held in September as scheduled. Since the revolution had won over the teaching staff, the debates in the faculty council meeting on July 11 were tense; some professors fell in behind the rioters, while others called for isolating the revolutionary minority so as to resume work. Jérôme took the floor and skillfully succeeded in countering the revolutionary motions. His speech was considered excellent by many confreres who did not have the courage or the talent to speak so clearly in those circumstances. So much so that, the next day, there was talk of appointing him dean of the faculty. Jérôme was stunned by this. That same evening, he wrote to Birthe, whom events had not prevented from leaving for Denmark:

> It's amazing to see that just saying what you think gets people so excited! I am quite struck by all this. The fact that these people think of asking me to lead them, simply because I dare to say what they think, is amazing.[20]

Jérôme had no desire to become dean and proposed other names. Birthe did not insist on it, either, and with her usual common sense and incredible intuition, she wrote back to him:

> I'm very flattered that they're thinking of you as dean, but I hope you won't accept it; it would be a shame to waste three years doing administration and dropping the research. Imagine the ordeal of quarreling with B. and H. instead of trying to heal the little ones.[21]

The letters that Jérôme and Birthe exchanged at that time showed their excellent knowledge of men and their stratagems. Obviously

[20] J. Lejeune, letter to Birthe, July 12, 1968.
[21] B. Lejeune, letter to Jérôme, July 16, 1968.

Jérôme was not naïve, and yet he was sad to discover a few days later that one of his collaborators, whom he had not had the heart to dismiss several months earlier, despite his poor professional conduct, had appeared on a revolutionary list. A collaborator, in his own department.... For Jérôme, it was a severe blow.

In the midst of this disorder, he reflected on a total overhaul of the faculties of medicine and worked hard to obtain recognition of human genetics as a discipline in its own right, distinct from pediatrics, to which it was still attached: He hoped to nominate new professors and organized a comprehensive genetics curriculum as well as a cytogenetics certificate. But he was in constant demand for upcoming appointments to the faculty council, and he knew that his opinion was decisive. What a waste of time, but how could he avoid it without failing in his duty to the faculty? Finally, in the face of mounting pressure to appoint him dean, Jérôme wrote to Birthe:

> Above all, don't think that I'm letting myself be intoxicated by visions of power; all this leaves me truly indifferent, and I would prefer a thousand times more to be left in peace to conduct my research. The truth is that it is difficult to know where duty lies and to judge wisely where one will be most useful. Ultimately, I will return to our beloved studies, but when they don't come pestering me all the time, because in this case it is better to take direct responsibility, even if it means making a mistake.[22]

In August, the government regained control, the situation calmed down, and Jérôme could honor two invitations he had received, one to India for conferences in the faculties of science of Calcutta and Benares, on August 15 and 16, and the other in Japan for the International Genetics Congress in Tokyo, August 17–23. In Calcutta, Jérôme responded to the invitation of one of his former interns, who had managed to set up a cytogenetics laboratory with ridiculously inadequate equipment, which he admired. This trip was also an opportunity to meet Mother Teresa, that little woman and great nun, whose deeply lined face reflected pure charity.

The faculty elections were held in October, and Jérôme was finally chosen as dean. He accepted out of duty but already feared these additional, essentially administrative responsibilities.... On the other

[22] J. Lejeune, letter to Birthe, July 22, 1968.

hand, he refused the benefits in kind attached to the office: he did not accept the magnificent apartment in the heart of the Latin Quarter—reserved for the dean—or the cook or the driver who went with it. When his children were already rejoicing about this new way of life, Jérôme announced to them his decision:

"My darlings, we will have none of this, we will stay here on rue Galande."

"But why, Papa," one of them exclaimed, "since this is offered to us, and you have the right to it?"

"Yes, that would be great!" said another.

"Of course, it would be very pleasant," replied Jérôme, "but I prefer that we not take on these luxurious habits, because it is difficult to get rid of them. And when you are too attached to them, you lose your freedom. We do not need that comfort to be happy; we have everything we need, and I prefer my freedom of speech to these material advantages."

His children looked at him, half convinced, but suddenly aware of the importance that their father attached to his freedom of judgment and action. They understood that he preferred not to amass wealth that would divert him from his commitments. His work protected them from need, and as for the unforeseen circumstances, he confidently entrusted himself to Providence.

Jérôme began the academic year of 1968–1969 by assuming, at the age of forty-three, the position of dean of the Faculty of Medicine at the Collège des Cordeliers (now Paris Descartes University). However, this responsibility very soon weighed heavily on him, and although he exercised it conscientiously, he did not excel at it, not being attracted to administrative obligations. In the months following his appointment, he tried to obtain from INSERM [Institut national de la santé et de la recherche médicale, National Institute for Health and Medical Research] the creation of a research group, unfortunately without success, since the budgetary restrictions of this institute allowed no creation of that type until 1970. In addition, he was appointed by the Rectorate to sit on the commission in charge of organizing elections in the departments of Biomedical Research, Medical Law, and Medical Ethics.[23]

[23] J. Roche, letter to J. Lejeune, January 16, 1969.

In 1968, he created the certificate of cytogenetics at the Collège des Cordeliers and fought in May 1969 to obtain final examinations for this certificate.[24] He fought also for the recognition of medical genetics as a separate discipline and for the elimination of the gap between histology, on the one hand, and pediatrics, on the other.[25] Without this reorganization, genetics might disappear from the curriculum of medical schools, and he could not resign himself to such a catastrophe.

Jérôme worked also to create a certificate of general human genetics that did not yet exist, for lack of teachers. He ardently hoped to set it up for the academic year 1970.[26] In December 1969, he asked the rector of the Paris Academy for two university fellow positions that were indispensable to the teaching of human genetics in Paris.

Jérôme made only three brief trips to lecture at the Royal Society in London and in Oxford, then Geneva and Athens, while his extensive network still brought him a tremendous amount of mail from all over the world: Australia, India, Japan, Argentina, Chile, Brazil, Uruguay, Canada, United States, Finland, Germany ... on the most varied subjects: internships, publications, genetic advice, scientific questions, plastic surgery, a study on the "assassin's chromosome", the Adamic hypothesis.... He always replied to this mail within a week. Despite this burden, Jérôme still found time to defend the reputation of a colleague that had been sullied by the press, between two appointments. This time, Jérôme took up his pen to write to *Le Nouvel Observateur*, and the insult to his colleague appeared to him so serious that he did not mince his words:

> Dear Sir, in his article entitled "The Damnation of Father B."[27], one of your collaborators tries, by base insinuation, to dishonor a physician and his patient. Having known Doctor B. for a long time and having had the privilege of esteeming the admirable character of Father B., I have the duty to demand that you denounce, in your own newspaper,

[24] J. Lejeune, letter to the director of higher education, May 16, 1969.

[25] Letter to the minister of higher education, May 28, 1969. The letter is co-signed by R. Berger, B. Dutrillaux, S. Gilgenkrantz, J. de Grouchy, H. Jérôme, J. Lafourcade, J. Lejeune, M. Prieur, and M.-O. Rethoré.

[26] J. Lejeune, letter to a physician, December 9, 1969.

[27] The name was noted in the article, but we chose to delete it here, out of discretion.

> these despicable allusions. I do not know whether your associate imagines that such infamy could pay off, but it is difficult for me to believe that you can agree to capitalize on it. Formally asking you to publish this letter in full in the next issue of *Le Nouvel Observateur*, I ask you to accept, Sir, the expression of my very exact consideration.[28]

In May, Jérôme agreed to give a lecture at the college of a medical federation in Bordeaux, and his well-publicized speech was enthusiastically received by the physicians. The organizer, a gynecological surgeon, warmly thanked him:

> I can assure you that all the confreres present were particularly touched by your openness and the kind, smiling simplicity with which you answered their questions. You could not believe how effective your quiet and competent testimony was ..., and in the discussions that followed it helped us to finalize many things. Do I need to tell you that they were struck by this harmonious mixture in your presentation of science and respect for the human person and his suffering? That is to say that you have done much good, both from a scientific and from a moral perspective.[29]

On his return from Bordeaux, he learned that he had been appointed a member of the American Academy of Arts and Sciences, a distinction that proved once again the American scientific community's interest in his work. And a few months later, McGill University in Montreal consulted him as they established an International Federation of Genetics.[30]

Jérôme went through the academic year 1968–1969 accumulating all these responsibilities, but with his heart and mind attached to his twofold activity of care and research.

The summer of 1969 was quieter than the previous one; the university vacation offered Jérôme a few weeks of peace conducive to scientific and personal reflection. While Birthe and the children were in Kerteminde, he willingly stayed in the deserted laboratory beyond the usual hours to finish a demonstration or to delve into a problem.

[28] J. Lejeune, letter to the editor of the *Nouvel Observateur*, October 30, 1969.
[29] R. Traissac, letter to J. Lejeune, May 2, 1969.
[30] J. W. Boyes, letter to J. Lejeune, September 19, 1969.

When he returned in the evening to rue Galande, in the quiet apartment he still gave free rein to his curious and inventive mind, and this perpetual intellectual activity softened the rigor of his lonely evenings. It was also one of the moments chosen by Jérôme to read and reread the Bible calmly, without fanfare; he liked to study it and meditate on it in the light of his science and his faith. The in-depth knowledge of Sacred Scripture that he acquired in this way, little by little, sharpened his mind. In the absence of his family, Jérôme also changed his eating habits ... This meant that he was content with nothing, or almost nothing. A can of sardines and a handful of rice were enough to keep him happy. The sobriety of Jérôme's altogether monastic summer life-style revealed that what he had written to Birthe at the time of their engagement was not just a lyrical and romantic flight of fancy:

> Our love will be the only baggage and our religion will be the inexhaustible provisions that will allow us to live.[31]

Jérôme had no taste for money; he never had any on him, and if Birthe had not been there to meet their large family's minimum needs for comfort, he would have lived all year long in this very austere way.

After dinner, Jérôme took up his pen to tell Birthe the details of his day and covered with his beautiful handwriting the little sheet of paper bordered by a tricolor and light as a stamp, which would be carried to Denmark by air mail. This exchange of letters with his wife fortunately overcame his loneliness, and, in addition to the tender conjugal bond that they thus forged, despite the absence, it was a true family journal that they wrote together year after year.[32]

On that beautiful August evening, Jérôme was in a joyful mood and recounted his domestic chores:

> My dear darling, this afternoon, instead of going to Saint-Hilaire as planned, I thought it more useful to stay here and rest, given the

[31] J. Lejeune, letter to Birthe, February 8, 1952.

[32] Birthe treasures all these letters in a suitcase. There are two thousand of them, spanning more than forty years of history.

> weather. So I did my own wash, because the laundry was closed, and this machine is absolutely fantastic.
>
> To start with, in the first load I found a charming pastel sky-blue shirt, the kind I always dreamed of having! I was all the more pleased that the underwear then came out in a matching color, a little bolder however, and here I am, the happy owner of a completely revamped wardrobe. As for the socks, there is no risk of mishaps now: they are all a uniform, deep dark blue, which makes it very convenient to pair them. Even the pajamas, which were already sky blue, are now deep blue. All the same, when we say that the Japanese make socks of poor quality, what a slander!
>
> For the second load of wash, all whites (I would have liked some pink shirts, but I had no more socks available), it got stupidly stuck because one shirt had escaped from the drum through the half-open port. Fishing it back out was very simple. Turn the hole back toward the bottom, fill it with water, the shirt floats and comes back into the drum. Just a half turn and *voilà*. Took about half an hour. My foot still hurts, so I'll do some ironing tomorrow. I'll let you know.[33]

Before sticking the edges of the tricolor envelope one against another, Jérôme quickly went through his letter and amused himself by imagining Birthe reading these lines aloud to the three eldest children: "They will laugh at me, and they will have good reason to!"

But the next day, Jérôme sent his wife quite a different letter. He had received good news in the mail, and he hastened to relay it to her:

> The American Genetics Society has just bestowed on me the Allen Award. It is the highest prize offered to a geneticist.... All this is lovely, but I will have to go to the ceremony in San Francisco from October 1–4! Of course, I accept, and tomorrow I will compose a beautiful thank-you letter.[34]

The very prestigious Allen Memorial Award was the highest recognition of a geneticist, the world's greatest prize for genetics, and Jérôme, at the height of his career, was delighted to receive it.

However, Jérôme's joy was not without reservations. It was clouded by a worry that he could not manage to drive away. For

[33] J. Lejeune, letter to Birthe, August 7, 1971.

[34] Ibid., August 11, 1969.

some time, he had observed at international congresses an evolution among his geneticist confreres that deeply concerned him. Many of them let themselves be won over by the eugenics current, which was growing more widespread, and simply proposed the abortion of children with disabilities. Instead of treating them, they would put an end to these children's lives because they were sick. It was a solution far removed from the medicine of all times. And the children with Down syndrome were precisely the first ones targeted, those that could be detected *in utero*, thanks to his discovery of trisomy 21. But besides the oath of Hippocrates, which was imperative for him as a doctor, Jérôme loved his patients unconditionally. Regardless of age, weight, height, infirmity, or illness, even the most handicapped, even the least wanted. What was the point of a medical profession that looked after healthy people only? What an idea to try to eliminate the patient when we do not know how to eliminate the disease! "This is medicine *à la* Molière",[35] he remarked sadly. Alas, this time, Molière was not making people laugh. Jérôme felt, in every part of his being, that he could not collaborate in the extermination of these children who were sick or different. The horror of this prenatal selection struck him as self-evident, and the deadline—before or after birth—did not change a thing: it was the opposite of Hippocratic medicine and the opposite of any human brotherhood. He could not go along with it and never would be able to. In the depths of his heart he had that *non possumus* [Latin: "we cannot"] which so many men had pronounced before him when they could not agree to betray their conscience. These words are stronger and freer than the most powerful emperors. And this *non possumus* demanded today that he give witness, because he could not fail to say that he saw, behind this extra chromosome, a child with her joys and sorrows and to tell what he knew about her humanity and her inalienable rights. His conscience demanded more than a silent refusal, which would already be courageous: it asked him to defend these voiceless children by proclaiming the truth for them and for their parents.

Jérôme had been meditating on all these things for a few months. And now the Allen Memorial Award offered him the unique opportunity to speak to the most influential geneticists in the world, those

[35] Ibid. [Alluding to the comedy *Le Malade Imaginaire* (*The Imaginary Invalid*).]

who worked in the best hospitals and in the most efficient departments. If only he could succeed in making them understand that not only the death of children, but also the death of medicine was at stake—a total medical misinterpretation! Perhaps this purely rational argument would touch them more than compassion for sick children. Jérôme was clear-sighted: he knew that his peers would not forgive him for taking that liberty, but if he had the slightest chance of stirring their hearts and minds, he wanted to take it. The stakes were too important. The award ceremony was scheduled for October 3 during the solemn ceremony of the congress of the American Genetics Society. Jérôme had a month for mature reflection on his decision.

In the last days of September, with his speech meticulously prepared, he flew to San Francisco, his soul at peace, his heart pounding.

CHAPTER 8

THE ADVOCATE OF THE VOICELESS

1969–1973

As Jérôme climbed the steps of the hotel, a van parked a few steps away from him caught his attention: a Volkswagen bus, its sides painted with multicolored flowers. "I really am in California", he thought with amusement while lifting his little suitcase mounted on two wheels held on by an elastic strap. Indifferent to the mocking expressions of the passersby who considered that coach unfashionable, Jérôme congratulated himself on having invented before its time a terrific rolling engine that relieved his poor back. Then, too, he did not dislike provoking those astonished glances. "Vanity or a sense of self-ridicule? I will have to study that more closely", he promised himself. For the moment, though, sensing an oncoming wave of fatigue after the twelve-hour flight from Paris to San Francisco, he had only one wish: to rest and to collect his thoughts for the banquet that awaited him.

One hour later, when he entered the comfortable dining room of the hotel, Jérôme received a warm welcome from the two organizers of the Congress of the American Society of Genetics, which was awarding to him the Allen Memorial Prize: Doctor Charles Epstein and Doctor Kurt Hirschhorn. Jérôme was pleased to meet Hirschhorn again; in Paris, in the excitement of the discovery, he had shown to him the extra chromosome of trisomy 21 under his microscope in 1958. The conversation went well about the earthquake that had shaken the city that morning; then they gave Jérôme the final useful information about the ceremony on the following day. It all seemed very easy. Until Hirschhorn asked Jérôme the question that had been tormenting him for several weeks:

"Dear friend, during our last exchange to prepare for your arrival, you confided to me that you are anxious about the modern evolution of genetics. Besides the fact that I do not share your ideas—should a geneticist not be open to movement and to evolution, like life itself?—I suggested that you choose another forum in which to defend your viewpoint, so as to keep this event festive. I hope", he added, eyeing Jérôme, "that you have followed my advice."

Jérôme, who remembered his friendly warning perfectly well, let a few seconds of silence pass and then answered calmly: "I thank you for your advice. I valued it. But tomorrow I will say what I think I must say."

Epstein and Hirschhorn looked at him, incredulous. "Is it possible?" Epstein wondered, somewhat disturbed. "How can this sympathetic Doctor Lejeune, this young French phenomenon, dare to brave the whole scientific community?" he asked himself with a bit of admiration, while Hirschhorn, who understood Lejeune's determination from his calm tone of voice, tried halfheartedly one last time to convince him to back down. Both men understood the risk that the ceremony might take an unaccustomed turn, which they did not like, and this nonconformism frightened them, but Jérôme's smile remained set. And the evening ended less lightheartedly than it had begun.

The following day, in the really fancy grand ballroom of the Sheraton Palace, Jérôme gave his speech, in English. In the presence of that prestigious audience, he publicly announced his disagreement with eugenic practices and presented the reasoning magnificently:

> To kill or not to kill, that is the question. For millennia, medicine has striven to fight for life and health and against disease and death. Any reversal of the order of these terms of reference would entirely change medicine itself.... Our duty has always been, not to inflict the sentence, but to try to commute the pain [i.e., penalty].[1]

Taking the logic of eugenics to its conclusion, he then proposed that the National Institute for Health be replaced by a National Institute

[1] J. Lejeune, "On the Nature of Man", *American Journal of Human Genetics* 22/2 (March 1970).

for Death, the name of which would indicate more accurately its activity. He concluded by saying: "In any foreseeable genetical trial, I do not know enough to judge, but I feel enough to advocate."

The text was reasonable, with a relentless logic. So relentless that the audience was dumbfounded. He returned to his place in an unforgettable silence, without any applause or handshake. A young physician said to his neighbor, "Wow! That is the second earthquake in two days in San Francisco!"[2]

The shock wave would spread, and Jérôme knew it. At the age of forty-three, he had just ruined his career. It was a decisive act, and there was no going back.

Jérôme returned to the United States two months later, in late November, for a series of conferences in New York, Chicago, and Baltimore. His fears intensified: heartbroken, he observed in the discussions the growing casualness with which abortion was being proposed in cases of malformation of the preborn child. On the evening of December 1, the eve of the conference that he was to give in Baltimore, he wrote to Birthe:

> My little Darling, thank you for your two nice letters, which I found when I arrived here. After this long week, it was a very great pleasure to have news from you and to learn how the children are doing.... All afternoon today, I saw lots of people who showed me lots of things. I refused to go out for dinner in town because I wanted to rewrite the end of my conference tomorrow. I have given up the idea of revising it now because I need rest too much....
>
> Here at Johns Hopkins they do amniocenteses nonstop and blithely abort all the children they don't like. I very much fear that my conference tomorrow, which alludes to abortion only in passing, will be a big fly in the ointment! At any rate, I will say what I believe is true.
>
> Forgive me this hurried handwriting and this disjointed style. My little Darling, all these charming and extremely interesting people have almost worn me out!
>
> I kiss you with all my heart and also our five, my darling. Your loving Jérôme.[3]

[2] V. Riccardi, interviewed by F. Lespés, in *Jérôme Lejeune: Au plus petit d'entre les miens*, documentary film by F. Lespés, April 2015, and C. Epstein, "From Down Syndrome to the 'Human' in Human Genetics", *American Journal of Human Genetics* 70 (2002): 300–13.

[3] J. Lejeune, letter to Birthe, July 3, 1970.

Upon his return to Paris, shaken by what he had observed in the United States, Jérôme took up his journal, which he had abandoned for three years, to confide to it his anxiety and suffering:

> I have stopped proofreading an article on "The Nature of Man" so as to record two things. One is tragic: chromosomal racism is being waved around as a flag of freedom: they will kill the abnormal ones *in utero* since they can recognize the abnormal karyotype by a simple amniotic sample. The fact that this denial of all medicine, of all biological fraternity that unites human beings, should be the only current practical application of the knowledge about trisomy 21 is more than heartbreaking. As I read the article by Madame Escoffier Lambiotte on the plane that brought me back from New York, tears came to my eyes. Killing children because they are not beautiful—this is the application that the great minds on the left find for cytogenetics.... Either we will cure them of their innocence, or else it will be the massacre of the innocents.... To protect the deprived—what a reactionary, backward, fundamentalist, inhumane idea! I saw this quite clearly in San Francisco, where, after my *spiel* about "the nature of man" on the occasion of the William Allan Memorial Award, the crowd parted in front of me without saying a word, leaving the way clear for me, without a word or a handshake. I know for a fact and have known for a long time in advance that the scientific world will not forgive me that misdemeanor! To be anti-conformist enough to believe still in Christian morality and to see how it is in complete agreement with modern genetics is just too much. If chromosomes ever had a vague chance to win the Nobel, I know that I twisted its neck with that warning. But between that and twisting the necks of little children, was there really an alternative?
>
> Children with trisomy 21 will soon be killed in their mother's womb, that is certain, and I will only be able to postpone the day a little. But although that battle has been lost in advance, I know that the war against the disease can still be won. There are very few of us on this planet who think so. But there are many among the parents who have confidence in science and perhaps see much farther than the scientists![4]

Jérôme knew that other geneticists shared his anxiety, but so few said so openly.... However, just that week, as though to encourage

[4] J. Lejeune, *Journal intime*, December 14, 1969.

him, he received a letter from James Neel from the department of human genetics at the University of Michigan, echoing his speech in San Francisco.[5] This letter was followed by another from Joshua Lederberg, professor of genetics at the University of Stanford, in California, who wrote to him quickly after the prize was awarded to tell him how moved he had been by it:

> I was very impressed by the great sensitivity with which you addressed the most delicate and the most important questions. It taught me a lot. Some of your reflections were in keeping with some arguments that I, too, have developed for my part.[6]

Urged on by the threat looming over trisomic children, Jérôme had to proceed quickly. Trisomy, although not fatal, had become a terminal illness with abortion, and Jérôme had no illusions about the subject:

> Either we will cure them of their innocence, or else it will be the massacre of the innocents.

He had to find a way to cure them quickly, not only to relieve them of their malady, but to save them. His previous hypotheses had reached an impasse, and he was beginning to despair, when just at that time, in 1970, he discovered a new avenue of research concerning the mechanism of the synapses and the role of enzymes in the functions of the brain and immediately fashioned a molecular model, made up of thousands of brown, blue, and red wooden balls that could be fitted together, which he could disassemble and reassemble at leisure to simulate the form of molecules. They invaded his desk and his mind like a gigantic puzzle, and he spent hours handling them skillfully in search of the solution. That was also the time when he elaborated a large and minutely detailed diagram of the chemical cogs of the human brain, helping him to identify the place and the manner in which a trisomic patient's brain is dysfunctional. Having isolated some molecules likely to affect the brain's mechanism, he had some substances produced by the Rhône-Poulenc laboratory, intensely

[5] J. Neel, letter to J. Lejeune, December 9, 1969.
[6] J. Lederberg, letter to J. Lejeune, October 27, 1969.

hoping that they would yield positive results. In order to save time, he tried treatments with existing molecules, of course those without side effects but which might produce a slight improvement for those trisomic children, for example, folic acid.

Still very much in demand with the international community, Jérôme gladly accepted trainees from all over the world, to the point of being swamped by them, but he was compelled to turn down many publications and conferences. He had no time available in his schedule for at least five months and sacrificed his research only for a few trips that he deemed indispensable, which took him to the United States, Canada, Spain, and Italy. More eccentrically, Jérôme also received an invitation to give a conference to the Dominican friars of Saulchoir, which offered the prospect of listeners quite different from his usual scientific audience. He accepted the engagement with interest.

After the very busy first half of that year, Jérôme relished the tranquility of the laboratory in the first days of July and took advantage of the summer calm to make progress in his research. Birthe had just left for Denmark with the children, and some colleagues were already returning from their vacations. On July 3, in the evening, he wrote enthusiastically to Birthe:

> My little Darling, I came back very early this evening, after taking Marie-Odile to the old Dupont Café for a cup of coffee! This time it is an important gadget, the model that renders all the active molecules and makes the distinction between the brain and the nerves. It is enormously complex and, at the same time, absolutely marvelous in its economy.... For the moment, I see being sketched gradually a diagram of the functioning of the synapses between the nerves, as simple as the structure of DNA, but prodigiously more ingenious.... To tell the truth, the diagram is of course not completely finished, but the general mechanism is approximately like that....

Then, remembering that Birthe liked to have news about his coworkers, too, he related a story.

> This morning Berger returned from vacation in excellent condition and charming. In contrast, Dutrillaux was disheartened because they hospitalized his little girl. And so I invited him and his wife and

Marie-Odile to lunch at the Chinese restaurant for a change of pace. I don't know whether it was the curry or the hot peppers, but the effect on our work was not bad. I kiss you but regret that unfortunately I must leave you. I would like so much to tell you all about it and to say many tender things to you at the same time. Kiss the five for us both. Your loving Jérôme.[7]

Jérôme was happy, a prospect was emerging; maybe he had an interesting therapeutic method and the whole summer to work on it. Finally! Alas, that favorable moment was very short-lived. A few days later, reality jostled his plan and his tranquility.

On that hot day in mid-July, Jérôme, sitting near the window of his office, the newspaper *Le Monde* unfolded between his hands, stopped breathing for a moment. He quite simply could not manage to believe what he was reading. He stared at each sentence to make sure that he understood it correctly. He wished so much that he had misread it. But he had to face the facts: these words written in black on white were from the president of the national association of physicians and it was a statement at a press conference. After a moment's reflection, Jérôme put out his cigarette, which with its curls of smoke was incensing that day that had started so beautifully, sat down at his desk, and in his full, nimble handwriting composed in one draft his sober, intense, and clear letter. For once he did not need to work and rework his phrases; he wrote from the heart, with his intellect and with every fiber of his being.

Mister President, my reading of *Le Monde* informs me that during a press conference you are said to have committed the national association of physicians to the abortion bill. It is difficult for me to believe that the text of *Le Monde* is lying, but I cannot imagine that it is faithful.

It would be a major abuse if a simple statement by the president could commit the entire association on such a serious point of medical ethics.

In the name of all the children afflicted with genetic anomalies and who are in danger of being killed by physicians, I have the honor of ceremonially asking you to convene the high council of the association about this plan, and I have the duty to ask you to let me be heard personally, as one of the specialists on this question.

[7] J. Lejeune, letter to Birthe, July 3, 1970.

It goes without saying that if the council of the association were to agree to this chromosomal racism, I would ask to be struck from the register of this association.

One cannot preside over the association and perjure one's oath as a physician.[8]

He reread it, well aware of the import of his words, and signed it. He knew what the consequences would be for him to be expelled from the association, but he did not stop there. The important thing was his patients. Several days later, he received the response: they had granted him a meeting with the president of the association, Professor Lortat-Jacob, on July 24.

Jérôme had a lot of respect for Professor Lortat-Jacob, and if the subject of their discussion had not been so serious, he would have been delighted about this next encounter with him. The meeting went very well and reassured Jérôme: the association of physicians had not said its final word, and its president was definitely a great man. Jérôme hurried to write about this important news to Birthe.

My little Darling, this morning I paid a visit to Lortat-Jacob, president of the council of the association. He was very unhappy, especially when I told him that I was ready to resign from the association unless he allowed me to appeal to the Council of State. In fact the conversation went very well, and this man is honest. He allowed himself to be duped, that is all, and he knows it very well. He told me that he regretted that I had not been there, because he had spoken against his heart, thinking that science had spoken the final word!

Then Jérôme told her that Lortat-Jacob had first been convinced by Turpin, who "actually proposed to him abortion for children with trisomy 21!" But having gathered his wits, Jérôme continued, "he decided to write to Deputy Peyret", who had initiated this proposed law, and "he is ready to ask the Academy [of Sciences] for its opinion so as to be able to retract his statement entirely." "And that took only thirty-five minutes! It is chilling to see the [flimsy] sort of basis on which these momentous decisions are made!"[9]

[8] J. Lejeune, letter to Lortat-Jacob, July 1970.

[9] J. Lejeune, letter to Birthe, July 24, 1970.

Jérôme calmed down and eagerly dived again into his molecular meditations, but reality once again cut him short. This time it was to participate in a very popular television program hosted by Armand Jammot, *Les Dossiers de l'écran*. The debate would be about euthanasia: a trial balloon in the middle of summer. Jérôme accepted the invitation, reluctantly, and quickly regretted it. That evening he wrote to his dear confidante:

> My little Darling, today, after a very busy morning of consultations, I went to the television studio. The program was very mediocre. There were three women on it, one of whom, the mother of a retarded boy, was superb.... I was not "good". I agreed to discuss euthanasia in order to reject it firmly, but it was not my field.... All in all, mediocre, and I am not happy with myself. I was too unprepared, preoccupied as I am by my chemical speculations. As far as that is concerned, it is making progress. Slowly, with difficulty, but there is progress, and it is more important in a different way.

Jérôme explained, however:

> The producer of the program, Guy d'Arbois, a discreet, intelligent young man, immediately proposed that I do two programs in September.[10]

Jérôme was surprised by these invitations and promised himself, if he accepted them, to check carefully beforehand the sequence of guests and topics and the arrangement of the set, but above all he learned one lesson from that first performance, which he considered poor: he should never let himself be drawn into a field that was not exactly his own.

Now to his great surprise, he received the very next day a phone call from his brother Philippe, telling him that it was a very good program and that his message had been well received, and a few moments later, when he left for the hospital, he was stopped in the street by a woman who thanked him "for saying true things that they never say on television". Jérôme was left dumbfounded. It seemed to him that the people understood what he did not actually say but

[10] Ibid., July 28, 1970.

meant to say! "Definitely, I will always remain a child in these matters, and just as well",[11] he thought as he mounted his big black bike.

Before the program, Jérôme had jotted down on paper a few hasty reflections in order to pin down his ideas and to elaborate the clear, concise formulas that had been occurring to him for several months, ever since he first felt the storm approaching. A strangely global storm, as though all the countries had spread the word.... The French media were still discreet, but Jérôme had a foreboding that this simmering phase would not last very long. It was necessary to get ready for a wave of programs, interviews, debates.... Thus, in his journal he wrote:

> A few reflections jotted down here that may be used later, when the battle over the life of the deprived will have started definitively.... A supply of ammunition is a necessary precaution.[12]

Then he noted some simple sentences that ought to touch the minds and hearts of his listeners.

> If a human being does not begin at the moment of fertilization, he never begins, because where would he get any new information?
>
> Whether you like it or not, the fraternity of human beings is an obvious fact. Human beings are brethren, quite simply [*tout bêtement*]: like one animal [*bête*] and another from the same species.

And this elegant response denouncing all forms of racism:

> What was the color of Adam's skin? He was the color of a human being.

Several days later, in late July, feeling the wind getting stronger, he confided to his journal:

> Here we go; the battle is approaching. It will be raging by September. They acquit a poor man who killed his retarded daughter, and they say that *euthanazi* (I spell [the French word] *euthanasie* that way

[11] Ibid., July 29, 1970.

[12] J. Lejeune, *Journal intime*, July 25, 1970.

> [phonetically] for the rhyme, to show what it rhymes with) is a crime of love!... We must not kill the guilty (I agree) because they are human beings (I agree), even though they are bad (again), but we must kill trisomic children, because they will be bad human beings! And this is catching on. To the point where the council of the association has given its preliminary approval, and how difficult it will be to go back on it!
>
> Therefore, one way remains, the only way: cure them and cure them fast. There! I'm all for it, wholeheartedly, full-time, pharmacology, biochemistry, molecular models five hours a day, all so as to try to design during my vacations—the only respite I have, when I can finally dedicate myself to something—a coherent plan of attack so as to deploy all our forces on as yet untried paths. I do not want to write anything down this evening; it is all vague and uncertain. The sure thing is that the machine is running coolly and that it cannot yield more.[13]

Fortunately, the month of August was calmer, and Jérôme was able to take advantage of several weeks of tranquility before leaving again for Kerteminde, where he joyfully saw his family for a few days. Then, with the start of the school year approaching, he brought back the children and Birthe, who, having spent the summer on the beach and in the water, were as dark as chocolate. He had to admit that the least ray of sunshine tanned the tribe, and the frequent rains made no difference.

What Jérôme had foreseen occurred in October 1970. A law proposing abortion for handicapped children was introduced by Deputy Peyret, president of the Social Affairs Commission of the National Assembly, and the media campaign aimed at preparing public opinion was launched. Jérôme was invited once again to the talk show *Dossiers de l'écran* to debate with the deputy, Doctor Peyret, on a subject that hit home: "These children are not like the others."[14] During the program, Doctor Peyret presented abortion as a prophylactic act, and when one of the guests, Jacques de Fenoyl, judiciously questioned him about the meaning of the word "prophylaxis", he

[13] Ibid., July 25 and 27, 1970.

[14] *Les Dossiers de l'écran*, program hosted by Armand Jammot, on the topic: "Ces enfants qui ne sont pas comme les autres", October 9, 1970. With J. Lejeune, J. de Fenoyl, J. Meyer, C. Peyret, et al.

explained without batting an eyelash, in front of thousands of television viewers: "Prophylaxis means preventing an infection; in the present case, it means interrupting a pregnancy to prevent the child from being born malformed."

Jérôme, who could not hear such a thing without reacting, intervened while stressing each word forcefully:

> Prophylaxis does not mean killing sick people. It will never mean that. You are asking us to play the role of Pontius Pilate. I am not speaking from a lofty professorial chair [*chaire*] but about children made of flesh [*chair*] and bone. And I do not want to kill these children. They are sick patients.[15]

Jérôme hit the bull's eye. His inimitable tone of voice, his simple, true words, chosen carefully and pronounced firmly, his demeanor—kindly but unwavering against the opposition—touched the listeners. Including the humblest of them. The very ones whom he was defending understood that this great professor was their friend, a true friend who loved them as they were.

In the days following the program, Jérôme received hundreds of letters of thanks and support.[16] One of them was written by a trisomic girl, Hélène:

> Dear Doctor Lejeune, I listened to the TV. Thank you for loving the mongoloids.[17]

And her mother explained:

> I am still experiencing the emotions of the television program yesterday evening, which I listened to with Hélène beside me. How can I tell you how grateful I am for your words, which expressed so well what I was feeling.... Hélène understood so well that I wanted to tell her to leave the room when she said, "What are those imbeciles saying? Do they want to kill the mongoloid girls?" But she hung on

[15] Ibid.

[16] Jérôme would receive three thousand thank-you letters after his broadcasts.

[17] "Cher Dr Lejeune. J'ai écouté la télé. Merci que vous aimez les mongolienne." The plural ending "s" of the word "mongoliennes" is missing in the girl's letter; the French edition reproduces it as it was written.

> to the sofa to stay and clapped her hands because you were defending the mongoloids. It distressed me so much I was in tears; she wanted to write to you. I let her do so and just told her: "Tell the Doctor what you like." I think that her letter needs no commentary and that the term "delighted" that was used in the past is quite correct. What is happiness, if not enjoying everyday joys to the maximum, not worrying about the future, being sensitive to all demonstrations of love, brimming with gratitude, knowing neither hatred nor jealousy nor ambition? If happiness is a predisposition to be happy, then these children are much happier than we are. Unfortunately our experience is incommunicable; you have to have lived it, and if they tempt a woman pregnant with a child who is surely abnormal, will she be able to accept the path that appears to be uniquely painful?[18]

Although they were wounded in their intellect, Jérôme's patients had developed an uncommon intelligence of the heart, and while persons with degrees spoke shamelessly on television about eliminating them, no doubt believing that they could not understand, another of Jérôme's little patients would prove the contrary to him. The day after that televised program, which had an unusually large number of viewers, Jérôme saw during his consultations a young boy, around ten years old, accompanied by his parents. No sooner had the child seen Jérôme than he threw himself into his arms and said to him, in words heavy with emotion: "My Professor, defend us!"

Jérôme, surprised by this heartfelt cry, hugged him and, turning to the parents, asked, "What happened? Why is he so upset?"

Then the father, with a catch in his voice, explained seriously that their son had heard the program on television and that he had understood very well that children like himself were the ones who were no longer wanted. And he added: "Since then he has been afraid."

Jérôme tried to reassure the child; then, when his morning of consultations was over, he went home for lunch, as he did every day. But this time, when he arrived at rue Galande, his face was so white that Birthe and the children immediately understood that something serious had happened. With tears in his eyes, he announced to them: "I will be obliged to speak up publicly to defend our patients. They are going to use our discovery to eliminate them. If I do not defend

[18] H. A., letter to J. Lejeune, October 10, 1970.

them, I will be betraying them and will abandon what I have in fact become: their natural advocate."

In recalling the duties and the beauty of Hippocratic medicine, which for 2,400 years had served all the sick, without distinction and unconditionally, Jérôme touched not only the hearts of his patients, but also those of physicians who were faithful to the oath of Hippocrates. His words strengthened and consoled, and the young generation was particularly sensitive to them. Thus a colleague wrote to him:

> Dear Professor, I thank you with all my heart as a young physician for the extremely firm positions that you are taking with regard to the problems of abortion and respect for life, despite the bombardment of correct opinions and so-called realist arguments. On the day when it is legal for a physician to deal death knowingly, we will have lost our soul and denied our most solemn commitments. Because demeaning one demeans the community. Thank you again and again. Very cordially, your colleague, Doctor Bernard B.[19]

After that first television program, which foreshadowed months of difficult debates, Jérôme flew to Quebec. He was scheduled to give a conference in Montreal, then one in London, Canada, at the University of Western Ontario. The day after his arrival, he received an important letter from Paris, hastily written by Birthe:

> Jérôme, my dear, yesterday was a hectic day, and I waited and am still waiting for your telephone call or telegram in response to mine. I will explain to you in detail. H. telephoned me yesterday morning to say that at the meeting where he substituted for you, they were supposed to vote for the replacement [of the president of Les Cordeliers faculty of medicine]. Your name was proposed.... If you had been there, you would have been elected right away. Now the vote has been postponed to Tuesday the tenth, at 18:00, and if you cannot be back by then, it is important for H. to have a telegram—which you will address to me—to confirm your acceptance. H. cannot be a candidate, and besides, he would not be elected. The employees' association is in quite a state, Milhaud, Jacques, etc. You can hear them say it: "He has to accept, it is very important, it will save Les Cordeliers, etc."

[19] B. B., letter to J. Lejeune, June 2, 1970.

> H. is willing to do all the work with you, provided that you are president in name.... Now I hope that you will make a sacrifice; I think that it is true: this is the only way of saving Les Cordeliers.[20]

Jérôme reflected for a short moment and, since he was leaving the next day for Colorado Springs, decided to respond to his wife immediately. As Dean of Les Cordeliers, he had seen how crushing these duties became when they were added to a threefold activity of care, research, and teaching. Therefore, without hesitation, he informed her of his refusal to accept the presidency of Les Cordeliers faculty of medicine as an extra responsibility.

> The gift is too dangerous. It is very good for Les Cordeliers, but H. would have to accept it. That will give me too much work, and I will do it badly.[21]

As Dean of Les Cordeliers, professor of the first chair of fundamental genetics and director of the department of cytology-genetics at Necker Children's Hospital, Jérôme spent a lot of energy getting the government to recognize genetics as a completely separate discipline. The national minister of education, whom he solicited expressly, wrote to him in reply:

> You were so kind as to call my attention quite particularly to the current interest in giving human genetics an individual status among the medical disciplines. I asked my departments to subject this question to an in-depth examination.[22]

Jérôme hoped that these lines were telling the truth. "It is becoming urgent to give to French genetics its true letters patent of nobility!" he thought with some impatience. Although to Jérôme it seemed incomprehensible that this academic recognition should come so slowly, he rejoiced, on the other hand, in the efficiency of his laboratory, where the team was doing excellent work. Although

[20] B. Lejeune, letter to Jérôme, November 6, 1970, and his response the same day.

[21] J. Lejeune, letter to Birthe, November 6, 1970.

[22] M. Benoist, national minister of education, letter to J. Lejeune, July 13, 1971.

he loathed the favoritism that puts friends in the best positions in spite of all justice, given the exceptional quality of his coworkers he considered it his duty to ask the administration on their behalf, repeatedly, to promote them and to give them a raise in salary. Several months earlier, he had already asked for a promotion for Roland Berger, emphasizing his "exceptional qualifications":

> Doctor Berger has been working with me for long years, and I have been able to evaluate his qualifications as a researcher and instructor. I do not know whether the step that I am venturing to propose to you is in keeping with the usual rules, but I thought it my duty to explain to you my entire interest in the work and in the human qualities of Doctor Roland Berger.[23]

The response came without delay, and a few weeks later a position of lecturer, hospital biologist of cytogenetics, was offered to Doctor Berger.[24] Jérôme decided now to obtain a promotion for Bernard Dutrillaux, whose exceptional qualities merited extraordinary treatment. On May 20, 1971, in the evening, while the whole family was in bed, Jérôme sat down at his desk and wrote:

> Dear Friend, the committee for experimental pathology and pharmacodynamics of the CNRS will soon hand down a decision on the appointment of Doctor Bernard Dutrillaux to the rank of researcher. I make so bold as to draw your attention to the fact that the report of Doctor Dutrillaux' activity is incomplete, because since that document was sent, this young, very high-quality researcher made a discovery destined to modify profoundly all of human cytogenetics.... These initial results were presented to the Academy of Sciences in Paris on April 25, 1971. Doctor Bernard Dutrillaux, who has always demonstrated exceptional dedication, is truly a "discoverer". I personally would be happy if his remarkable qualities as a human being and a researcher were rewarded from now on by an exceptional promotion.[25]

For his part, Jérôme continued to be rewarded for his work. He won the City of Paris Prize, for which he was deluged with

[23] J. Lejeune, letter to Professor Clavert, December 10, 1969.

[24] Letter to J. Lejeune, January 16, 1970.

[25] J. Lejeune, letter to J.-P. Bader, May 20, 1971.

congratulations, and, for the second time, his name was proposed for the Nobel Prize in medicine.[26]

The laboratory functioned as well as possible with the resources that it had, but Jérôme had to find additional financing to develop their research projects. He decided, therefore, to turn to Eunice Shriver Kennedy, who had always promised her financial aid. Not only did Eunice keep her word and allocate a subsidy for him, but she also asked him several months later to assume the vice-presidency, in France, of FAVA, a new federation that organized Olympics for mentally handicapped persons. Jérôme gladly accepted and became the best supporter of these young athletes, whom he encouraged and applauded each year on the bleachers in the stadium where the games were held. It was a great moment to celebrate sports and humanity, and Jérôme rejoiced to see these delighted, proud athletes receive their medal from the hands of the president of the French Republic.

While immersed in his research projects and faithfully continuing his medical practice, Jérôme remained attentive to the political debates and stood ready to take up the defense of his patients when necessary. The Peyret law did not pass, but he was aware that this initial victory was only provisional. He therefore gladly accepted the invitation that was extended to him to give a conference on March 5, 1971, at the Institut catholique [Catholic Institute] in Paris. This was the first time that he had given a major public conference in Paris, and such was his renown that a huge crowd came to hear him.

Weary from his day, during which he went from consultations to laboratory work, Jérôme had just enough time to have his dinner before leaving again. Fortunately, the Institut catholique was not far away, and that allowed him a little time to exchange a few words with his children before going out with Birthe, who had decided to accompany him. When he arrived on site, Jérôme found a conference hall bursting at the seams, with people of all ages in the audience. "Perfect", he thought while ascending to the stage. The organizers introduced the evening, the crowd fell silent, and Jérôme began:

> The tale of Tom Thumb has always enchanted children, because it is a true story that women in all countries composed, or rather

[26] M. Derot of the Académie de médecine, letter to J. Lejeune, December 14, 1971.

> rediscovered, well before modern techniques had shown us the dance of an eleven-week-old child. At two months, our dancer is less than an inch tall, from the top of his head to the base of his pelvis! He could easily make his bed in a nutshell, just like the one in the fairy tale! And yet everything is there, extremely miniaturized; his hands, his feet, his head, his brain, everything is in place and will only grow. As for his heart, it has already been beating for a month!

A woman then stood up in the back of the hall and starting shouting: "Boo, boo! Bastard Lejeune!" Her infuriated neighbors chided her: "Ssshhh! Be quiet!" Jérôme, who had scarcely heard the intrusion, continued:

> Moreover, we can record it with modern equipment, and every mother is amazed to hear the heart of her two-month-old child before feeling his first movements. He is, in fact, so small and so much at ease in his amniotic bubble that he can do acrobatics there without his mother feeling the slightest touch.

The shouts resumed, scattered through the hall: "Bastard Lejeune, women will have your hide!" "Free and legal abortion!"

Several projectiles flew. Jérôme dodged a piece of meat, supposedly representing an aborted fetus, that was thrown in his direction. Strangely calm, he demanded silence at the microphone, but in vain. He noticed at the back of the hall several immense, horrible signs with drawings depicting trisomic children sticking out their tongues, with the inscription: "Death to Papa Lejeune and his little monsters!"[27]

It was heart-wrenching for him to think of the pain experienced by the parents of trisomic children who were present in the hall as they discovered those signs. "What is to be done?" Suddenly he had an idea! Since no security personnel were provided to keep the peace, he announced in a loud voice at the microphone: "Those who are with me, leave! All those who want to hear my conference, leave the auditorium!"

After a moment of astonishment, everyone stood up and left the auditorium. Soon no one was left but a dozen persons shouting; they

[27] These insults and calls for murder are authentic. They were, in fact, shouted and posted against Jérôme that evening.

were arranged along a diagonal to create the impression of being present in great numbers and to prevent the conference from going on. They were led by a defrocked priest. Unmasked, the disrupters were soon obliged to leave the premises, and the conference could resume in peace. Then Jérôme, who had not lost his serenity, calmed the audience by his tranquility and continued.

> Today we have experienced what he feels, listened to what he hears, and even tasted what he relishes (because he can tell sweet from bitter very well), and we have seen him dancing full of youthful joy. Thanks to technology, the tale of Tom Thumb has become a very true-life story.
>
> But not only science describes this first world to us; artists sometimes are wiser than scientists and, in a way, remember what all the others have apparently forgotten.
>
> To get some idea of this, let us make a brief excursion: let us go into a discotheque, a vaulted shelter scarcely lit by reddish gleams. The atmosphere is humid and hot, the odor is strong, and bodies move, sometimes imperceptibly, sometimes whirling around. A tremendous noise overcomes us: the head vibrates to the sharp rhythm of the maracas, and the whole chest cavity trembles with each deep, muted stroke of the string bass. And the people who are there, apparently, like it. Why? Because they remember, at least unconsciously.
>
> There was a time in their lives when the first world that they inhabited was a vaulted shelter, too, scarcely lit in red, the shelter of the mother's womb. The strong odor and the hot, humid atmosphere were almost the same. And while they were dancing, their head vibrated to the beats of their own heart (140 to 150 per minute, the rhythm of maracas), and their whole body trembled to the muted, reassuring hammering of their mother's heart (60 to 80 per minute, the rhythm of the string bass). It is no accident that the specialists in pop music have adopted these two rhythms, which are mixed together, incidentally, by all primitive forms of music, from any country whatsoever.
>
> It is indeed a form of music, the most primitive kind there is: it is the first music that each human ear ever heard in its life. A symphony of two hearts, that of the mother and that of the child: that is the song of this first world, the one from which we all come.[28]

[28] J. Lejeune, "Le premier monde", published in the bulletin *Tom Pouce* 4 (December 1985). The story of Tom Thumb was related by Jérôme, not at this conference, but on other occasions. We quoted it here for the purposes of the biography.

The evening was a great success. The intimidation did not upset Jérôme, and the crowd was enthusiastic. But Jérôme and Birthe were still surprised at the violence and the hatred that they observed in those agitators.

"You could say that you had your baptism by fire, my dear", Birthe said to her husband as they returned to rue Galande.

"It all goes to show that there are terrible stakes for society and that truth disturbs the promoters of this new world in which those who are well will decide the fate of those who are ill", Jérôme replied pensively.

"It also shows that the feminists have identified you as the best advocate for the preborn children", Birthe added.

One month later, on March 5, 1971, Jérôme was expected to give another major conference on life at the Maison de la Mutualité, just a few steps from his house. Also on the stage with him was Denise Legrix, an astonishing, tiny woman, a painter, who had been born without arms or legs, whose *joie de vivre* was an extraordinary testimony.[29] The hall was packed, and the atmosphere was joyous. Alas, Jérôme had scarcely started to speak when once again opponents started shouting. An impossible brouhaha set in at the back of the hall, as at the Institut catholique. Jérôme continued to speak as though nothing were happening. His tone remained calm. He only raised his voice so that everyone could hear, despite the shouts of the fanatics:

> "Choice" is not determining whether we will agree with the racism of those who are well and try to eliminate sicknesses by eliminating the sick.

Several minutes passed, and Jérôme continued his conference, unflappable in an atmosphere that had become electric. He had to raise his voice again to make himself heard:

> A physician can conquer sickness only if he respects the sick person.[30]

[29] Denise Legrix, born in 1910, died in 2010 at the age of one hundred. Her parents' unconditional love, she says, was what gave her a magnificent philosophy of life, the source of her overflowing joy of living. Her last book, *Ma joie de vivre*, recapitulates her whole life.

[30] J. Lejeune, conference at the Maison de la Mutualité in Paris, March 5, 1971.

The screaming started again, even louder. Once again someone aimed a piece of meat at his face. Jérôme then interrupted his conference and said in a stern voice at the microphone:

> I ask those who do not approve of throwing projectiles to applaud.

His calm was absolutely extraordinary. The sustained applause that resounded proved that there was only a handful of agitators. Several security guards then tried to make them leave, but given the turn that events were taking, they ended up calling the police. Fortunately, the station was right nearby, and the police intervened quickly, soon followed by firemen and ambulances. A few steps away in the apartment on the rue Galande, the five children were spending the evening tranquilly when they heard the procession of sirens. They looked at each other, frightened, and Anouk exclaimed: "It is surely because of Papa's conference! Let's hope that nothing happens to him or to Mama!"

Then she immediately suggested: "Let's start praying that the Good Lord will protect them!"

Immediately the five knelt down in the living room and begged God for their parents' safety and that no one would be injured. When Jérôme and Birthe came back a little later, exhausted, the children rushed to the door to greet them.

"Thank God! You are okay!" Damien exclaimed, reassured to see his parents unharmed.

"Yes, my darlings, don't worry", Jérôme replied, his face drawn.

"What happened?" Karin asked, all ears.

Birthe told about the evening and the intervention by the police. Then Anouk, intrigued by her father's calm expression beneath the fatigue, asked him: "But Papa, aren't you afraid? Those people are crazy! They could have hurt you!"

"My darling, of course it is not pleasant," he answered, "but don't worry; we are in God's hands."

"The most astonishing thing about all this", Clara said, "is that the media are trying to make you the violent bad guy! When you only talk about the beauty of human life and the value of each human being, even the handicapped, even the unwanted! And you are the one taking hits!"

In confronting these annoyances, he remained serene because he was not worried about his personal interests; his sole, insistent concern was the urgency of saving those children. All those intimidations did not make him swerve one millimeter from his course: again and again, he spoke about the beauty of life and the right that every human being has to enjoy it.

Jérôme gave witness for his patients, and this unconditional love was his strength. At his consultations, he saw behind all those faces, smiling despite the illness, the child or the adult full of dreams and hopes, of desire and joy. He saw the beauty of the person behind "the incompletely chiseled features" and knew that the condition that affected their intellect did not affect their heart.

The day after that memorable evening, his children, with the impetuosity of their age, told him: "Papa, you have to defend yourself! Those people are wicked!" Jérôme replied:

"Children, they can say and do what they want; it does not matter much. I am fighting, not for myself, but for my patients. Those people are violent, yes, but wicked? It is not up to me to judge. We have to judge acts, but never persons. Remember that, it is important. Acts, but never the persons. I fight against wrong ideas but not against men."

"Maybe, my darling," Birthe interrupted him, "but one thing is certain: to do what you are doing takes the hide of a hippopotamus!"[31]

And while they all started to laugh, she went to get the hot coffee that was waiting in the kitchen.

Strange to say, simply because he explained that the embryo is a living human being, from the moment of conception, and recalled that every human being is "my brother", he was accused of making mothers feel guilty, of trying to impose a "dictatorship of the moral order". Jérôme was only defending preborn children, the weakest and most vulnerable, without ever stigmatizing the women who have abortions. He showed that it was inhumane to pit the child against the mother: it is necessary to save them both, with the same gesture of compassion. The woman in distress and the child in peril. The man who hated no one, who always said: "I am not fighting human beings, I am fighting wrong ideas", was thrown into an unusually

[31] Birthe Lejeune's exact words.

violent battle because he wanted to work for the cause of truth and to serve the most fragile human life. No doubt because his tranquil strength, unconcerned about what is "politically correct", his oratorical talent, and his scientific aura made it difficult for those who were promoting abortion.

After those two terrible evenings, there was soon another gathering that promised to bring Jérôme great joy and immense consolation. With the full force of his renown, he very actively promoted the first official pilgrimage of mentally handicapped persons, and this pilgrimage was scheduled to take place in Lourdes on April 12, 1971. It was organized by the association Foi et Lumière [Faith and light] at the instigation of Jean Vanier and Marie-Hélène Mathieu. Jérôme was very glad to participate in it. He knew also that his presence was useful because it silenced the criticisms that were beginning to be raised against the idea of that particular gathering.

Getting away from Paris for forty-eight hours in order to accompany the pilgrimage, Jérôme was happy for a time of recollection in the midst of so many of his patients, who came to greet him with big hugs. Not far from the grotto where the Blessed Virgin performs miracles, Jérôme remained for a long time looking at those thousands of pilgrims, whose smiles warmed frozen hearts and innocently defied the proud. The scene reminded him of an admirable "Adoration of the Infant Jesus" produced in the sixteenth century by a Flemish painter.[32] Snuggled against the heart of the Blessed Virgin, a young trisomic angel stands near Jesus, discreetly toward the back of the circle of cherubim. His illuminated face reflects the gentle light of the Infant, and the painter's talent depicts with incredible accuracy his characteristic, tender languor. While Mary and the other angels hold their hands folded toward Jesus, he crosses his delicately over his heart, in a gesture of interior recollection that only an artist's genius can capture. And there is the even more extraordinary picture by the famous Mantegna. The trisomic child is none other than the Infant Jesus, snuggling against His mother's heart, under the gaze of a privileged witness chosen by the artist, Saint Jerome, Doctor and Father of the Church.

Five centuries later, leaning on the balustrade, Jérôme looked in turn at the trisomic children crowding in faith and hope, in the springtime

[32] *Adoration of the Magi*, anonymous Flemish painter, 1515.

sunshine, around Our Lady at the grotto. As close as possible to her motherly heart. This multitude of infirm people processed, candle in hand, or formed a convoy of disabled persons in their wheelchairs—a crowd made up of children and adults who placed all their hope in Our Lady of Lourdes. Although he did not shed tears, Jérôme felt a profound compassion for these "poorest among the poor". Mingled with that silent, manly suffering was a feeling of shame because of the powerlessness of medicine and the folly of society that was considering an attack on them.[33] He prayed for each one of them. That they might find "the full freedom of their mind".

Two months later, in June, Jérôme would have a completely different experience. This time he flew to Japan for a series of meetings. With great interest, he visited Saint Luke's International Hospital in Tokyo, then after a meeting in Nagoya, spoke in Nagasaki to the Atomic Bomb Casualty Commission.[34] For this third stay in the Empire of the Rising Sun, Jérôme had the honor of being received by the imperial prince. He emerged from it struck by the strict etiquette of Japanese protocol and somewhat amused. Amused, not by those rules of delicate politeness, which he spontaneously respected, but by the embarrassing situation in which his guide put him when he deferentially announced:

"Honorable Professor, I invite you to take off your shoes so as to appear before the emperor. You can leave them with me, and you will get them back at the conclusion of the audience."

"Dear Lord!" Jérôme fretted. Quite ignorant of these customs, he had not thought that morning to check the state of his socks, and his fears materialized: two holes at the tips allowed his big toes to air themselves quite comfortably but not very aesthetically. "Especially in an audience like this!" he thought, laughing inside. He refrained from confiding this amusing worry to his guide, who would have had difficulty tolerating this crime of lese-majesty, and approached the emperor with his big toes painfully curled up. He was focused more on his unusual little steps, which had an almost Japanese air, than on the solemnity of the moment, but the magnanimous sovereign seemed not to notice anything, and so the audience could

[33] J. Lejeune, interviewed on the program *Radioscopie* by Jacques Chancel, December 13, 1973. Jérôme described his feelings at the grotto in Lourdes during that pilgrimage.

[34] Atomic Bomb Casualty Commission, June 1971, Nagasaki.

begin. As he left, Jérôme was delighted by the success of his acrobatics: "This at least was one meeting that did not unravel!" he congratulated himself.

Since abortion had won over the public forum in many countries, and it was only a matter of time in the legislatures, Jérôme from now on addressed this question relative to the protection of his patients during scientific congresses. Whenever he deemed it necessary, he asked the physicians to fight the right fight and to attack the sickness rather than the child. Thus he carefully prepared the conference that he gave to the International Congress on Human Genetics that took place in Paris in 1971. The title that he chose for his eminent colleagues was as simple as his message: "On the Correct Use of Genetics". This was the first time that he officially addressed this reflection, in France, to a scientific congress, and he succinctly presented to his peers the arguments that he had already developed in San Francisco:

> To modify the destiny of human beings is a formidable power.... Given the inexorable character of hereditary illnesses, the oldest use of our discipline was to predict these decisions of destiny.... All the discoveries that have been reported to this congress, whether the new deciphering of human chromosomes, the precise screening of a biochemical disorder, or a statistical forecast about entire populations, can and must work toward this goal: to anticipate as much as possible the genetic risks that future human beings will have to endure. And for two thirds of a century, this prudential use was practically the only one. Very recently, however, a technological achievement, the analysis of cells obtained from the fetus by amniocentesis, has led some to preach and to practice another use of our knowledge: the selective destruction of fetuses that have been recognized as carriers of an illness that we do not know how to cure. To measure the right to life by the age or the height or the health of any human being whatsoever cannot be discussed objectively, since such metrics of man are not at all accessible to scientific logic.
>
> The strangest thing about such a use is that it would be desperate. For only despair could drive physicians to eliminate sick people in order to fight against a sickness. We know, moreover, that the ones who conquered the plague and rabies were not those who burned the plague-stricken in their houses or suffocated the rabid between two mattresses. To what point would the use of genetics be reduced if it went from warning about sicknesses to deliberately aggravating the

sufferings, from Cassandra to Carabosse [the wicked fairy godmother in "Sleeping Beauty"]? Human genetics is a science like the rest, but it can show that it is humane in the presence of the sick person.[35]

In October Jérôme left again for the United States, to Warrenton, Virginia, then to Bethesda, to the Fogarty International Center of the National Institutes of Health (NIH). Here again, there was debate about selecting the trisomic infants in the womb, and here again he did not hesitate to oppose it and to ask his colleagues to reflect. An unexpected occasion was offered to him since, besides his first conference, which had long since been scheduled, they assigned to him a second one for the following day. Quickly, in his hotel room, he prepared his speech. Quite simple. And two years, almost to the day, after his speech in San Francisco, he gave in English this unexpected conference:

When we are talking about adults or even children, the "National Institute for Health" is generally preferred [nomenclature]. But when it is a question of young individuals, especially when they are not yet born, the "National Institute for Death" finds some supporters. The reason for this discrepancy seems to depend on this question: Are they human beings or not? My personal opinion is that we ought to make our decision solely on scientific bases and by utilizing all scientific information together.

Let us take the example of trisomy 21 observed by amniocentesis.... We saw not only an extra chromosome 21; we also saw the forty-six other chromosomes and concluded that they were human, because if they had been from a mouse or an ape, we would have noticed it. Genetically speaking, we have therefore two responses: first, it is a human being in the developing stage; then, that it is suffering from trisomy 21.

What seems obvious to me, based on what we know in genetics, is simply this: if a fertilized egg were not by itself a complete human being, it could never become a man, because something else would have to be added to it, and we know that that does not happen.[36]

[35] J. Lejeune, *Du bon usage de la génétique* (Paris, 1971).

[36] J. Lejeune, conference prepared one day in advance in 1971 for the National Institute of Health, in Bethesda. Plans were made for the conference to be published in the summer of 1972 by Plenum Press in New York.

The strength of his witness to the truth had a visible effect on the audience, and, unlike in San Francisco, after this speech several physicians came to thank him for saying out loud what they were thinking very quietly. Jérôme was astounded by this, as he had been in May 1968. Astounded to see that so many people did not dare to say what they thought, out of fear. Among the physicians who shared his analysis, Jérôme recognized Professor Joseph Warkany from Cincinnati, who had come to see "his beautiful chromosomes" when the team was still in Trousseau. Jérôme had a lot of respect for that man, who was older than he, and was pleased to accept his invitation to dinner. During their friendly exchange, Warkany confided a family memory to him:

> One night, the night of April 20, 1889, my father, who was a physician in Braunau, Austria, was called for two deliveries. In one case, it was a fine little boy who howled quite loudly; in the other, it was a poor little girl who had trisomy. My father followed the lives of these two children. The boy had an extraordinarily brilliant career; the girl had a rather somber fate. And yet, when her mother was afflicted with paralysis on one side of the body, that daughter, whose intelligence quotient was very mediocre, kept the house with the help of neighbors, and she gave four years of her happy life to her bedridden mother. I no longer remember the name of the little girl. But I could never forget the name of the little boy: his name was Adolf Hitler.[37]

This exchange of views with Warkany consoled Jérôme a little but did not dissipate the feeling of horror that had seized him while reading documents that he had had in his hands that afternoon. After dinner, Jérôme returned to the hotel, eager to confide this weighty information to Birthe. He took his pen and, with a lump in his throat at the thought of what he was about to tell her, wrote:

> My little darling, what a day! This morning I gave my very short oration, seventeen minutes, but I think that it struck home for a lot of the listeners. Ultimately, I am the only one to have a precise position that is logical and consistent. All the others do agree with it but tend to change one point or another in order to deal with a difficulty.

[37] J. Warkany, quoted by J. Lejeune.

The discussions were all extremely dense and closely argued, but very courteous and not at all unpleasant.

Only one speaker was very good: Kass, a man around the age of thirty, with an extraordinary intellect and a lively mind.... I was not able to talk to him this evening, but I do hope to have a long conversation with him. He thinks very correctly, does not dare at all to reach a decision, but he is a very important figure. The others talk; he thinks.

When I see all these decent people (because they are decent people) ready to eliminate patients with trisomy, I tell myself that every hour spent in debating is an hour wasted and many a child killed (well, fortunately they have not yet reached that tempo). The future, though, is extremely dark.

I just looked at a draft by the NIH [National Institute for Health] on rules to apply during experiments on five-month-old fetuses "removed" by Caesarean section and put on artificial blood circulation to survive so that they can do experiments in physiology or biochemistry. The document says to treat them like any other tissue or organ sample, but explains that it is necessary to kill them after a short time; their survival must not be prolonged. And this text meets with the approval of very likable people!

They asked me my opinion. I read the text attentively and could not offer any revision to it. I simply said that it was written well enough, but that no text could regulate crime! I kiss you very tenderly, my little darling, and our five with you. Your loving Jérôme.[38]

Despite the horrific practices that were explained, Jérôme judged the acts but not the persons, and this position had become so natural for him that he would never abandon it.

However, as the days went by and the conferences and discussions followed one another, Jérôme observed a slight variation in the tone of this talk. Some were beginning to wonder about the real significance of prenatal screening. The atmosphere was less triumphalistic. On the evening of the final day, Jérôme confided this glimmer of hope to Birthe:

My little darling, another day loaded with words, words.... This evening S. painted for us a terrible picture of babies in flasks, manipulated

[38] J. Lejeune, letter to Birthe, October 12, 1971.

genes, the Brave New World, as if all that were necessary, or useful, in any case inevitable. In the discussion, I quoted Pascal on the children who are frightened to see in a mirror the mask that they have put on their faces. But why wear a mask? It is truly a strange world. They do not see that the fetus that they are torturing is a human being, and they claim to be improving the human species. There are no limits to the pride here because it encroaches largely on the stupidity.

Finally, Neel, who observes a lot and says almost nothing, told me that now 90 percent of the people think that I am right (I don't want to say "I" because it is only the idea that I express and not me). That was not the case on the first day.

I kiss you very tenderly, my little darling, and our five with you. Your loving Jérôme.[39]

When he returned to Paris, Jérôme was more determined than ever to find a treatment to save trisomic children from programmed death. He devoted the following months to his consultations and his research projects, and the few trips that he made, to Sweden, Germany, or the United States, and his recent appointment to the French Society of Biology did not distract him from that objective. With renewed energy, he plunged into his meditations and was relieved that he could take advantage of those long, relatively calm months.

At home, the family was flourishing. Anouk, who was already twenty years old, was pursuing her studies in literature. Damien, aged eighteen, was valiantly battling against epilepsy, which had become manifest a few years earlier, and he hoped to become a physical therapist. Jérôme had compassion on his son and asked for advice from colleagues who were specialists so as to give him the best treatment, and it actually did have an effect. As for Karin, she had no lack of eccentric ideas for a sixteen-year-old. Jérôme remembered with amusement the conversation that he had one evening with his daughter.

"Papa, Robespierre was an awesome man, and I have become a Marxist."

"That's interesting", he answered. "May I ask why? What is it about Marxism that you like? Let us see your arguments, then I will give you mine."

[39] Ibid., October 14, 1971.

Karin presented to him the ideas that she had heard at school, and the discussion was on. One by one, Jérôme repeated her arguments and showed her their limits and contradictions, leading his daughter to lift her sights so as to see, beyond the immediate advantages, the consequences.

Another time she announced at dinner: "Papa, Mama, I have decided to stop studying. School is worthless."

Even before Birthe had time to react, Jérôme answered calmly: "If you don't study, then you will look for a job to earn your living. What are your plans? But people who work have much less vacation time. Especially in the summer; you will no longer be able to go to Denmark for two months. Did you think about that before making your decision?"

Her expression suddenly turned gloomy, and Karin fell silent, disappointed at such an unhappy prospect, and the matter stopped there. The method that Jérôme used with his children, in which he favored dialogue over the argument from authority, defused many minor conflicts of their adolescence, which unfolded without rebellion.

When Jérôme came home in the evening, with a lot on his mind, he had an incredible ability to make himself available to his children and the parade of friends who visited them in their welcoming house. Birthe, who prepared simple, generous meals, was always willing to add one or more place settings around the table. Raising his eyes from his newspaper or his documents, taking off his glasses so as to see the inquisitive person better, Jérôme never put off a question for lack of time and always proved ready to engage in a conversation with his interlocutor, whether he was seven or twenty years old; "Papa, how were the stars born?" "Papa, how old were you during the Hundred Years War?" "Can you help me with my history assignment?"

Despite such a busy work schedule, he jealously guarded every day these special moments for his family. First, the daily family midday meal. When he was not traveling, Jérôme arranged his activities so as to return to rue Galande for lunch each day with Birthe and the children. As for the dinners, Jérôme and Birthe gave such priority to family life that they very seldom accepted an invitation to dine out: no society life, unless they truly could not escape from it, which was rare. So much so that one day one of his children said to him:

"Papa, why don't you take advantage of all these invitations? Why don't you go out into society? We could go, too; it would be great!"

To this Jérôme responded: "You have to be very careful with that whole world; it is better to remain outside, so as not to fall into temptations. That whole world with its money is a world that I do not want to enter into deliberately."

After dinner, during which everyone could tell about his day, Jérôme was the one who gathered the children, whatever their age, and recited the daily prayer with them, while Birthe attended to her chores. Kneeling in front of the crucifix, Jérôme took the littlest one between his knees and folded his hands; then all together they recited an Our Father and a Hail Mary. Then Jérôme concluded with a blessing for the family and for the sick: "My God, bless our whole family; thank you for having given it to us; heal all the sick." Before sending the younger ones off to bed, Jérôme managed to have another little affectionate moment with his children, in that shared peace created by their common prayer. Then, while Birthe went upstairs to bed and quickly fell asleep, Jérôme sat down at his desk, on the third floor of the house, which now had a few more rooms, and immersed himself in a conference that he was preparing or in his meditations.

In the summer, when the house in Paris was empty, it was also for Jérôme an opportunity to take some time with a few dear friends for fine long evenings of exchanging views calmly. Thus, he told Birthe about one of his evenings with Marcel Clément:

> Marcel Clément and I stayed to discuss at the table and then in armchairs. Toward 11:30, Clément told me that he was leaving. Then we chatted for another five minutes, and it was 2:30 when he noticed the time! To tell the truth, we got through a tremendous amount of work, or maybe scoured the countryside, because it covered everything, from Adam and Eve to the astonishment of the stigmatists!... All in all, a charming evening, but what a state I'm in this morning![40]

It was also an occasion to dine with his brother Rémy and his wife, Odile, or with Philippe, with whom he spent a lot of time after Geneviève's departure.

[40] Ibid., July 10, 1973.

Besides the close or distant friends who would come for a meal or to stay for several days, every Saturday the house welcomed for lunch Jérôme's three colleagues and intimate friends: Jacques Lafourcade, Jean de Grouchy, and Henri Jérôme. They shared the family lunch and discussed the laboratory and current events. This was exciting training for the children and tactful consideration for Birthe, who was thus at the heart of the discussions. After that weekly meeting, the family piled into the car and finally left for the country, to the great joy of the children of all ages! They wished so much that they could leave in the morning! One day one of the boys asked him:

"Papa, why can't we leave on Friday evening, as many of our friends do? Why do you work on Saturday morning?"

"Because that is the only time when the parents can come for a relaxed consultation for their child, without having to make special arrangements with their job, especially if they come from a distance. I know already how much effort it costs them to come to the hospital."

This was also the reason why Jérôme did not want to have a private practice. Some people would be willing to pay a fortune to benefit from his expertise, but he did not want to deprive the less well-to-do families of the help that he could offer them. More than one family was astonished when it came time to pay and he said: "Go to the hospital cashier's desk."

"That's all? Nothing else?"

"No, nothing."

In the country, in their little White House, which was rather modest with its two rooms on the ground floor and on the upper floor, into which the children cheerfully squeezed, the family was in seventh heaven. In the back of the studio that Jérôme set up in a shed in the garden, he could happily prolong his meditations and exercise his fingers with some tinkering, for which he had the knack. From the perfect geometric forms woven by his friends the spiders, whom he contemplated with admiration, to the medieval castle that he made out of wood for his sons; from the one-decade rosaries that he sculpted delicately from bone to the majestic feathers that he used for calligraphy: he let his eyes and his hands follow the train of his thoughts, from one hour to the next. The lightness of the air, the weightlessness of the spiders, and the silence made that studio a unique place for recollection . . . often disturbed by an active wife or by children in tears over a broken bike or a thorn in the foot. Jérôme then transformed his bucolic retreat into a multi-purpose studio.

He loved to tinker, to repair, and to invent and did not hesitate to make his entourage laugh with his motley inventions. He was from the generation that had experienced the war and spontaneously recycled. And when it came to throwing away a bit of well-worn rope or a basin with a hole in it, he would say: "No, let's keep it; there's a use for everything." The agility of his fingers was heightened by an inexhaustible imagination, and he launched into the oddest inventions with confidence and enthusiasm. One of his best ideas was the "weed burner" that enabled him to recycle an old iron while beautifying the yard. While waiting to win the Lépine Prize, he demonstrated it to his children, and his discovery was definitely a success among the family and won the prize of general hilarity.

CHAPTER 9

THE BATTLE FOR THE CHILDREN OF FRANCE

1973–1974

The clouds announcing the storm loomed now over Paris. The battle begun in 1970 resumed more intensely, magisterially orchestrated in the courts, the media, and the political arena. This time, the offensive was serious and dangerous. It was launched on November 8, 1972, by the media coverage of the Bobigny trial, at the conclusion of which the court acquitted a sixteen-year-old girl who said that she had had an abortion following a rape. This girl was defended by Gisèle Halimi, the lawyer who had founded the association Choisir [Choice], which promoted abortion and performed it clandestinely. The well-honed technique was effective, and the general public was shaken. The noticeably partisan media presented a series of unilateral statements and positions, especially the famous *Manifesto of 331 Physicians* who had performed abortions when they were illegal, which appeared on February 3, 1973, in the weekly news magazine *Le Nouvel Observateur*. It followed the *Manifesto* of the 343 women who had had abortions, published in 1971. Nevertheless, the minister of health, Jean Foyer, firmly resisted these demands and absolutely refused to modify the law in any way. The preceding summer, in July, he had summoned Jérôme to study with him methods of defending it. The political offensive, therefore, had to wait until Foyer left the government, in March 1973, in order to resume with new intensity.

On March 18, Jérôme was invited to a colloquium on abortion, in the former Royaumont Abbey, which he would never forget. The day was organized by the Cercle français de la presse [French press association] around journalists and feminists, including Gisèle Halimi, but the Cercle also requested appearances by Cardinal Renard, Archbishop of Lyon, and Professor Lejeune. Unwilling to leave the cardinal alone for the debates, which promised to be difficult, Jérôme accepted the invitation and traveled there with Birthe. On his arrival, however, he discovered that the cardinal had had to cancel his appearance because of health problems: therefore, he would be the only one defending the preborn child. The speakers followed one another at the podium, all of them, except Jérôme, demanding access to abortion, and during this series of speeches, Birthe noticed that a woman seated in the first row, not far from her, was directing the interventions like the conductor of an orchestra. With little signs she would invite one to speak, another to keep quiet, whispered phrases to these and to those: called the dance. Suddenly, when one of the speakers had just finished his talk, this influential woman stood up and declared:

> We want to destroy Judeo-Christian civilization. To do that, we must first destroy the family. In order to destroy it, we must attack it at its weakest point, and this weak point is the preborn child. Therefore we are in favor of abortion.[1]

The statement made a great impression on the journalists who were present, and when they asked this woman her name, she refused to give it, then sat down and did not speak again.

Quite remarkably, not one of the journalists referred to that quotation, although it was essential, in the papers published following the colloquium, nor is it found in the acts of that day, which omit both that intervention and the one by Jérôme. One sentence at the conclusion of the acts explains: "The speech by Professor Lejeune will be published later." A "later" that would never take place.

Jérôme knew that the statistics and the arguments set forth by the promoters of abortion were only snares to tip the scales of public

[1] This story and this quotation were related many times by J. Lejeune, notably in a letter to the Jesuit scholar Michel Schooyans dated December 18, 1984, a letter to Pastor Randall dated February 8, 1989, and in the speech that J. Lejeune gave to the Synod Fathers on October 8, 1987, which was published in *L'Osservatore Romano* on October 20, 1987: "La science seule ne peut pas sauver le monde" [Science alone cannot save the world].

opinion,[2] and naturally, humanly speaking, Jérôme could not understand that anyone would present abortion as a solution. As if the death of an undesirable human being could be a solution worth considering! Who would ever think to propose such an option if the human being to be eliminated were not a preborn child? If such a political philosophy were applied, it would have considerable human and societal consequences. As for the physician, if he became the instrument of that lethal act, he would sign the death notice of Hippocratic medicine. The argument of the promoters of abortion, then, was to say that the embryo, the fetus, was not a human being but only a mass of cells. But here again, the human intellect clearly shows, to anyone willing to see it, that the embryo is a living human being, one so extraordinary that it has in it everything necessary to develop and to become Paul or Leah, without the addition from outside of any essential part. Every first-year student of biology or genetics knows that as of the fusion of the gametes a human embryo is a human being in the first stage of his development, the stage through which everyone passes. At the stage of the embryo, then the fetus, childhood, adolescence, and old age, it is still the same human being who develops, grows, then dies. Therefore, in the name of the "biological brotherhood that unites human beings with each other", and as a physician, Jérôme could not accept such a policy. Society must find true ways of helping women in difficult situations, but it cannot reasonably propose abortion as a solution.

That woman in Royaumont, by presenting so clearly the philosophy hidden behind the pro-abortion campaign—of which the vast majority of the public was absolutely unaware—corroborated Jérôme's analysis. The roots of the battle being waged around human life are spiritual. It is a battle of man who, out of the desire to have full power over life and death, rejects the authority of the Father and condemns the Infant Jesus.

[2] This tactic of promoters of abortion was described by Norma Leah McCorvey, better known under the pseudonym Jane Roe, whose widely publicized trial ultimately led to the legalization of abortion in the U.S. in 1973. After her conversion, McCorvey militantly defended respect for the life of preborn children and worked to have abortion outlawed. She wrote her story in *Won by Love: Jane Roe of Roe v. Wade, Speaks Out for the Unborn as She Shares Her New Conviction for Life* (Nelsonworld Publishing Group, 1997). This tactic was also described by Doctor Bernard Nathanson, one of the physicians who pioneered abortion in the U.S. and author of the film *The Silent Scream* after his conversion.

"In order to kill the Infant Jesus, Herod was obliged to kill all the infant boys of Bethlehem without exception. In order to love the Infant Jesus, I would be obliged to love all the infants of Bethlehem without exception", James Haggerty would later write.[3] This meditation admirably sums up Jérôme's conviction. He knew that behind every human child who is loved, the Infant Jesus is venerated, and that behind every human child who is threatened, the Infant Jesus is attacked. Jérôme confided this sure truth to Birthe:

> If they really want to attack the Son of man, there is only one way, and that is to attack the sons of men. Christianity is the only religion that tells you "Your model is a child"; when you have learned to despise the child, Christianity will no longer exist.[4]

With the intellect of the heart, Jérôme loved to meditate on the Prologue to the Gospel of Saint John, a source of profound inspiration for him in his life as a physician, scientist, and Christian:

> In the beginning was the Word, and the Word was with God, and the Word was God.... In him was life, and the life was the light of men.... He was in the world, and the world was made through him, yet the world knew him not.... And the Word became flesh and dwelt among us.[5]

Everything begins through the Incarnation of the Word. Jérôme knew that this mystery, which was revealed to human beings by the birth of a tender infant who was venerated by the Magi and condemned to death in the first days of his earthly life, is the foundation of the Catholic faith. Aware that this mystery of the Incarnation is the epitome of the Christian religion, it became obvious to Jérôme that one cannot believe in God without loving Christ incarnate and all our human brethren with him. How could someone say "I love the God whom I do not see, but I do not love my brother whom I do see"?

[3] J. Haggerty, *Quitter Dieu pour Dieu* (Paris: Éditions Mame, October 2009).

[4] J. Lejeune, *Le respect de la vie*, speech given at the major seminary in Montreal, April 12, 1993.

[5] Jn 1:1–18.

This attention to the Incarnate Word, which was central in Jérôme's spiritual life, took concrete form, naturally, in his professional life. He knew that the charity that judges everything judges by the fact that we have been made neighbors to everyone, to all flesh, regardless of skin color, age, sickness, disabilities, while recognizing the Word of God in them. In caring for his patients, Jérôme served the Incarnate Word. He did not turn away from the suffering flesh of the sick, of the rejected patient; he did not flee.

This attention to the body also had a very simple pedagogical virtue: realism. This was one of Jérôme's great strengths when he advocated. He spoke on behalf of his patients, who had a name, a face, a body, sometimes deformed, and not to defend an abstract, imaginary humanity. Thus, after the conference in Royaumont, while they were dining together as a family and the conversation turned to the opinions of that colloquium, Jérôme pointed out to the older children:

> There is no Man with a capital M. There are men, individual human beings, and each of them deserves respect. Although everyone is willing to shed a tear about the condition of Man, although great minds pride themselves in speaking with great verve about the dignity of Man or the rights of Man, they care very little about every human being, much less the elementary law of charity, a word that is much disparaged these days and yet is irreplaceable: it applies to everyone and to each person and, above all, to the first one who shows up, the one who is right nearby, the neighbor, as the catechisms that actually taught something used to say. For the physician, there are indeed only individuals, persons, subjects, and never objects.[6]

While the older children listened attentively, Jérôme reflected, then went on:

> Basically, that woman said it all. She said exactly why some people wanted it to be legal in France to kill children. It is not so much in order to attack the children; it is because she knows, along with those who are conducting this campaign, that there is a theorem—how can I put it, of supernatural physiology—namely, that the supernatural virtues

[6] This statement, placed here in a dialogue for the purposes of this book, is in fact excerpted from a working document by J. Lejeune, D9-4, undated, Fonds Lejeune [an archive].

can flourish only among the natural virtues, on the soil of the natural virtues, and that the day when women no longer love their children will be the day when there will no longer be any supernatural virtues.[7]

Possessing this clear view of the situation, Jérôme naturally became the inspiration and the reference point for defenders of human life. The association Laissez-les-vivre [Let them live] soon asked him to be its scientific advisor, and Jérôme very willingly agreed. In that association, he met a remarkable woman, Geneviève Poullot, sister of the Dominican Father Ambroise-Marie Carré, a member of the Institut, who had participated actively in the Résistance against the Nazi occupiers. Adopting that same principle of effective, discreet action in order to protect the identity of the young women, Geneviève Poullot created with little funding the association SOS futures mères [S.O.S. for future mothers], a mutual assistance network for pregnant women in difficult situations: a telephone hotline and material aid throughout France before and after they gave birth. It was the start of responsive, effective, and concrete aid, but it was not enough. It was necessary to devise a strategy.

While the resistance movement was being organized in France, Jérôme departed again in May 1973 for the United States, where he was scheduled to give scientific conferences in Los Angeles, at the University of Southern California, then in Pasadena, at the California Institute of Technology. But three days after his arrival in Los Angeles, he received from Birthe a long, hastily written letter. From the very first words he understood that something serious had happened.

My darling Jérôme, I hope that you arrived safely, that everything is going well and that you have success. Yesterday was an eventful day.... The police had discovered a Choisir center in Grenoble: 500 abortions in ten months.... The woman doctor had been charged, and Choisir announced with great fanfare a public abortion in Grenoble for this evening, with Gisèle Halimi and others participating. This was staged, because at the same time Jean Bernard, Milliez, and Royer were demanding freedom for physicians to abort *ad experimentum* for five to eight years. Moreover, the radio and the newspapers

[7] J. Lejeune, conference in Lorient, November 28, 1989. Jérôme tells about the conference in Royaumont and gives this explanation for it.

announced that Neuwirth [Editor's note: the deputy responsible for the 1967 French law liberalizing contraception] was going to speak at the assembly and that Ponia [Editor's note: Michel Poniatowski was the minister of public health from April 1973 to May 1974] had to respond that he agreed.

This morning there was a telephone call at dawn from Georges M., who was furious because of Jean B[ernard]. He wanted me to telephone you so that you would protest with him; I advised him to call Hervet. Then the day was like the day of the 330 [*sic*; the *Manifesto of the 331 Physicians*], telephone calls from journalists, horrified people, etc.

As early as 9:00 A.M., Clément prepared a telegram to send to [French President] Pompidou and to release to the press. We telephoned this text to all of France this morning, so that prominent people in each town can send it directly to the Élysée [official residence of the president of the French Republic]. Rheims, Grenoble, Bordeaux, Rennes, Lyon, etc. Clément, Madame Vaur, and I were hanging onto two telephone lines for hours, but by noon Pompidou had received many telegrams, and at 3:00 P.M., abortion was forbidden. Laissez-les-vivre [Association] had even found out the exact address where the abortion was supposed to take place; they sent it to the prefect, to Pompidou, etc., to "save this child who was going to be killed this evening".

Malinas telephoned me in the afternoon to tell me that the district was sealed off by the police and that Choisir had given up; he also spoke on the radio several times today. He is very good. Hervet will be on TV tomorrow. I also had a phone call from the minister of the interior who wanted to know what Laissez-les-vivre was.

After all that, we managed to put in alphabetical order the first 2,000 cards so as to give them to the lady this evening.... This evening we were all dead tired.

Ponia spoke for hours about information on birth control, and to the great disappointment of the abortionists, he said, in less than fifty words, that it was necessary to revise the 1920 law and that commissions would deal with it.[8]

It was becoming really urgent to make the public understand, if there was still time, that these militants, despite their apparent feelings of compassion for women, were preparing a brave new world in which the child would be the fuse that detonates human passions

[8] B. Lejeune, letter to Jérôme, May 11, 1973.

at will. And that the fate reserved today for children would be that of the elderly next. "The initials IVG [*interruption volontaire de grossesse*, voluntary interruption of pregnancy] have a terrible meaning", Jérôme reflected. "*Interruption d'une vie gênante*, [interruption of an inconvenient life], and age makes no difference; the elderly are threatened just as much as the youngest."[9] Jérôme got down to work with Jean Foyer, who had just resigned as minister of health and taken his place again as president of the Commission on Laws at the National Assembly, then the historian and demographer Pierre Chaunu and the philosopher Marcel Clément, public figures and staunch Christian intellectuals. They would try to stop the movement by acting at every possible level.

Together with Marcel Clément, Marie-Odile Rethoré, and Marie-Hélène Mathieu, Jérôme wrote a document that was faithful to the Hippocratic Oath and formally ruled out abortion and euthanasia and submitted it to be signed by physicians. This *Declaration of the Physicians of France* said simply and firmly:

> The physician's duty is to do everything possible to save the mother together with her child. This is why the deliberate interruption of a pregnancy for eugenic reasons or in order to resolve an economic, moral, or social conflict is not the work of a physician.

In a few days, it had been signed by 10,000 and then by 18,000 French physicians. More than half of the physicians in France.

The Supreme Court of the United States had just legalized abortion in January with the *Roe v. Wade* decision. Not unaware of the global dimension of the pro-abortion movement, Jérôme decided to make the resistance international by inviting eminent foreign physicians to sign this *Declaration of Physicians* in their own country. In April 1973, he wrote to Doctor André Hellegers, director of the Bioethics Center of the Kennedy Institute at Georgetown University and one of the pioneers of bioethics, a new academic discipline that was emerging in the United States. Jérôme greatly valued the clarity of his thought. He also sent this invitation to join the campaign to Gedda in Italy, Cruz Coke in Chile, and Halpern in Portugal:

[9] J. Lejeune, letter to Guillaume, Easter Monday, 1985.

> My dear colleague, in order to fight the incessant propaganda of the abortionists, we have submitted the attached declaration to the majority of physicians in France.... Being a simple explanation of the Hippocratic Oath, this document formally rules out abortion and euthanasia.... Do you think that a translation of this declaration could be sent to the physicians in your country? The advantage of a common declaration, repeated by many countries, would be to give an international dimension to our efforts to uphold medical morals, in other words, to protect the individual human being.... I would be extremely glad to have your opinion about this possible international collaboration of physicians against a scourge that is threatening all countries.[10]

The publication of the *Declaration* signed by 18,000 French physicians was a thunderbolt. Public opinion and the political authorities understood that the vast majority of medical personnel were opposed to abortion, contrary to the talk usually reported by the media. The 330 physicians who had signed a pro-abortion manifesto in *Le Nouvel Observateur* three months earlier were swept away.

The press conference was held on June 5. Professor André Hellegers immediately agreed to travel from Washington for it, and there were Frenchmen like Doctor Henri Lafont, who had created the Association des médecins pour le respect de la vie [Association of pro-life physicians] in 1971 and was fighting side by side with Jérôme. This time the media were obliged to talk about this *Declaration of the Physicians of France*, and Jérôme tirelessly explained in front of radio microphones that "The physician's duty is to do everything possible to save the mother together with her child." He invited society to offer genuine material assistance and counseling to mothers in distress and to promote every initiative that respected the mother and the child. The declaration by the French physicians was soon followed by other statements, including one by mayors and local elected representatives, then one by lawyers and judges.

After this initial success, Jérôme was exhausted. "This harassing campaign, conferences, interviews, meetings, radio, television, etc., hardly left me any time for reflection",[11] he said regretfully. "When will I be able to go back to my scientific projects and have a little time to think?"

[10] J. Lejeune, letter to Luigi Gedda, April 12, 1973.

[11] J. Lejeune, *Journal intime*, August 17, 1973.

In fact, during the previous few months Jérôme had sacrificed much of his time for this public commitment, which he extended with numerous conferences. He was invited everywhere, to speak on various subjects and to very diverse audiences. Sometimes all he had to do was to nourish the hearts and intellects of committed Catholic listeners, for example, at the big annual congress in Lausanne, which was remarkably well organized by the association Ichtus [French spelling of the Greek word *Ichthys* = the Christian symbol "fish"]. Other times, he spoke to his peers, to whom he offered a top-flight scientific reflection. For example, at the Institut de France, at the heart of the prestigious Academy of Moral and Political Sciences, where he guided academics in his "Reflections on the Beginning of the Human Being". With virtuosity, Jérôme addressed the topics in it: *Logos* and matter, the symphony of life, the brotherhood of human beings, neo-Darwinism. It was an admirable document, considered "one of the most brilliant sessions of our Academy in many years",[12] and earned him enthusiastic congratulations. He witnessed also, before the National Assembly, to the beauty of human life and the duties of society toward the child and the mother in distress.

After all these speeches, Jérôme received many thank-you letters, like this one from a former student:

> Dear Sir, you are my teacher. I will respect Hippocrates so as to be worthy of the honor of having been your student.[13]

Jérôme spoke as a scientist and addressed intellects. When journalists tried to confine him to religious talk, he replied that he spoke as a physician who had taken the Hippocratic Oath. By recalling that Hippocrates lived four hundred years before Jesus Christ, he showed them that respect for human life is commanded by the natural law, even prior to the Christian law. And in order to force his interlocutor to reflect, Jérôme went so far as to say: "If the Catholic Church ever said that abortion was not murder, I would no longer be a Catholic."

Thus, he made it clear to the scientific community that to transgress this prohibition is to regress intellectually and medically and is not a victory of scientists over the Church.

[12] A member of the Academy to Jérôme Lejeune.

[13] Letter to Jérôme Lejeune from a former student, 1973.

Jérôme was a guest for several debates broadcast on radio and television in which pro-abortion feminists and physicians participated; they sometimes used astonishing ways of asserting their ideas, for example, during the televised program *Aujourd'hui madame* [Today, Ma'am] in June, with Professor Paul Milliez. No doubt short on arguments, the latter tried to discredit Jérôme with a statement that was unexpected, to put it mildly. While Jérôme was speaking about the role of the physician, Milliez interrupted him and asked him:

"Do you see sick patients? Do you see women?"

"Yes, sir", Jérôme replied.

"Do you seem many of them?"

"I see many of them."

And Milliez went on the attack: "That is not true. You lie. Because you do not see patients; you are a biologist. You are not a physician."

The argument was so wrong that Jérôme was staggered, but his astonishment was imperceptible. He answered politely but firmly: "Monsieur Milliez, would you like to retract the statement that you just made?"

"No, I do not retract it."

"You are wrong, sir", Jérôme commented.

"Well, then, I'm wrong. But that is how it is."

"You are wrong", Jérôme repeated in the midst of the brouhaha on the set, because this broadcast was becoming ridiculous. "I am not in the habit of lying. This gentleman has treated me as a liar. That is a serious error on his part. I ask him to apologize."

When Professor Milliez refused to apologize, Jérôme went on: "Let us be clear about this. Yes, there are physicians, and the vast majority of physicians refuse to perform abortions because their profession is to care and not to kill. Monsieur Milliez' opinion will not change that at all. We are at the service of both the mother and of the child at the same time."

Then, when Professor Milliez asked him a question, Jérôme, astonishingly calm, responded by speaking to the journalist: "I will not answer Monsieur Milliez, who treats me as a liar. I will not answer him, but I will gladly answer these women [in the studio audience] if they want to ask me questions."[14]

[14] Verbatim citations from the exchange between Jérôme Lejeune and Paul Milliez during the televised program *Aujourd'hui madame*, June 1973.

Since Professor Milliez was at that time Dean of the Broussais-Hôtel-Dieu University Hospital Center, it is difficult to believe that he was unaware of Professor Lejeune's renown and the international reputation of his practice at Necker Children's Hospital. Since the beginning of his career, Jérôme had consulted with four thousand patients ...

Another time Birthe accompanied him to a televised debate. While she remained behind the scenes, without attracting the attention of the journalists, who had no idea that that modestly dressed woman with a cigarette on her lips was Professor Lejeune's wife, she heard one of them exclaim while listening to Jérôme debate on the set:

"The bastard! He is too good. They won't invite him again!"

After the broadcast, a friend heard about those remarks and took offense at them, but Jérôme told him:

> Nowadays trying to speak French [*français*] and especially to speak frankly [*franc*] is a dangerous experiment; if everything you say is in no way global and universal and consciousness-raising, if you don't reify ideas or reduce persons to things, that endangers everything among the intelligentsia, because there is a risk that people might then understand.[15]

From then on, Jérôme was no longer invited to the television sets or the radio studios. Only Jacques Chancel interviewed him on France Inter [a public radio station] for the program *Radioscopie*, in which the journalist's well-meaning questions contrasted with the usual tone of his colleagues. Jacques Chancel questioned him in particular about his commitment to serving human life.

"Professor Lejeune, how is it that you have become the leader of those who are fighting against abortion?"

"I do not think that I am a leader, not at all."

"When Gisèle Halimi, for example, speaks about her battle and the fact that she is facing an adversary, you are that adversary, because you represent the others."

"That seems to me indeed very strange, because the others are the ones who choose me as their adversary; I do not feel at all that I am a leader, a little Napoleon in the pro-life campaign, not at all. The reason why I spoke up as soon as there was a question about

[15]J. Lejeune, working document D9-4, undated, Fonds Lejeune.

abortion may be very precisely because I am a physician, and I care for sick patients whom medical science does not know how to cure. At the beginning, two years ago—it seems quite old now—a bill had been written to permit the elimination of children who would be abnormal—the very same children whom I care for, the children who have a chromosomal anomaly."

"You are well positioned", Jacques Chancel added.

"I know them", Jérôme agreed. "These children are extremely lovable, but sick; they are severely handicapped, and it is very hard for the parents to bear, but they are real children, real little human beings. The idea that anyone in our country could campaign to kill children because they are sick is really something that I could not bear, and this is the reason why I responded right away when they asked me: 'Will you state your opinion on the radio, on television?' I said 'Yes'. I don't usually do that, I am not a star, but in such a serious case, 'Yes'. And I realized that it corresponded to something extremely deep, not only in me, but precisely in my little patients. You cannot imagine the extremely simple, poorly written letters, with spelling mistakes, but truly from the bottom of the heart, saying simply: 'Oh, thank you, you are not abandoning us.' That, that explains a lot of things."[16]

Jérôme was also invited to speak at the National Assembly on November 23, 1973, to the task force doing preliminary study of the proposed bill concerning the "voluntary interruption of pregnancy". He took advantage of this occasion to recall that "the quality of a civilization is measured by the respect that it has for the weakest of its members."[17]

The battle was not just in the media and the legislature, but also on the ground, in the hospitals that were illegally performing abortions, and here again Jérôme was in demand. During the month of December, he received a phone call from the nursing nuns at the Parisian hospital of Notre-Dame du Bon-Secours [Our Lady of Good Help], who had discovered to their great sorrow that abortions were being performed in their hospital. The Mother Superior asked him to help

[16] *Radioscopie*, interview of Jérôme Lejeune by Jacques Chancel, December 13, 1973. Verbatim quotations.

[17] J. Lejeune, interviewed by M. Leclercq, "Oui il faut les laisser vivre" [Yes, we must let them live], *Paris Match*, November 7, 1980.

put an end to that practice, which seemed all the more obvious since abortion was still illegal then. Jérôme immediately requested a meeting with the archbishop, Cardinal Marty, since the hospital was Catholic. The cardinal did not receive Jérôme personally but referred him to his auxiliary, Bishop Pézeril, who was in charge of such matters. When Jérôme met him to present to him the Sisters' call for help, the auxiliary bishop told him: "Leave them alone; it will be voted into law soon."

Then, seeing the expression on Jérôme's face, he said to him: "You are as intolerant as [the conservative Catholic journalist] Louis Veuillot, as relentless as [the philosopher] Bergson, and as tough as [the novelist] Mauriac. I tell you, with God as my witness, that you are a bad Christian."[18]

It was a brutal blow. Reeling inside, Jérôme stood up and left the bishop's office. When he arrived at rue Galande, Birthe immediately noticed from his pallid complexion that the meeting had gone badly.

"What is wrong, Jérôme?" she asked anxiously.

With tears in his eyes and his voice quavering, Jérôme reported the conversation to her and ended with the most painful part: "Then he told me: 'I tell you, with God as my witness, that you are a bad Christian.'"

It was Birthe's turn to be shocked. "Oh! And what did you say?" she asked.

"Nothing", Jérôme said. "Because I was always taught that you have to respect bishops."

In May 1974, Giscard d'Estaing, who had just been elected president of the French Republic, appointed [Magistrate] Simone [Jacob] Veil minister of health, in order to prepare the law on abortion. With Pierre Simon,[19] Grand Master of the Grand Lodge of France and co-founder of the Mouvement français de planification familial [French movement for family planning], as her official expert advisor, she quickly presented an abortion bill to the National Assembly. Jérôme, Chaunu, Clément, and Foyer, president of the parliamentary

[18] Quotation cited by Madame Lejeune in a letter written for Cardinal Lustiger, February 16, 1986, but never sent.

[19] P. Simon was grand master of the Grand Lodge of France (Freemasons) from 1969 to 1971, then from 1973 to 1975. He is the author of the book *De la vie avant toute chose* (Paris: Éditions Mazarine, 1979).

Commission on Laws, joined forces to try again to stop the process. But this time they had little hope. The president of the republic and his minister wanted this law; it was a campaign promise to buy votes.

Jérôme was unhappy to see the hesitation of some of those in charge of the Church in France, whose words would have had considerable impact on public opinion and the many Catholic parliamentarians who were getting ready to vote on that law. This silence of the Church in France left committed Catholics quite isolated. Jérôme knew also that there were many reasons that partially explained this position of retreat from political debates. The [historically] complicated Church-State relations [in France] had to be taken into account. It had to be acknowledged also that a wind of protest was sweeping through the Church in the 1970s, upending landmarks. May 1968 had been experienced by many Christians as a liberating experience, and so the challenging questions within the Church in France made it difficult to find a common, consistent language. Since the end of Vatican Council II, which had invited the Church to be more open to a changing world, many priests and lay faithful believed that this was an unprecedented opportunity to innovate freely. Some saw in it an occasion to revolutionize the Church, as this appeal from the newspaper *Témoignage chrétien* [Christian witness] shows:

> The presence of Christians in the revolution presupposes and requires the presence of the revolution in the Church, in her ways of life and in her customary thinking, as expressed both collectively and individually.[20]

The malaise was universal: thousands of priests left the priesthood, the seminaries were empty, and the churches, too. In the parishes, everyone felt free to interpret the conciliar documents as he pleased. The omnipresent relativism won over many minds, replacing the proclamation of the truth with subjective, emotional "witness" and the tolerance that levels all judgment to the ground. The rejection of authority led to the rejection of the Magisterium; decisions from Rome were criticized, magisterial documents were ignored, and the

[20] "Appel aux chrétiens" [Appeal to Christians], published in *Témoignage chrétien* on May 21, 1968.

absence of religious formation for Christians did not make the task any easier for the pastors. In these circumstances, when Pope Paul VI published the encyclical *Humanae vitae* on July 25, 1968, the condemnation of contraception in the midst of the sexual revolution landed like a bombshell. When the debates about abortion began in France, the episcopate, therefore, found itself disarmed and loath to react. Troubled by the testimonies of Catholics who had had abortions or performed them, influenced by the arguments of the promoters of abortion, some of whom were Catholic, the French bishops did not dare to condemn publicly the law that was being prepared. One part of the clergy even thought that it was a lesser evil. It must be said that the proponents of abortion did not hesitate to parade in front of the bishops asserting the distress of the women as the main argument. Simply forgetting that you can never kill someone in order to relieve the suffering of someone else, many pastors were so politically naïve as to be unaware that transgressive laws always start with exceptions that, once allowed, are extended and generalized.

The Veil law decriminalizing abortion, which was primly rechristened "the voluntary interruption of pregnancy" [*interruption volontaire de grossesse* (IVG)], was presented to the National Assembly in November 1974, and, after three days of debates, it was finally adopted, then promulgated on January 17, 1975. In this tragedy, Jérôme's only consolation was that Jean Foyer had courageously succeeded in adding a first article to the law, which explains: "The law guarantees respect for every human being from the beginning of life." At least the principle was recalled. It was a severe trial for Jérôme. He knew that it was a terrible blow for the children of France. That was what he explained to the journalists who questioned him about this defeat: "It is not our defeat but the defeat of the children of France."

On that day, Jérôme's voice trembled slightly at the microphone. As though he were already in mourning for those millions of babies who would perish.

In that battle, Jérôme managed not to harden his heart by way of protecting himself from the blows that he received, and in this defeat he did not become bitter. On the contrary, during those long months, a change was taking place in him. Whereas during his early travels to the United States, in the late 1950s, he sometimes emphasized with humor or annoyance, in his letters to Birthe, unpleasant character traits in some individuals or others, this tone disappeared little by little. Jérôme, who was quick-witted and lively in debate and could crush an opponent with a word, seems to have reached a state of interior peace and a high-minded perspective that allowed him spontaneously to judge acts and not human beings and to proclaim the truth with serenity. This extraordinary benevolence toward the people whose dangerous ideas he fought vehemently only increased over the years. To the point where those close to him were sometimes astonished by it and admired his restraint.

One day, one of his children asked him the question: "Papa, how do you stay calm and not insult your opponents when they attack you?"

Jérôme answered his young interlocutor gently: "I do not fight against the man, but against his ideas; he has his reasons for taking that position. Then, too," he added after a moment of silence, "it is more difficult to be an unbeliever than a believer. When you are a believer, you have hope; when you are an unbeliever, there is the void, nothingness—it must be very difficult to endure."

His son, pensive, asked him: "And is it because you forgive them?"

"In order to forgive them, it would be necessary for them to have done me some harm; I would have to have something to blame them for, but they have nothing against me; they are against the reality that I remind them about. It does not matter what they say against me."

All the efforts made by Jérôme in this political battle on behalf of human life did not dampen his ardor for his research projects and his practice, because the central point that united his whole life were his patients, those whom he cared for and for whom he sought a treatment, those whose right to life he defended. These commitments, although different in their expression, were connected and ongoing. And strengthened by the presence of Birthe at his side, Jérôme could devote himself totally to this threefold and unique cause.

At the Institut de Progénèse, things were going smoothly. One of the original studies underway had to do with the sensitivity of children with trisomy 21 to various medications. In order to avoid all experimentation that might be dangerous or unpleasant for the patients, they measured the reactions of the iris after putting a drop of liquid in the eye. This method allowed them to measure the effect of extremely reduced dosages, and in this way they discovered a hypersensitivity of the patients to certain substances. With the help of this data, they were able to bring to light what could be a major difficulty in the mechanism of the mental disability of these children.[21] This study, conducted by Doctor Prieur, was made possible thanks to a subsidy of 15,000 francs from the Foundation for Medical Research (FRM), which very helpfully supplemented the insufficient funds allotted by the Research Administration. These expenses, although moderate, were not budgeted by the administration. A part of the subsidy also made it possible to keep employing a female colleague, a technician, whose work was indispensable to the projects of the Institut de Progénèse and whom the French organizations National Institute of Health and Medical Research (INSERM) and National Center for Scientific Research (CNRS) had not rehired at all for the previous two years.

Another research project conducted by Odile Raoul, Marie-Odile Rethoré, and Bernard Dutrillaux dealt with partial trisomy 14q by maternal translocation.[22] It was published in 1975 in the *Annales de génétique*, a scientific journal founded in April 1958 at the initiative of Professor Turpin and Jérôme. The team was very active and also published a case of trisomy 14 mosaicism, which Sophie Carpentier was working on, two cases of trisomy 11q by translocation,[23] a study conducted in particular with Alain Aurias and Pierre-Marie Sinet, trisomy 10q24 10qter, syndrome 4p- by paternal translocation,[24] et cetera.

These efforts, which were crowned with important publications, manifested the caliber of his coworkers. Jérôme, aware of their exceptional merit, continued to ask the administration repeatedly, indeed insistently, to promote some and to increase the salaries of others. In 1974, he requested for Marie-Odile Rethoré a position as director of research:

[21] Report of the activity of the Institut de Progénèse for the Fondation de recherche médicale, 1975.

[22] O. Raoul, M.-O. Rethoré, B. Dutrillaux, L. Michon, and J. Lejeune, "Trisomie 14q partielle: I. Trisomie 14q partielle par translocation maternelle, t (10; 14) (p15.2; q22)", *Annales de Génétique* 18/1 (1975): 35–39.

[23] A. Aurias, Cl. Turc, Y. Michels, P.M. Sinet, D. Graveleau, J. Lejeune, "Deux cas de trisomie 11q (q231 ter qter) par translocation t (11; 22) (q231; q111) dans deux familles différentes", *Annales de Génétique* 18/3 (1975): 185–88.

[24] J. Lejeune, M.-O. Rethoré, B. Dutrillaux, J. Lafourcade, J. Cruveiller, and P. Drillon, "Syndrome 4p- par translocation paternelle t (4; 20) (p15; p12)", *Lyon médical* 233/3 (1975): 271–74.

Sir, and dear colleague, having had the privilege of assisting in the flowering of the scientific status of Mademoiselle Rethoré, who has worked at the Institut de Progénèse for almost twenty years, I wish quite simply to inform you of the very high esteem that this exceptional researcher merits.... Her contribution to human cytogenetics is extremely important, and her discovery of trisomy 9p, even before the use of modern techniques of marking chromatids, is a model of both cytological and clinical analysis. Her initial descriptions were then confirmed in all countries, and her international renown makes her one of the most famous cytogeneticists.... Combining a very rare subtlety of heart with exceptional competence, she is at the same time an accomplished physician and an exceptional researcher. Certain that I am acting in the interests of science, I make so bold as to ask you with the most confident insistence to support her candidacy for the position of director of research, which she has fully deserved for a long time.[25]

He supported that recommendation with other letters to various colleagues in which he explains concerning Doctor Rethoré:

Among the genetic anomalies that she was the first to describe—most of which were confirmed later, both in the U.S. and in Europe—I will cite only these: trisomy 9p, trisomy 4p, partial trisomy 8q and 8q-, and the localization of the gene of the LDHB on the short arm of chromosome 12.

Then Jérôme added:

As head of research projects for more than ten years, Mademoiselle Rethoré suffered from serious prejudice in the unfolding of her career because of grave errors committed by a former commission of INSERM. My intention, in making so bold as to address this letter to you, is not to fulfill my duty as a department head sponsoring one of his most brilliant coworkers, but rather to enlighten some colleagues about the originality and importance of the work of a researcher of the highest caliber.[26]

[25] J. Lejeune, letter to Professor Jean Bernard, February 7, 1974.

[26] J. Lejeune, letter to Professor Baulieu, June 4, 1975, and letter to Professor Varangot and response from the latter on June 16, 1975.

In June 1975, after a hearing that made a great impression on the Scientific Council of INSERM, Marie-Odile Rethoré was appointed director of research.

Jérôme continued to support the promotion of Bernard Dutrillaux, so that he would finally be appointed to the level of head of research projects. He explained once again in his letter of recommendation to the administration:

> Doctor Dutrillaux is indeed a "finder". A tireless researcher with exceptional technical skill, he has demonstrated since the beginning of his career an extremely sure judgment combined with great inventive ability.
>
> Very well-known abroad, having already trained many, many researchers of high caliber, he is without dispute one of the most brilliant cytogeneticists of his generation. To mention only his principal discoveries that have renovated cytogenetics, I will note simply those having to do with chromosomal marking, the dynamic of chromatids, the evolution of the karyotype among primates. [Jérôme describes them.] This substantial list gives only an imperfect idea of the exceptional contribution of Doctor Dutrillaux to human cytogenetics. The appointment of Doctor Dutrillaux to the level of head of research projects would only be an acknowledgment, and alas a belated one, of his exceptional merits.[27]

Aware of how important it was for his young coworkers to take part in high-quality international congresses, he often proposed them as participants to the organizers, as in the case of Doctor Sinet for the Ninth Meeting of the Nobel Prize for Chemistry in Lindau, Germany:

> A doctor in medicine, a confirmed geneticist, and a very competent biochemist, Monsieur Pierre-Marie Sinet recently discovered the excess of the superoxide dismutase enzyme caused by trisomy 21. A researcher with a great future, and a very hard worker, Monsieur Sinet would be capable of deriving the greatest benefit from the irreplaceable lessons that so many very highly competent scientists will give on this occasion. I personally would be extremely happy if this valuable opportunity were granted to him.[28]

[27] J. Lejeune, letter to the CNRS, 1975. This request was reiterated in a letter dated May 3, 1976.

[28] J. Lejeune, letter dated April 23, 1975.

Nor did Jérôme forget the advancement of the technicians on the team, like Madame Lenné, so that she might get a permanent contract and be promoted to the position of specialized laboratory aide.

Concerned about advancing science by training younger generations, Jérôme also accepted many interns, from all over, giving his time and advice unsparingly. He kept no secrets from them and very willingly shared his "little tricks". Thus, a young intern from Marseilles, Doctor Jean-François Mattéi, who had already done an internship at the laboratory, asked him:

> Monsieur, my dear teacher, on the occasion of the New Year, please accept this expression of my faithful devotion. Since we spent time in your laboratory, our tissue cultures are much more manageable and the problems less insurmountable. If you would still have us, my wife and I would like to spend a few days again at the Institut de Progénèse in May or June.[29]

Jérôme gladly accepted their offer.

For his part, Jérôme continued to receive prizes and distinctions in France and abroad. Appointed to the French Society of Biology in 1972, he then received honorary doctorates from the University of Düsseldorf in 1973 and the University of Navarre in 1974, and his name was proposed for the second time to the Academy of Sciences in France.[30] Since his election to the Academy had been blocked the previous year, he had few illusions about the results of this new nomination, after his public pro-life stance. But so what!

The public role that Jérôme assumed did have consequences for his professional life. Although he was still invited to international scientific congresses, he observed a gradual decline: now he was only rarely in demand to preside over a congress or a session or even as a speaker, for instance, at Berkeley or in Vienna, where his conference was rejected.

Birthe was aware of this too. One evening she asked him: "Jérôme, I get the impression that you are being invited less often to scientific congresses, especially in the United States. Is this true?"

"Yes, you are right. I have noticed it too." Then, after a moment's reflection, he told her: "From my first major trip to the United States

[29] J.-F. Mattéi, letter to J. Lejeune, December 31, 1973.

[30] Professor P. G., letter to J. Lejeune, September 2, 1975.

in 1958 until my speech at the Allen Memorial Award in San Francisco in 1969, in other words, over the course of ten years, I spoke at fifty work meetings, congresses, and courses in the United States. And since 1970 to today, around five years, I have participated in only five scientific meetings there. And that is not going to improve, because for two years I have not received any purely scientific invitation. From now on, in the United States, only the Kennedy Foundation regularly requests my expertise, because we share the same analysis of the situation."

"But it seems to me that you are still very much in demand for scientific congresses in other countries", his wife remarked.

"Yes, a lot of them: Canada, Belgium, the United Kingdom, Argentina, Portugal, et cetera. But some of my contributions have not been accepted, for instance in Vienna, and our friend Neel told me frankly that it is because I reject abortion."

"I must say", Birthe replied, smiling, "that with the speech that you gave them in San Francisco and the equally frank one that you gave to the National Institute of Health in Bethesda in 1971, you have dealt with the subject directly. And you are the one who forced them to look reality in the face. That is not always pleasant, even if it is said tactfully."

"That is true," Jérôme replied, "but we cannot perpetuate this confusion of minds by our silence, because what is at stake is the abortion of hundreds of thousands of handicapped children in future years. And if I say nothing, I will give the impression of being complicit in my silence."

Despite the decrease in the number of invitations from the scientific community, Jérôme still received from all over the world important correspondence asking for his opinion, his expertise, or his collaboration. Thus Johns Hopkins University in Baltimore proposed to him a collaborative study, based on two of his publications, on the markers of several chromosomes,[31] the New York hospital Cornell Medical Center asked his expertise on the biochemical approach to trisomy 21,[32] and Yale University asked his advice about the choice of new researchers for its expanding department of human genetics.[33]

[31] D. S. Borgaonkar, Johns Hopkins University, letter to J. Lejeune, March 21, 1975.

[32] A. G. Bearn, Cornell University Medical College, letter to J. Lejeune, December 1, 1975.

[33] Doctor Maurice Mahoney, Yale University, letter to J. Lejeune, November 9, 1976, and Jérôme's response dated November 16.

Although Jérôme's commitment was rewarded with ostracism by the scientific community, it won him the admiration of pro-life people, from the lowliest to the most learned, and extended his fame to all corners of the earth. While some doors closed, other larger, better ones opened, and without trying to or even being aware of it, Jérôme inspired pro-life witnesses throughout the world, becoming their moral support and example.

Now almost half of his abundant correspondence concerned questions of ethics, especially the defense of human life. Indeed, at the highest scientific level, for instance, the renowned *Encyclopedia of Bioethics* of the Kennedy Center at Georgetown University in Washington, D.C., which solicited his expertise concerning the choice of topics to treat and asked him to be so kind as to sit on its advisory board.[34]

Jérôme's international experience prompted him to promote a worldwide movement of Catholic physicians. Therefore, he suggested the creation of the International Federation of Associations of Catholic Physicians (FIAMC, Fédération internationale des associations des médecins catholiques) and took part in founding it. He worked on this project with Philippe Schepens, a Belgian professor of medicine. During one of the first meetings in Holland, which laid the foundations of this federation, Jérôme gave prudential instructions: "Start with the medical basis, do not try to convince well-known opponents because you will not succeed; first, work at the grass-roots level, among physicians to start with, so as to form a group."

One of the doctors asked him: "And on what sort of message should we focus?"

Jérôme answered, "Indeed, it is really not very complicated; we just have to state the facts on the scientific level, on the moral level. All this is logical; we just have to say what is. They are the ones who are doing all the dirty tricks, trying to make abortion, euthanasia, et cetera, acceptable. They have to make evil seem good in order to convince people, while we only have to state the facts. We must say nothing but the truth, always the truth, and again the truth." Then the group asked him to be so kind as to serve as the president of this brand new federation, but Jérôme refused the office, along with the other official

[34] W. T. Reich, editor-in-chief, *Encyclopedia of Bioethics*, letter to J. Lejeune, January 24, 1974.

positions that they proposed to him. "It is up to you to do it. I can help you, give you my advice, but it is up to you to preside and to direct."[35]

Letters poured in from France and the whole world, thanking him, congratulating him, and asking his advice. Whenever he returned to rue Galande, he would find them, placed by Birthe on the little table in the living room. Sometimes Birthe read them to him while he sat down and lit a cigarette. "Listen, Jérôme, here is a professor of neurology at the hospital in Washington who is asking your advice about a conference that he will soon give about the ethics of genetics."[36]

Then, taking another envelope, she said to him, "Oh, this one is funny; just listen. It is from a Canadian journalist, Françoise Gaudet-Smet, who writes to you in these surprising words: 'Well, we have just started thinking about you, referring to you, using you, and following you! Lucky boss! . . .' "[37]

Amused, Jérôme smiled and commented: "You see: at least one journalist appreciates me!"

These letters expressed the senders' admiration for his courageous example and sought his enlightened opinion. Students, physicians, priests, and even mothers of families requested his advice and arguments on subjects as varied as abortion, priesthood for women, and gender ideology, and some even asked him to collaborate in composing a catechism. The deference and the immense respect manifested in these letters indicate how much his truthful statements enlightened and strengthened those who heard or read them. For example, this Frenchwoman who wrote to him the day after a conference:

> Allow me to express my amazement and my gratitude to you for the presents that you gave yesterday to our Church of Today. I had the good fortune of getting some bracing, dazzling ideas from it.

Or this Protestant woman, a seeker, who told him:

> It is so rare to hear voices like yours that have the courage to go against the current fashions, and I thank you for it. I cannot help telling you how much I admire your courage.[38]

[35] Conversation of the author with Philippe Schepens.

[36] Sean O'Reilly, letter to J. Lejeune, November 8, 1973.

[37] F. Gaudet-Smet, letter to J. Lejeune, May 21, 1974.

[38] Letter from P.B., December 4, 1975.

Or this physician from Guatemala, who wrote to him expressing

> ... the devotion that you, with the close collaboration of Señora Lejeune, deserve because of your defense of the human life of the preborn child and the preservation of the values of the French family. The battle that you are waging is already having repercussions in many other countries.[39]

In a few months' time, he became the point of reference for pro-life activists in the farthest corners of the world. From then on, from Canada to New Zealand, via Brazil or Australia, he received endless invitations. Jérôme would take the defense of the weakest human beings, not to the podiums of scientific congresses now, but to the very heart of political and juridical institutions.

[39] E. Cofino, letter to J. Lejeune, May 27, 1974.

CHAPTER 10

WITNESS FOR HUMAN BEINGS

1974–1977

"Jérôme, Jérôme, there is a letter for you from the Vatican!"

Birthe rapidly climbed the old wooden staircase that led from the street to their apartment, a cigarette at the corner of her mouth, and as she came back into the kitchen where Jérôme was finishing his cup of coffee, she presented the envelope to him, her eyes gleaming.

"Open it, open it!" she said impatiently while rummaging in the drawer for a plain-edge knife.

"My dear, of course you can open it!"

Birthe did not wait to be asked twice and slipped the blade of the knife under the flap of the envelope, taking care not to tear the stamp with the image of Pope Paul VI or the postmark from the Vatican Post Office, dated June 24, 1974. Jérôme put down his mug, intrigued as well by this letter from the Vatican, then took the beautiful thick paper and read aloud:

> Dear Professor, I have the honor and the joy of informing you that His Holiness, Pope Paul VI, in consideration of the great merits that you have gained in the international scientific world, decided to appoint you a member of the Pontifical Academy of Sciences, assigning to you seat no. 57. The Holy Father is pleased to think that this lofty distinction will be for you a reason for deep satisfaction and a title of honor for the Academy of which you will be a part.

Jérôme stopped and looked up toward Birthe, who was so raptly attentive as to be motionless.

"Finish reading it, please, and tell me who signed it."

Gladly allowing himself to be rushed by his wife's impatience, Jérôme continued:

> I inform you that the apostolic brief of nomination will be sent to you during an extraordinary session of the Academy, which will take place solemnly on a date that will be communicated to you at the opportune time. I am happy to join my personal congratulations to this testimony of esteem given by the Supreme Pontiff, and I ask you to be assured, dear Monsieur, of my respectful and cordial devotion.[1]

Finally Jérôme announced: "It is signed by Jean-Marie Cardinal Villot."

"The one who was archbishop of Lyons before Archbishop Renard?" Birthe asked curiously.

"Yes", Jérôme replied. "Then he was called to the Vatican and worked in various dicasteries. And now he is secretary of state of the Holy Father, and I have learned that he is also *camerlengo*."

"*Camerlengo*? What does that mean?" Birthe asked, surprised to hear that Italian word for the first time.

"It is a very high-ranking prelate who plays an important role, especially at the time of the Holy Father's death. He is the one who certifies and announces his death, retrieves and breaks the Fisherman's Ring, in other words, the ring with the personal coat of arms that the pope wears on his finger. And when the See of Peter is vacant, he is the one who looks after the temporal goods and civil law of the Holy See."

"And this Pontifical Academy of Sciences", Birthe asked, "is it made up only of Catholic scientists?"

"No", Jérôme answered, standing up from the table after glancing quickly at his watch. "The Holy Father appoints to it the best specialists in their scientific field, so that they can inform him of the latest status of the research in the world and on the developments to be foreseen: in physics, mathematics, astronomy, the neurosciences, chemistry, agronomy, et cetera. Whether or not they are Catholic does not come into consideration, because science is not denominational. The purpose of this academy is also to promote a moral development of science for the

[1]Jean-Marie Cardinal Villot, letter to J. Lejeune, June 24, 1974.

good of mankind and to encourage dialogue between faith and science. Most of these scientists have won the Nobel Prize. I even think", Jérôme continued with a laugh, "that the Academy has the largest concentration of Nobel Prizes in the world!"

"That means that the Holy Father is very well informed about scientific advances", Birthe remarked in astonishment.

"You are quite right. Contrary to what many people believe, the Church loves science very much, since she seeks the truth and is very well informed. This Academy started with the Academia dei Lincei, founded in Rome in 1604. It was the first scientific academy in the world. And do you know who was promptly appointed a member?"

"No!" Birthe replied with interest.

"Galileo. He was appointed a member of the Academy in 1610."

"Incredible!" Birthe said, greatly amused. Then she exclaimed enthusiastically: "It is terrific that you have been appointed to it!"

"It is a great honor for me", Jérôme replied with a hint of seriousness in his voice, "and a great joy, because I will be able to put my knowledge and my competencies directly at the service of the Holy Father. No nomination could make me happier."

Then, handing the letter to Birthe, he said to her, "Till this evening, darling. I must go, because I do not want to keep my little patients waiting."

And while his wife relit her cigarette with a lighter and, letter in hand, walked over to a claret-colored velvet armchair wedged in beside the window, Jérôme opened the door and disappeared into the little poorly lit staircase.

Several weeks later, on Friday, July 26, Jérôme flew to Rome, not for the Pontifical Academy of Sciences, but for a mission that the pope wanted to entrust to him. He had been named a member of the official delegation of the Holy See to the World Conference on Population in Bucharest, and since that conference was to take place August 18–29, he was invited to join in the preparatory meeting that now called him to the Eternal City for an intensive weekend of work. When the plane landed on the runway at Fiumicino Airport, Jérôme allowed himself to be overcome by a new emotion: "This is the first time that I am coming to the Vatican, not for a congress, but to work with the Holy See. Lord grant that I may do my best to serve it."

But his reflection was soon interrupted by the voice of the stewardess: "*Signore, Signori, benvenuti a Roma.* [Ladies and gentlemen, welcome to Rome.] The temperature in the sunlight is 38° C [100° F]. We thank you for flying with our airline, and we wish you a pleasant stay in Rome."

With his small suitcase in hand, Jérôme soon left the cabin and, setting foot on the gangway, was struck by the oppressive heat of the Roman summer. The thick mugginess that hit his face made him hope for an instant that it was due to the exhaust from the engine. "Unfortunately not! This is, indeed, the local temperature", he noted with surprise while walking down the metal steps.

In the taxi that brought him at high speed along the highway lined with parasol pines—clouds of greenery in the azure sky—his eyes contemplated the pleasant Roman countryside. The rose-colored light of that late afternoon awakened the ocher palette of the land and the houses. Everything seemed to vibrate in the creative light of a first day, while the repose of the first evening was already announced in the outstretched shadows of the cypress trees. Even the suburbs blended harmoniously into the decor under that celestial light. Then suddenly, straight ahead, the dome of Saint Peter's loomed, like a blue diamond offered to heaven by human genius, the velvety colors of which are wedded to beauty. It attracts all eyes, until the heartrending moment when the imposing walls of its fortified enclosure snatches it from view. The taxi, hurtling down the via Aurelia, was pitted against those kilometers of Leonine fortifications and, conquered, went off toward the Centro storico [historic district], where Jérôme's hotel was waiting for him, a few steps from the Pantheon.

The next morning, while walking cautiously down the via di Torre Argentina toward the Ponte Sisto, Jérôme tried to gather the ideas that he had exchanged with two friends and advisors in Paris before his departure. On Tuesday, he had taken a bicycle ride to the Basilica of the Sacred Heart, Sacré-Coeur, on Montmartre, to meet Father Gaudillière, with whom he had conversed for three hours and who had given him some very good advice, along with an out-of-date papal yearbook to help him navigate the organizational chart of the Curia. That evening, he had invited Marcel Clément to dinner to discuss with him this conference in Bucharest, some prospects on his return, and the presentation that he had to give to the synod the following October.[2] But this morning, in the little Roman alleys, Jérôme quickly forgot those wise thoughts and glanced with astonishment in all directions. As though delighting in a crèche, he observed with a smile the shivering of the city and the joyous light of morning awakening the façades of the palaces and churches that were still asleep, and he enjoyed losing his way in the maze of alleys in the Trastevere district. A quarter of an hour later, when he finally managed to wrest himself from the charm of these places and arrived in front of the Palace of Saint Callixtus, he was immediately brought to the floor where the meeting would begin.

The delegation was made up of six persons: Father Riedmatten, a Dominican whom Jérôme immediately considered "superb, natural, and funny",[3] Jean Gayon, whom Jérôme liked a lot and who was in charge of the delegation, a very efficient female physician, an Indian sociologist, an African demographer, and Jérôme. The purpose of the delegation was to present the doctrine of the Church intelligently and intelligibly, and the discussions among the members dealt with the best way of developing the arguments, in keeping with the spirit of *Humanae vitae*. During the morning, Archbishop Benelli, the deputy secretary of state, came to say how important he thought this conference was and explained what was at stake for the Holy See. Jérôme was supposed to give a speech on the family and would speak, if necessary, during other sessions. Each one left with three kilograms [6.5 lbs.] of documents in U.N. jargon to digest as quickly as possible.

In Bucharest, Jérôme observed the debates and stood ready to transmit the message of the Holy See. Besides his scheduled speech, he was appointed reporter for an essential session and had to play a much more important role than he had expected in composing and defending the resolution presented by the Holy See.[4] At the conclusion of those longs days of work and debate, which extended from August 18 to 29, Jérôme was satisfied because it seemed that he had been able to get everything necessary into the documents and to avoid what should not appear in them. With this sense of a duty

[2] J. Lejeune, letter to Birthe, July 24, 1974.
[3] Ibid., July 28, 1974.
[4] Ibid., August 8, 1974.

accomplished, he was happy to return to Denmark, where he would finally meet his family again.

Over the next few days, sitting on the pebbles of the beach in Kerteminde, he told Birthe in detail about everyone he had met and the gist of their discussions.

The effusive thanks that he received from Cardinal Villot several weeks later indicated that the Holy See, too, was quite satisfied.

> It is for me a pleasant task to express the Holy See's satisfaction and gratitude to you for the effective way in which you participated in the work of this conference. Your competence and devotion, the team spirit and friendship that animated the delegation of the Holy See, while remaining faithful to Church teaching, allowed it to offer a special contribution to that event. I am anxious to note in particular the help that you gave to the delegation as a man of science due to your information about questions of genetics and by your highly valuable scientific and moral considerations concerning the grave problems of abortion. This is why the Holy Father, who followed closely the development of the conference and the activities of the members of the delegation, asked me to convey to you his heartfelt thanks for your collaboration and for the competence with which you set forth and defended the moral and human arguments of the Holy See.[5]

On October 1, 1974, Jérôme was once again in Rome for his first session of the Pontifical Academy of Sciences and to make an intervention at the Synod of Bishops. After being welcomed at the airport by a French prelate, Msgr. Jacqueline, whom he quickly came to respect as a remarkable man of great faith, he had the pleasure of meeting at the hotel the eminent Professor Carlos Chagas, a physician, biologist, specialist in neuroscience, and son of the famous Brazilian physician by the same name. Chagas was president of the Pontifical Academy of Sciences, and Jérôme was glad that he could continue, during their dinner, the long conversation with him that had started in Paris the preceding August. Their points of view were very close, and the discussion went well.

The next day, Jérôme made use of a free morning to attend Mass in Saint Peter's Basilica, then climbed the countless steps that led him

[5] Jean-Marie Cardinal Villot, letter to J. Lejeune, October 18, 1974.

to the top of the dome, from which he could enjoy a splendid view of Rome and the chain of Appenine Mountains to the east, in the sunlight. From the lantern turret, from which he surveyed the Vatican Gardens with their fountains, their precision-trimmed shrubbery, and their incredible flower beds forming the Holy Father's coat of arms, he could make out, behind a clump of greenery, the Casina Pio IV, the beautiful sixteenth-century pavilion that now housed the Pontifical Academy of Sciences where he was to make a presentation at noon. "The Casina, decorated with remarkable mosaics and frescos and its oval courtyard adorned with fountains and statues, is without the slightest doubt the most delightful academy imaginable", Jérôme reflected, since he knew the reputation of the place. "Moreover, it is time for me to go back down, unless I want to arrive late for my meeting in that charming edifice!" At the Porta Sant'Anna, where he appeared in order to enter the Vatican, Jérôme had the unpleasant surprise of meeting with some difficulty from the Swiss Guard, who conscientiously barred him access. It must be said that Jérôme had nothing with him that proved that he was expected. He had left everything at the hotel that morning when he set out at dawn for Mass. No invitation or nomination on his person! The matter was resolved anyway, and Jérôme was finally accompanied to the Casina, where he was welcomed by the chancellor, Father Rovasenda, whom he described that same evening to Birthe as a "charming, refined, and cultivated" man.[6]

The session at the Academy was followed by a luncheon at the residence of Cardinal Villot, who placed Jérôme at his right and questioned him at length about science, abortion, and respect for life. Jérôme reported French current events to him and shared with him his reflections on the true roots of this battle. He was struck by the charming courtesy and the obvious skill of that sensible man. After that interesting and warm luncheon, Jérôme still had a long afternoon, for he was expected at the Synod of Bishops, where he was to speak at 17:00 [5:00 P.M.]. This conference[7] had demanded of him a lot of work. To speak within the Vatican to the successors of the apostles

[6] J. Lejeune, letter to Birthe, October 1, 1974.

[7] J. Lejeune, "Le message de vie", Synod of Bishops, reprinted in *L'Homme Nouveau* (October 1974).

was a responsibility that he did not take lightly. At the podium, while the moderator was introducing him and highlighting certain aspects of his career, Jérôme observed those attentive men with such diverse physiognomies. Then he spoke and elaborated for them his reflection on the message of life, the natural law, and the appearance of man on the biological scene, taking good care to explain that his Adamic hypothesis was not proved but merely plausible. He also addressed another question that he had at heart: the evangelization of the scientific world. And he spoke frankly. He did not hesitate to say that it is necessary to send missionaries who have the faith and not "ectoplasms that are always ready to renounce it for the latest theory".[8] After the conference, Jérôme was surprised and moved to see so many cardinals and bishops come over to congratulate and thank him. That evening, before going to bed, he wrote to Birthe:

> Some of them were jubilant about some passages. Never have I spoken to such a studious and sympathetic audience. Some heads are admirable, very diverse, but with an astonishing depth. If Philippe had been there, he would never have stopped gazing at them.[9]

Since he was now a member of the Pontifical Academy of Sciences, Jérôme could admire close up the scientific work of the Church in her search for the truth, and he decided to write an article on the subject. In July 1975, he published in the fortnightly French Catholic magazine *L'Homme nouveau* a beautiful essay entitled "Paul VI and Science". The article was read in Rome, and several days later Jérôme received a letter from Cardinal Villot conveying the deep thanks of the Holy Father.[10]

Having successfully carried out the first missions entrusted to him by the Vatican, Jérôme now received regular requests to make a scientific contribution to the Church's reflection on the moral implications of new medical techniques. Cardinal Seper, prefect of the Congregation for the Doctrine of the Faith, asked him for several

[8] These words are a quotation from Jérôme's letter to his wife telling about the conference, and not from the text of the conference itself.

[9] J. Lejeune, letter to Birthe, October 1, 1974. [He refers to his brother, a professional artist.]

[10] Archbishop Benelli, letter to J. Lejeune, July 24, 1975.

notes, in 1975 and 1976, and the Secretariat for Non-Believers, in the person of Monsignor Jacqueline, questioned him regularly, especially about the relations between faith and science.[11] Finally, although Jérôme collaborated like the other academicians on the work of the Pontifical Academy of Sciences, his scientific expertise was specifically solicited by the president of the Academy in order to enrich the Church's reflection on the moral import of certain medical practices.

The Vatican was not the only State to call for his talents. Jérôme was also called on by various countries to testify before their parliaments, which were preparing to modify laws about the beginning of human life. On May 7, 1974, he spoke before the U.S. Senate and appeared there once again in 1976 before the commission on the separation of powers. He was urged also to testify before the Austrian parliament, and he gladly made that trip to Vienna and back in 1976. In the United States, the Bishops' Conference asked his opinion on the apparent neutrality toward abortion of the March of Dimes, an American organization that campaigned for sick children. Jérôme wrote back to Father James T. McHugh, director of the Catholic bishops' committee for pro-life activities:

> Having listened to some representatives from the March of Dimes, I do not think that they reject abortion. There is no doubt that they accept it fully, since they do not reject it at all.[12]

At the same time, Jérôme saw his "dance card" filling up with an increasing number of invitations to give conferences. For his fellow physicians, for students of major schools such as the Polytechnique or Navale, or for the general public in Limoges, Sénanque, or at the church of Saint-Louis-des-Français in Rome on May 19, 1975.

Of all these requests, one in particular would impress Jérôme by the warmth of the welcome that he received and the dynamism of the local community. Whereas the West had closed, with the declining number of invitations to the United States (where, from the vantage point of France, the Far West meets the Far East), new

[11] Monsignor Jacqueline, letter to J. Lejeune, May 16, 1975.

[12] J. Lejeune, letter to Father James T. McHugh, July 21, 1976. These words concern the March of Dimes in 1976; they do not prejudge the situation at the moment when this book is being written.

venues opened up for him: New Zealand and Australia begged Jérôme to pay them a visit and extended his horizons.

It all started with a letter that arrived at rue Galande, dated August 30, 1974, and sent from Wellington, New Zealand.[13] It was from Doctor Bergin, a neurologist and a member of the Guild of Saints Luke, Cosmas, and Damian and vice-president of the Society for the Protection of the Unborn Child created by Sir William Liley, who ten years earlier had performed the first intrauterine blood transfusion in the world. Quite aware of Jérôme's reputation through his meetings and lectures, he wanted to invite him to be the featured speaker at their next congress on respect for life the following year, and the program promised to be packed with conferences, interviews, and scientific meetings. Jérôme accepted and, therefore, flew to Wellington in October 1975.

To the originally scheduled series of events, the organizers had added a new, important speech, and this program left Jérôme no respite. As soon as his plane landed in New Zealand, he was welcomed by the Royal Commission in Auckland to testify scientifically about the beginnings of human life. Despite the fatigue of the journey and the change of time zone, Jérôme endured four straight hours of hearings and answers to objections, which were exhausting but obviously appreciated. On the evening of that first day, drained, Jérôme had just enough strength to write to Birthe:

> My little Darling, what a rough day! This morning a hearing at 10:00 before the Royal Commission. I thought it would take me a half hour. But at half past noon, the cross-examination had not ended. It is just like in the Agatha Christie novels: each group, the Right-to-Life and the abortionists, has its appointed attorney who grills the witnesses. The one who attacked me was a certain F. He tried to sweet-talk me,... but he was out to earn his fee. It resumed at 2:00 and ended, with a knock-out of said F., at around 2:40. As soon as I returned to the Lileys' house, I was making a film with all the neighbors' children and the little trisomic girl. Scene after scene. That brought us to dinner. Then at 7:30, cocktail hour with the local Laissez-les-vivre [Let them live] group and then a long session with a conference. I was exhausted, and my speech was mediocre. They were very nice

[13] J. Bergin, letter to J. Lejeune, August 30, 1974.

anyway and thanked me profusely. It was already midnight, and I could no longer keep standing, or even sitting! With all my heart I kiss you, my little Darling, and our five with you. Your loving Jérôme.[14]

On the following days, Jérôme gave one conference after another to the local associations. He was impressed by the people whom he met: "All these Catholic New Zealanders are solid, brave, and devout", but he observed also that "they let themselves be maneuvered by the 'tricks' of the pro-aborts." He therefore made use of that series of meetings to "put them on guard, to vaccinate them",[15] hoping that they would resist the pressure better than the French had done. He also gave conferences at the medical school and at the laboratory for human genetics, where he was awaited impatiently by Doctor H.R. McCreanor,[16] whom he had taken on as an intern in Paris in 1973, and, since he was in that part of the world, he accepted the invitation from the University of Sydney in Australia. That first journey to New Zealand and Australia, at the initiative of Sir Liley, who hosted him and would become a dear friend, was for Jérôme the beginning of a long and productive collaboration with the local Christians, whose devotion he admired. This successful trip earned him another invitation a few months later, this time from Patricia Judge, a member of the Right to Life association in Sydney, who requested that he make a grand tour of Australia.[17] Jérôme's work schedule was so busy that he gladly accepted, but for 1978, two years later!

Birthe, who was not afraid of fatigue but knew the limited resistance of her husband, sometimes wondered how he kept up that pace: "He used to say that he was weak and lazy, yet he became the support, the inspiration, the hope of thousands of people in France and throughout the world. He never stops, and he strengthens everyone." She admired his fortitude, a virtue that she did not recognize in him when they were first married. "How does he do it?" she wondered.

In order to bear up under the pressure of that flood of activities and tribulations, Jérôme relied on the love of his wife and children.

[14] J. Lejeune, letter to Birthe, October 7, 1975.

[15] Ibid., October 10, 1975.

[16] H.R. McCreanor, letter to J. Lejeune, March 25, 1975.

[17] P. Judge, letter to J. Lejeune, September 1976, and Jérôme's response, dated September 20, 1976.

His family was his source of energy. But it was not the only one. In the agitation of his life, he prized the time set aside for prayer, so as to draw from the very source of love. That love is what kept him going. In his very heavy schedule, he always found some way of participating in Sunday Mass, praying, and meditating on the Bible. His fidelity to the Mass impressed his professional entourage. One of his colleagues remarked to him one day, "I don't know how you do it. At congresses in the United States or elsewhere, you always find the time to go to Mass. We never do!"[18]

When returning from his travels, if he had not been able to attend Sunday Mass before catching the plane, Jérôme went in the evening, at the Cathedral of Notre-Dame, despite the fatigue and jet lag. In the summer, in Denmark, this diligence was not always easy, either. The Catholic church was several dozen kilometers [more than 15 miles] distant, and it was rare to find young Danes present at Mass. Therefore his children, who felt the appeal of the beach, were not always motivated. One day one of them asked him: "Papa, what good does it do to go there? We don't understand a thing, the priest is Polish, he says the Mass in Danish, and the people there are Vietnamese; it is complicated to follow!"

Jérôme replied: "Yes. But it is important to go there. We have a date with the Lord, and when you love someone, you don't skip dates. You must never give way in this."

On Sunday morning, at departure time, Jérôme was always the first one ready and was waiting at the wheel for the stragglers to arrive finally. When they were in Paris, they attended Mass at Saint-Séverin, unless they were in the country, in which case they went to the little parish church of Chalo-Saint-Mars. For years they used to participate in the Mass in Étampes, where Jérôme sang wholeheartedly in the ranks of the beautiful choir directed by his old friend Raymond Legrand. Then a new priest, a zealous liturgical reformer, chased all those musicians away; they found refuge in the church in Chalo-Saint-Mars, where the pastor, Father Santa Catarina, joyfully welcomed them. Jérôme liked to get involved in the parish, and, wearing his rugged corduroy trousers and the thick sweater that Birthe had knit for him, he was happy to swell the ranks of the choir

[18] Conversation of the author with that scientist, A. B.

or to read the second reading, after Monsieur Leriche had read the first. Jérôme liked that simple, prayerful ambiance. Very often, after Mass, Birthe and Jérôme invited their parish friends to savor their Sunday rest over a good aperitif, served in the garden or beside the fireplace, depending on the season.

On weekdays, too, from time to time, when he could, Jérôme participated in an evening Mass. Before returning to rue Galande, when his multiple responsibilities allowed him, he would then stop at Saint-Sulpice or Saint-Séverin to attend Mass there and, during that special time of recollection after the whirlwind of the day, to draw the strength to continue his fight for human life.

As a physician, Jérôme was particularly sensitive to the physical presence of Christ in the Eucharist. This corporeal dimension of the Real Presence in the Host fascinated him, and he received Communion very devoutly. After Communion, he would recollect himself, his head bowed slightly, as though he wanted to hear Him better. His attention to Christ's Body was manifested also in the smallest things. One day he found in a trash can a crucifix without arms and could not bear it. He retrieved it so as to make wooden arms for it in his studio in Chalo.

He also spent precious moments meditating on the Word of God; he was drawn particularly to Genesis, the Prologue of Saint John, and the Gospel of Saint Luke because, as a good physician, the latter Evangelist gave astonishing details. Little by little, biblical references were woven into his letters, personal reflections, and conferences, whether or not they were explicit, and sometimes he confided the fruit of his meditations to an attentive audience:

> The most famous of all physicians, the one whose written work remains a best seller in all categories—I am speaking about Saint Luke—reveals to us in a few words the marvels of the most tender infancy. Reread the Visitation. How old was the little prophet who jumped inside Elizabeth at the approach of Mary, who was carrying Our Lord? Six months *in utero*. Saint Luke as a good physician recorded this detail for us; the angel himself, moreover, had told Mary this. But how old was the human form of Jesus then? Saint Luke does not say but simply notes that right after the announcement by the angel, the Blessed Virgin hastened to visit her cousin: *Maria festinavit*. In that land of Galilee, distances are not very great and journeys are not long, even on a

> donkey, even on foot. At the moment of the Visitation, therefore, the human form of Jesus was incredibly young, only a few days, maybe a week.... And yet John, the little prophet—six months older, it is true—jumped for joy at his arrival! If doctors nowadays reread this Gospel passage, they would understand with their hearts that science does not deceive them when it forces them, by reason, to acknowledge that Being starts at conception. Like the Magi, like every human being, doctors have everything to learn in the school of Jesus.[19]

Perhaps because of the influence of Father Balsan, his teacher at Stanislas College who invited the boys to pray the rosary in order to become men, Jérôme had great devotion to the Blessed Virgin, whom he explicitly chose as his guide when making a difficult discernment, and his affection was expressed in simple gestures. He prayed to her unostentatiously during his long Sunday walks in the fields of wheat that overlooked the little house in saint-Hilaire, and when he found a bit of tranquility in his studio, in the back of the garden, he could spend hours meditating and minutely sculpting a decade rosary out of bone or boxwood, which he then offered to a relative or friend with these instructions: "This rosary is guaranteed not to wear out; you can use it as often as you like. And you can say one Hail Mary for the craftsman."

As a contemplative, Jérôme appreciated the calm of their country house, hidden in the hollow of a green valley, and happily surveyed the golden fields that stretched out lazily on the plateau beneath the village. Everything was a cause for wonder: the instinct of the partridge protecting her little one against the importunate stroller and the gracefulness of the hawthorns in flower. Those close to him knew that those long walks were a prayer, a moment of eternity in the midst of the whirlwind of life. From it, Jérôme derived his inspiration and thanked God, who had created everything so beautifully. This interior dialogue between the Christian scientist and his Creator was a prayer that engaged the whole man. Jérôme then became a poet:

> The weather had suddenly cleared, and a splendid sky enshrined the fields, which, already harvested, were turning yellow with stubble and

[19] J. Lejeune, "Les docteurs devant Jésus" [Doctors in the presence of Jesus], a text cited many times, for example, in *Le sourire de Marie*, a parish newsletter, 1977, or at a conference of the Catholic Family Association in Lorient on November 28, 1989.

> cut straw. Stretched out on a pile of straw in the middle of the field, I spent a delicious moment observing the subtlety of the atmosphere that surrounds the planet.[20]

In 1977, during one of those beautiful summer days, Jérôme welcomed a young priest from the vicinity of Étampes who wanted to interview him for his parish newsletter, *Le Sourire de Marie* [Mary's smile]. Jérôme gladly took part in the exercise and for the first time confided in an interviewer in his answers about the faith. He took care to explain by way of an introduction:

> You ought to have questioned the little catechism of our childhood and not the physician and geneticist that I am today. Faced with the mysteries of God, the biologist is just as poor as the juggler of yore who, in order to honor Our Lady, naïvely resorted to the finest acts of his art! Although science has fewer charms than a grateful acrobat, and less skill, too, allow me to answer you in the language that is familiar to me.

With a notebook on his knees and a ballpoint pen in his right hand, the priest started the little tape recorder and, slightly intimidated, began:

"Tell us, Professor Lejeune, what would you say if Jesus Christ asked you: 'And you, who do you say that I am?' "

Jérôme reflected, then answered: "The true son of Being. All the information, present and gathered, animating matter in a human form."

After hastily scrawling the answer, the young priest continued: "Professor, do you love Mary? If so, why?"

"This is the wonder of all wonders. Biology teaches us that every living being owes its nature to the genetic message that animates it and gives it life. In order for the whole message (the working of the Holy Spirit) to be able to find a place and to take flesh (Incarnation) in Mary, the Virgin had to be conceived in the state of perfection itself (Immaculate Conception), free from all hereditary imperfection (original sin) ... and the theologians already knew that before genetics was even invented!"

The priest, intensely interested, quickly checked to make sure that the tape recorder was working, then, turning to Jérôme, posed the following question to him: "For you, what does the Eucharist represent?"

[20] J. Lejeune, letter to Birthe, August 5, 1973.

After a moment of silence, Jérôme said, with a smile: "Jesus. But the mystery of the Real Presence is experienced in very different ways, as we see from the following crude, clumsy comparison: the antenna of a broadcasting radio, vibrating to the electromagnetic message conveying the most beautiful music, let's say the *Magnificat*. Three observers, each armed with a transistor radio, discuss this phenomenon. The first, who is not tuned in and therefore receives nothing, says that positively and materially nothing is happening. The second, better informed, tunes his apparatus and hears the *Magnificat*. But if he turns his receiver off, he no longer hears anything. He says that the message is only potential and protests that it exists only for the one who receives it. Finding this argument not very catholic, the third decisively remarks that his transistor radio still works even when his neighbor has turned off his own. From this he concludes that the message really exists even if no one captures it. Of course, the Real Presence is completely disproportionate to a radio emission, but, however much it may limp, this comparison helps us to define transubstantiation: during the emission, the most careful examination of the antenna would show that the atoms of the metal are quite unchanged in their chemical properties or in their position. An electronics expert speaking the language of the theologians (you see that wonders hardly intimidate me) would say that 'under the species [or appearances]' of the metal there is a message that absolutely transcends them."

Finally abandoning his notes, which have become useless, in order to concentrate on the implications of these words, the interviewer continued: "Do you love the Church? What is it, in your opinion?"

"A family that recognizes itself, since the faithful know that they are children of the same Father. The expression 'Holy Mother the Church' is an objective description."

"Professor, what value do you assign to prayer?"

"It is tuning one's interior transistor, connecting with the Creator."

The formula made the young priest smile. "Well, well! I could use that formula for the youth group that I direct!" he said to himself before asking another question:

"Professor Lejeune, what is the ideal of holiness and the way to attain it?"

"Holiness is the ideal. We reach toward it and scarcely arrive at it. But we can allow ourselves to be led to it."

"Do you like the Bible? Why?"

"It is the Book, the only one that has no need of a title.... Genesis says more about [human life] in three pages than all the treatises do."

"What does the pope represent for you?"

"The authorized representative for the whole family."

The priest smiled again at this unexpected answer, then announced: "Professor, this is my last question: In the Church, what should be the role of the priests, the religious, and the lay faithful?"

This time Jérôme did not have to reflect for long in order to answer with enthusiasm: "The priests must be faithful, and the faithful—religious."[21]

[21] J. Lejeune, interviewed in *Le sourire de Marie*, a parish newsletter, 1977. The interview, presented for the purposes of this book as a conversation, in fact took place in writing. All of Jérôme's answers reprinted here are exact quotations.

CHAPTER 11

THE GRAIN OF SAND

1978–1980

"Mama, can I come to lunch today with a friend from the Poli-Sci [Paris Institute of Political Studies]?"

"Of course, my dear", Birthe answered spontaneously. "Just be on time!"

"Yes, yes, don't worry", Clara answered, laughing, before kissing her mother on the cheek. "My little Mama, you are really great. The house is always full of people that we bring in from all over, and you find that quite normal! And even when ten of us turn up for dinner, without warning you, it is no problem at all. You are incredible! Thanks!"

Then she ran out of the house and rapidly went back up the rue Dante and the boulevard Saint-Germain to arrive on time on rue Saint-Guillaume.

At lunch, Clara introduced to her parents her guest, Kacim Kellal, and a conversation quickly started between Jérôme and the young man she had invited. The children were used to it, because every time they came with friends, the latter, captivated by their father, would bombard him with questions, which he would answer gladly, with great kindness. At dessert that day, the conversation was about the natural law, and Jérôme humorously gave his opinion:

"From my personal experience, I get the impression that human nature is obvious to everyone, provided he does not refuse to see. When I am in a city that I do not know, I visit, if I can, two equally instructive places: the university and the zoological garden. In the universities, I have always met extremely learned people who shake their heads, wondering whether, all things considered, their children, when they are very young, are not some sorts of animals. But in the zoological gardens, I have never observed congresses of chimpanzees wondering whether, all things considered, their children, when they are grown up, will not become academics!"[1]

They all burst into laughter, including Kacim, whose reserve, dictated by his good education, melted like snow in the sunlight when it met the family's simplicity and warmth.

"I conclude from this", Jérôme continued more seriously, "that human nature is obvious to everyone. On this planet, man is the only being to ask himself where he comes from, who he is, and what he has done with his brother."[2]

Then Clara asked: "If there is a human nature, does that imply that there is a natural law?"

"Yes," Jérôme replied, "and a sensible man would derive great profit from respecting it, since it is the instruction manual of his own nature."

"And yet," he said, smiling, "morality has never gotten good press. It has always embarrassed the people who would have liked to get rid of their neighbor when he bothered them, to rob him of his things when they envied them, to take his wife, et cetera.... Look at the usual behavior of drivers: generally they do not read the maintenance notes, they neglect the user's manual, and, as for the rules of the road, as soon as they can break them, they do. This is exactly what happens in the field of morality. Still, we cannot imagine rather heavy traffic without rules of the road, without maintenance notes, and without a user's manual. In the same way, we cannot conceive of the life of human beings without some morality."[3]

Kacim, whose Muslim faith agreed very well with this observation, then asked: "And what do you see as the consequence of this on the political level?"

"Political leaders have immense responsibilities", Jérôme replied. "In order for civilization to last, politics will necessarily have to conform to morality: to the morality that transcends all ideologies

[1] J. Lejeune, testimony to the Parliament in Ottawa, March 21, 1990.

[2] J. Lejeune, "The Human Condition and Supernatural Morals", conference in Rome, November 1989.

[3] J. Lejeune, "Je n'aime pas qu'on parle d'éthique quand il s'agit de morale" [I don't like talking about ethics when it is a matter of morality], *France catholique* 1993 (March 1985).

because it is inscribed in our inmost depths, by that impenetrable decree that governs both the laws of the universe and the nature of human beings."[4]

Then, before someone in the party could speak again, he added: "The quality of a civilization is measured by the respect that it has for its weakest members. There is no other criterion of judgment. All the love, all the devotion, all the money that is expended to protect those whom life has handicapped are the price, and the fair price, that a society must pay in order to remain humane. We can envisage, certainly, a technocratic society in which they would kill the elderly and the abnormal, and in which they would finish off those who were injured in a traffic accident. That society would perhaps be economically efficient, but that society would be inhumane. It would be completely perverted by a racism that is as stupid and as despicable as all the other kinds, the racism of the well against the sick."[5]

Karin asked in turn: "Papa, people often talk about ethics but never about morality; are ethics and morality two different things? What do you think?"

Jérôme answered: "When I hear talk about ethics, I am on guard: the people who talk about ethics often want to throw out morality. Although these two words, one Greek, the other Latin, designate exactly the same thing, namely, the science of morals, we have noticed for several years a distortion of the meaning: the one who speaks about morality understands that morals ought to conform to higher laws, whereas the one who speaks about ethics implies that the laws ought to conform to morals ... even very inferior morals!"[6]

When he left the house after lunch, Kacim could not get over it. He wanted to call all his friends to tell them about that incredible encounter. Deeply moved, he said to Clara: "Clara, I have to tell you something."

She looked at him, intrigued, and he went on:

"Listen, it is incredible. You kindly invited me to meet your father. I had heard a lot about him from my friends who are studying medicine; for me, it was almost as though I were meeting Professor

[4] J. Lejeune, "Hommage à Sakharov", Moscow, June 29, 1987.

[5] J. Lejeune, interviewed by M. Leclercq, "Oui il faut les laisser vivre", *Paris Match*, November 7, 1980.

[6] J. Lejeune, "Je n'aime pas qu'on parle d'éthique".

Fleming, who discovered penicillin. I was completely intimidated. Then, as soon as your father spoke to me, it was all gone. He, the great scientist, spoke to me as though I were bringing him all the news in the world, as though I were going to open to him all the doors in the world, in the universe. Such a great man welcomes you, listens to you, makes jokes, and when he speaks to you, you have his attention, he is not somewhere else, he is not lost in his thoughts! When he looked at me, I had the impression that I was the center of the world, that there was no one but me! I will never forget his look."[7]

Clara started to laugh: "You seem to be captivated!"

"Yes, that is the word, I was completely captivated by him", Kacim replied seriously. "What's more, you all welcomed me as though I were a child of the family, with incredible warmth and cordiality. You have extraordinary parents. In Arabic we would say: 'Your house is the house of God.'"[8]

Clara looked at him again and said, this time seriously, "Yes, you are right. I am very fortunate."

One of the acquaintances whom the children regularly invited to the house was a friend of Damien, Aimé Ravel, whom he had met at the students' Mass; he was in his second year of medical school and was taking the courses in genetics given by Professor Lejeune. And so, when Damien invited him to come to lunch on rue Galande, Aimé accepted enthusiastically, although the idea of sitting at the table of that great professor frightened him terribly. During the lunch, Aimé was stunned to see the simplicity with which Jérôme welcomed him and took an interest in him. Like Kacim, he had the impression of being unique in his sight, and he was very surprised when, at the end of the meal, Jérôme suggested that they continue their discussion from time to time at his laboratory. From then on, Aimé, the young second-year student, met Professor Lejeune month after month to converse with him on a wide variety of topics.

That was also the time when Anouk announced to her parents her desire to marry a young philosopher, Jean-Marie Meyer, with whom Jérôme and Birthe had been well acquainted ever since his father, a physician, had participated with Jérôme in a television program

[7] These are the exact words of Kacim Kellal telling the author about his meeting with Jérôme Lejeune.

[8] Ibid.

on respect for human life. The marriage took place in 1976 to the great joy of everyone. While they were celebrating the newlyweds, another Jean-Marie, whose surname Le Méné reveals his Breton origins, took his first steps in the family circle that day. He was a guest of Karin, a student friend whom she had met shortly before at the Journée du livre d'Assas [a book fair] and who hoped to become a captain in the navy. Invited more and more frequently to the house on rue de Galande, he relished these meetings with Jérôme, to whom he had already listened with admiration at the congresses in Lausanne that he had attended as an adolescent with his father.

Although Jérôme and Birthe had not been surprised when Anouk had announced her engagement, they were when Damien informed them of his decision. He had just received his diploma in physical therapy and, when they were discussing with him the future and his job prospects, Damien told them: "In a week I am leaving for the seminary. I am going to the Saint Martin community."

When the moment of surprise had passed, Jérôme expressed his joy and said to his son: "If God is calling you, it is an honor for the family. I am very proud." And Damien left Paris to enter the seminary the following week.

While the children were taking flight, each according to his age, Jérôme continued to work on the development of his laboratory. In January 1977, he received a letter from the administration informing him that the director of the CNRS was renewing his associated research team. Alas, this almost automatic notification was not accompanied by any sign of an increase in financing for his research projects. Jérôme was therefore compelled once again to apply to French and foreign organizations for subsidies in order to make the laboratory function effectively.

In April, Jérôme flew to the U.S.S.R. for a mission entrusted to him by the Ministry for Foreign Affairs. He was to meet his Soviet colleagues in Moscow and Leningrad. He started with the School of Genetics in Leningrad. Since his interview with Professor Davidenkova, scheduled long before, was cancelled at the last minute, without explanation, Jérôme continued his visit with the Institute for Genetics in Moscow, directed by Professor Bochkov, who proved to be extremely active. He observed that many studies on the replication of chromosomes were being conducted there very skillfully, and he congratulated himself on the fact that the scientific cooperation between the Moscow Institute and his laboratory at the Institut de Progénèse was so effective. In the report that he sent to the Ministry for Foreign Affairs upon his return, Jérôme explained:

> Our Russian colleagues asked me to present the state of our research projects at several conferences in the Institutes in Moscow and Leningrad, and the desire among them for an overture is quite palpable. On several points, our Russian colleagues need our help, both in rare chemicals and in the exchange of young researchers. It seems to me that the most important service that we can render to them would be to promote travel to Paris by young (or not-so-young) researchers who wish to familiarize themselves with the most recent methods. Although the French scientific literature reaches Moscow and Leningrad, it is extremely difficult for them to keep up with the latest developments, and visiting French laboratories is of prime importance for them.[9]

Then he concluded by explaining:

> Out of friendship and subsequent to this mission, our colleagues proposed that I act as vice-president of the next congress on general genetics in Moscow (August 21–30, 1978). I very gladly accepted this responsibility, which is more honorific than active, considering that Western scientific thought can give much to a country that not long ago subjected all geneticists to the intellectual dictatorship of one Lysenko.[10]

Besides those travels in the U.S.S.R., Jérôme participated in several congresses during that first semester, in Finland, Switzerland, and Belgium. After the summer, he had to depart again for New York and Washington, where he had been invited by Professor Hellegers to give a conference for the Kennedy Foundation at Georgetown University.[11] Upon return from a short trip to the United Kingdom for a speech at the Center for Cancer Research and at La Maison

[9] J. Lejeune, report sent to the Minister of Foreign Affairs, December 19, 1977.
[10] Ibid.
[11] A. Hellegers, letter to Jérôme, July 28, 1977.

Française [French house], Jérôme received an invitation to speak in Milan, in June 1978, to a congress on the family. This congress would be inaugurated by a young Polish cardinal, Karol Cardinal Wojtyła, but Jérôme, unable to accept all the increasingly numerous invitations throughout the world to testify in favor of human life and the family, did not know whether he could participate. He declined invitations when there was a schedule conflict with scientific congresses or when he had to concentrate on his projects. The search for a treatment for his patients was his priority, and that meant giving up some things. And so he confided one day to a female friend who sent him requests for articles and conferences:

> I am truly sorry that I cannot give you a better answer. But I am so swamped, with all the articles and conferences that I have to prepare, that I am not managing to face up to all my duties. The work at the laboratory is going full speed ahead, and I think that it is more important to be operational on the medical level so as to help the children who are threatened than to tell other people what they ought to do for them.[12]

Besides these minor, everyday discernments, the month of November 1977 was for Jérôme the opportunity for a more radical choice. In mid-November he received at the laboratory on rue de l'École de Médecine a nice letter postmarked Washington. With a smile on his lips, he opened the envelope quickly, because he rarely received bad news from the United States, more often some help, and in these difficult times for the laboratory, any financial aid would be welcome. But this time the lines that he scanned surpassed his wildest imagination. They were from Sargent Shriver, the husband of Eunice Kennedy:

> Dear Doctor Lejeune,
>
> I have a little free time this morning and want to take this opportunity to assure you that you could render a great service to genetics and to the Church by spending an academic year as a visiting professor at the Kennedy Institute and at Georgetown Medical School.

[12] J. Lejeune, letter to P. Judge, October 1, 1978.

Once again I send you my most cordial invitation.... Washington, D.C. offers an extraordinary concentration of physicians and excellent scientists.... Your scientific ardor and your renown would also be an inspiration for the Catholic scientists of the United States.... Our great poet William Shakespeare wrote [in *Julius Caesar*]: "There is a tide in the affairs of men which, taken at the flood, leads on to fortune." I think that this moment has arrived here, in America, and I also think that you can help in an exceptional way to derive the maximum benefit from this extraordinary scientific, intellectual, and religious opportunity. The United States holds such an influential place in the intellectual world and in science that we should not miss this chance to take a position there, and from there, like Archimedes, we could lift the world.

Cordially yours, Sargent Shriver.[13]

For a moment, Jérôme was disturbed and moved by so much enthusiasm. These lines opened up for him the royal doors of a scientific paradise. "The offer is tempting. It seems that there is in fact a historical conjunction that would allow me to nudge things to a higher level, without totally abandoning my ongoing research projects. What should I do?"

Jérôme took several days to reflect and then replied:

Dear Monsieur Sargent Shriver, I was very moved by your very kind letter, and your description of a stay at the Kennedy Institute strongly resembles a scientific Eden.[14]

Then he declined that magnificent invitation, explaining to Sargent Shriver that he had to complete an ongoing therapeutic study on trisomic children and his research projects on the congruence code. He was aware that he was passing up an offer that would not be repeated, but his decision was clear. Right there in Paris was where he could best advance his research projects, and that was the primary factor in his decisions. Upon reading that reply, Sargent Shriver was greatly disappointed, but he promised aid for Jérôme's research projects. He subsequently kept his promise. From then on, the Kennedy

[13] S. Shriver, letter to J. Lejeune, November 10, 1977.

[14] J. Lejeune, letter to S. Shriver, November 22, 1977.

Foundation would regularly allocate to Jérôme subsidies that would very quickly prove to be indispensable ...

In February 1978, Jérôme departed for Australia, where he was invited for the second time. Patricia Judge,[15] who was very devoted to the pro-life cause, organized this tour and prepared for him a program of conferences and interviews in Sydney, Darwin, and Melbourne, which did not leave him a moment of respite. Universities, associations, televised panels: he responded successfully and devotedly to all these requests and received once again an incredible reception in that part of the world. One of the organizers confided to Jérôme at the end of his trip:[16]

> I would like to tell you how much I appreciated your participation in the seminar on trisomy 21 at the University of New South Wales in Sydney. Scientifically, your contribution was fascinating, and the audience present at your conference included most of the specialists in cytogenetics in Sydney. They told me that few among them had ever had the chance to hear a speaker with your knowledge, experience, and very creative way of thinking. Even more important was your intervention at the end of the day, and the fact that such an eminent scientist should defend handicapped preborn children greatly encouraged those who share that opinion and led those who thought that aborting those children was the best possible treatment to reconsider their position.[17]

Jérôme had scarcely returned to Paris when he received a long letter from Patricia Judge thanking him warmly and inviting him to come back as soon as possible to crisscross the country, this time with Birthe.

In the following months, Jérôme responded to several invitations that led him to Sweden, where he was officially received as a new member of the Royal Academy of Sciences, to Egypt for a symposium on genetics, to Germany and the Academy of Sciences in Munich, then in late June to Italy to visit the faculty of medicine in Milan, and finally in July to Canada for a conference at the medical school in Winnipeg.

[15] P. Judge, letter to J. Lejeune, February 22, 1978.
[16] B. Kearny, letter to J. Lejeune, March 9, 1978.
[17] University of New South Wales.

In August, Jérôme flew to Moscow to participate in the 14th Congress on Genetics; he had accepted the position of vice president the preceding year during the mission that he performed for the Ministry of Foreign Affairs. Unfortunately, political events would give an unexpected twist to this congress, and the scientists would be divided about what decision to make. One of their Russian confreres, the biologist Sergei Kovalev (sometimes spelled Kovalyov) had been arrested because of his dissident opinions and sentenced to seven years detention in a work camp with a stringent regime, then to three years in exile. In order to make known their deep disagreement, some physicians decided to boycott the meeting. Jérôme chose another path that seemed to him to correspond better to the needs of science: he would participate in the congress, so as not to do the Russian geneticists an injustice, but would inform the political authorities of what he thought. He offered to be the official bearer of the petition denouncing that arrest and asking for the release of Kovalev, which he would deliver to the organizers of the congress. On the scientific level, he also intended to refute the errors of the Marxist genetics of Lysenko, as he had done in his preceding speech in Moscow. Science is not always as objective as people think ...

In Moscow, as planned, Jérôme demonstrated during his conference the serious errors of Lysenkoism and delivered the petition to the congress authorities, which won him warm thanks from those in charge of the committee in defense of the biologists who were imprisoned for their opinion:

> Dear Professor, you were so kind, during the 14th Congress on Genetics, to deliver personally to Professor Bochkov the petition for the release of S. Kovalev, a petition launched by our committee. We are anxious to convey to you our thanks for this gesture, which, we hope, will help S. Kovalev and with him all those in the Soviet Union who are deprived of their liberty because of their opinion.[18]

How astonished he was, then, when after his return, while browsing through the newspapers that had piled up during his absence, he discovered in the August 21 issue of *Le Quotidien du Médecin*[19] an

[18] D. Anxolabehere and G. Periquet, letter to J. Lejeune, September 15, 1978.

[19] M.-C. Tesson Millet, "Est-Ouest", *Le Quotidien du Médecin*, August 21, 1978.

article stating that Professor Lejeune was one of the few physicians who had refused to sign the petition in favor of releasing Kovalev and that he did not denounce Lysenkoism during his conference.... Finally, Jérôme discovered in that article that he would gladly have participated in a congress in Nazi Germany.... Quite a bit scandalized by such a tissue of untruths, Jérôme took up his pen and composed on September 7 a firmly worded letter addressed to the attention of Doctor Marie-Claude Tesson Millet, editor-in-chief of *Le Quotidien du Médecin*, of whom he requested the right to respond:

> Madame, upon my return from the Moscow congress on genetics, I was surprised at the smear campaign conducted by your newspaper. In an initial article (no. 1741) Doctor G.K. put into my mouth the words: "I would have traveled to a congress in Nazi Germany in 1939"; an ambiguous phrase that you reprinted in your editorial (no. 1743) and that *Le Canard enchaîné* [a satirical weekly newspaper] did not fail to reprint, too! If your coworker had honestly intended to inform his readers about the telephone interview that I had granted to him, he would have to have included a more complete citation. Here it is: "In speaking about general genetics at the Moscow congress, I will not feel that I am approving the gulag any more than I get the impression of approving of the Veil Law [which decriminalized abortion] when I practice human genetics in France. I would have traveled to a congress on genetics in Nazi Germany in 1939 to say that racism is a scientific error." And in that spirit I accepted the vice-presidency of the Moscow congress.
>
> My short speech at the plenary session in the palace of the Kremlin denounced the imposture of Lysenkoism, which put all Russian biologists under the reign of a pseudo-scientific dictatorship. In an article in issue no. 1749, your correspondent Nicolas Miletitch, reporting on that inaugural session, regrets that there was no discussion of Lysenkoism! Either that gentleman was absent during the session of which I am speaking, or else he understands neither English nor Russian (French was not the official language of that meeting).
>
> On the other hand, he proves to have a remarkable imagination when he has me declare, again in that inaugural session: "The meeting in Moscow offers great opportunities on the level of personal contacts and the exchange of ideas." Now, in my forty-minute presentation, I spoke about only two things: first, Lysenkoism and, then, mental handicaps, without a single word about the congress. Perhaps the commentator reads the local daily newspapers too much!

But the most surprising thing is that speaking about the petition to release the researcher Sergei Kovalev, that same Monsieur Miletitch notes without batting an eyelid: "The French delegation supports this initiative except for a few individuals, including Professor Lejeune." But I am the one who, on behalf of the French delegation, delivered the petition signed by 160 French scientists requesting an end to the detention of our colleague Kovalev into the hands of Professor Bochkov, the president of the committee that organized the congress!

I by no means mix politics and science, but given this systematic distortion of the facts, you will understand, I think, Madame, that these false articles bordering on defamation call for a complete correction. This is why I demand that you publish on the front page, as your editorial, the present letter without modification or omission.

Please be so kind as to accept, Madame, the expression of my distinguished consideration.[20]

This was not the only occasion on which Jérôme had to assert a right to respond. He sent several similar letters over the course of those years, including one to a Christian newspaper that never allowed him to write a column for them but cited his words only to distort them. True to his custom, Jérôme sought, not to defend himself, but to correct the errors or the lies that were uttered against him. For he knew that, through him personally, they were seeking to discredit his activity in the service of the trisomic children and the preborn children. He could not consent to that. Therefore, he responded conscientiously and firmly, whenever he considered it useful for his patients and for the pro-life cause.

While Jérôme was treated that way by the French media, he was regularly solicited as an expert before courts and tribunals in the United States. The first case occurred in the month of May. Jérôme received a letter from the Right to Life Association,[21] requesting his assistance in the "Barbara Lee Davis affair" that was shaking Illinois. The courts had to give a decision in the case of an abortion performed after the legal limit of the twelfth week of pregnancy. Although it was not the first time that an abortion was performed outside of the legally prescribed period, it was the first time that the size of the fetus

[20] J. Lejeune, letter to Doctor Tesson-Millet, *Le Quotidien du Médecin*, September 7, 1978.

[21] The Right to Life Association, letter to J. Lejeune, May 15, 1978.

made it possible to prove that it had passed the age limit for abortion. The whole dossier was sent to Jérôme, who confirmed:

> Given the medical dossier, the fetus is sixteen weeks old, and in no case can it be eleven weeks old, as the gynecologist claims, unless it was suffering from a kind of gigantism never before observed in the human species.[22]

Several months later, his opinion was solicited once again in the United States, concerning a little boy, John,[23] whose parents did not want him to have a heart operation because he was trisomic. This time again, Jérôme did not need to travel; his written opinion would suffice in court. He studied the dossier attentively and responded:

> It seems to me that the decision must be based on two simple and universal principles of medicine:
>
> –Every human being has the right to receive the full care of the medical arts, including a delicate operation, that is available in the current state of our knowledge. This applies regardless of age, sex, race, or any psychological or genetic characteristic that human diversity may present.
>
> –Any decision concerning a life-saving operation, such as cardiac surgery, can be made only after having weighed prudently the advantages and the disadvantages of the operation, and the advantages and disadvantages of refraining from it, for the life and well-being of the patient himself.

Jérôme continued:

> Applied to John, these two principles mean, in my opinion, that the reasons for refusing to have him undergo surgery are not acceptable.

Then he concluded with his characteristic logic:

> Every human being has the right to receive the full care of the medical arts. John's life must be protected, as it is, just like the life of

[22] J. Lejeune, letter to the Right to Life Association, May 1978.

[23] The name has been changed.

any person. If a person's handicap could be a reason to refrain from obtaining care for him, that would lead to the conclusion that only persons in excellent health could receive excellent medical care.[24]

In February 1979, Canada called on his expertise in the "Borowski case" which pitted the minister of justice, who favored abortion, against the Canadian Bill of Rights, which protected the life of every individual. Jérôme had to demonstrate when the human life of an individual begins and stand ready to testify in court.[25]

A new solicitation from the United States required Jérôme's presence this time. He was invited as the observer of the Catholic Church to participate in a meeting of the Council of Protestant Churches concerning the relations between faith and science. The extremely long congress—lasting two weeks—took place at the Massachusetts Institute of Technology (MIT), near Boston. Jérôme attended all the sessions conscientiously. One day, a young Argentine researcher whom he met at the event and with whom he struck up a friendship, Antonio Battro, told him:

"I just came back from an artificial intelligence laboratory where my friends have solved an interesting problem. They found out how a young man with cerebral palsy can use a computer to write a letter. It is an amazing thing! Come see it, because I think that medicine these days has just changed!"[26]

Jérôme immediately followed him, and the two left on foot for the laboratory. When they arrived, the patient was no longer there, but the engineer in charge of the program related the facts to them. Then Jérôme sat down and said: "This is an innovation that will change the education of sick children."

Then, immediately, he encouraged Antonio Battro to use that machine for trisomic children. Antonio did not forget that suggestion, and a few months later he came to Paris as a collaborator with the global computer center directed by Nicholas Negroponte[27]

[24] J. Lejeune, letter to Randy Engel, January 10, 1979.

[25] Morris Shumiatcher, letter to J. Lejeune, February 5, 1979.

[26] Conversation of the author with Antonio Battro, physician, psychologist, specialist in mathematical logic, who published *Un demi cerveau suffit* (Paris: Odile Jacob, 2003).

[27] Nicholas Negroponte created in 2005 the association One Laptop per Child. [The association shut down in 2014.]

and took the occasion of Jérôme's proposal to work with several of his patients.

When he arrived for the first time at Necker Children's Hospital, Antonio had difficulty believing what he saw. Along the walls of the corridor leading to Jérôme's office, he found graffiti so violent that he was scandalized: "Lejeune wavers, the MLAC watches!" "Lejeune the assassin!"

The MLAC, Mouvement de libération de l'avortement et de la contraception [Abortion and contraception liberation movement] had been created in April 1973. Jérôme was one of its prime targets. Antonio stopped, aghast: "My God, how is it possible to say things like that?!" he exclaimed to himself. "Lejeune! The very one who refuses to kill!"

Several moments later, still upset, Antonio entered Jérôme's office and immediately explained to him why he was emotional, but his astonishment increased even more when Jérôme was content to reply soberly, "Yes, that's what they say about me. In 1973, some people had also written on the walls, in red letters: 'Kill Lejeune and his little monsters.'"

"And what did you do?" Antonio asked.

"I erased those words and took away the insulting placards", Jérôme answered calmly.

Antonio was amazed. "That is hard to take! How can he remain so calm? This man is serenity itself."[28]

It should be noted that Antonio Battro arrived in Paris in 1979, the year in which the Veil Law that had passed provisionally in 1975 for five years was being revised. The debates for or against the decriminalization of abortion had started again, and Jérôme, still at the heart of the resistance movement, remained the principal opponent of that philosophical, medical, and social revolution. Although he was no longer invited to the television studios, he was still on the radio, particularly on the France Inter programs *Le Téléphone sonne*, *Journal du matin*, *Inter actualités*, but his was still a very isolated voice.

Jérôme was not welcome, either, in the Association of Catholic Physicians in France ever since a congress that the association held in

[28] Conversation of the author with Antonio Battro, who quotes this remark by Jérôme that had made an impression on him.

1972, during which he replied to a speaker who presented abortion as a necessary evil by explaining to him that killing an innocent patient was an evil, yes, but no, never necessary. Especially for Catholic physicians. The end does not justify the evil means. Following that intervention, Lejeune's name was stricken from the list of the editorial committee of the association's magazine, *Médecine de l'Homme*. In 1979, the situation had not improved, because the association still did not dare to recall the Church's message about respect for human life and published, in the April issue of *Médecine de l'Homme*, an article that was at least ambiguous. This text, signed by the president and the chaplain of the association, in the middle of the debate over renewing the Veil Law, might influence the opinion of many physicians, and Jérôme gagged upon reading those lines. The stakes were considerable, and he decided to take up his pen. Despite the situation, he wrote gently:

> My dear Colleague, allow me to tell you in all friendship the sorrow that I felt while reading the latest issue of *Médecine de l'Homme*. Your introductory essay is quite good natured, but the effect that it has produced in the press is terrible. President Abiven and the chaplain, Michel Roy, present a series of questions, it seems, but this bundle is very close to being an opinion. The journalists were not mistaken about that.... This is no longer posing questions; it is describing in paraphrases a position in favor of keeping the law. I know that Maurice Abiven, Michel Roy, and you yourself speak quite conscientiously, and I would just like to say to you in all friendship that this is why I am writing to you. Science without conscience is nothing but the ruin of the soul, we all agree about that. But conscience without science is nothing but the ruin of the intellect. It is necessary to agree on this, too.... Let us leave to others—to those outside, Saint Paul would have said—the schizophrenic language. We should let the others quibble about beings that are human-already-but-not-yet, the little men that are non-human or dehumanized. If we Catholic physicians let people think that we doubt, we are just leading the others astray. Who will speak for the children if we do not dare to do so? Now, in all these arguments, the child is never mentioned!
>
> Allow me to remind you how the pro-aborts set out to change people's minds at this point (you will grant that no Catholic magazine would have published an article of this sort even less than ten years ago). First, they highlighted the most deprived, the deformed,

> the unwanted, the unloved, and from the day when some Catholic physicians accepted the idea of killing, of killing *in utero* some very little patients who are seriously afflicted, it became possible to speak openly and finally to demand abortion for all: the sick and the well. The question posed by the two articles in *Médecine de l'Homme* is no longer whether Catholic physicians must demand a revision of the Veil Law at all. To read their arguments, you might think that it is altogether "tolerable". The question that they intend to raise is only how to apply it loyally!...
>
> This letter, my dear colleague, is an appeal, not a critique, much less a polemic. I ask you: have Abiven read it, and Father Roy, Doctor René, and other colleagues, too. Among our colleagues who teach on the faculties, I am unfortunately the odd man out. Being resolutely, absolutely on the side of the little ones who have no voice, who are without visible form, is paradoxical today. Oh, that is old-fashioned, outmoded! But this outmoded truth still has the same youth that it did almost two thousand years ago. Why would we not all be resolutely, absolutely on the side of life? Will you join us? Amicably.[29]

Yet despite all the efforts of the pro-lifers, the law decriminalizing abortion in France was passed on December 31, 1979, not for five more years, but in a so-called definitive way. As in 1975, Jérôme suffered for all the children who would never see the light of day and for the mothers who were being confined to that choice because they "have no choice".

For those who still were unsure about the nature of those laws, it was enough to consult the very explicit book that Pierre Simon, Grand Master of the Grand Lodge of France[30]and expert advisor to the minister of health, Simone Veil, had just published in 1979: *De la vie avant toute chose* [About life above all else].[31] In it, he describes in detail the patient strategy of Freemasonry, developed starting in the 1950s, to obtain the legalization of abortion. The Masonic author enjoys describing to the public the full extent of the stakes and encourages his readers not to underestimate the decisive influence of Freemasonry in this campaign for abortion. Simon explains

[29] J. Lejeune, letter to Professor Laroche, April 11, 1979.

[30] P. Simon was grand master of the Grand Lodge of France from 1969 to 1971 and then from 1973 to 1975.

[31] P. Simon, *De la vie avant toute chose* (Paris: Éditions Mazarine, 1979).

that since French society was opposed to abortion in 1950, his Masonic confreres proceeded by stages to change minds by obtaining, first, the legalization of contraception as a step toward legal abortion. According to them, as soon as women were accustomed to controlling life through contraception, so as to have a child exactly "when they want", they would no longer accept an unexpected pregnancy and would be ready for abortion.[32] He also announced their next battles, which they would wage starting in the 1980s, in favor of medically assisted procreation and euthanasia. Strange to say, this very instructive book disappeared from the libraries fifteen years after its publication ...

Birthe and Jérôme, nevertheless, were able to obtain a copy of it [in 1979]. What they read confirmed their analysis: the roots of the battle are spiritual. Page after page, the book shows that medicine is utilized as a weapon with which to liberate the world from God, a world in which man becomes his own measure. Pierre Simon is quite explicit:

> For the first time, science and technology opened up for society the possibility of detaching itself from the laws of nature.
>
> Gynecology acquired the dimension of a weapon for the great battle of knowledge. It would extend man's dominion, change life, and refuse to consider the current human condition as definitive.
>
> Medicine was one of the means of lifting up the world, or bringing down the old order.[33]

Life is no longer received from God; it does not exist by itself; it is a "material" that human beings are in charge of.

[32] This logic explains why in France today, a country where the rate of contraception is very high, the rate of abortion is also very high (220,000 per year, eight million since 1975, without counting the ten thousand abortions of handicapped children each year, which brings the total number of abortions to 9.5 million over forty-three years). The development of contraception leads to the development of abortion: on the one hand, the contraceptive mentality encourages a "liberated" sex life, in other words, one disconnected from its procreative dimension, and thus multiplies the occasions of unwanted pregnancy; on the other hand, in the contraceptive mentality, the child appears as a risk, and in the relatively frequent cases of "contraceptive failure", in other words, in cases of pregnancy, abortion becomes the solution to remedy the error. Recall that in France today the abortion of handicapped infants (primly called "medical interruption of pregnancy", IMG) is legally authorized, with the agreement of physicians, throughout the nine months of pregnancy.

[33] P. Simon, *De la vie avant toute chose* (Paris: Éditions Mazarine, 1979), 34.

> It is not the mother alone but rather the whole community that bears the child in its womb. The community is the one to decide whether it should be conceived, whether it should live or die, what its role and its development are.
>
> This responsibility for life has its corollary: see to it that this material is not degraded. That would be to degrade ourselves and to ruin the species.
>
> To bring non-handicapped children into the world: that is what it means to give life.[34]

The control of births should allow total mastery of the living thanks to an improvement in their quality of life, without handicapped persons, with liberated sexuality.

> Contraception, therefore, has a threefold role to play. In the first place, the preservation of the genetic heritage, the property of all human beings.... Blocking the transmission of known transmissible hereditary defects is a duty of the species. The second role is the qualitative management of life; health has become a collective property. We contribute to Social Security for the quality of life and the health of the community. Each one has solidarity with all. The third role of contraception is to fine-tune the new design of the family.[35]

Simon, who participated in the creation of the French branch of Planned Parenthood in 1960, personally subscribes to the eugenicist views that underlie the ideology of Planned Parenthood, created by Margaret Sanger in 1921 in the United States. In her various written works, Sanger is very clear in affirming that it is necessary to prevent the "undesirable" from reproducing.

> All the miseries in the world can be blamed on the fact that we allow irresponsible, ignorant, illiterate, and poor people to reproduce without having the least control over their fertility.

Birth control "must lead ultimately to a cleaner race; it is truly the greatest and most authentic eugenic method."[36] It is the first step in

[34] Ibid., 15, 16, 54.

[35] Ibid., 96.

[36] Margaret Sanger, *The Pivot of Civilization* (1922), chapter 8.

improving the race, while waiting for the second stage to be implemented: selective eugenics.

> Before the eugenicists and all who work to improve the race can succeed, they must first facilitate the control of births.... Both pursue the same goal but insist on different methods.[37]

This thesis did not crop up overnight; it was rooted in the ideologies of the late nineteenth century and had been developing in the scientific world right before Jérôme's eyes since the late 1960s. First, Darwinism played an important role by supporting the hypothesis of an improvement of the human species in the name of evolution, which tacitly presupposes the elimination of the weakest members. Darwin emphasized "how harmful this perpetuation of the feeble-minded must be to the human race", and by that reasoning, when nature accidentally fails to eliminate "the feeble-minded beings", physicians have to take over. That was when the word "eugenics" appeared for the first time, coined by Galton, Darwin's cousin.

In 1892, ten years after Darwin's death, Charles Richet, who was a Nobel Prize winner in medicine and a staunch eugenicist, foresaw with frightening accuracy the applications of that philosophy:

> Around the year 2000, when the laws of heredity and their practical applications are well known,... they will not be content to perfect rabbits and pigeons; they will try to perfect human beings. It will be necessary then to prepare the foundations for a sort of artificial selection, by dint of which human beings will become stronger, more beautiful, more intelligent.

Four years later, in 1896, the Frenchman Vacher de Lapouge suggested that this selection should be facilitated by developing "the skill of artificial fertilization", which separates love, sexual pleasure, and fertility.... Eugenics then spread rapidly in university circles, and a chair in eugenics was created at the University of London in 1904. Curiously, the Nazi exploitation of this ideology did not check the enthusiasm of scientists, and, in the wake of World War II, it was

[37] Margaret Sanger, "The Eugenic Value of Birth Control Propaganda", *Birth Control Review*, October 1921: 5.

fashionable to be a member of an overtly eugenicist association. In order to dispel misgivings, it was enough to say that Nazi eugenics had nothing to do with scientific eugenics.[38] So much so that in the 1960s Francis Crick, the co-discoverer of DNA and a winner of the Nobel Prize for medicine, blithely declared:

> No newborn infant should be declared human until it has passed certain tests regarding its genetic endowment. If it fails these tests, it forfeits the right to live.

The medical revolution that resulted from the cultural transition that began in the nineteenth century, therefore, was under way, and anyone who opposed it had to play the role of David against Goliath.

At the end of the 1960s, Jérôme found himself exactly at the historical confluence of the eugenicist and Malthusian trends, which for the first time, thanks to advances in genetics and gynecology, had the means to implement their policies on an international scale. As a witness to this revolution, Jérôme quickly understood that his discovery of trisomy 21, combined with the procedure of amniocentesis due to Sir William Liley, would make it possible to carry out this eugenicist policy, and he dreaded it. Two discoveries that had been made in order to care for patients were diverted from their objective; this was a tragedy for their authors and "heartbreaking" for Jérôme. Therefore, he had spoken up in 1969, in San Francisco, to denounce the misdeed and the violence of such scientific conduct, and after that he never stopped doing so. Despite the intimidations and insults. What was worse, for the promoters of those eugenicist and Malthusian laws, Jérôme's international renown grew steadily and thus made his witness more and more convincing. Which is to say that he was becoming truly bothersome. A grain of sand in the gears of a machine that was running at full speed.

Aware that the battle was not over, and isolated in his position within the Church in France, during those trying months Jérôme had the consolation of maintaining good relations with the Vatican. Monsignor Jacqueline, from the Secretariat for Non-Believers, questioned

[38] On this subject, read the book by Daniel Kevles, *In the Name of Eugenics* (Cambridge, Mass.: Harvard University Press, 1998).

him regularly about the relations between faith and science and on the hesitations of scientists with regard to the faith. Jérôme proposed an analysis based on his observations.

> The scientific mentality and the practice of the positive sciences certainly do, as a secondary effect, lead some to believe that the only objects of reflection worthy of interest are those that can be grasped by the scientific method. This is what I call a professional deformation. A true accountant knows only the figures. A scientist ultimately knows only the experimental results confirmed by repetition and analyzed by the logic of non-contradiction. This professional deformation is extremely harmful to the mind and excludes not only religion and metaphysics but everything that is not repetitive or measurable. That terribly amputates reality. A scientist who is deformed into an adherent to scientism cannot take an interest in art, poetry, or history. Scientists who are not deformed have no more difficulty than other human beings in bowing down before religion or inquiring about metaphysics. But it is necessary first to kneel down. Pascal said it for the ages.

Then, concerning the discoveries of science, Jérôme explained: "Not one of the current conclusions of science appears to me to cause any difficulty for the faith." He took several examples to illustrate his statement:

> Concerning the origin of life and evolution. First the marine animals, then the birds, then the beasts, then man—Genesis is a marvelous summary of the evolution observed by paleontology. Since it could not be done in a shorter or clearer or more evolutionary way, clerics seem to forget deliberately the sequential aspect described by the Bible. At no moment was religious thought "fixist". And yet it is accused of being so! Dobzhansky, who was one of the great theorists of modern evolutionism, confided to me: "The Christian religion is the only possible one; first, it is evolutionary (before and after Christ); secondly, it is incarnate; and, thirdly, it is historical!"

Then Jérôme addresses the following point:

> To my knowledge, no system of thought leads by a scientific procedure to the rejection of faith and of religion. For the ideologies

just noted—neo-positivism, structuralism, Marxism, Freudianism, and others—the rejection of all faith and of all religion is logically prior to the development of the ideology itself. In rereading Marx or Freud or Comte, or [Jacques] Monod, the reader can understand what they mean only by reading the invisible phrase placed as an inscription for every chapter: Since God does not exist, ... therefore.... The "therefore" means that this supposed absence must be replaced by a particular system constructed for this purpose. Since these theories contradict each other, this "therefore" appears to be very weak in correct logic. Nothing can be concluded from a null hypothesis!

Finally Jérôme concludes:

Science is, first of all, a school of modesty; technological success is what makes it vain. Theories must be subjected to the facts of creation. In acknowledging that scientific ideas are like the successive stages of a multi-stage rocket, historians of the sciences indicate that there is a more general viewpoint toward which knowledge tends.[39]

In November 1979, Jérôme departed again for Rome to attend the plenary session of the Pontifical Academy of Sciences, scheduled by way of exception around November 10, so as to celebrate the centenary of Albert Einstein's birth. For the occasion, the Academy organized a big ceremony; also among the invited guests were the cardinals residing in Rome and the diplomatic corps accredited to the Holy See. It was expected that the members of the Academy would be introduced at the conclusion of the audience, for the first time, to the Holy Father John Paul II, who had been elected to the See of Peter the previous year, on October 16, 1978.

Jérôme had a very vivid memory of that election. By a stroke of luck or an act of Providence, he just happened to be in Rome with Birthe for a session of the Pontifical Academy of Sciences. He recalled that, as they were meeting in the Casina Pio IV, the academicians received a phone call from a Vatican official who announced to them: "Habemus papam!" And all the respectable academicians started running through the Vatican Gardens so as to arrive first on Saint Peter's Square!

As he passed a Swiss guard, Jérôme asked him: "Who is pope?"

[39] J. Lejeune, letter to Monsignor Jacqueline, extracts, May 28, 1979.

The latter answered, pouting with disappointment: "Un Polacco!" ("A Pole!") Then he gave the name of the cardinal who had just been elected: "Karol Wojtyła".

That answer meant nothing to Jérôme or to any other member of the Academy. Not one of those eminent scientists recognized the name Karol Wojtyła. Jérôme remembered also the absolutely extraordinary spectacle on Saint Peter's Square and the astonishing joy that emanated from it. When the Holy Father said in Italian: "If I make mistakes in your language, in our language ...", extraordinary enthusiasm was unleashed; people threw their handkerchiefs and hats into the air. Then, when he said that they were going to pray to the Blessed Virgin, Jérôme turned to a friend and said to him: "We have a good pope, a man who speaks about the Blessed Virgin at the moment of his election has to be good."[40]

After the election, Jérôme heard high praises of the new pontiff from Wanda Poltawska, his psychiatrist friend whom he had met during a scientific congress in Poland, who had worked so much on pastoral care of the family and the pro-life cause with Karol Wojtyła when he was still a young bishop, then cardinal of Kraków. Jérôme greatly rejoiced, therefore, on this when he met him for this congress of the Academy.

In the magnificent Clementine Hall, ornamented with wonderful frescoes, he waited patiently. Suddenly the invited guests stood up as one man, and Jérôme did the same. The two-paneled door had just opened, revealing the tall, white, athletic silhouette of the Holy Father, surrounded by Swiss guards and busy prelates. The pope walked briskly over to the apostolic chair, and, while everyone tried to see him, he looked kindly at that silent assembly, then sat down, soon imitated by all present. From the first words of the speech that John Paul II gave in Italian with his slight Slavic accent, Jérôme was deeply touched in both mind and heart.

> I feel in full solidarity with my predecessor Pius XI and with those who succeeded him in this Apostolic See in calling upon the members of the Pontifical Academy of Sciences, and all scientists with them,

[40] J. Lejeune, *Entretien sur Jean-Paul II* [interview about John Paul II] with E. Ostian, not dated.

> to bring about "the progress of sciences more and more nobly and intensely without asking anything else of them, because the mission of serving truth, with which we charge them, consists in this excellent intention and in this noble labor" (Pius XI, *In multis solaciis*, 1936). The search for truth is the task of basic science. The researcher who advances on this first slope of science feels all the fascination of Saint Augustine's words: "Intellectum valde ama", "He loves the intellect very much", and the function that is characteristic of it, to know truth. Pure science is a good that is worth loving, because it is knowledge and, by that very fact, the perfecting of man in his intellect.[41]

At the conclusion of the audience, the academicians were presented, one by one. When his turn arrived, Jérôme bowed down with profound joy before that pope whose stature he intuited. The Holy Father looked attentively at this Professor Lejeune, for he was acquainted with his merits, so often praised by his friend Wanda Poltawska. Their smiles matched.

June 1980. John Paul II came to Paris. It was the first journey of a Roman Pontiff in France since the coronation of Napoleon! Jérôme and Birthe prepared enthusiastically for that visit. What an honor for the Church of France! And what a joy for Jérôme, who was so happy to see again this pope whose kindness and intelligence had won him over.

"We have to give him a magnificent reception", he said one evening to his family, who had gathered for dinner.

"Yes, you're right!" said Birthe. "Moreover, I get the impression that the authorities are not very convinced about it and are not motivating the crowds!"

"Exactly. Some friends and I want to organize a pilgrimage", their daughter Karin said enthusiastically. "We plan to leave in the evening to arrive at Mass in Paris in the early morning. We will walk all night, with as many people as possible."

"Terrific!" Birthe exclaimed.

"We will come!"

Several days later, Karin announced to her parents that the enterprise was a success.

[41] John Paul II, speech to the Pontifical Academy of Sciences, commemorating the birth of Albert Einstein, November 10, 1979.

"Thanks to the networks of friends and of Ichtus,[42] we have already gathered almost a thousand people. Especially young people. It's great! We learned through the nunciature that the Mass will finally take place in Bourget. So we are looking for a place from which to start our pilgrimage, 25 kilometers [15 miles] from Bourget."

That same evening, at the headquarters of the organization, a young man spread out on the floor a map of the vicinity of Paris with a compass in his hand set at a radius of 25 kilometers. With the point of the compass planted on Bourget, the circle that it described passed over the village of Champlatreux.

"It would be terrific if we could meet at that place and leave from there!" he said to the group.

So it happened that on Saturday evening, May 31, a thousand pilgrims, including Jérôme and Birthe, gathered for a great prayer vigil in Duc de Noailles Park, which had been designated by the compass to accommodate them. They prayed for the Holy Father, the Church, and France, and then set out courageously on their journey. The falling rain did not dampen their joy, and the songs intoned with full voice cheered that long nocturnal march of a thousand ponchos. Having covered the 25 kilometers during the night, they reached the esplanade of Bourget well before dawn and the Holy Father, whose arrival was expected much later in the morning. Everyone tried to sleep a little, sitting or stretched out on the ground, amid puddles of water. At 11:00, finally, the Holy Father arrived, amid the applause of several hundred thousand courageous people. However, the welcome was not proportionate to the event. Fewer than 400,000 French Catholics were there to welcome Pope John Paul II for his first visit in France. But the Holy Father, braving the cool reception, turned the situation around. The homily that he gave on June 1, 1980, shook Christian France out of its torpor. He, the son of Holy Poland, invited France to rediscover her vocation.

> In conclusion, allow me to ask you: France, Eldest Daughter of the Church, are you faithful to the promises of your Baptism? Allow me

[42] *Ichtus* [the French spelling of *Ichthys*, Greek "Fish"], also known as Ictus or Rue des Renaudes, is a center for civic and cultural formation according to the natural and Christian law. In particular, it organizes large congresses in Lausanne, at which Jérôme spoke regularly.

to ask you: France, Daughter of the Church and teacher of nations, are you faithful, for the good of man, to your covenant with Eternal Wisdom?

These enlivening words shook the yoke of spiritual indifference and fears. Reconnecting with the prophetic witness of Saint Remigius, they announced a new day for France, and Jérôme was profoundly moved by them.

That evening, Jérôme rejoiced to be able again to hear the words of truth that came from the mouth of the Holy Father, at the Parc des Princes, during the prayer vigil for young people. Alas, he found the ceremony neither beautiful nor recollected, with unfamiliar, poor-quality songs and texts. It was almost an affront to the pope. But suddenly, from various stands in the stadium came the *Salve Regina*, chanted in chorus by hundreds of young people. They were the pilgrims of the previous day, scattered throughout the stands, singing full voice, and soon joined by the Holy Father, who sang with them, for long minutes, visibly happy. A moment of grace.

As in Rome during the congress of the Pontifical Academy of Sciences, Jérôme was deeply touched by the words of John Paul II. The Holy Father expressed what Jérôme carried in his heart. They were in unison: a profound spiritual and intellectual understanding, which had on him the effect of a soothing balm. Jérôme, for the first time, felt less alone and, happy about this new grace, dared to take up his pen, as soon as the apostolic journey was over, to write to the pope, expressing his gratitude.

Most Holy Father, allow me to thank you for having come to bring us the truth. France is sick in her soul. A self-styled intelligentsia has hold of the news media and misleads minds. Some have promoted "merciful" abortion and thus have endangered the lives of hundreds of thousands of children. Now a country that kills its children kills its soul. Today the great minds that claim to be the conscience of the nation come to indoctrinate the physicians, assuring them: he who cares well kills well! We are dying of that intelligentsia which is leading us to abortion and euthanasia. And yet we want to live. It is absolutely necessary for enlightened intellects to dare to cite Catholic doctrine openly.

People pretend to fear that modern science is opposed to faith. That is false, and I agree completely with what Monsieur Chaunu said. But in order to give some semblance of reality to this nonexistent opposition, they reveal only one part of the facts, while the other is deliberately hidden. [For example, when the English physicians successfully performed an *in vitro* fertilization followed by the birth of a healthy little girl, they said, "You see, technology makes us the masters of life." Now the true scientific conclusion was quite different. Extra-corporeal fertilization is the visible, experimental proof of a fact that morality has always taught: "Human life begins at fertilization."] This mask put over one part of our knowledge disfigures science and gives it a terrible countenance. This is the sickness of the intelligentsia. And this amputation of reality leads to disdain for love and the loss of respect for life. This is the sickness of our country. The enormous task, which must constantly be restarted, is to rebuild intellects, because falsified reason makes man insensitive to the appeals of the heart.

This is why, Most Holy Father, I am anxious to express to you our immense gratitude, because you are finally bringing to us, loud and clear, the words of life.[43]

Jérôme set out again on his scientific battle, fortified by the joy of that encounter. A joy that would soon be of great help to him.

[43] J. Lejeune, letter to John Paul II, June 5, 1980.

CHAPTER 12

A PROVIDENTIAL FRIENDSHIP

1981–1982

Head in hands, alone in his office, Jérôme reflected on the danger of the situation: "What is to be done? I really am afraid that this silence of the administration concerning my repeated requests is deliberate.... I already spent a year without a secretary, and I had to fight in order to obtain one at last! With all this mail, the meetings, and the publications to produce, it was impossible! It slowed down the work of the whole team! And now the CNRS announces to me that it will reduce its financing again! With the little money that it gives us, I can no longer pay our temporary worker who has been with us full-time for more than four years. What is to be done?"

Overcome with worry, Jérôme sought a solution. "Fortunately," he said to himself, "I still have something left from the Kennedy Award; I can pay her for a few more months. After that I will have to find something else. Or I will not be able to keep her. What a mess! Everyone will be the loser." Suddenly the alarm clock went off. Raising his head, Jérôme looked at the clock, which said 7:00 P.M. He extended his arm and with a quick gesture stopped that noisy call to order and smiled, well aware that without it he would often miss the family dinners that were so important to Birthe. He stood up hastily, took his jacket, and went out, glad that he would soon be with his loved ones and could share his concerns with his wife. Right after dinner, he told her about his worries.

She, too, was concerned, and suggested to him: "Why don't you write to the general director of INSERM? Might he be able to help you? At any rate, nothing is lost by trying."

"Good idea!" Jérôme replied, then added: "All this time that I waste fighting to obtain funding for our work is that much less time for research. What stupidity!"

Jérôme wrote his letter and a few weeks later received a reassuring response.[1] To his great relief, the position would be financed by INSERM. With the renewed subsidy from the Kennedy Foundation, which allocated $5,000 to him that year, and the one announced by the Michael Fund, Jérôme was relieved: he would be able to keep the team's activity going in 1981. "After that, we will see. Tomorrow is another day", he said to Birthe.

In his race against the clock to save the sick children, Jérôme had only one desire: to dedicate as much of his time as possible to his research so as to find at last the medication that would not only cure them but save them, because trisomy, which was not a fatal illness, was going to become one if prenatal screening became systematic. Jérôme saw in the United States that "the massacre of the innocents" was on the agenda, and he observed that the only way to save them was to cure them. He knew also that children with Down syndrome were not the only ones threatened. All children who presented malformations that are detectible *in utero* would soon be in danger, all the children carrying a chromosomal anomaly, often more serious than trisomy 21. Jérôme was personally acquainted with so many of them. He had seen four thousand of them in his practice since the beginning of his career. His appointment calendar was full. Four thousand whom he knew by name and whose case histories he knew, because he did not see them just once in their lives, but once or twice a year, for regular, personal follow-ups. With their parents and their brothers and sisters. Jérôme also kept up an exchange of letters with the families; his letters show the extent to which he was acquainted with each of his patients. Thus, he answered one mother who questioned him about her young adult son, who was an artist and a painter:

> In more than a thousand other particular ways, which indeed define him, Matthieu[2] is a painter. Others are musicians (or, rather, music

[1] J. Lejeune, letter to Doctor Laudat, general director of INSERM, April 22, 1981.
[2] The name has been changed.

lovers, since few of them are instrumentalists), others are writers, poets, or storytellers. Still others have the precious talent of making people happy and are content to be charming individuals. Like every happy person with trisomy 21, Matthieu is a bit of all that. But how it happens that Bruno is a poet, Chantal a writer, and Matthieu a painter, I do not know. This nature of the artist, flourishing in spite of the mental deficiency, is not so surprising after all. Abstract, reasoning intelligence, the kind that is measured by tests and that can be programmed on a machine, this admirable and almost mechanical logic is wounded in trisomic persons. None of them can claim to have [Pascal's] spirit of geometry beyond a very simple level. But this other reason that is seated closer to the heart, in the place where emotions approach reality, where one must feel correctly under penalty of not feeling at all, in that more intimate and more privileged domain, persons with trisomy 21 are no more hindered than others. In this field of the mind where children, lovers, and poets meet, they are as free as we are, to the extent that human beings can be.[3]

Jérôme worked furiously in search of the medicinal solution for his trisomic patients, and his studies, which were not partitioned off, led him in the direction of other chromosomal aberrations, such as fragile X syndrome, the most common illness after trisomy, which is due to a fragile site on the X chromosome. Jérôme spoke explicitly about illness with regard to these chromosomal aberrations because he thought that it was possible to find a treatment. He attacked the problem ardently, and his research projects made rapid advances. For the first time, he succeeded in modifying a chromosomal anomaly *in vitro* [in a petri dish] and *in vivo* [in a patient].[4] The results seemed conclusive, and Jérôme agreed to speak about it to a journalist from *Paris Match*. The article appeared on December 11, 1981, under the title: "On the third day, Ludovic finally started talking."[5] Jérôme was always very careful not to give false assurances to the parents, and he

[3] J. Lejeune, letter to a mother, 1981.

[4] J. Lejeune, letter to Doctor Laudat, general director of INSERM, April 22, 1981. They succeeded in modifying *in vitro* and *in vivo* a chromosomal anomaly: the fragility of site q27 of the X chromosome.

[5] J. Lejeune, interviewed in *Paris Match* by Monique Cara, "Au troisième jour, Ludovic se mit enfin à parler.... Un espoir dans la lutte contre la débilité mentale: le professeur Lejeune guérit à Paris deux enfants anormaux", December 11, 1981.

regularly wrote to journalists who were drawn to sensational stories and talked about a cure within reach.[6] He insistently asked them to be extremely prudent so as not to "torment the parents with hope". He explained:

> It would be thoroughly unjustified to let them believe that these advances correspond to the development of a treatment that is yet to be discovered.[7]

But this time he was the one speaking enthusiastically about the change in Ludovic's behavior, which the child's relatives and he himself observed. Alas, a little later these spectacular results that he announced to the journalist turned out to be wrong, and Jérôme was deeply mortified to have made that announcement prematurely. He, of all people, who was always so careful not to give false assurances to the parents!

This error upset him but did not shake his determination: he prepared a new study. This one was to determine whether folic acid has beneficial effects on persons who carry a fragile-X chromosome, not by curing them, but by accelerating their metabolic reactions.[8] Jérôme was a firm believer in the benefits of folic acid, especially during pregnancy, so much so that he already recommended it to the pregnant women with whom he was acquainted, to the great surprise of his colleagues. He was therefore ready to start the clinical trial with more than a dozen patients.

His research projects, during the years 1980 and 1981, were interspersed with several scientific congresses. Jérôme went to Israel and gave conferences on genetics in Chile, Argentina, Portugal, the United Kingdom, and Italy. In Chile, he was made an honorary professor of the University of Santiago. In Argentina, he was appointed a member of the National Academy of Medicine and received an honorary doctorate from the University of Buenos Aires.

[6] J. Lejeune, letter to R. Norris, December 21, 1981, etc.

[7] J. Lejeune, letter to the president of ANAPEI, January 28, 1981.

[8] J. Lejeune, letter to R. Gribble, November 24, 1982. In it, Jérôme explains this study: although patients carrying a fragile X chromosome do not have a folic deficiency but have, rather, a block in their metabolism of carbons, he hoped that folic acid could, if not cure them, at least accelerate their reactions.

On the political level, those two years since the Veil Law had been passed and confirmed were relatively calm for Jérôme. He therefore had considerably fewer requests, but still made speeches because the media continued to question experts regularly on whether or not handicapped persons should be kept alive. When Jérôme was invited to a debate, he agreed to participate in it, even though he found the questions out of place and violent for the persons concerned, in order to take up their defense. He was their advocate, "the voice of the voiceless". And so he answered a journalist from *Paris Match* who planned to publish two contradictory interviews under the headline: "Should We Persist in Saving Them?" In his interview, entitled "Yes, We Must Let Them Live", Jérôme reaffirmed the immense value of every human life, even if severely handicapped. He forcefully restated the principle: "We must always be on the patient's side, always."[9] The article appeared on November 7, 1980. A few days later, Jérôme received a thank-you letter from a thirteen-year-old girl whose charming words express the hope that his pro-life testimony awakened in the childlike hearts:

> I would like to congratulate you, Professor, from the bottom of my heart, for your article in *Paris Match*. Your ideas are marvelous, and it will be thanks to you, thanks to all those who work with you, that medicine and genetics and especially life [i.e., the pro-life cause] will make a spectacular leap forward. I admire you, Professor; I would like to be like you, to save lives, to give hope for the future. I am only thirteen, but already I am very interested in medicine and especially in genetics. It may just be an adolescent idea, but I want so much for it to take root and to become my vocation. In twenty, thirty, or forty years, I would like to be what you are today and to continue the work of my elders.... This article made an impression on me and on many other youngsters as well. You have given me personally a lot of hope in the future.[10]

The many conferences that he gave throughout the world left a fragrance of joy and courage wafting in the countries that he visited;

[9] J. Lejeune, interviewed by M. Leclercq, "Oui il faut les laisser vivre", *Paris Match*, November 7, 1980.

[10] M. Rusnac, letter to J. Lejeune, November 15, 1980.

they also earned him hundreds of letters of thanks and congratulations from the most distant countries. Such as these words by a Hungarian physician whom he met in Innsbruck, who took the trouble to write in French:

> Never in my life have I found a document like this, combining so wonderfully the faith and the science of a physician.[11]

Or this letter from Doctor Battro, which he received shortly after his tour in Argentina, where he had had such a good reception:

> Dear Jérôme, your visit to Buenos Aires was deeply moving for us. You brought us an extraordinary light. May God bless you!... You gave us not only the beginnings of the greatest medical discovery of our age but also the joy of understanding and loving life in its most intimate mystery. "The integral humanism" of the Christian, thanks to you, can finally incorporate the biological dimension that it was missing. The philosophy of the mind now discovers an "unformed matter" that allows it to understand better the unity of soul and body. You have opened for us a window onto the sublime phenomenon of the human intellect, and these little infirm patients are the ones who caused you to discover the greatness of the human spirit. Thus you followed the Gospel, and the Good News led you to the truth.[12]

In April 1981, Jérôme was expected in the United States, not for a scientific congress, since for eight years he had not been invited to one single medical colloquium in the United States, but rather to testify before the American Congress and Senate. As a scientific expert, he was questioned on a draft bill emphasizing that human life starts at conception and that this fact must be considered by law. On April 23, before the American Senate Subcommittee on the Separation of Powers, Jérôme chose simple words to explain the current state of the findings of embryology to an audience more specialized in law than in experimental science:

> When does a human being begin? I would like to try to bring to this question the most precise answer that science can currently provide.

[11] P. Cholnoky, letter to J. Lejeune, April 2, 1981.

[12] A. Battro, letter to J. Lejeune, November 2, 1981.

> Modern biology teaches us that ancestors are united to their descendants by a continuous material link, since a new member of the species emerges from the fertilization of the female cell (the ovum) by the male cell (spermatozoid). Life has a very, very long history, but each individual has a very neat beginning, the moment of its conception. The material link is the molecular thread of DNA. In each reproductive cell, this ribbon, about one meter [one yard] long is cut into pieces (23 in our species). Each segment is carefully rolled up and packaged (like a magnetic tape in a minicassette) so well that it appears under the microscope like a rod; a chromosome. As soon as the 23 paternal chromosomes are joined with the 23 maternal chromosomes, all the genetic information necessary and sufficient to express all the innate qualities of the new individual is collected. Just as placing a minicassette into a tape recorder makes it possible to reconstitute a symphony, so too the new human being begins to express itself as soon as it is conceived.... The chromosomes are the tablets of the law of life, and when they are collected in the new human being ... they completely describe his personal constitution. The astonishing thing is the miniaturization of the writing. It is difficult to believe, although possible beyond all doubt, that all the genetic information necessary and sufficient to build our body and even our brain—the most powerful problem-solving engine, capable even of analyzing the laws of the universe—can be summarized to such an extent that its material substrate can stand on the point of a needle!

Jérôme stopped for a moment, observing the faces of the members of the Subcommittee, then resumed his presentation. He explained that the genetic formula is so complex that every new being is totally unique and irreplaceable. Then he described the autonomy of that little living human being, a dancer and an astronaut:

> Within his life capsule, the amniotic sac, the new human being is exactly as viable as an astronaut on the moon inside his spacesuit; the replenishment of vital fluids has to be furnished by the mother-ship. This food is indispensable for survival, but it does not "make" the child, any more than the most sophisticated spaceship can produce an astronaut. This comparison is true even more when the fetus moves. Thanks to very refined ultrasound imagery, Professor Ian Donald of England succeeded last year in producing a film showing the youngest star in the world, an eleven-week-old baby dancing in utero. You might say that the baby is playing on the trampoline! He bends his knees, pushes on the wall, rises, then falls again. Since his body has

> the same density as the amniotic fluid, he scarcely feels his weight and dances very slowly with a grace and elegance altogether impossible in any other place on earth. Only astronauts in their state of zero-gravity achieve such smoothness in their movements. A propos, for the first space walk, the technicians had to decide where to attach the pipes carrying the vital fluids. They finally decided on the belt buckle of the space suit, thus reinventing the umbilical cord.

The audience seemed dumbfounded. Never had they heard anything like it. A scientist who presented such complex findings with so much simplicity ... Jérôme finally arrived at his conclusion:

> Accepting the fact that after fertilization a new human being has come to exist is no longer a question of taste or of opinion. The human nature of the human being, from conception until old age, is not a metaphysical hypothesis but, rather, an obvious fact of experience.[13]

Upon his return to Paris, Jérôme had a few days in which to see his patients and monitor his research projects before packing his suitcase once again. This time he departed for Rome, with Birthe, right in the middle of the Italian debate on abortion. Abortion had been legalized in 1978, but the Movimento per la Vita (Pro-life movement) was organizing a referendum on the subject for mid-May. Several days before his departure for the United States, Jérôme had received a letter from Cardinal Benelli, archbishop of Florence, inviting him to speak:

> Dear Professor, while apologizing for the little time that I leave for you to decide, I take the liberty of writing to you to invite you to give a "press conference" in Italy on the topic of abortion, and to do so before May 17 of this year, the date of the referendum. It would be a matter of speaking against abortion and in favor of the referendum of the "Pro-Life Movement" (Movimento per la Vita) which, as you know, proposes the partial dismantling of the law, since the Constitutional Court has prevented us from having a referendum in which we were demanding the abrogation of said law. This is only a first step, but it is essential for the dismantling of that unjust law.[14]

Jérôme immediately accepted.

[13] J. Lejeune, testimony before the U.S. Senate Subcommittee on the Separation of Powers, April 23, 1981.

[14] Cardinal Benelli, letter to J. Lejeune, April 14, 1981.

In Rome, at the end of their short stay, a surprise was awaiting them. While they were preparing to travel back to Paris, they received an invitation that was as unexpected as it was fortunate. A message left at their hotel informed them that the Holy Father was inviting them to have lunch before their departure the next day, Wednesday, May 13. They should appear at the Bronze Gate, under the Bernini colonnade, to the right of Saint Peter's Square, at 12:30. Jérôme's emotion was so strong that he was speechless, while Birthe already thought to order a taxi that would pick them up directly at the Vatican to bring them to the airport. Fortunately, their plane was to take off in the late afternoon.

They were aware of what an extraordinary privilege this was. The next day, when they entered the pope's apartments, escorted by one of his secretaries, they were immediately won over by the warmth of the Holy Father's welcome. During the luncheon, which was attended also by two Italian guests, including the journalist Alberto Michelini, the conversation turned to the upcoming referendum on abortion, scheduled for the following Sunday. The subject greatly concerned John Paul II, who had just created, on May 9, the Pontifical Council for the Family in order to intensify that pastoral outreach which held such an important place in his heart. He was persuaded that the family, intimately connected with pro-life advocacy, was the future of the world. The Holy Father questioned each one attentively with great kindness.

During those two hours of wonderful discussions with him,[15] it seemed to Jérôme that time had stopped. Alas, that was not the case at all; the clock actually struck, and the Holy Father soon had to leave his guests for an audience on Saint Peter's Square. While the pope met the thousands of pilgrims who were waiting for him, Jérôme and Birthe departed for Fiumicino Airport, slightly anxious about missing their plane, because Father Grimaud had made arrangements for Jérôme to give a short conference to some students that same evening in Paris, and he did not want to disappoint them by his absence.

When they arrived at Fiumicino, they discovered to their annoyance that all flights were suspended, without explanation. Their wait

[15] J. Lejeune, letter to E. Shriver, June 1981.

lasted almost three hours. Total silence about the reasons for the delay. Then finally they were invited to board, and their plane took off. A good two hours later, in Paris, in the taxi that was bringing them to rue Galande, Jérôme and Birthe heard on the radio a series of condolences. Not knowing who was meant, they asked the driver, and he told them, laconically: "The pope is dead."

This made a terrifying impression on Jérôme. The driver continued: "He was assassinated during the audience on Saint Peter's Square."

Jérôme could not believe it. The shock of that horrible news was too violent. As white as a sheet, he turned to Birthe: "To think that we were speaking to him a half hour before he was assassinated by that bandit...."

Then he fell silent without finishing his sentence and then went on to say, with infinite sadness, "We were the last ones to speak to him."[16]

Immediately he felt faint and ill. When they finally arrived home on rue Galande, they dashed to the television set. Images of the Holy Father collapsing gently into the arms of his secretary went by in an endless loop. A thin, dark-complexioned man, standing three meters [ten feet] from the pope had fired three shots, then was grabbed by a nun who prevented him from fleeing. The people on Saint Peter's Square were shouting. John Paul II passed for the second time in the popemobile back again at the Bronze Gate. He had just hugged a little girl and put her back into her mother's arms when the pistol shots rang out. Under a radiant sun.

Jérôme was pale. One of his daughters heard him murmur: "If only it had been me...."

Then he was seized with sharp pains. He would have liked to rest but could not: he was expected that evening with the students. He kept his word and went to the event, but he was very weary. He could only speak to them about the Holy Father. Brought immediately from Saint Peter's Square to the emergency room at Gemelli Hospital, the pope was still in the operating room at the hour when Jérôme spoke. His injuries were life-threatening. He had lost a lot of blood, and vital organs had been hit. It would take almost a miracle for him to survive. Jérôme, distressed, wrote this testimony of faith on a piece of paper offered to him by the students:

[16] J. Lejeune, *Entretien sur Jean-Paul II*, with E. Ostian, no date.

> On this May 13, in the evening when we learned about the assassination attempt against the Holy Father, we spoke about love, as the Holy Father teaches us every day. May God preserve him for us.[17]

When they returned to rue Galande, Jérôme felt so sick that Birthe had to call an ambulance. It brought him in the middle of the night to the Hôtel-Dieu. His anguish had caused a painful stone to form in the common bile duct, a kind of gallstone, which required emergency surgery. The next day, when Birthe went to visit him at the hospital, Jérôme was still unconscious. Not until two days later did he regain consciousness. Birthe announced to him that the Holy Father, too, had revived. After five hours of surgery, John Paul II seemed to be saved. It was a resurrection for the pope and for Jérôme, who nevertheless had to stay in the hospital. During each of her visits, Birthe observed with astonishment that her husband had the same medical bulletin as the pope's, which was announced on all the radio stations. From day to day, the progress that they made was similar: temperature curve, first steps in the corridor, et cetera. Distressed by these coincidences, the family saw in them the sign of their friendship and of Jérôme's active compassion for the Holy Father. But Jérôme retorted: "No, there is no sign!"

He refused to make any comment, allowing himself only to acknowledge, "Yes, it is a strange story."

It would take him another several weeks of convalescence to be able to work again full-time.

Several months later, in September, having recovered from his operation, Jérôme received a request from the Pontifical Academy of Sciences. Because of his studies on the genetic effects of forms of ionizing radiation, the Academy asked him to participate in a task force on the consequences of an atomic bombardment. The little group of around ten experts would meet in Rome on October 7–8 and reflect in particular on the medical and hospital care that could be given to the victims in the case of an atomic war. Jérôme accepted and with great interest participated in these important studies in the middle of the Cold War. At the end of the meeting, the conclusion appeared to be brutally obvious:

[17] J. Lejeune, May 13, 1981. This sentence is framed in the staircase of the house on rue Galande, next to photos of Pope John Paul II receiving Jérôme in audience.

> Living conditions following a nuclear attack would be so harsh that the only hope for humanity is the prevention of any form of nuclear war.[18]

The academicians proposed to meet with the heads of state that possessed atomic weapons to explain to them the dangers of an atomic war. The Holy Father, who had already insisted several times in his speeches on the danger of such a conflict, accepted the suggestion immediately.

Upon his return to Paris, Birthe bombarded her husband with questions, and Jérôme confided to her his thoughts about the Holy Father:

> He is a basically good man, and I have not seen many men about whom I dare to say that they are good. When he speaks with someone, whether a child or an old man, a member of the Academy or someone who is mentally handicapped, he speaks to him as though that person had suddenly become the only one on earth whom he was addressing, and he is in fact the only one on earth for John Paul II at that moment. That is altogether extraordinary. In my life I have seen many important people, in any case they thought that they were important, but never this degree of presence to each human being personally.
>
> My second impression is that he is astonishingly intelligent. The quality of his intellect is exceptional.... A small group of us from the Academy were in his office, and we had composed a document about the dangers of an atomic war.... There was an Englishman, a Spaniard, an Italian, two Frenchmen, a Ukrainian, and a Portuguese. A discussion started between the Holy Father and each one personally on a topic that is unusual for him. He spoke with each one in his language without any apparent difficulty going from one to the next. I have never seen such facility in anyone who is not a certified translator. As a specialist in infirmities of the intellect, and therefore of its good health also, I must say that I had never seen such a performance. The Holy Father is therefore a good man, totally good, and on an intellectual level that I have not yet seen in any other member of humanity.[19]

Birthe looked at her husband, whose voice betrayed a particular emotion. His face was shining. "These meetings with the pope are

[18] C. Chagas, letter to J. Lejeune, November 23, 1981.

[19] J. Lejeune, *Entretien sur Jean-Paul II*, with E. Ostian, no date.

very comforting", she said to herself joyfully. "I have never seen him return from a trip so happy."

Jérôme went on softly: "I might add that he is naturally charming, he is very kindly, and he has a sense of humor and is always humorous. This is not a man who says a few clever words. When you see him, you understand what Saint Francis meant: 'A saint who is sad is a sad excuse for a saint.' This pope is not a sad pope."[20]

"And what did he say to you about your studies and the risks of an atomic war?" Birthe inquired.

"He seems to be in favor of a meeting with heads of state, but we are awaiting his decision", Jérôme replied.

In order to convey the message from the Pontifical Academy of Sciences to the heads of state who had an atomic bomb at their disposal—President Reagan, Secretary General Brezhnev, President Mitterand, Mrs. Thatcher, Mrs. Indira Gandhi, Deng Xiaoping, and the Secretary General of the United Nations, John Paul chose his ambassadors from among the academicians. To speak to the ruler of the Kremlin, he designated three members of the Academy: Lejeune, Marini-Bettolo, and Duve.

Jérôme received the letter commissioning him in the last week of November and had a few hours to reply. Before December 1. After that date, his silence would be taken as acceptance. You do not take a special mission lightly ... Jérôme sent his affirmative response. On December 14, with his Vatican diplomatic passport in his pocket, he flew off to Moscow. Everything had been organized by the Vatican services: the contacts with the Kremlin and the practical aspects. But they had not foreseen a political event that occurred in Poland, throwing that meeting into particular relief: in the night of December 13–14, Lech Wałęsa and the leaders of the Solidarity Movement were arrested by the police, and on the 14th, General Jaruzelski declared martial law. Jérôme heard this news on the morning of the 14th, as he was departing. He would conduct a decidedly thorny mission ... He was being sent by the pope to see Brezhnev, while the Holy Father's moral and spiritual support was encouraging the peaceful revolution of the workers of Solidarność against the Polish Communist regime ... In reflecting on the delicate circumstances surrounding his

[20] Ibid.

journey, Jérôme also remarked with pleasure: "We have a pope who knows how to fight against oppression with the powerful weapons of prayer, justice, and truth. He is teaching us the cultural and spiritual revolution of love."

At Roissy Airport, before going through the checkpoints, Jérôme looked for a phone booth in order to make an extremely important call. Before selecting the number, he glanced one last time at his watch: "Yes, this is the right hour", and put the coin into the slot.

"Hello?"

"Hello, this is Professor Jérôme Lejeune."

On the other end of the line, a voice replied: "Good morning, Professor!"

"May I please speak to your superior?"

"Yes, certainly, Professor. I will tell her right away."

Several moments later he heard a clear voice say to him: "Good morning, Professor."

"Good morning, Reverend Mother. I am at the airport, about to leave for Moscow, to meet Brezhnev at the Holy Father's request. May I commend this difficult visit to your prayers and those of your whole community?"

"Certainly, dear Professor. May God go with you."

The Carmelite assured him of the prayers of her community, as she had done every time he had presented difficult intentions to her. Jérôme hung up, confident that his trip was now in God's hands.

Jérôme arrived in Moscow right in the middle of a snowstorm. The meeting with Brezhnev was set for December 15, but the little delegation—made up of the Italian Marini Bettolo and Jérôme, since their colleague Duve had canceled his trip—was received early on the evening of the 14th by colleagues from the Soviet Academy. The reception went very pleasantly, and, after the dinner, according to the local custom, everyone proposed a poetic toast. The academician Bochkov quoted with literary talent from *War and Peace* and *Anna Karenina*, and then it was Jérôme's turn. He stood up, paused for a moment, then alluded to a familiar story in those days leading up to Christmas:

> Long, long ago, three wise men set out from the East to pay a visit to a very powerful prince. They had observed signs in the sky that, they

> thought, announced good news, peace on earth to men of good will. Almost two thousand years later, some scientists from the West are in turn paying a visit to a very powerful man. We scientists know that if by some misfortune immense signs unleashed by men were to appear in the sky, it would be the announcement, not of good news, but of the massacre of the Innocents.[21]

His Soviet colleagues were listening intently. Jérôme said "Salut" and sat down, while they all congratulated him.

The next day, officials came looking for Jérôme and Marini Bettolo to drive them to their meeting with Brezhnev. The first secretary of the Party received them in a very friendly fashion despite the stiff protocol. The journalists' flashbulbs popped. Brezhnev read a fifteen-minute text on the politics of the U.S.S.R., and Jérôme noticed the words that had been chosen to introduce that long speech. In them, Brezhnev emphasized the unusual character of their meeting and explained that this was the first time that he was receiving envoys from the head of the Catholic Church. He added: "It is not impossible that this is connected with the difficult and dangerous times that humanity is going through."

The atmosphere grew warmer. Then, having led the pope's envoys into a private room, Brezhnev let them speak, and Jérôme finally addressed the reason for their visit.

> Mister President, if we have come to visit you at the request of the Holy Father, it is because we scientists have reached the conclusion that there is no technological, military, or medical solution to ward off the disasters of an atomic war. We scientists know that, for the first time, humanity finds itself confronted with the fact that its survival depends on the acceptance, by all the nations in the world, of moral precepts that transcend all systems and all speculation.[22]

When the interpreter heard the words "moral precepts", he turned to Jérôme and asked him: "Do you really want to use the words 'moral precepts'?"

Jérôme said "Yes", and the interpreter translated them faithfully. When Jérôme stopped speaking, Brezhnev remained silent for a

[21] J. Lejeune, report of the interview with Brezhnev, December 15, 1981.
[22] Ibid.

moment then answered "Da" (Yes). At the end of the one-hour interview, Brezhnev expressed his very great respect for this step by the Vatican and acknowledged "a serious moral and political obstacle on the path to unleashing a world war".[23] Then Brezhnev, who did not seem to be in a hurry to dismiss his guests, continued the conversation in a less official tone. He announced to them that it was his birthday and said to Jérôme, "Thanks to God and to my physician, I am in good health."

When he heard Brezhnev giving thanks to God, the interpreter was left gaping. Jérôme, too. Oddly, there was no commentary on that extraordinary mission in the French press,[24] but it was widely reported by the official Russian newspapers and television networks, in keeping with the extraordinary reception reserved by the Soviet authorities for those envoys of the pope.

In 1982, Jérôme ardently continued his research on fragile X syndrome. The folic acid treatment seemed to give appreciable results, but those observations were still too uncertain to be announced. Twenty patients were now receiving the treatment, and Jérôme had thirty-six other patients likely to join the research protocol. He corresponded with Doctor Randi Hagerman, from Children's Hospital in Denver, Colorado, who inquired about this program:

> Dear Doctor Hagerman,... I would be very interested to see you and your team plan a systematic study on the possible effect of folic acid on patients afflicted with fragile X syndrome.... Cooperation is certainly necessary, and I am ready to give you access to all our data, if that interests you.... It is much too early to speak about an improvement of intelligence; no doubt in five months I will have the first set of data.[25]

Jérôme had the distinct impression that the results of the clinical trial on behavioral troubles went beyond a mere statistical fluctuation. He devoted himself with redoubled efforts to this promising research project. "If only we could finally find something for the patients!" he said to himself joyfully.

Still, he was prudent, because since 1952 he had been seeking a treatment for children who suffer from a mental handicap, and how

[23] Ibid.

[24] J. Lejeune, "Mon entrevue avec Brejnev", *France-Soir Magazine*, January 23, 1982.

[25] J. Lejeune, letter to R. Hagerman, June 14, 1982.

many times had he thought that he had the solution, only to see it slip away? Each time, it was months of work lost and hopes dashed. The dream of his life. But his determination was renewed each morning by the smiles or the tears of his little patients. Every morning he would start again, with a new avenue of research, new energy, new hope. And still greater determination.

This time he really had good hope of obtaining positive results, and this dynamic was very helpful at the laboratory, where difficulties were proliferating. For some time now, he had noticed a change in his coworkers. His own ambition had not changed, but their enthusiasm was no longer the same. Most of them no longer supported his research projects. As though they no longer believed in them. Now, for Jérôme, the stakes were crucial. One day he confided to Birthe:

"You understand, darling, my team is the only one seeking a treatment for patients afflicted with an intellectual disability. Well, if my coworkers give up the cause, the hope of finding one will be terribly diminished."

Jérôme did not know how to motivate them once again, how to get them to realize what was at stake in this research, which was his whole life. After much hesitation, he decided to write them a letter in which he confided his fears, doubts, and hopes for his research. That evening, after the house on rue Galande had fallen silent, he sat down at his little desk and, choosing each word carefully, wrote these disarmingly simple lines:

> Personal letter to the attention of Monsieur Couturier, Monsieur Dutrillaux, and Monsieur Aurias:
>
> Dear friend, your hesitation, not to mention your refusal, to begin with me a very promising research project is doubly painful to me. On the one hand, I see you thus neglecting a line of work in which your discernment and your competence would have great weight. On the other hand, I sense that in our team, which until now has been very amicable and cooperative, a sort of separation is forming that greatly concerns me. Certainly I understand your doubts, and perhaps from the beginning I ought to have associated you more closely with these research projects. I think that I have tried to do so several times without success, and the fact that I was so unconvincing is costing me dearly today. But think about it. The stakes are extremely important, because we are talking about nothing less than a possible improvement

of a psychosis that until now has been incurable. Moreover, the theoretical model allows us to think that other afflictions besides fragile X may also be susceptible to this sort of investigation. The reason why I put these few words into writing is so that you can think about this at your leisure. I cannot let a possibility like this slip by without exploiting it thoroughly. Of course, you are not acquainted with P..., or P..., or G..., and the spectacular improvements observed by their parents seem to you like pipe dreams,... and these intellectual gains seem uncertain to you....

I very deeply regret that, since you are finishing your thesis and wish to devote yourself to the fine structure of chromosomes, you are neglecting this possibility for study. Above all, I deplore the fact that you did not consider returning to strict participation in our clinical activity, which is the logical outcome of human cytogenetics. I do not wish to omit any way of bringing you to reconsider that proposal. In the interests both of the laboratory and of the patients.

What is at stake is so serious that I am obliged to make a decision in the very near future to recruit assistants who are determined truly to help me in this research. It is obvious that I will be led to restructure the Institut de Progénèse and to modify thoroughly the type of work in progress. The activity of the hospital's laboratory assistants is admirable, and their devotion is quite praiseworthy. But I cannot let the personnel of the Institut de Progénèse, sheltered in its little ecological niche, stay aloof from this type of investigation....

Consider, dear friends: you are abandoning me midstream because you no longer believe in what I have seen. Certainly, you are not the only ones. My friend de Grouchy does not believe in it, either! To be perfectly frank, I understand you, and I encountered the same difficulty twenty-five years ago with regard to trisomy 21. The cosigners accused me then of risking their reputations with a note in which they did not believe. Moreover, you will have to resume the whole study of pharmacology and of molecular structures in order to work without difficulty on this project that is new for us. All this is not as daunting as it appears....

And then, let's speak plainly, it is not usual for the boss to give directives here and, what's more, ideas. A boss is a has-been; the best proof of this is that he has a past as a researcher. How can anyone admit that he could propose a new life today! And don't you know that all that very difficult experimentation on serine, porphine, and hydroxyproline in patients with trisomy 21 ended with no results? No discernible effect. Isn't that a death sentence for the monocarbons model, a demonstration of the weakness of the observations that made me believe, two years ago, in a slight but real beneficial effect of serine? And don't you know, too, that the whole code of molecular congruence on which I worked furiously five years ago is left without a future? You have all these things, all these failures in mind, and you consider (who could hold it against you?) that mounting my new hobby horse would be an error in judgment that you do not want to commit.

Dear friends, I know all that just as well as you do. I share your hesitations, and I share your revulsion at the thought of counting hundreds of thousands of fragile X chromosomes. But—and this is the conclusion that I propose to you—it is necessary to choose: either the humdrum existence of cytogenetics as we know it (a new syndome here and a new evolutionary filiation there) or else a hand-to-hand combat with the unknown in order to snatch a shred of knowledge on which to base a potential treatment.

In all simplicity, I await your response. If you want to stay aloof from the venture, I will leave you completely free. But I do not want you to be able to accuse me in two years of having neglected to urge you to set out with me. Forming a new team, training new students, creating a new spirit—I will do that anyway, with you, please God, or without you if I cannot convert you.

This, my dear friends, is what I wanted to tell you quite plainly, quite simply, quite bluntly. I would be so happy to lead you to participate in these discoveries! I await your response by the end of next week. Very cordially, your friend.[26]

Jérôme put down his pen, relieved after having said what was on his heart. Sincerely.

"But is it judicious to send it?" he wondered.

He was still hesitant. Too tired to decide, he decided to go to bed. "I will see tomorrow, when I am rested and my head is clear."

The next day he did not send it, nor did he on the following days.

Despite that internal difficulty, Jérôme continued his research projects and devoted so much effort to them that he was obliged to turn down several trips, including one planned for Uruguay. His appointment book was full for a year in advance. He participated,

[26] J. Lejeune, letter to M. Dutrillaux, M. Aurias, and M. Couturier, March 24, 1982. This handwritten letter was found in the personal archives of J. Lejeune; it was never sent; the note "non envoyée" is written by hand near the heading.

nevertheless, in August in the major international congress on the family in Mexico, where once again he met Mother Teresa, who was as receptive as the first time. He was captivated by her incredible work and wrote to Birthe: "What she is accomplishing is literally unimaginable."[27]

During that congress, he also made the acquaintance of a woman who was very involved in the pro-life cause, Mercedes Wilson, who would become a great friend of his family.

Swamped, Jérôme agreed to give only a few conferences now, ones that he deemed important, like the one scheduled for October at Notre-Dame in Paris. This particular speech took a lot of work, and he entrusted this intention to the prayers of his priest friends.[28] As always, he prepared it meticulously, because his oratorical ease was the fruit of long labor, but this time he applied himself even more so as to chisel and polish a speech worthy of the place. He would speak in the presence of the delicate smile of Our Lady ... Therefore, it was with some emotion that he prepared to speak beneath the vaults of the cathedral, on October 10, 1982, in the evening. Nevertheless, the meeting took an unexpected turn. Some not very scrupulous protesters managed to cut off the microphone, and it proved impossible to restore the sound system. Jérôme was therefore compelled to go down to the basement to give his conference to an audience that was much smaller because of the cramped quarters. Nevertheless, this mishap did not diminish the force of his speech:

> It is a great honor and a great blessing to be able to say at Notre-Dame Cathedral in Paris these simple words: "My dear brethren". An honor, because this brotherhood comes to us from God, who made us in His image, and a blessing because modern biology helps us to recognize our common origin. Far from being a sociologist's utopia, this brotherhood is a fact of nature. God created man *ish* and *isha*, man and woman He created them. And although our species is quite specialized in one or the other sex, human nature is fully common to both, and even by its origin, as we will soon see.[29]

[27] J. Lejeune, letter to Birthe, August 22, 1982.

[28] J. Lejeune, letter to Father Patrick Chauvet, October 1982.

[29] J. Lejeune, "Biologie, conscience et foi", conference at Notre-Dame Cathedral in Paris, October 10, 1982.

Then Jérôme led his listeners to the farthest reaches of time, to the creation of the world, of light, and of life, so as to bring them as far as the Garden of Eden to meet Adam. Jérôme reread Genesis in light of the facts of science, admitting that the mechanism of evolution is still unknown, contrary to the received ideas of neo-Darwinism, and proposed his Adamic hypothesis to explain the appearance of man on earth; in doing so, he showed with great mastery and with poetry how science is an ally of faith and how complementary the two are in their search for the truth. This conference, which admirably sets forth his thinking, met with great success and earned him effusive thanks. He received many congratulatory letters from persons who had been able to hear the speech or to read the text of it, which was published in the following days.

> This enabled us to read and reread it with a clear head and to derive from it spiritual profit that you may not suspect.... Through all that we experience and live, who can boast of never having had a gnawing feeling of insidious doubt or spiritual dryness? Now your lecture radiates such a luminous certitude that all we can do is humbly leave it up to someone who is so much more enlightened than we are. Be assured, Monsieur, of my infinite gratitude to you for this calming of the soul.[30]

But it also evoked criticism, because he was accused of trying to make science coincide with revelation. Jérôme, however, had carefully shown the dangers of concordism "for this reason, always the same one: science evolves, and therefore theories pass, while what is true abides."[31] Several days later, he submitted this observation to Father Jules Carles, who taught at the Catholic University of Toulouse and with whom he conducted a friendly correspondence.

> Please find enclosed the text of a conference that I gave at Notre-Dame. I received on this subject a very angry letter from Father D. that professes a holy horror of concordism. But what are we to do if genetics refuses to contradict revealed truth! I would very much like

[30] M. A., letter to J. Lejeune, December 31, 1982.
[31] J. Lejeune, "Biologie, conscience et foi".

> to have your opinion, and I ask you to be assured of my very deep and very respectful affection.[32]

In the laboratory, work continued. In July, Jérôme welcomed as an intern a young Mexican woman, a physician, Pilar Calva de Vazquez, who was writing her thesis with him and sharing in his consultations, and in September the young Aimé Ravel joined his team. They brought new enthusiasm to the heart of his laboratory, which was invaluable for Jérôme, who could not manage to motivate his coworkers, who were increasingly detached from his projects. On the research side, there was no noticeable progress. Jérôme confided to a friend:

> The work on fragile X is advancing slowly. Several new treatment methods are under way, but I know nothing yet. It takes so many months to see any results![33]

Jérôme still hoped. But this time, his words revealed a certain weariness, which was unlike him. It was like a premonition ...

[32] J. Lejeune, letter to Father Jules Carles, December 31, 1982. Jérôme was frank with his friends and did not hesitate to tell them when he disagreed. Thus, on July 28, 1986, he wrote to Father Jules Carles to tell him how disappointed he was in reading the priest's article "Embryons et personnes", which appeared in the June 19, 1986, issue of *La Croix l'Événement*: "I cannot conceal my sorrow from you.... To say that a person does not exist until the age of seven years ... so as to draw a lower line at the age of five years is literally incredible! As for the remark, 'In Heaven we will find only those who have merited it': don't you know that in that case it would be empty? It is impossible to refuse the Kingdom of Heaven 'to the least of my brethren'. They are the ones to whom He belongs, well before the age of reason! Forgive me for writing to you in this way, Father.... With my very respectful, very faithful, and very sorry affection."

[33] J. Lejeune, letter to Father Jules Carles, December 31, 1982.

CHAPTER 13

CROSSING THE DESERT

1982–1984

In early November, the situation reached the tipping point. Jérôme learned that a law that directly concerned him had just been passed. This law forbade a director of a research unit to hold that office for more than twelve years. Regardless of his age, his merits, or the importance of his research projects. This law concerned only three directors in France, including Jérôme. When he returned to rue Galande on the evening of that important notification, he was exhausted and confided to Birthe:

"My darling, this is a catastrophe for my research projects and for the patients. It means that my team will be dissolved in a year."

Birthe, frightened by this news, looked at him anxiously. He continued, in a flat voice:

"Now we are the only ones seeking a treatment for these handicapped little ones. I will fight as much as possible; maybe I can gain another year, but surely no more than that."

Then he became pensive, and she did not dare to interrupt that silence. He knew very well that in striving to find a treatment for his patients, he was implicitly demonstrating his rejection of a public health policy based on abortion and that this stubbornness was highly displeasing to the administration. Why look for a treatment for illnesses that can be eliminated by abortion? The very objective of his work was what displeased them. He was judged at best useless, at worst dangerous because he did not conform. Since the pressures on his career had not been enough to bend him—besides being kept in the background, he had not had a promotion or a raise in salary for more than ten years, and when nominated several times for a Nobel Prize, his name was set aside because of his advocacy[1]—he was now being attacked for his research itself. In order to neutralize him, they had decreased his funding, and now they were ousting him. Suddenly lifting his head, he said to Birthe, who was still sitting beside him in silence:

"I am going to fight hard, you can be sure of that.[2] I don't yet know how, but I will find some way to continue."

Birthe, too, quickly pulled herself together.

"Surely there is someone who can help you", she said. "Someone who understands the importance of your research projects. At the CNRS, at INSERM, at the Ministry."

Jérôme reflected for a moment. "Could I perhaps try to write to Professor Boiron? He is president of the specialized scientific commission on biology and cellular pathology. Maybe he will be able to help me, even though we do not share the same pro-life ideas at all. You know that he was technical adviser to Simone Veil when the law was being written and that he started the first abortion center at Saint-Louis Hospital. But he may understand the importance of our research projects and act for the good of science."

"Write to him right away", Birthe continued, glad to have the start of a solution.

"Not this evening," Jérôme replied, "I am too tired."

Then, after another interval of silence, he went on to say: "I will try to convince my colleagues to collaborate with my ideas, but if there is a lack of money, that will be difficult.[3] It will be necessary for me to find financing, too. I will mention this difficulty in the United States, when I go to Chicago in December to give a conference at the medical school, and in New York. Maybe they will be able to help me financially.

[1] P. Chaunu, *Hommage à Jérôme Lejeune*, April 6, 1994. Excerpts: "Eligible for the Nobel Prize, without the slightest doubt; there is testimony to this from everywhere. Eligible but not a winner of the Prize; sometimes it is difficult to be a prophet in one's own country, especially in one's all-too-close family, when such stakes enter into the calculations. This is why I am sensitive, yes, to the titles that he did receive, but even more so to those of which he was deprived as a sanction for his refusal to capitulate to the powers that be and the horror of this era." Professor P. Kamoun, interviewed by F. Lespés, in *Jérôme Lejeune: Au plus petit d'entre les miens*, documentary film by F. Lespés, April 2015.

[2] J. Lejeune, letter to H. Ahern, November 16, 1982. Jérôme predicted this law to his correspondent and told him: "I will fight hard", and "I will not abandon them."

[3] J. Lejeune, letter to R. Engel, November 1982.

Birthe looked at her husband with compassion and thought sadly: "This man never has a franc on him and is not attracted to money at all, and here he is obliged to pass the hat around. He will have to beg in order to continue his research projects. And to think that he would have all the money he needed if he were in the United States. He wants to stay and work in France, and look at how France treats him. My God, what an odd situation...." The next day, November 15, 1982, Jérôme wrote to Professor Michel Boiron:

> Since the discovery of chromosomal pathology in our species, this new chapter of medicine has developed rapidly, and ERA 47 was created by the CNRS in 1967, affiliated with the Institut de Progénèse and the chair of fundamental genetics. This decision by the CNRS made it possible to create the only existing program in France designed to focus the available disciplines—cytogenetics, clinical genetics, and biochemistry—on a single objective: research into a possibility for treating mental disability. In spite of the stages that have already been covered, with some successes in the cytogenetic, biochemical, and clinical areas, noted more particularly in two afflictions, trisomy 21 and fragile X syndrome, this objective has not yet been reached.
>
> The suppression of ERA 47 would mean the passing of this multidisciplinary approach, the only one possible. Requesting that you be so kind as to take this fact into account, I ask you to be assured, Monsieur le président, of my very high esteem.[4]

Then Jérôme flew to the United States. In New York, when he described the situation at his laboratory in Paris, he found that a position was offered to him immediately.

"It would be so easy to accept! No more wrenches in the works. Some money for my research projects...."

Jérôme let himself be lulled for a few seconds by this prospect but then turned down the offer without hesitation. Once again, he refused because, despite all the difficulties, France was where he wanted to conduct his research.

In Paris during that time, the administration proposed to his coworker, Doctor Dutrillaux, that he become the director of a new CNRS research unit, while taking with him all the members

[4]J. Lejeune, letter to M. Boiron, November 15, 1982.

of Jérôme's team. Bernard Dutrillaux hesitated, then accepted.[5] The news was a heavy blow to Jérôme. Doctor Dutrillaux, however, proposed integrating that new unit under Jérôme's authority, but the latter refused, because that would assure the permanence of his position but not of his studies. Now the position was not the object of his concern.

At the age of fifty-six, he continued his practice and remained professor of the chair of fundamental genetics on the faculty of medicine. He therefore already had a lot of work! Not to mention all his talks in France and abroad. No! What worried him was his research. He knew that in taking away from him the directorship of that research unity, the administration was tolling the death knell of the multidisciplinary studies necessary to find a treatment. He was angry. A wounded, helpless anger. "How can they not understand the importance of these research projects?" he wondered sadly. It was a terrible blow. Terrible because his scientific hopes and projects were failing. He was angry because he felt powerless to prevent this disaster. The task was so great that it was absolutely necessary to deploy all his forces in the battle, and now he lacked troops! His team was the only one in France searching for a treatment for these patients, and here he was now without a team, compelled to search in greater isolation than ever.

The break was consummated. Dutrillaux and Jérôme separated. Dutrillaux kept with him the laboratory equipment and all of Jérôme's coworkers, except for Marie-Odile Rethoré and Aimé Ravel,[6] who faithfully remained at his side. Jérôme preserved only the microscope paid for by the American foundations as well as some smaller items. They packed their boxes, left the rue des Cordeliers, and settled the Institut de Progénèse at 45 rue des Saint-Pères. It was a strange situation, which Marie-Odile Rethoré did not fail to emphasize:

"Monsieur, here we are, the two of us, as at the beginning, when everything was just getting started. Do you remember?"

Sitting on a crate, visibly exhausted, Jérôme lightly nodded his head. "Yes. At the age of fifty-six, I will have to start all over again", he thought. "Recreate everything, find new coworkers, find money.

[5] B. Dutrillaux, interviewed by F. Lespés, in *Jérôme Lejeune*.

[6] Today Doctor Aimé Ravel is medical director of the Institut Jérôme Lejeune.

It is necessary to begin from zero. Less than zero, because when I started in Turpin's practice, just thirty years ago, I had more means at my disposal than today." His anger had subsided. He no longer resented his coworkers, his former coworkers. He understood that, despite their friendship and respect for him, they had little by little divested themselves from his research projects, out of disinterest and weariness and a lack of confidence in his unusual methods. And then he knew that it was not easy for them to be labeled "Lejeune's collaborators"—that Lejeune who had been placed on the Index of the scientific community. "They, too, have mouths to feed, a career to pursue. How can I hold it against them?" he said to himself.[7]

As though these difficulties were not enough, Jérôme became at the same time the target of a smear campaign that was as violent as it was unexpected; the outrageous claims would have been amusing had the stakes not been so high. The blow was even more painful because it involved friends.

It all started with a visit. One from a representative of the European Worker's Party in France (POE, Parti ouvrier européen), Jacques Cheminade. During their conversation, he asked Jérôme to combine the associations Laissez-les-vivre and SOS futures mères, to which Jérôme gave his moral and scientific support, with an association to which he, Cheminade, was very close: the Club de la Vie.

Jérôme listened and then replied: "Sir, I do not commit my friends without having asked their opinion. Therefore, I cannot take this initiative without speaking to them about it."

But after having listened to Jacques Cheminade, Jérôme was convinced that combining the groups was not desirable. He did not go into political calculations, but he gauged what people said. And he did not like Jacques Cheminade's words very much. Several days later, Jérôme received a telephone call. Quite surprised, thinking that the matter was settled, he heard the voice of a man speaking American English, who introduced himself as a member of the organization of Mister Lyndon LaRouche. Jérôme, who knew neither this Mister Lyndon LaRouche—an American politician and activist and a former

[7] B. Dutrillaux, who dimly understood that Lejeune had been marginalized while he was working for him, very quickly saw proof of it. The moment he separated from him, he started receiving invitations and being courted. Then he understood the extent to which Jérôme was being ostracized and related this in the documentary film by F. Lespés, *Jérôme Lejeune*.

Trotskyite—nor his interlocutor, listened politely. Then the tone changed, and the man warned him in extremely threatening terms that if he persisted in spreading the rumor that their organization was an offshoot of the KGB [Soviet security agency], his international scientific reputation would be destroyed. Jérôme hung up, dumbfounded. "Who *are* these people?" he wondered, while returning to the table with his family. Preoccupied with many other things that were more important for his laboratory, Jérôme soon forgot that call.

Several weeks later, Jérôme started to receive from various English, Italian, German, American, and Spanish colleagues newspaper clippings that were strange, indeed, to read. He learned from these multinational publications[8] that he had Nazi friends in Sweden, Fascist friends in Spain, and others in Brazil who were fundamentalists and in Rome who were Malthusians; that he was "a KGB viper"; that he had invented male pregnancy; that he was moving ideologically from the Third Rome [i.e., Moscow] of sinister memory to a Fourth Reich in an undisclosed location, and that he had dubious friendships with the pope's assassins. He was also said to have met with President Brezhnev to finalize with him the methods of the assassination attempt on Saint Peter's Square.... With a supporting photo of a man training to shoot, in the woods, at night, with Jérôme mentioned in the caption.... The fact that the assassination attempt took place several months before Jérôme went to meet Brezhnev in Moscow did not seem to bother the authors of these allegations, who claimed to inform the reader with a host of details and conspiratorial cross-checking. These accusations were soon reprinted in France by the newspaper *Nouvelle solidarité*, which sold its issues in front of the Lejeunes' house, and by documents distributed at the exits from the subways and in front of the Faculty of Medicine. During the month of June, Jérôme and Birthe, sitting in their living room, received through the window from the street a leaflet folded into a paper airplane. Birthe picked it up, unfolded it, and read the screaming headline: "Jérôme Lejeune supports the KGB line."[9] Then she looked at her husband. After a moment of surprise, he commented laconically: "Surely they claim to have seen it all ..."

[8] "Jérôme Lejeune: entre la IIIe Rome et le IVe Reich", *Nouvelle Solidarité*, May 27, 1983.

[9] "Jérôme Lejeune soutient la ligne du KGB", leaflet by the Club de la Vie, June 1983.

Birthe folded the document up again and went upstairs to file it in a large carton that already contained a pile of more than a hundred similar articles. Each one of them was spine-chilling.

The strangest thing was that, despite that campaign, the association Laissez-les-vivre, with which Jérôme had worked so well in the run-up to the Veil Law, and for which he was still a scientific advisor, did not want to break ties with Jacques Cheminade. Jérôme, therefore, found himself compelled to resign from the association and asked his attorney, Jacques Tremolet de Villers, Esq., to sue Cheminade for defamation. Jérôme had to protect not only himself personally but also the cause that he represented. For he was not gullible. Why would anyone engage in such a broad international campaign? It was not simply on account of him. They were aiming at him for some further purpose. He observed that all the victims of this campaign, Professor Chaunu, Father Paul Marx, O.S.B., Geneviève Poullot, and he himself, had one thing in common: they were "true" defenders of human life. Marcel Clément, who actively supported him during those difficult months, proposed an analysis:

> The operation as a whole is obviously intended to establish a parallel intellectual and moral hierarchy in the worldwide anti-Communist right.

A hierarchy that would then be easy to manipulate.

> They denounce the KGB so as to attract those who are anti-KGB and to link them up with structures that are manipulated by the KGB. Jérôme Lejeune was chosen because he polarizes almost all those whom they want to divide: the friends of the Polish pope, the Catholic and/or anti-Communist scientists; the men capable of warning against the Soviet arms race, etc.[10]

The stakes were high; the violence of the attack showed it.... The French police intelligence service (Renseignements généraux) took these attacks very seriously and came to rue Galande several times to investigate. As all this unfolded, Jérôme stood firm, but he was still affected by the divisions that ensued. It is always surprising

[10] M. Clément, letter to J. Lejeune, June 17, 1983.

to see how some people let themselves be influenced by such crude accusations.... Although Jérôme won the lawsuit against the POE, the difficulties continued for several more long months. As late as 1985, Jérôme used to receive insulting letters that accused him of compromising. He always answered, often laconically, as he did to this member of Laissez-les-vivre:

> Dear friend, having no relations with Masonry and never having had any, I admit to you that I do not understand the object of the warnings that you send to me. Kind regards.[11]

Although Jérôme had reasons to worry during that year 1983, he also had numerous occasions to rejoice with his family. After the blessing of Damien's diaconal ordination in 1982, which he received as a grace, he had the joy of attending the wedding of Karin with Jean-Marie Le Méné. In order to celebrate the entrance into the family of this new Jean-Marie, a naval officer, Jérôme, who loved plays on words, nicknamed him Jean-Maritime, while his other son-in-law, the philosopher, was promoted to Jean-Maristote [*Aristote* = French spelling of Aristotle].

Jérôme also delighted in the everyday trivialities, especially if they were shared with those near and dear to him. Everything was conducive to his happiness. Thus, in July 1983, he wrote to Birthe, who had already settled in Kerteminde for the summer, to relate to her the quiet happiness of the evening that he spent in Chalo:

> After dinner, while Clara, Loïc, and Marie-Alix were picking gooseberries at sunset (a delightful rural tableau), I set out with my cane, my horse, and my dog (both of which are sculpted on the knob of the cane) to watch the sun set on the Beauceron plain. The harvest is ripe. Some fields have already been cut; the air is redolent with wheat, barley, and rye, and at sunset the whole earth is golden. The trills of ecstatic joy emitted by the larks were even more deafening than usual. Had it not been for the late hour, I would have played the sub-prefect on the fields. That is to tell you that after this incessant activity, comforted by your telephone call, which gave me great joy, all I have left to do is to get some rest.[12]

[11] J. Lejeune, letter to a representative of Laissez-les-vivre, November 25, 1985.
[12] J. Lejeune, letter to Birthe, July 14, 1983.

One month later, Jérôme allowed himself a pleasant getaway at the other end of France. The pope had announced that he would come on pilgrimage to Lourdes on August 15, for the Feast of the Assumption. Jérôme had decided to greet him there. Since Birthe was in Denmark, he departed alone for a trip by car as far as Angoulême, where he stayed with cousins, and then continued his journey by train. At his destination, he was happy to see the Holy Father and returned to Paris delighted by those twenty-four hours. Although nothing had gone as planned, since Birthe was not there.... Knowing how much this story would amuse her, he hurried to write to her about it.

> Lourdes, this August 15, '83, 7:30. Since the train's arrival abruptly interrupted my writing, I am continuing it at the friendly café that I found while leaving the station. The town is decorated very prettily with flags bearing the colors of Lourdes and with the White and Gold of the Vatican.... Since you know that I am not very resourceful (the stationmaster ... asked me whether you were here and looked at me with some commiseration when I answered in the negative, like someone who is thinking, "The poor man; how is he going to manage, all alone like that!"), it is not certain that I will succeed in delivering to the Holy Father the letter from APEL in Paris. I will strive to do my best, though....
>
> Lourdes, this August 15, '83, 18:30. Well, you won your bet, my little darling; I did not succeed in giving the letter from APEL to the Holy Father. I will mail it from Paris! To tell the truth, I didn't try awful hard, as children say! Upon reflection, it seemed to me so stupid that there was not one single placard of the APEL that I gave up on such a complicated adventure.
>
> But I will tell you about the day. When I arrived on the esplanade with which you are familiar, the meadow, on the other side of the River Gave, I met lots of people; above all, Spaniards from Pamplona and even from Santiago de Compostela!... The Holy Father was in superb form, and Don Stanislas, too. I was along the route, walking with some kids ... while shouting hearty "Vivats!" ["Long live the pope!"]. I'm not sure that the Holy Father saw me, but it is possible.... The Mass was superb, very recollected and quite long. To go to Confession, I came across a charming priest ... who recognized me immediately! I saw a dozen physicians whom I do not know but who know me. One of them, from the emergency medical service, stopped

his ambulance to say hello to me, which won for me the great esteem of my neighbors! Then a security official came to suggest that I go ahead of everyone to the official places. Since you were not there, I thanked him profusely for his gracious attention and remained there planted on the lawn. To my great displeasure, moreover, since I can't stand for long. I did not think that I could manage to go back into the Basilica of Saint Pius X where the Holy Father was speaking to the youth. Quite by chance, I had turned up at one of the entrances, and suddenly an official came to say that there were still seats and that they could absorb a bunch of people who were collapsing—including me—but without any right of way, given the immediate rush!... It was at the same time a bit folkloric and deeply moving to hear that inverted nave resound; the other speakers were midgets next to the Holy Father. Of course I missed the train for which I had a reservation, and if all goes well, God willing, as our old pastor used to say, I will be in Angoulême sometime past midnight, after a trip standing in the aisle, and in Aunac a little before 1:00 in the morning. If I find the car again. But everything is perfect, exactly as expected. I kiss you affectionately. Your Jérôme who loves you.

P.S. I think that I have forgotten a lot of things, but my legs have receded into my body so much that it bothers me a bit to write![13]

After that short summer excursion, Jérôme fervently took up his work again and confronted the paucity of his resources. He had to form a new team and to find equipment in order to restart his research projects. While he was striving to rebuild a laboratory in great destitution, the new academic year at the university brought him another unpleasant surprise: the CNRS announced to him that, starting on January 1, 1984, it would no longer provide him with any financing. Not content to have eliminated his team, the administration, therefore, continued its demolition work by cutting off his funding. Jérôme had no other option but to find some money quickly if he wanted to continue his work. Fortunately, the Michael Fund granted him a subsidy that allowed him to hold on for another few months, but he had to prepare for the sequel. He confided this difficulty to Martin Palmer, an American attorney who had contacted him after his deposition to the American Senate and was

[13] Ibid., August 15, 1983.

writing a screenplay about the story of Tom Thumb as related by Jérôme. The words that Jérôme wrote at the conclusion of his letter to Martin reveal his firm intention:

> After next summer, we will be in a very difficult if not disastrous situation. But I have high hopes and great determination. We will never give up.[14]

The attitude of the CNRS was so unfair that it disturbed several leading figures in France. The municipal government of Paris, scandalized by such discrimination, decided with the support of Jacques Chirac, then mayor of Paris, and thanks to the efforts of Bernard Billaud, his chief of staff, to allocate to Jérôme a one-time research subsidy, while he was being elected to the Academy of Moral and Political Sciences and to the Academy of Medicine. Jérôme became a member of those two prestigious institutions in 1983 and 1984 respectively. He was also named a member of the *Accademia Scientifica dei Lincei* in Rome and received their Feltrinelli Prize.

The situation did not escape the journalists' attention, either. Thus, on March 19, on the occasion of his election to the Academy of Medicine, *Le Parisien libéré* commented:

> Rather oddly, although he has been director of research since 1963 with the CNRS, the subsidies that had been allocated to him have just been discontinued. The Americans, who are very interested in his studies, have decided to help him, since France has cut off his funding. No doubt his pro-life stance is not unrelated to the official decision. His election will perhaps console him for his "abandonment" by some.[15]

And while other newspapers, such as *Le Monde, Le Quotidien du Médecin* or *La Croix*, were content to mention the election, the weekly *Valeurs actuelles* reported the whole story by saying:

> The election of Professor Jérôme Lejeune to the Academy of Medicine is a response to the CNRS, which just deprived him of funding

[14] J. Lejeune, letter to M. Palmer, October 25, 1983.

[15] "Le professeur Lejeune, élu à l'Académie nationale de médecine", *Le Parisien libéré*, March 19, 1984.

> for his laboratory. Other reactions favorable to the French geneticist and opponent of abortion: the C&A Society enabled him to continue his research projects immediately by financing a position of researcher, and the Michael Fund in Pittsburgh has just launched a campaign in the United States to collect $100,000 for the benefit of Professor Lejeune's practice at the University of Paris V.[16]

The election of Jérôme to the Academy of Moral and Political Sciences, one of the five academies of the prestigious Institut de France, softened the harshness of that ostracism. It was recognition by France of the extraordinary value of his work and the occasion for a very beautiful and solemn ceremony for the conferral of his academician's sword. On November 28, 1983, a crowd filled the magnificent hall of the Chancery of the Universities of Paris.

Jérôme greeted with a broad smile the numerous invited guests who had come to give him their official or friendly support. He recognized in the first row, on either side of Birthe, Father Rovasenda and Professor Chagas, from the Pontifical Academy of Sciences, Monsignor Oliveri from the Apostolic Nunciature, Father André Vingt-Trois, vicar general of the cardinal archbishop of Paris, Jean Tiberi, deputy-mayor of the Fifth Arrondissement, Bernard Billaud, from the City Hall of Paris, and Jean Foyer, the courageous former minister of health. Also present was his friend Pierre Chaunu, already a member of the Institut. Not to mention the rector and the deans of the Universities of Paris. He recognized also André Clément, Geneviève Poullot, Virgil Gheorghiu, Jean Daujat, and others. So many, many friends![17]

A series of speeches followed, tracing Jérôme's scientific career and the moral importance of his work. Marie-Odile Rethoré recapitulated thirty years of fruitful collaboration, while Pierre Debray-Ritzen, professor of child psychiatry at Necker Hospital, congratulated him for being admitted beneath the *Coupole* [Dome] with the words that everyone had in mind: "Dear Jérôme, this is it! You are entering into the Promised Land. That is your reward. You certainly deserved it."

[16] "Réactions en chaîne", *Valeurs actuelles*, March 19, 1984.

[17] "La remise de l'épée d'académicien au Pr Jérôme Lejeune", *L'Homme Nouveau*, December 18, 1983.

Then, when Marcel Clément took the podium, he emphasized the many dimensions of Jérôme's work, which extended well beyond the sphere of the experimental sciences:

> Following the very logic of his reflections, the geneticist became an anthropologist. The researcher found himself compelled, so to speak, by his discoveries to become a moralist. The physician, finally, one day, became in France and throughout the world the herald and the hero [*héraut* and *héro* are homonyms in French] of a pro-life policy.... Today you perhaps appear just as well known for your contribution to anthropology, to the moral disciplines, to the political common good, as for your scientific work. Anthropology owes a lot to you. You have brought to it a new scientific foundation, which until now it had replaced by often risky hypotheses: you asked yourself how genetics, for its part, could contribute to the definition of human nature.

Finally, under the watchful eyes of Birthe, who was beaming in the first row, Jean Fourastié approached to confer the sword on Jérôme. But before handing it to him, he turned to the audience and declared:

> This is a sword from 1830, which has been restored and provided with new symbols. These symbols, as is customary, summarize the scientific work and the human work of Jérôme Lejeune.... We can distinguish on its cross-guard four series of motifs: the upper one is the double helix, to the right and to the left, of DNA.... The main motif is related to the experimental scientific mind, to science. It is made up of a half-field of a microscope, and in that half-field we see three chromosomes, an obvious and direct allusion to trisomy and to chromosome 21. But science is not only observation; it is intuition, it is creative imagination. And here Jérôme Lejeune wished that the words *Deo juvante*, "With God's help", be written on the parchment on which science writes its results. To the right of these symbols, therefore, of science-observation and science-intuition, I might almost say "revelation", there is a telescope to the right, and to the left—a fetus that Jérôme Lejeune made known worldwide, that two-month-old infant who was already sucking his thumb. Dear Monsieur and Friend, I have the honor therefore, in the name of the committee of honor that Mademoiselle Rethoré brought together, to confer on you this sword.

Thunderous applause. Then silence fell again, and Jérôme, in turn, went up to the microphone:

> For the last thirty years, we have gradually learned to recognize this mind that is hindered by an imperfect body. We have learned to love Pierre, or Jacques, or Paul, or Madeleine, or Françoise, whereas the science of pathology saw only a syndrome. And our profession as a geneticist presents this paradox that we are perhaps the last family physicians since, over the course of the years, the affectionate patients and their admirable parents quite naturally become friends.

After responding to the preceding speeches, he concluded:

> A statement by Saint Irenaeus sums it all up: "Gloria Dei est homo vivans", "The glory of God is man fully alive." And the attempt to give to everyone this fullness of life that we call intellectual freedom is a task for us, for our successors, and for their successors. And if I had to sum up for you in one word the scientific program that will lead to this achievement, I would simply borrow it from Saint Vincent de Paul. Just one word: "More".[18]

As she listened to these words being uttered by her husband, Birthe knew that they were fraught with great meaning. Beyond their oratorical effect, they revealed his most intimate disposition: "Despite the difficulties that accumulate, he does not surrender", she thought admiringly. Then, observing her husband's smile, she thought, "How can he be so peaceful and cheerful? I know very well that this serenity that he displays this evening is not just a façade. I have never seen him perturbed. His rare moments of discouragement are quickly swept away by the hope that guides his life. He has an absolutely astonishing interior strength. He acts as though everything depended on him, then abandons himself as though everything depended on God."

Hope had, in fact, become for Jérôme a concrete virtue; its specific connection with the art of medicine led him to practice it daily. Not only did it help him pick himself up again and persevere despite the failures and adversities, but it guided his medical practice. It was evident in the way he looked at his patients and in his conviction that

[18] Ibid.

their lives had value, despite their suffering, and he conveyed that certitude to them. Not by words, but by his way of being. In serving his patients, who were bent under the weight of suffering, Jérôme, in a way, took on their pain so that it might become his own. This ability to have compassion, to console, day after day, uplifted them and manifested his own interior attitude toward the cross. He knew that, behind the scandal of suffering, there is "a path of hope".[19]

Then, too, Jérôme did not seek to replace God—neither in the care that he gave to his patients nor in his research for a treatment. He did as much as his strength allowed him to do, with modesty like that of Ambroise Paré, who used to say: "I bandage, God heals." As a scientist and a Christian, he recognized that "heaven is not empty", that "life is not a simple product of laws and the randomness of matter", and that there is, above all, "a Spirit who in Jesus has revealed himself as Love".[20] This led him, as a physician, to seek man's salvation, not in science, but in God. He refused to substitute scientific hope for biblical hope; he stood in his place and did not put on a lab coat too big for him. He was only a physician; he was not God. He was not the one who saved or prolonged life; he was at the service of life. Therefore, he fought to comfort his patients but did not think that he had to eliminate the sick person in order to arrive at a world without suffering, because he did not hope for the establishment of a perfect world in which suffering would be eradicated thanks to advances in science.[21]

Jérôme was aware of the spiritual stakes of this scientific attitude. He wrote it to the pope the day after he had come to Bourget: "A society that kills its children has simultaneously lost its soul and its hope."[22]

No, he had chosen and chose once again solemnly, on that day of his election to the Academy, the hope of a Christian scientist, the hope that relies on God, which he had engraved on his academician's sword: *Deo juvante*.

[19] Benedict XVI, encyclical *Spe salvi*, no. 38: "Indeed, to accept the 'other' who suffers, means that I take up his suffering in such a way that it becomes mine also", Benedict XVI says. "The individual cannot accept another's suffering unless he personally is able to find meaning in suffering, a path of purification and growth in maturity, a journey of hope."

[20] Ibid., no. 5.

[21] Ibid., no. 30.

[22] J. Lejeune, letter to Pope John Paul II, June 5, 1980.

Jérôme, who as a young fiancé had admitted to Birthe that she was the one who had brought him hope, had taken hold of it since then. "Hope . . . , that little daughter of nothing at all . . . she alone, carrying the others. As the star led the three kings from the farthest reaches of the Orient",[23] this joyous little flame, which is described so beautifully by the poet Charles Péguy, illumined his life from then on.

Jérôme, preoccupied in late 1983 by the difficulties of his laboratory, had little time to devote to the requests that poured in from all over the world. With great regret, he turned down some invitations. Thus, in October, he received a letter from Monsignor Carlo Caffarra, president of the new John Paul II Institute for Studies on Marriage and Family, which had been created by the Holy Father the preceding year—a letter in which Monsignor Caffarra asked him to be so kind as to be a permanent collaborator on their official academic journal. Alas! Jérôme, who was in complete agreement with all the topics studied by the Institute, had to turn down that collaboration and agreed to participate only occasionally.[24] God knows that he would have loved to be able to do more for that work of John Paul II, whose prophetic commitment to families he could see!

"They say that the Holy Father signed with his blood the creation of the Pontifical Council for the Family that he was supposed to announce on the day of the attempted assassination", Jérôme remembered. "But I cannot commit myself to contribute regularly; I must concentrate my efforts in order to rebuild everything at the laboratory."

Nevertheless, despite his duties, Jérôme decided to participate in a prayer group that met every week in the early morning. Christian Chabanis, a writer and journalist, used to gather several Catholic intellectuals to have a prayer breakfast. He invited Jérôme to join them. They met to pray and to discuss spirituality before going to their professional activities. Jérôme quickly came to value those weekly appointments where he met committed laymen and a few clerics, like Father Georges Berson, with whom he struck up a friendship.

In February 1984, Jérôme received a call from the Holy See. They asked him to be so kind as to board a plane to Rome and then to Moscow so as to lead the papal delegation to the funeral of Andropov,

[23] C. Péguy, *Le porche du mystère de la deuxième vertu*.

[24] Monsignor C. Caffarra, letter to J. Lejeune, October 15, 1983, and Jérôme's response.

who had died on February 9. This new mission to Moscow lasted only three days. Jérôme agreed and, at dawn on February 13, arrived in Rome, where Monsignor Tauran from the Vatican diplomatic services was waiting for him. When the young prelate saw the rough, military-looking jacket that Jérôme was wearing, he worried:

"Professor, don't you have anything more formal to wear to the funeral?"

Jérôme admitted, "Alas, no! I brought the warmest thing I have. I had nothing else but a raincoat."

Monsignor Tauran replied: "Very well, we will find for you a coat that will be suitable and warm. I will give you a *shapka*, too, because you are going to be standing for hours in the icy wind of Red Square, and I would not like to have your death on my conscience!" he explained with a smile.

Jérôme gratefully accepted. A few moments later, he was equipped with a heavy wool coat, a fur cap and a diplomatic passport from the Vatican. Then they led Jérôme, together with the other members of the Vatican delegation, to the Italian delegation, which had reserved seats for them on the presidential airplane. At 11:00, President Pertini welcomed them on board, in the company of Signore Andreotti. They then made a stop in Budapest, where they quickly met with the local Soviet ambassador. Then the airplane finally landed in Moscow, where the papal delegation was immediately welcomed and entrusted to a "special attaché" who did not leave Jérôme and his colleagues alone for an instant, even in the corridors of the hotel.

On the afternoon of the 13th, Jérôme was invited to visit the room where the remains of the late President Andropov were lying in state in the Trade Union House, which was draped in red and black. That evening, he participated more lightheartedly in a warm, beautiful dinner at the Italian embassy. The next day, February 14, at 11:00 in the morning, all the delegations were on Red Square. The funeral ceremonies began. Despite the sun, the temperature was 12° C below zero [11° F]. Jérôme curled up in his comfortable coat and silently thanked Monsignor Tauran for his prudent attention.

While the delegation's special attaché was explaining to them that the ritual was identical to the one employed at the time of the death of President Brezhnev, Jérôme observed the leadership team's painful ascent to their places on the mausoleum.

"This expresses, not sorrow, but disarray, given the inevitable dwindling of a band of men that is not being renewed", he thought. "Despite an almost stereotypical reproduction of the Brezhnev ceremony, one gets the impression of attending, not a revival, but a dress rehearsal."

Furthermore, several comments that he heard during the brief polite exchanges at the end of the ceremony confirmed that unease. Pierre Mauroy, who represented France, remarked, "I was here a little over a year ago, and we will meet again soon, I fear."

While another delegation let loose with the observation: "They are making embassies and industries out of funeral ceremonies!"

The next day, the papal delegation departed again for Rome, where Jérôme was awaited by Monsignor Tauran. The latter kindly drove him back to the airport right away, where Jérôme returned to him the coat, the cap, and the visa and gave him a preliminary report of the situation.

In Paris, his family was very impatient to hear what had happened on his mission. He had scarcely come back to rue Galande when Birthe peppered him with questions:

"My darling! Whom did you see, and what did they tell you?"

While Thomas asked: "How is this Chernenko now at the controls?"

Jérôme, exhausted but happy to be back in the warmth of his house, told them about his trip in detail.

"Secretary General Chernenko seems to be in a physical state similar to that of President Brezhnev in December 1981. I got the impression of a junta still in power although its life is slipping away. When he gave his speech, his delivery was uncertain, hesitant, occasionally interrupted. He has respiratory problems. He sometimes swayed. In contrast," Jérôme added, laughing, "Marshal Ustinov seems martial and Mister Gromyko—oratorical."

Then, turning to Birthe, he said to her: "Do you remember when I went to visit Brezhnev in 1981, that he received us with his chief of staff, Mister Alexandrov?"

"Yes, of course", replied Birthe, whose memory never failed.

"Well, when I went forward to present our condolences in the big white and gold hall, just before arriving in the central apse, I noticed him standing in the previous small apse. And I saw that he was giving instructions to people attentively huddled around him. After the ceremony, we met for luncheon at the Italian embassy, where we arrived very late after going back to the hotel. Since I was seated on the ambassador's right, my lateness was unfortunately very conspicuous. During the luncheon, I told them that Alexandrov seemed to be playing a subdued but very persistent role. My statement was considered very unlikely. But that evening, after dinner, we heard on television that Alexandrov had just been chosen as Chernenko's chief of staff!"

"Incredible!" Birthe interrupted. "They will think that you were very well informed!" she said, laughing.

"Yes, that's the funny thing! Whereas all you had to do was to look at what was happening right before our eyes in the great hall during the condolences."

Then Jérôme went on: "I deliberately informed our special attaché, who was watching television with us, about the excellent impression that I had of Mister Alexandrov because of his courtesy during our interview with President Brezhnev in 1981. I confided to him also that during the handshaking, I had almost stepped out of line to greet Mister Alexandrov, but that fear of a breach in protocol had prevented me from doing so."

Then Jérôme added, laughing, "The special attachés are a very useful institution, since they are a constant and inevitable means of communication. May as well use it without complaining about it!"

"And the Italians to whom you had made your remark about Alexandrov: What did they say about it?" Birthe asked.

"Ah, that is even funnier", Jérôme replied. "On the return plane, as soon as we had departed from Moscow, a member of the Italian embassy asked me which officials I had met. 'Only the ones from the Academy of Sciences', I said, but apparently he did not believe me. During the stopover in Vienna, another member of the Italian delegation asked me insistently which Soviet leaders I had been able to meet and what I thought about them. I replied that I had taken a great interest in the discussion with my fellow academicians. It seems that our late arrival at the Italian embassy, my remark about Alexandrov during the luncheon, and the news, six hours later, of his appointment caused some to suppose that there were unexpected contacts between the delegation of the Holy See and certain Soviet leaders! It was a good thing I had not greeted Alexandrov in the great hall!" Jérôme concluded, laughing.[25]

A month later, the Holy See called on him again, this time to have his scientific opinion on the "bio-medical aspects concerning sexuality, love, and the family".[26] For its part, the Pontifical Academy of Sciences, which was forming a small task force on *in vitro* fertilization, asked Jérôme for some contacts and his expertise.

When Birthe questioned him on this subject, Jérôme told her: "Since the birth of the first baby conceived in vitro, little Louise Brown, who was born on July 25, 1978, in England, I have already been called on several times concerning this subject."

"Yes, I remember", Birthe said. "Last year you went to testify before the Royal Society of Medicine in London."[27]

"Indeed", Jérôme replied. "And do you recall that I had been at a congress in Toronto, long before that, in October 1979, for 'The Tiniest Humans Conference'? I spoke there along with Sir William Liley."

In mentioning his friend who had recently died, Jérôme had a moment of anguish. "With the death of Sir Liley, the pro-life movement lost its greatest champion",[28] he said sadly to Birthe. "He was a big, strong New Zealander who had an extraordinary career", he explained. "A neuro-biologist at first, he became an obstetrician to protect babies from risks associated with birth. We owe to him the discovery of amniocentesis. He took care of infants endangered by an Rh-factor incompatibility, because the mother produces antibodies capable of injuring the infant's cells, especially the red blood cells. He was daring—the first to use a large needle to perforate the mother's abdominal wall, go through the uterine wall, and remove a sample of the amniotic fluid in order to examine the infant's condition. If the child was very sick, they could induce early labor right away, at around the seventh month, so as to give the child a transfusion and save him. Then he had the courage not only to pierce the child's dwelling place, but to perforate the abdomen of the child himself and

[25] J. Lejeune, *Compte rendu sur les funérailles d'Andropov*, February 15, 1984.

[26] Cardinal Baum, letter to J. Lejeune, March 13, 1984.

[27] J. Lejeune, *Test Tube Babies Are Babies*, testimony before the Royal Society of Medicine in London, 1983.

[28] J. Lejeune, letter to P. Vignes, 1984.

to insert a minuscule plastic tube within the abdomen of the little fellow, who kept wriggling, so as to give him a blood transfusion and to save him *in utero*."

"And the baby did not die?" Birthe asked in astonishment.

"No, no!" Jérôme replied. "He was also the one who discovered that when you inject a bitter substance into the amniotic liquid, the infant refuses to swallow, whereas, on the contrary, if you inject a sweetened substance into the amniotic fluid, he swallows much more often than usual ... and of course gets the hiccups."

"He was a great physician!" Birthe commented admiringly.

"Yes. Liley was the founder of intrauterine infant pathology and treatment. The Queen of England ennobled him, but the medical profession had ennobled him much earlier, acknowledging him as the father of modern fetology."

Jérôme stopped for a moment, then confided to his wife: "Liley suffered profoundly, because through his remarkable discovery he was the pioneer of a technique that was designed to give care but was diverted from its purpose. When we spoke about it, I had the same feeling. When I saw for the first time the extra chromosome 21 in trisomic persons, it was a sign of a sickness, but since then some have made it a sign of death."

Jérôme let a few moments of silence pass by, then added with conviction: "He certainly was the best pro-life orator on all the continents, in all circles."[29]

Birthe looked at her husband with some surprise and thought, without telling him: "That is what people generally say about you...." But Jérôme paid no attention to his wife's astonishment; intent on his account of the congress in Toronto, he related a humorous anecdote.

"I had started my conference by taking the unexpected example of George Bernard Shaw, the Irish author and wit who received the Nobel Prize for literature, and the very beautiful American dancer Isadora Duncan. Do you remember that story?"

"No!" Birth replied.

"Maybe I did not tell it to you", Jérôme said. "Just listen, you'll find it amusing. During a dinner where they met, Isadora Duncan, who was known much more for her beauty than for her wit, told Bernard

[29] Ibid.

Shaw, who was extremely intelligent but obviously no Adonis, 'Let us have a child together. He will be the most extraordinary of all. I will give him my beauty. You will give him your brains.' Bernard Shaw looked at her, quite interested, and asked her pensively, 'Yes, but what if he had my body and your brains?' And the whole auditorium started to laugh."

Birthe laughed, too. She did not like French humor very much, but this sort of story amused her. Then, becoming serious again, she asked: "Wasn't that the congress where you met Chuck Dean?"

"Yes, you are right. Charles, alias Chuck, Dean, as president of the Virginia Society for Human Life, was asking about the licitness of extra-corporeal fertilization, so as to know whether he should encourage or curb the creation of *in vitro* fertilization centers in his state. He is courageous. He subsequently tried to prevent these clinics from being established. That was at the very beginning of the big procreative market."

"And Chicago?"

"Yes, that's right. I spoke in Chicago, also. The following year", Jérôme agreed.

"Therefore, you are well prepared to reply to the Pontifical Academy of Sciences", Birthe concluded as she stood up to look for a cigarette.

Jérôme, who had not smoked for several years, having stopped from one day to the next in order to protect his voice, took a licorice drop and said, "That's right. But for the Pontifical Academy of Sciences, I have to go into things in greater depth."

Jérôme therefore inquired among his international contacts about the best scientific and technical studies relating to this question.

Meanwhile, he received a letter from Monsignor Caffarra, who wrote to him, with the agreement of Cardinal Ratzinger, prefect of the Congregation for the Doctrine of the Faith, asking him to submit a text with his critical opinion "as scientific devil's advocate".[30] Now Birthe was no longer surprised to receive at the house on rue Galande fine envelopes with Vatican postage stamps. They had become quite frequent in early 1984! In March, Jérôme received another letter. This time it was written by Cardinal Ratzinger, who asked him to list "in

[30] Monsignor Caffarra, letter to J. Lejeune, and Jérôme's reply, February 1984.

a scientifically incontestable way all the questions that genetics poses, now and in the immediate future, for man's moral conscience."[31]

In his reply, Jérôme noted: "Of all these subjects, the one that demands the most serious decision is this: Is extra-corporeal fertilization illicit per se?"[32]

The exchange continued until August with Archbishop Bovone,[33] secretary of the congregation, who asked Jérôme for a new critical analysis. In October, a second letter from Cardinal Ratzinger thanked Jérôme for this exchange.[34] During that difficult year, the congratulatory and thank-you letters that Jérôme received from men like Cardinal Ratzinger, Archbishop Tchidimbo,[35] former ordinary of the Archdiocese of Conakry who had been imprisoned for eight years by his government, or, in France, Bishop Jean-Charles Thomas[36] of Ajaccio, who congratulated him on his pro-life commitment, were particularly heartwarming for him.

Jérôme tried also to be available for other requests, especially those that arrived from his new friend, the attorney Martin Palmer. This time, in June, Martin asked him his opinion on the project of Doctor Bernard Nathanson, an atheist American physician who had been one of the promoters of abortion in the United States. He himself had performed more than five thousand abortions, and the "clinic" that he directed performed sixty thousand in two years. Then, having suddenly understood, thanks to the latest scientific techniques, the marvels of extreme youth [i.e., the earliest stages of human life],[37] he converted. He did not convert to religious faith; he converted to Life. He became one of its most courageous defenders and planned to make a film showing the reality of an abortion, in order to enlighten minds and hearts. This was the project that Martin submitted to Jérôme in June 1984. Jérôme replied at first:

> I am frightened by this film project. That is not my method, teaching by horror. I prefer to convince by describing the beauties of nature

[31] Cardinal Ratzinger, letter to J. Lejeune, March 5, 1984.
[32] J. Lejeune, letter to Cardinal Ratzinger, March 1984.
[33] Archbishop Bovone, letter to J. Lejeune, August 24, 1984.
[34] Cardinal Ratzinger, letter to J. Lejeune, October 26, 1984.
[35] Archbishop Tchidimbo, letter to J. Lejeune, June 12, 1984.
[36] Bishop Jean-Charles Thomas, letter to J. Lejeune, December 1984.
[37] J. Lejeune, "Le cri silencieux", *Tom Pouce* 2, June 1985.

rather than by showing the diabolical suggestions of unnatural techniques. But this is only a personal opinion.[38]

A few days later he clarified:

Nathanson surely has right on his side. If the video could be shown to every abortionist, every nurse who works in an abortion center, to every pro-abortion militant, it could do them a lot of good. This video could probably convert the abortionists, and Doctor Nathanson is no doubt the most eminent person to do it.[39]

Jérôme also found a little time to speak at a congress in Rome, during which he made the acquaintance of Angela de Malherbe, who was very committed to promoting family life. She would become a great friend. He also gave a conference in Ostende, the title of which, "Physiology of the Intellect", indicates the theme of his meditations during it: the freedom of the intellect. During that congress, he met Monsignor Michel Schooyans, a doctor in philosophy as well as in theology and professor at the Catholic University of Louvain, as well as Carlo Casini, an Italian Christian Democrat deputy who was very involved in pro-life work. Jérôme corresponded at length and struck up a friendship with each of them.

Three months later, among his important mail from the United States, Jérôme received a letter that was different from the usual requests. This time it was a professor of history at the California Institute of Technology (CIT), Professor D.J. Kevles, who sent to him the manuscript of a book on the history of genetics that he was preparing to publish. Jérôme was quite touched by that sign of respect and replied, giving several clarifications:

Dear Professor Kevles, I thank you for your courtesy. Your historical account is very carefully written, and I recommend only that you make some minor clarifications, as you will see. Only one of them, the last, is rather important, and, confidentially, I must tell you why. In fact, Turpin did not advise me at all to publish the data. When I suggested that he co-sign, he hesitated because he had never looked at the chromosomes, and he said, "Well, I think that I will sign, just because in

[38] J. Lejeune, letter to M. Palmer, no date, probably in June 1984.
[39] J. Lejeune, letter to M. Palmer, July 3, 1984.

the current state of ignorance, no one will pick a quarrel with you if it is not true." Moreover, at the time of the publication, Marthe Gautier was on vacation, and when she returned, she told me that I had taken too much liberty in putting her name in second place on a publication by which she was not convinced. These memories absolutely must not be mentioned in a printed document. It would show a great lack of tact toward Turpin and Marthe Gautier, and I would detest such critiques [in print]. Because I trust your honesty as a historian, I thought that I should give you this information privately, so as to explain to you why I modified the text slightly. With my thanks for having most courteously submitted to me your excellent book.[40]

Jérôme, in fact, had never recounted those facts before, out of respect for his boss Turpin and out of tact toward his former colleague Marthe Gautier. Only his family and a few close friends knew of the situation.

In late 1984, a new trial awaited Jérôme. Not only did the material situation of the laboratory remain precarious—he still had no computer to work with—but once again he had to face a major disappointment in his scientific research. And this time, the letdown was particularly painful. After enrolling several trisomic children in a clinical trial, he observed with indescribable joy that the cranial circumference of the patients following his treatment developed much more than the others. Finally, he had found something! But he did not dare to believe it and meticulously repeated all the results before proclaiming victory. After checking one last time, he realized, alas, that it was nothing but a stupid error due to imprecise tape measures: the cranial circumference after treatment seemed larger because the tape used to measure it was not the same as the one used at the beginning of the trial, causing a slight variation in the readings given by the two tapes. After so many years of hope and intense work, the disappointment was on the same scale as his earlier joy: immense. Although it was not his first disappointment, this time it was different: Jérôme had not only hoped, he had believed that he was seeing and measuring the effects of the treatment.... It was a rough blow. Jérôme confided to his journal:

[40] J. Lejeune, letter to D.J. Kevles, 1984, the month is not indicated but probably in September.

> This is why, all things considered, I feel crestfallen at the previous technical failure, uneasy about my results, and intimidated by the decision that has to be made.[41]

This new disappointment, added to the major financial difficulties and the fact that he had become the object of ostracism in France, marked two years that were particularly trying for Jérôme. His close friends looked at him and understood that, despite his cheerfulness, he was experiencing a genuine desert crossing in his professional life. But behind his calm and serenity, did they notice his extreme intellectual and professional solitude? Not that he was completely alone—his correspondence shows the countless scientific exchanges that he was having with researchers from all over the world—but the professional invitations had grown scarce, and his honors were forgotten. Even his former scientist friends were gone. With regard to his career, the fact was overwhelming: he, who had revolutionized genetics by his successive discoveries, from which the new discipline of cytogenetics emerged, the discipline for which he created the first university course; he who had been courted and honored throughout the world for his work as a whole; he who had trained generations of French and foreign geneticists, on the faculty and in the laboratory, apparently no longer meant anything to the French scientific community. Now he had neither team nor financing, and he was no longer invited to events.

Internationally, although he was in regular contact with many researchers, those exchanges were as a private person, and his career was deadlocked. All that would have had little importance if he had found the much-desired treatment. But here, too, the reality weighed heavily. The bottom line, after all those years spent in looking for a way to cure his little patients, seemed very meager. Thirty-two years of efforts that yielded no therapeutic success. He had made discoveries to identify sicknesses, but still had no treatment to offer. He had some leads, of course, but he had followed so many of them since 1959! And they had all unraveled; they had all proved to be without a future. Now this was the very purpose of his life. Not to speak of his political failures. All his efforts to try to save the handicapped children,

[41] J. Lejeune, *Réflexions personnelles*, December 7, 1984.

the preborn children, had not prevented the vote on the Veil Law. Here, too, he had failed. The overwhelming fact was painful.

Jérôme had apparently lost all his glory and saw everything that he had built professionally taken away from him. Already detached from the goods of this world, he was now divested of all professional or worldly vanities. But, curiously, this destitution did not shake his serenity. Jérôme remained true to himself. He peacefully accepted the events of life, and the interior freedom that had already been manifested in the past was revealed here with a new brilliance. Freed from everything that was not absolutely essential, Jérôme was afraid of nothing except of offending God and of not doing enough for his brethren. He had placed his life in God's hands, and now he commended his future to him. Like the useless servant. In that confident abandonment, his life took on another dimension. From now on, he was called to care not only for bodies, but also for intellects and hearts. Again, with that little flame of hope that guided his soul. *Deo juvante.*

CHAPTER 14

PHYSICIAN OF HEARTS

1985–1989

> Dear Professor, You don't know me, but I know you. Twenty years ago, without knowing it, you changed my life, and today I want to say thank you.

Jérôme stopped reading for a moment and read the signature. The family name certainly meant nothing to him. Only when he looked back at the beginning of the letter did he notice the maiden name, written in parentheses.

"Oh, yes! I remember that poor woman who had come to see me. But how is she related to the one who is writing to me today?"

Intrigued, Jérôme continued his reading.

> My father and mother are farmers, breeders on a small farm.... They really worked a lot and had lots of problems with their children because both of my parents were Rh positive, and we children are all Rh negative.... Mama had seven children. Their first child, whose name was Marie, born in 1949, died at birth.... Then my big sister Marie was born on June 4, 1950, and she was normal. Then the twins were born, my sister Françoise and my brother Henri, Rh negative of course, on March 26, 1951. They were born prematurely, at seven and a half months. They weighed one kilogram [2.2 lbs.]. Henri died right after his Baptism, and he was able to have a Christian burial. My sister survived. Françoise was put into a special little bed lined with cotton by the fireside, and the doctor said: "We will see whether she lives"! She survived, but you can imagine with what aftereffects. One year later, on June 2, 1952, I arrived. I was a large baby weighing 3.7 kg [8 lbs. 2 oz.], normal, no one knows how, and Rh negative. Mama had another child, who died prematurely in 1956. And on January 2,

1963, my little sister Marie-Gabrielle was born trisomic. She was very damaged; they did not want to show her to Mama right away; she was in an incubator for a month.

I still remember her birth; I was ten and a half years old. I remember the visit from the doctor who came to my parents' house, into the farmyard, and I had hidden behind the window. We children were all looking forward to the birth, and suddenly I saw my father, who was a giant, a farmer, doubled over and bent down, weeping, and I thought that my sister had died. She survived, and I was immensely happy. I said to myself: "She did not die, she is alive!" ... She survived, but for my father, that was a catastrophe....

For me, that baby was one of the loves of my life, truly one of the loves of my life. She is the one who taught me the invisible, essential things.... What pained me was not her illness but the way others looked at her. The accusing look of others: "Your father drinks", which he never did, or "Your mother has something abnormal." I had doubts about my mother, I had doubts about my father. It was necessary to hide her; they told us to put her in an institution because otherwise the rest of us would not get married.... For my father, that was a genuine castration in his lineage. He was completely destroyed.

As for me, I was compared to my sister Françoise, who was handicapped.... The boys ran away from us during our adolescence as if we had the plague.... But Mama used to say to us, "Don't worry, your sister will pick the right man." And, in fact, I met my husband, and my sister fell completely in love with him. As for my parents' condition, they were blamed; that is what Mama told me: "I was very much to blame." They were crushed: so many dead children! Humiliated. At the very least, they were being punished by God for a hereditary sin. People pointed at us all the time. They asked us not to come with our sisters to weddings in the family. Therefore, there was always one of us who stayed to watch the others. And then Mama's sister-in-law had a trisomic child ..., and she met you, and she told Mama to come see you, also....

Therefore Mama went to see you, with my two sisters.... Mama was transformed; my mother was transformed. Because you restored her dignity to her. She had become obese, she weighed 87 kg [191 lbs.]. By restoring my mother's dignity, you restored the dignity of the whole family, and for me, kid that I was, that was my backbone. I looked at my sisters; I had always loved them, but that supported me when others looked at us. It was my backbone: "Professor Lejeune said that ... therefore it is because ..., and if the professor did that, it is so that I can get on in life, without being ashamed", or rather being less ashamed, because in adolescence you are always a little ashamed. You held me up by the arms; that enabled me to stand up and to be able to look at my sisters. No, I personally did not see you, but that is the effect that it had on me. It was colossal. I personally was normal and therefore had no reason to go see you. You comforted Mama. We were no longer banished. People brought up this hereditary story. Me, too; I told myself that I could not get married because I had that heredity. Therefore, there was no more heredity or deviant behaviors by my parents, alcoholism, or things like that. It could be understood and explained scientifically. The extraordinary thing about you is that you dealt not only with my two sisters but with us and with my mother. You told Mama, "Take care of your two normal daughters, because psychologically it is very difficult for them." At that time, there was no psychologist in these regions....

When you took my little trisomic sister in your arms for the first time, you revived my mother by exclaiming, "Oh, how cute this little girl is." I still remember Mama telling us about that. The consequence of those repeated visits is that you found a remedial program for my sister Françoise. You gave some tests, you looked at how she was. She was very retarded; she was not able to go beyond the first few grades of elementary school. You gave a special treatment for my sister Marie-Gabrielle because she was not walking. She did not walk until the age of five. You gave her shots to strengthen her. You gave all of us our dignity back. You can image the state we would be in if we had not met you! My father started to love my little sister, to accept her, and ended up loving her a lot. So for me as a little girl, you were a backbone when shame or humiliation took hold of me when others looked at us, because we were banished. You brought us out of misery. You revived us. You took care of us all. My mother lost 30 kg [66 lbs.]. When they talk about the paralytic who was carried by four men, I think that you are one of those four.... And I, of course, am the paralytic.[1]

Jérôme put the letter down in silence. He knew the sorrow of those mothers, of those fathers, or of those siblings who suffered because of a handicap, but, above all, from the looks given to their

[1] This text was not sent to Jérôme Lejeune but is the exact account, word for word, related by Blandine S. to the author; it is published here with her authorization. (The only modification made by the author was to adapt the text by addressing it to Professor Lejeune.) This text is typical of the testimonies received by the author about the changes brought about by Professor Lejeune in the lives of the families that came to consult him.

child, from the fact that he was rejected, from the resulting fear about the future. "Who will take care of him when we are no longer there?" How many times had he heard that anguished question from parents? In order to be useful to them, to help even just one of those little children, Jérôme was happy to be in his position. He had refused to leave it for all the gold in the New World and was very happy about it. There was so much good to do here, so much suffering to relieve.

Many pregnant women, worried about expecting a trisomic child, also came to him to ask his advice and seek the reassuring presence of a physician.

"I remember that woman whom my friend Philippe had referred to me", Jérôme suddenly thought. "She came to see me right after her husband died. He was young, not yet forty. She was pregnant with her second child, and she knew that he was trisomic. She hesitated. What a joy when Philippe told me that she had welcomed her son and that now she headed an association to help trisomic persons enter into the mainstream of life!"

But sometimes the outcome was less fortunate. Jérôme remembered, too, that telephone call one evening at home on rue Galande. One of those many calls from worried parents or anxious women, at dinnertime, to get some advice or to experience a bit of support. The conversation sometimes would last a long time, and, despite the day's fatigue, Jérôme would always answer. But that evening, the conversation was short. It was a woman who announced to him that she had had an abortion, that she had not had the courage to keep the child. Jérôme returned to the table, his face pale. When his children asked him, "Who was it?" he answered, "A poor mother who did not find anyone to help her. All these tragedies are because we do not do enough to help the mothers."

And he sat down, wondering how to do more. His many concerns about the laboratory must not cause him to neglect direct aid to the "poorest of the poor", the sick children and the preborn children. To serve them as much as his strength allowed. At the place where he was the only one who could act. Without failing to perform any of his duties.

This willingness to advocate for the preborn children was quickly called on, then, in early 1985 from the other side of the Channel. In the United Kingdom, the Warnock Committee, established by the Department of Health and Social Security, had been interested for several months in human embryos, or, more exactly, in the possible use that researchers could make of them. On June 26, 1984, that committee had published a report in which it proposed experimentation on human embryos *in vitro* until the fourteenth day after fertilization. That date, corresponding to the appearance of the neural crest in the embryo, was chosen by consensus but arbitrarily, citing the future benefits expected from that experimentation.

In February 1985, the bill came before the British Parliament, and Jérôme was called to testify before the Chamber of Commons. Much was at stake, since it was the first European country to propose legalizing research on human embryos. Jérôme did everything he could in this new Battle of England, aware that if England lost, the world would follow in the debacle. On February 6, 1985, standing before the Chamber, he demonstrated that, contrary to the allegations of the Warnock Report, experimentation on embryos less than fourteen days old would not lead to any therapeutic solution for hemophilia, myopathy, cystic fibrosis, or trisomy 21.[2] Jérôme doubted that the members of the Warnock Committee, who knew how empty their own arguments were, would forgive him for having demonstrated it, but so what!

To Jérôme's great joy, at the conclusion of those first debates, the vote by the Chamber of Communes was positive. The Unborn Children Protection Bill protecting the preborn child was passed. It still had to go through several stages before becoming law, but it was an initial victory. The English friend who had requested Jérôme's deposition congratulated him. But Jérôme responded:

> I am absolutely certain that the members of the Commons did not vote for Enoch Powell's text in order to please me or because I had made them change their opinion!... The idea of protecting little Englishmen was not imported from abroad. It is the simple application of habeas corpus, which established the dignity of the English nation! Habeas corpus is the thing that must be highlighted (because it is true).

[2]Jérôme Lejeune was right. Thirty-four years later, research on human embryos has provided no therapeutic solution whatsoever.

His friend feared reprisals, but Jérôme calmly told him:

> As for attacks against my work or yours, they are inevitable but of no interest at all, because that is not the subject of the law that is to be voted on in May.[3]

In Paris, Jérôme tried to get his laboratory up and running again, little by little. He continued his studies of fragile X and trisomy but was still very cautious. To his English colleague who asked him about this subject, he answered:

> I have published nothing about the therapeutic trials in the case of Down syndrome. No one can say that I claim to cure them. I am convinced that it is possible, but I don't yet know how![4]

1986 was somewhat calmer than the two preceding years. The situation at the laboratory stabilized. Jérôme managed to form again a little team with young physician-researchers like Doctor Marie Peeters, who came from the hemato-oncology department of the teaching hospital in Nancy and had just published an interesting study on leukemia in trisomic persons. Doctor Pilar Calva, whom he had welcomed as an intern in 1983, came back from Mexico to work with him for two years, and her husband, an anesthetist, helped them from time to time. Many French and foreign interns also expanded the team. Similarly, another great assistant for Jérôme was Monique Baroni, whom he had taken on as secretary at the faculty in 1979 and whose help with his correspondence was invaluable.

In the area of finances, too, things improved a little. Jérôme found that he was less constricted thanks to the generosity of his American and Australian friends. The catastrophe had been avoided. Nevertheless, the team and its finances remained very fragile.... This poverty summoned each collaborator to dedicate himself to the essentials, and Jérôme went forward, still driven by a terrific hope: "Our conduct can be summed up in one sentence: whatever may be and whatever happens to us, we will never give up."[5]

[3] J. Lejeune, letter to R. Brinkworth, March 26, 1985.
[4] Ibid.
[5] J. Lejeune, *Du bon usage de la génétique*, 1971.

What struck the visitor when he arrived at Jérôme's new laboratory was the atmosphere that prevailed there. They worked hard, soberly, and in Jérôme's office there was a black cross on the white wall. A lab-oratory.... Although Jérôme did not talk about his faith with his collaborators, they, by observing him, understood what motivated him. Especially at the hospital, with his patients.

One day an intern asked one of the young physicians in the department: "Don't you find that there is something special in his manner? There is something that supports him in the difficult moments so that he can give good advice to his patients. His look is very special, with them, with us. I sense that he sees someone special in each one of us."[6]

The young woman replied: "That is true. He does not have to give us great lessons in theology; we see it in his action, through his patients." Then, after a moment of hesitation, she confided: "His example was a real conversion for me. His witness of respect and love for life transformed me. I come from a family that is Catholic but not practicing. I was baptized, but I was not going to church. During the consultations with Professor Lejeune, his witness transformed me. And then his warmth, his humility, his delicate respect for women, his consistency.... I discovered that it is possible to be an extraordinary scientist and a great Catholic. I understood that it is possible to wear the cross and a white lab coat at the same time."[7]

After a moment of silence, the intern went on. "As for the cross, you know: the other day, a television journalist came to the laboratory, and the cross posed a problem. When the journalist arrived, he took the liberty of saying to Professor Lejeune, 'I would like to remove that crucifix', and Professor Lejeune replied, 'No, I insist on this crucifix. You will leave it there.' The journalist retorted: 'You do not know what the cameraman is going to make out of it; while you speak, he will zoom in on the black crucifix against a white background, and that will conjure up images for the television viewer.' I do not know how it ended, but I know that he had this debate, because the journalist himself related it to me, and Professor Lejeune

[6] Conversation of the author with that former coworker of Jérôme Lejeune.

[7] P. Calvà de Vazquez, testimony given to the author and in various media, such as www.amislejeune.org or American newspapers.

told him: 'No, I am not ashamed. If it is there, it is because it has to be there.'"[8]

Although careful to use arguments of reason and not of faith in discussions with his fellow scientists and not to make pronouncements about God while working with his peers, Jérôme did not hide what he was, what he thought, and whom he served. Therefore, when someone asked him to display a reassuring neutrality, so as to sail under the colors of civility, he would reply very naturally: "Putting my flag into my pocket turns it into a handkerchief."

He was tactful yet had integrity; the scientist was not one side of him and the Christian the other. It was all one. Not all his friends had his fortitude, though, and some worried for his sake about the animosity that his witness provoked in some scientists. To one of those warning letters, sent by an English friend, Jérôme replied humorously:

> Thank you very much for your kind letter. Mister W.'s anger is a curious phenomenon. I am Catholic, and I teach fundamental genetics; these two pieces of information are true. But how does Mister W. mix them in order to produce a "fundamentalist Catholic" outside of his test tube?... Charity tells us that errors must not be taken as insults. And a Catholic must be fundamentally charitable. Sincerely yours.[9]

Whether or not it was a mere coincidence, ever since Jérôme was excluded from the scientific scene, his renown among the defenders of human life had spread so much throughout the world that he was now swamped by invitations. People from all regions and walks of life turned to him to defend life, sick children, preborn children, embryos ... or the beauty of family and of love. He was invited to universities, high schools, courts, legislatures, the Synod of Bishops.... Plainly, it was not just the scientist whom they invited, but the wise man. One who transmitted, with scientific knowledge and faith, the words of Eternal Wisdom. As a layman and a scientist, he was now one of the principal moral reference points for those who defended human life and truth in the world, whether or not they were Catholic. A great apostle of truth in charity.

[8] Story related by the journalist to a close friend of Jérôme Lejeune, who repeated it to the author.

[9] J. Lejeune, letter to Elspeth, January 30, 1986.

The tone of the letters that Jérôme received indicates the very high esteem of his correspondents and their respect, which sometimes bordered on veneration. In the evening, though, he would not say a word about those invitations in his journal but would cover the pages with his scientific reflections and biochemical formulas. Despite the great number of them and sometimes their prestige, Jérôme's speeches were for him a secondary activity, certainly useful, but never as important as his research. While his appointment calendar displayed a public life made up of conferences and trips, his *Journal intime* became a scientific journal exclusively. It had evolved a lot since Jérôme started it in 1959. Today, there was not one word about his private life, his reflections, or his speeches. Only the search for a treatment for his patients occupies those pages of handwriting. It monopolized his thoughts; he was almost obsessed by it.

However, it was necessary for him to respond to some invitations. Jérôme could not avoid it without the fear of failing in his duty. It was always a difficult balance to strike, and it changed with the circumstances. Since the start of his career, despite appearances, Jérôme always had strived not to be away too often, so as to preserve the equilibrium in his department and in his family. He was aware that his travels disturbed his everyday work and, to a certain extent, that of his coworkers. But in 1986, things were very different. First, with regard to his family, because his children were now adults. Only Thomas still lived at home. Birthe, liberated from everyday chores, could now accompany Jérôme. Then, professionally: Jérôme had his consultations and his courses, and it was essential for him to continue them, but his travels had become indispensable for the survival of the laboratory. They allowed Jérôme to collect the sums necessary for it to keep running, thanks to all the money earned by his conferences and the financing that he obtained from new and generous donors. Obliged to go around the world begging for bread for his research, he would now conduct his studies thanks to funding from America, England, New Zealand, Australia, and Venezuela. He also received several private gifts in France, quite insufficient on the practical level, but expressing magnificent generosity. Such as the donation from this fifteen-year-old girl who wrote to him after hearing him at a conference:

I decided to collect the money that my family wanted to put toward my [Confirmation] gifts and to send it to you, so as to try to help you in your research projects that have become difficult.[10]

During the first trimester of 1986, he therefore flew to Australia. There he met his friend Patricia Judge, who was in charge of the Genesis Foundation in Strathfield, who organized a high-quality reception for him, as she had done previously. Jérôme was scheduled to appear before the Australian Senate, where he spoke in favor of the human embryo. Then he went to Brussels, to the European Parliament, and once again to the British Parliament, to defend again and always the human embryo. After Clara's wedding to Hervé Gaymard (whom she had met at the National School for Administration) on May 31, to the great joy of the whole family, Jérôme gave a speech in Munich, Germany, then left for Rome. At the request of Monsignor Caffarra, he gave a course there at the John Paul II Institute for the Family, then in August flew to Argentina. He was invited to Buenos Aires for the congress of the International Federation of Catholic Physicians, which had been organized together with Archbishop Fiorenzo Angelini, President of the brand-new Pontifical Commission for Pastoral Assistance to Health Care Workers,[11] of which Jérôme had just been appointed a member. His speech was greatly appreciated, and upon his return to Paris he received a very beautiful letter from the archbishop of Paranà, Archbishop Karlic:

Is it necessary to tell you that you were for us a real grace that the Lord granted us?... I hope to see you again before eternity, when, I am sure, I will hear the Lord call you to His side because you want to spend your life doing good to the littlest ones and you do so.[12]

During that summer, Jérôme participated in the final preparations for the Ninth International Congress of the Family, which was to take

[10] M. Deal, letter to J. Lejeune, May 17, 1989.

[11] This commission, created in 1985 by Pope John Paul II, would become the Council for Pastoral Assistance to Health Care Workers in 1988, still headed by Archbishop Fiorenzo Angelini.

[12] Archbishop Karlic, letter to J. Lejeune, August 18, 1986.

place several weeks later, September 11–14, in Paris. It was organized by Angela de Malherbe, with the encouragement of Mercedes Wilson, with whom Jérôme was well acquainted since the Congress in Mexico, and Christine Vollmer, whom he had met in Rome, then in Venezuela, where she had invited him to speak. Angela de Malherbe had launched into this courageous adventure, asking Jérôme for his help. Enthusiastic about the idea, Jérôme had supported the project as much as he could by putting Angela in contact with the necessary persons and by warning her about the pitfalls that are inevitable in such an undertaking. The team managed to line up exceptional speakers: besides Jérôme, Monsignor Caffarra, Archbishop Tchidimbo, Father Daniel Ange, and Mother Teresa were scheduled. Jérôme appreciated the work that had been accomplished and did not fail to express it with his customary warmth and gallantry. "Angela, I place roses at your feet!"

This congress organized by lay people did not receive much support from the Church in France, but they all hoped that Cardinal Lustiger would be able to come. On September 11, in the morning, despite the few advance registrations, the large amphitheater of the Palais des congrès was bursting at the seams. Four thousand seats, all of them occupied. The latecomers were standing or sitting on steps. The audience was touched by those giants of the faith who had come to speak to them about "the fruitfulness of love".[13] Cardinal Lustiger, too, made an appearance. The applause for him brought down the house. It was an immense success. Scarcely believable. More than four thousand persons gathered for four days in Paris to hear talks on the family in God's plan. A terrific reason for hope! Quite happy about a success like that for the Church, Jérôme flew the next day to the United States, where he would participate in the work of the United States Bishops' Conference meeting in Washington from September 15 to 18. He took away with him this magnificent memory: "This congress was the most important event of the last ten years. Five thousand persons spent four days affirming respect for human life and respect for its Creator!"[14] he thought while contemplating the marvelously blue sky through the window.

[13] Title of the Ninth Congress of the Family, Paris, September 1986.

[14] J. Lejeune, letter to T. Franquet, November 6, 1986.

In 1987, the little team of physicians and researchers that Jérôme had rebuilt continued to work valiantly. Although he no longer had the means by which to further the career of his coworkers, he nevertheless found an occasion to propose the candidacy of Marie-Odile Rethoré to the American Academy of Arts and Sciences.[15]

His travels continued. Before the summer, Jérôme participated in two scientific conferences, one in Yugoslavia, the other in Guatemala, to which Birthe accompanied him, then he went to Lebanon, the United States, and the United Kingdom.

In late June, Jérôme was sent to Moscow by the Academy of Moral and Political Sciences to honor there the famous and courageous Russian atomic physicist Andrei Sakharov, an exile in his own country. He had been elected a member of the Academy of Sciences and of the Academy of Moral and Political Sciences, but the Soviet authorities did not allow him to go to Paris. At the French embassy in Moscow, therefore, Sakharov received the insignia of his election from the hands of Jérôme, who was accompanied by three members of the Academy of Sciences. In his speech, Jérôme effusively paid homage to that free, courageous scientist who had been censured by the regime:

> Most illustrious and most honored confrere, it is an honor and a blessing to be the messenger of the Academy of Moral and Political Sciences to you.... And now the blessing that falls to me to thank publicly the man who labors untiringly for the survival of mankind. If we are united in the same crusade, it is because we stumble on the same obvious fact: there is no technological or medical remedy for the abominable ravages of atomic extermination. After the greatest honors, my dear confrere, you experienced the harshest disgrace ..., but ideas cannot be imprisoned. Your removal to a place that tourists rarely visit has conferred on you, if I may say so, a toponymic glory: all Frenchmen, however little inclined to geography, now recognize the name of that unknown town: Gorki? Oh, yes, Sakharov!...
>
> Political leaders have immense responsibilities, and scientists have the duty to tell them that there is no escape from this brutal observation: "Science alone cannot save the world; technology is cumulative, but wisdom is not." Just as in each one of us the heart and reason do

[15] J. Lejeune, letter to L. Smith, August 24, 1987.

> not always get along well, so too in nations morality and politics do not always live in mutual understanding. And yet, this understanding is the only possible hope: reason, too, can lose its temper, and the heart then reasons with it. In order for civilization to last, politics must conform to reality: to the morality that transcends all ideologies because it is inscribed in our inmost depths by that unfathomable decree which simultaneously governs the laws of the universe and human nature. Allow me, my dear confrere, to present to you this diploma of membership in the Academy of Moral and Political Sciences. Your life and your work show that the dignity of scientists is to connect politics, morality, and science, despite everything.[16]

Upon his return to Paris, Jérôme read in the daily newspaper *Le Monde* that Sakharov had been honored by three members of the Academy of Sciences. Not one word about him personally, the only representative of the Academy of Moral and Political Sciences. And not one word from his speech, either. Of course.

In August, it was a different atmosphere: Jérôme gave a speech at the famous Rimini Meeting in Italy, and the press covered it extensively. Then in November, he traveled once again to Italy, but this time to Rome, where he attended the congress of the Pontifical Commission for Pastoral Assistance to Health Care Workers and spoke at the Synod of Bishops on the Laity. As during each of his stays in the Eternal City, Jérôme had the privilege of being invited to participate in morning Mass in the private chapel of the Holy Father, who then had him stay for breakfast. It was, as always, a great joy for Jérôme, which he especially appreciated in those difficult times. And current events, particularly with the recent publication of the instruction *Donum vitae*[17] (The gift of life), provided them with many topics for discussion.

The Congregation for the Doctrine of the Faith offers in this instruction a reflection on respect for human life in its origin and on the dignity of procreation, and Jérôme, who was defending the

[16] J. Lejeune, "Si tu veux la paix, protège la vie" [If you want peace, protect life], *Tom Pouce* 11 (October 1987).

[17] J. Ratzinger and A. Bovone, Congregation for the Doctrine of the Faith, *Donum vitae*, Instruction on Respect for Human Life in Its Origin and on the Dignity of Procreation (Rome, February 22, 1987), introduction.

dignity of the human embryo before French and foreign parliaments, appreciated the quality, the moderation, and the beauty of that document:

> The gift of life which God the Creator and Father has entrusted to man calls him to appreciate the inestimable value of what he has been given and to take responsibility for it: this fundamental principle must be placed at the center of one's reflection in order to clarify and solve the moral problems raised by artificial interventions on life as it originates and on the processes of procreation.[18]

The instruction, however, was not well received by most of the public, including many priests and lay Catholics in France, who thought that the affliction of infertility legitimized recourse to techniques of medical procreation. The noble purpose—to give life—justified, in their view, the means. But the instruction points out the drawbacks of this practice, which introduces a third person into the conjugal act, and shows that this personal substitution is harmful to the couple. This was the first voice raised to alert families on the impact of these techniques, while the procreation market was starting to develop. The instruction, therefore, elicited strong reactions, and Jérôme was questioned by the Catholic media to explain it.[19] He defended it intelligently and confidently:

> Just as a technician cannot replace the husband, another woman cannot replace the mother without there being, here too, a personal substitution. Marriage consists of the union of two persons in order to procreate a third. If you have other persons intervene, you are no longer looking at a marriage but at a sort of social procreation. I think that this is the foundation of the Church's position. If Holy Mother Church ever admitted that there are cases in which extra-corporeal fertilization is legitimate, she would also be obliged to revise the theology of marriage completely. For example, an impotent man could perfectly well have an ovum from his wife fertilized *in vitro* with sperm that had been obtained by tapping his testicles. Whereas the Church

[18] Ibid.

[19] J. Lejeune, "Analogie", on Radio Notre-Dame, in which he explains the instruction *Donum vitae* and expresses his admiration for Cardinal Ratzinger, on April 26, 1987. See also "Attaques contre l'instruction sur le respect de la vie", *L'Homme Nouveau*, May 3, 1987.

has always considered that the non-consummation of a marriage is an absolute argument for its nullity, she would be obliged to revise her position totally, which would be a dreadful injustice for wives. For the biologist, therefore, the Church has an extremely logical position: either there is no theology of marriage, and conjugal union is only an imprecise contract, or else the conditions in which the sex cells can be joined can be established only in marriage and exclusively by the spouses themselves.

But of course, whatever the method of fertilization may be, legitimate or illegitimate, the child is always a gift from God. This is also true even if it is the child of an unknown father, of a donor, or is carried by a woman who is not his mother. What is illegitimate are the methods used to establish the conditions for the appearance of a new life. But this new life is incontestably that of a child of the Good Lord.[20]

Finally Jérôme explained:

Not only would the Church not condemn a technique—yet to be discovered—that would treat sterility, but she demands it of researchers. Personally, I am thoroughly convinced that this detour outside the mother's body—that is what extra-corporeal fertilization is—is a technical and by no means desirable complication. The real fight against sterility, within marriage, is not at all by way of extra-corporeal fertilization. Intra-corporeal fertilization will be the real response.

To say that Jérôme defended the instruction *Donum vitae* is to mention not just his interviews in the media but also the concrete, courageous interventions that he was called on to make, at the risk of becoming once again the lightning rod of criticism from the scientific community and the general public. This time Jérôme would have to confront a team of physicians at the Parisian hospital Notre-Dame-du-Bon-Secours [Our Lady of Good Remedy], which, as its name indicates, was Catholic and belonged to a congregation of Sisters. On behalf of this same hospital, before the Veil Law, Jérôme had gone, at the request of the mother superior, to see the auxiliary bishop of Paris so that he would stop the abortions there. In vain. But thirteen years later, with the new archbishop, things were going to change.

[20] J. Lejeune, interviewed by A. Bagieu, "Le Pr. Lejeune explique l'instruction *Donum vitae*", *Famille chrétienne*, April 9, 1987.

This time, Cardinal Lustiger called for an investigation of the hospital. The superior, Sister Jeanne, contacted Jérôme, begging him to take the seat that became vacant on the Administrative Board. She hoped that he could help them from within to put an end to the abortions and the *in vitro* fertilizations initiated in 1984 and performed by Doctor Chartier. The situation had become untenable, all the more since the physicians involved had signed an article in the *Lancet*, a major international scientific journal, presenting the new method of prenatal screening of trisomic children that they had perfected. Thus they made the Catholic hospital a world-renowned center for the screening of trisomic children, which Jérôme pointed out to Auxiliary Bishop Thomazeau,[21] who was working alongside Cardinal Lustiger.

Cardinal Lustiger appointed Jérôme to the Administrative Board of the hospital, and on September 15, 1987, the Administrative Board voted to stop the abortions and the *in vitro* fertilizations. The physicians responsible for those illegitimate acts in that Catholic hospital handed in their resignations and left, furious. Headed by Doctor Chartier.

Several months later, in early 1988, a press campaign started denouncing the obscurantism and arrogance of the Roman Magisterium, represented by Cardinal Ratzinger and his defender, Jérôme Lejeune. On the other hand, the media sang the praises of Doctor Chartier, who was presented as a practicing Catholic physician with a mind sufficiently open to criticize the Magisterium. The campaign in favor of Doctor Chartier was relayed by dozens of media outlets,[22] including the newspaper *La Croix*.[23] Once again, Jérôme's fidelity to the Magisterium earned for him a coordinated media attack.

"If only you criticized the Church, everything would be so much easier!" Birthe told him one day, laughing. "You would be invited to all the talk shows!"

"Yes, indeed! Especially if I attacked Church teaching about the family and about life", Jérôme replied, and he laughed, too. "But for

[21] J. Lejeune, letter to Bishop Thomazeau, November 1986.

[22] "La faute du Dr. Chartier", *L'Événement du Jeudi*, January 11–17, 1988.

[23] "Les médecins de N-D-de-Bon-Secours soutiennent le Dr Chartier", *La Croix*, January 23, 1988.

me that is impossible; the Church is truly an expert on humanity. I observe it every day."

These upheavals led to the cancellation of a conference that Jérôme was supposed to give on *Donum vitae* at the Catholic University of Lille, at the students' invitation. Two weeks before the scheduled date, Jérôme received a letter telling him that the rector, upon learning the name of the speaker selected by the students, had issued a veto with no appeal. "A fine example of freedom of speech on a so-called 'Catholic' faculty. The pope is on the Index, and it is forbidden to agree with him!"[24] Jérôme exclaimed when he learned the news.

Alerted to this series of incidents, the apostolic nuncio questioned Jérôme. The latter soberly related the anecdote about the Catholic University of Lille, showing the contradictions of such an attitude, which promotes dialogue except with Catholics who are faithful to the Magisterium:

> This interdict was of great interest to me, coming from a rector who was complaining in the newspapers about a lack of consultation in the Church, precisely on this point [*in vitro* fertilization].[25]

This rector, like other Catholics who were in favor of medically assisted methods of procreation, was in effect reproaching the Vatican for not having questioned the physicians who were performing *in vitro* fertilizations. But Jérôme was well positioned to know how unfounded those critiques were, since the Pontifical Academy of Sciences, as usual, had questioned the greatest specialists on the subject. Jérôme explained this to the newspaper *Famille chrétienne*:

> Doctor Edwards, the inventor of the technique, and Doctor Frydman, who promoted the method in France, presented their opinions to the Pontifical Academy of Sciences.[26]

Jérôme was also consulted about the instruction by many of his correspondents; he answered them in precise terms, as in this letter, which expresses the essentials:

[24] J. Lejeune, letter to a friend (name not given), 1988.
[25] J. Lejeune, letter to the apostolic nuncio, December 28, 1988.
[26] J. Lejeune, interviewed by A. Bagieu, "Le Pr. Lejeune explique".

> The *substitutio personarum* (substitution of persons) applies when the technician, replacing one of the spouses, performs an act that according to the Christian theology of marriage not only is exclusively reserved to the legitimately married spouses, but also is the basis for the indissolubility of the marriage. Christian marriage is founded on consummation + recognized consent.... The relentless opposition to *Donum vitae* is quite understandable; it is inevitable if what I encourage you to take stock of (the indissolubility of marriage) is called into question. It is inevitable also because of the temptation to conform to the opinion of *the world*, represented here by the newspaper of the same name (*Le Monde*).... With *Donum vitae*, Cardinal Ratzinger tells human beings true morality in an attempt to protect them from a terrible abuse of medical technology that is capable of bringing about a total collapse of morals. Reread Huxley's *Brave New World*, reread Goethe and part two of *Faust*, and you will see how immensely necessary it is to keep in mind the teaching of *Donum vitae* (for this procedure is not an innovation, but the destruction of all Christian morality).

Jérôme then made about Cardinal Ratzinger comments that were close to his heart:

> As for Cardinal Ratzinger: during a work session I saw and heard him endure—there is no other word for it—very harsh personal attacks and demented theological arguments, without wavering for a moment in his calm and his kindness! Then he summed up in a few minutes the whole subject that had been discussed and set right everything that was upside down, showing at every moment a respect for persons that his interlocutors had scarcely displayed. In the discussion, his was the clearest and most charitable mind that I have ever encountered. He bows only to the truth. But he knows how to look for it.[27]

When Jérôme participated in these debates, so as to defend the beauty of life and of the human family, he knew to what virulent criticism he would be subjected, but ignored it because it was only ideological. And he encouraged all Catholics to do the same by reminding them that the world's critiques are powerless against Eternal Wisdom:

[27] J. Lejeune, letter to a friend (name not given), 1988.

> It is quite necessary for us to have a reference point, and even a reference point much stronger than the natural law about which I spoke to you just now, and this reference point is very simple. You all know it; it can be summed up in one word, actually, in one sentence, but a sentence that judges everything, explains everything, contains everything, and this sentence simply says: "As you did it to one of the least of these my brethren, you did it to me."[28]

In fact, these words explain Jérôme's whole life.

Like John Paul II, he too encouraged people not to be afraid. Moreover, in these same terms, he addressed the bishops in Rome, at the Synod for the Laity, in 1987:

> You, who are for the family, will be mocked. They will wave in front of you the specter of science that is supposedly being gagged by an outmoded morality; they will raise against you the tyrannical standard of unlimited experimentation.... Bishops, be not afraid. You have the words of life.[29]

Jérôme easily refuted the argument that aimed to inhibit Catholics, and he invited them to carry out their civic duties by defending their moral values democratically.

> Then they will say to you: What you are doing is altogether intolerable! You, who respect life; in practice, they will say: "you who are Catholics ...". (It's curious; Catholics must have some special virtue, because when someone defends human life, they always ask him: Are you a Catholic? They never ask him: Are you a Freemason?) Then they will say to you: If you respect life, it is because you are Catholics, and if you are Catholics, you have no right to impose your morality on others. Well, that is very interesting, because that is the argument of a totalitarian.... You live, and I too live, in a country that is said to be pluralistic.... It follows from this that, in a pluralistic society, it is the duty—I am not talking about a right, I am talking about a duty—it is the duty of each citizen to try to incorporate into the laws of his country, as much as he can, legally, the morality that seems to

[28] J. Lejeune, "N'ayez pas peur d'aimer", conference in Lorient, November 28, 1989.

[29] J. Lejeune, "La science ne peut pas sauver le monde", speech given to the Synod Fathers, October 8, 1987, published in *L'Osservatore Romano*, October 20, 1987.

him superior, because if he does not do that, he betrays his democratic duty, since democracy will be accomplished only by the law voted for by the majority. Now if each citizen does not try to make the law the best law possible, that citizen is not doing his duty.[30]

And to those who thought that any positive change in favor of life was impossible, he replied:

They say that abortion has now become customary and that nothing more can be done about it.... [But] change can be made in the other direction, and even without playing the prophet, we can be certain that it will be made. Health through death is a ridiculous triumph. Life alone can win.[31]

He would need this courage of truth, this charity of truth again in the year 1988, because another threat against preborn children appeared, and Jérôme wanted to do all he could to prevent it. This was the abortion pill RU 486. After many unforeseen developments, the authorization to market this pill was signed in September. Jérôme was staggered. One month later, he was invited to a television talk show, *Duel sur la 5*, to debate with Professor Émile Baulieu, the designer of the drug. He went, hoping to make the listeners aware of the immense risks of that French invention. When the journalist asked Jérôme why he was opposed to that pill, RU 486, Jérôme answered gently and firmly, while looking at the television viewers:

For one very simple reason, because as a physician, I fight on the side of life and not on the side of death, and because the abortion pill, which kills children, is bad, like all abortion. What I wish with all my heart is that chemical warfare will not take place. For we are talking about a very curious product, you know, which has a toxicity specific to human beings who have reached a certain stage of development. That, incidentally, is why it does not attack the mother's health, but it prevents the child from surviving. To be exact, it is a specific poison; I would say that it is the first anti-human pesticide. And as a physician, I cannot accept an anti-human pesticide.

[30] J. Lejeune, "La nature humain est indisponible", conference in Montreal, March 20, 1990.
[31] J. Lejeune, "La santé par la mort", *L'Osservatore Romano*, April 2, 1976.

Then, after Professor Baulieu presented the pill as a medication, Jérôme went on:

> It is necessary to know that this product was registered and that the authorization to put it on the market was signed based on one and only one direction for its use—there is no other in the request, which simply says that it is an abortive substance....
>
> The number of doses that will be manufactured is enormous. I do not know the number, I am not an industrialist, but it means millions of babies will be eliminated. And I say this because the television viewers must understand it: if this product is for sale, or even—whether or not it is paid for is of no importance—if it is used, exploited industrially, millions of human beings will be destroyed each year. And I say this calmly because it is true, because it is necessary for people to know it: this product will kill more human beings than Hitler, Mao Tse Tung, and Stalin combined; that is a historic fact.... At least ten million human beings will be eliminated each year by this poisonous substance.... That is a real fact; why hide it?

In that debate, Jérôme displayed great professionalism. Now he was a master of the genre. He repeated the message that he wanted to get across, kept refocusing the discussion, and refused to digress to subjects on which he was not competent. For example, when Professor Baulieu tried to discuss the animation of the embryo, Jérôme answered: "We are not theologians to be talking about the soul of the embryo. I would be ready to discuss it, but with a theologian, not with you.... Let us discuss this product."

At the end of the debate, Jérôme concluded:

> On one point I am in agreement with you: I would not want our children to experience war. But I would not want them to experience chemical warfare. I claim, because this is the absolute truth, that we are talking for the first time about a pesticide against little human beings. This is the first time that that has happened, and I demand that, in the country of [Louis] Pasteur, we do not start killing children chemically.[32]

[32] J. Lejeune, on *DUEL sur la 5*, television program hosted by Jean-Claude Bourret, October 1988.

At the conclusion of the program, Channel 5 polled the television viewers, who could respond by Minitel [a viewer data service]: "Which of the two debaters seemed to you the more convincing?" 35.6% said Baulieu, 61.99% Jérôme. After the broadcast, Jérôme went home, exhausted.

On December 14, Jérôme participated in a hearing by the National Assembly, which wanted to study the subject. Unfortunately, the authorization to market the pill would not be revoked. Jérôme's close collaborators silently observed then how much he suffered anxiously. For he saw with the eyes of the heart and of the intellect the millions of embryos who would be killed by that "human pesticide". It was a carnal, almost paternal suffering. He knew and felt that each embryo destroyed was a child who dies. And these are not just words.

"It is absolutely necessary to help women in crisis pregnancies more", Jérôme said to himself. "To house them during their pregnancy, if they want. For as long as they want. So that they might find shelter. And material aid."

He decided to talk about it with Geneviève Poullot, who was working so effectively with pregnant women in distress.

"I have thought about that for a long time", she replied, enthusiastically. "But we need funding, which we do not have."

"We will find some, that is certain", Jérôme replied in turn.

Providence got wind of it, and a few months later a generous friend donated to them a large house, a few kilometers from Paris, to accommodate the first young women who wished to live in a shelter. Now they had to find a woman to direct the house. Here again, Providence got involved, and soon a lively, solid young woman volunteered; her first name, Marie-Noëlle was like a sign from heaven. The first Maison Tom Pouce [Tom Thumb house] could now open. To welcome the lives of hundreds of Tom Thumbs and to warm the hearts of their brave mothers. Jérôme was very happy about it.

Since congresses for the family were proliferating in the world, particularly at the instigation of the Pontifical Council for the Family, but also of dynamic local associations, Jérôme increased the number of talks that he gave in those friendly, lively settings. After the very beautiful congress organized by the Pontifical Council for the Family in Vienna in 1988, Jérôme spoke in 1989 in Strasbourg, then in Lorient and Brussels. In the latter city, his arrival created waves. At a congress for the family! A series of telephone calls asked the organizers to cancel the appearance of Professor Lejeune and warned them that if they refused, they would lose their financing. Despite these pressures, Jérôme's speech was kept on the program, and the congress was a great success. But, in fact, the sponsors, who were under pressure, withdrew one by one; it would take the courageous organizers a year to pay for their expenses.

In August, right after returning from his vacation in Denmark, where he left a good part of his family, to work on his research projects and to examine a few patients who were not put off by the summer heat, a telephone call from his American friend Martin Palmer changed his plans. When Jérôme heard Martin's fine voice, he was delighted.

"Hello, Martin!"

Martin was very glad to reach Jérôme directly, since he feared that he was on vacation, and told him immediately: "Dear Doctor Lejeune. We need you." Then without stopping, he related the reason for his call.

"In Maryville, a little town in Tennessee, a beautiful young woman, who is a model, and her husband are going to divorce, after ten years of marriage, with no children. They tried *in vitro* fertilization. Out of the nine embryos conceived, two were implanted but did not thrive. Before the subsequent embryos were implanted, the husband demanded a divorce. And now they are quarreling about the fate of their seven frozen embryos. The man demands that they be destroyed, arguing that they are not persons. As for the young woman, she demands that they be kept alive; she defends their humanity. The judge, Dale Young, who is to judge the case, is very confused, because never before has a court decided a case like this."

Jérôme listened very attentively.

"I called Mary's attorney, Christenberry", Martin continued, but was interrupted by Jérôme, who exclaimed:

"So many Gospel names are bending over these children!"

Smiling, Martin agreed with this remark, which was so typical of his French friend, then went on: "Christenberry needs the help of a great scientist to prove to the judge that these embryos are, indeed, human beings. Doctor Lejeune, this trial, *Davis v. Davis*, is of the utmost importance, because it will set a precedent. You have to come."

Jérôme then asked: "But what does the mother say?"

"She says that if she could have the embryos, she would provide shelter for them and would hope to have them implanted into her. And if that was not possible, because of the husband, she would want to give them to any woman who cannot have children, so that her embryos could live."

Jérôme exclaimed: "That is incredible! That is the judgment of Solomon! I didn't think that it would be repeated in all of history! But do you need me in person?"

"Yes!"

When Jérôme asked whether written testimony would suffice, Martin confirmed: "No. For this trial, your presence is necessary; a written testimony is not enough. Christenberry says that he can postpone the trial by one day to give you time to come. No more than that."

Jérôme reflected a moment, then said: "Call me back in a half hour. I have to call the airport and my wife, who is in Denmark, to warn her."

Martin hung up, his heart pounding. A half hour later, Jérôme confirmed that he would come.

"I will take the plane tomorrow afternoon. I don't want to cancel my morning consultations."

"Fantastic!" Martin exclaimed. Then, a bit uneasy, he asked: "What about the ticket? I'm afraid that the attorney cannot pay it for you."

"Don't worry", Jérôme replied. "It will be my personal contribution to help save Mary's seven hopes."

When Jérôme arrived in Maryville on August 11, he met Mary's attorney, J. G. Christenberry, Esq. The latter was still wondering whether he had done the right thing in accepting Palmer's proposal to have a French physician come to testify in court. He knew neither this Palmer fellow before his phone call nor this Lejeune.

"What a funny idea", he thought, a bit anxious. "Why did I agree? Let us see what this guy is like. Does he have the guts?"

Christenberry, therefore, took Lejeune aside for a private discussion, before the hearing. He carefully interrogated him. Very quickly, Jérôme's answers reassured him, then made him enthusiastic. Finally, the lawyer asked him: "Are you a Christian?"

Jérôme replied, "Yes."

Christenberry nodded his head, then, looking him right in the eyes, asked him again: "For whom do you work?"

Jérôme replied simply, "For my Lord."

Then Christenberry told Jérôme emotionally, "You will be my star witness."[33]

At the courthouse, hundreds of media representatives were waiting for them, and soon Jérôme took the witness stand before a packed courtroom. Carefully choosing his words in English, he recalled:

> We all know that if human nature was not entirely and completely inscribed in the fertilized ovum from the start, the embryo could never become that ever-renewed and forever irreplaceable wonder: a new human child.[34]

Then he described in detail, with the rigor of a scientist and the poetry of a contemplative, the development of the human embryo, a unique little living human being. Jérôme's testimony had considerable impact on Judge Dale Young and, broadcast by hundreds of media outlets, was followed by tens of thousands of Americans. At the end of the hearing, the judge announced that he would issue his decision in forty days.

Jérôme immediately took the plane to Paris, where he stopped over for twenty-four hours. Just enough time to repack his bag and to depart again, this time for Compostela, where he intended to welcome the Holy Father John Paul II with young people from all over the world. Besides the joy of seeing the pope, this trip gave Jérôme the great satisfaction of exchanging with Cardinal Lustiger words that warmed his heart. They met by chance at the airport, and the cardinal offered to bring him back by car. That same evening, he wrote to Birthe: "We are very close in our thinking." "That meeting alone was worth the trip."[35]

[33] J. G. Christenberry, Esq., interviewed by F. Lespés, in *Jérôme Lejeune: Au plus petit d'entre les miens*, documentary film by F. Lespés, April 2015.

[34] J. Lejeune, "Les sept espérances de Mary", *Tom Pouce*, October 1989.

[35] J. Lejeune, letters to his wife, August 17 and August 21, 1989.

After a month of deliberation, the judge in Maryville gave his verdict. Judge Dale Young concluded in favor of the humanity of the seven embryos, "children *in vitro*", and decided to grant custody of them to Mary, their mother. Jérôme was profoundly happy and relieved by this beautiful ruling, which could set a precedent. Several weeks later, Jérôme's deposition was published in English, under the title *The Concentration Can*[36] (a term used by Jérôme in his deposition, describing the containers in which the embryos are submerged in extremely low temperatures), then in French, and finally in Italian, Spanish, Catalan, and Danish.

Jérôme was happy about that outcome but did not know the whole story. In Maryville, besides the judge who had been very impressed by the attractive clarity of his testimony, a young man present in the courtroom had been overwhelmed. That young physician, John Bruchalski, who had come to hear Jérôme, worked at the Jones Institute of Reproductive Medicine in Norfolk, a cutting-edge laboratory of procreative medicine—the one where Mary's embryos had been conceived. They also performed many abortions of handicapped children, and John participated in them. But that day, he was in the audience because he wanted to see who this famous Doctor Lejeune was and because he was extremely interested in the subject. As a Christian, he was looking for a way to reconcile his faith and his work. The inconsistency of having to leave his religious convictions at the door of the laboratory every time he put on his white coat was becoming intolerable for him. "Maybe this Doctor Lejeune will enlighten me", he said to himself.

John Bruchalski experienced something like an electric shock when he heard Jérôme explain that life begins at conception and that the term "pre-embryo" does not designate any reality, because before the embryo, there are gametes. He knew very well that Jérôme was right, since in his highly specialized center, where they manipulated embryos and performed abortions, they used this term "pre-embryo" so as not to have to ask themselves questions. In hearing Jérôme explain very simply and scientifically these obvious realities, he felt

[36] J. Lejeune, *The Concentration Can: When Does Human Life Begin? An Eminent Geneticist Testifies* (San Francisco: Ignatius Press, 1990), 17–100. French edition: *Enceinte concentrationnaire* (Paris: Éditions Fayard Sarment, 1990). This deposition was reprinted again in French in *Embryon mon amour* by Céline Siorac (Paris: Éditions Edite, 2004).

his soul tremble as a physician, as a researcher, and as a man. The words that came from Jérôme's mouth helped him to see the truth:

"There is a better way to practice medicine", John realized joyfully, "and this guy is showing me the way. Instead of aborting trisomic children, we can help them; we can try to care for them."[37]

Awakened spiritually by Jérôme's scientific testimony, John Bruchalski understood then that he had to make a choice. Jérôme's words and his example gave him the courage he needed to liberate himself. Several days later, he announced to his boss that things had changed; then, in the following weeks, he submitted his resignation and launched a project of creating a network of state-of-the-art clinics to help pregnant women in difficulty. John explained to anyone who would listen:

> Doctor Lejeune said: "We are certainly more powerful today than ever before, but we are not wiser. Technology is cumulative, but wisdom is not." With Doctor Lejeune, I looked for a new way, and I found that my conscience and my faith were as important in my relationship with my patients as my stethoscope and my prescription. Dotor Lejeune is a realist and a visionary, a man of profound faith and rigorous science. He served as a catalyst in my life, so that I might practice medicine by serving others and by serving Our Lord. He conveyed to me the love of Christ as experienced in medicine. Lejeune's genius is to show that life is a blessing, a gift![38]

At that same time, in France, a woman named Anne made exactly the same discovery. Married and completely absorbed by her profession in which she was passionately interested—trading on the Paris Stock Exchange—she did not want children. When asked about this, Anne used to reply: "I really find the world very ugly. I see no good reason to transmit life." Some friends then brought her and her husband to a series of conferences organized by the formation center Ichtus. Anne took an interest. Over the course of several months, she found these reflections enriching. One Saturday, she decided to

[37] J. Bruchalski testifies very frequently to this conversion. He gave this testimony to the author. A short excerpt is available also [in French] on www.amislejeune.org. Doctor Bruchalski received the *Un de nous* [One of Us] Prize celebrating Pro-Life Heroes in 2017 in Budapest.

[38] Ibid.

participate with her husband in a whole day of talks. The last conference was Jérôme's. They were tired and talked about leaving. They were not acquainted with this Professor Lejeune, but finally they decided to stay and listen to him. Anne no longer remembers Jérôme's exact words, but she will certainly never forget the effect that they had on her:

> I remember very well—and this was decisive at the end of the conference—I stood up and said to myself: "If I am convinced by what I have heard here, I have to put it into practice in my life." Then I decided to transmit life, if God allowed it. That was the point of departure for my complete change. That conference-debate was the point of departure, which had been in preparation for several months. I did not imagine that that could be so radical. I had the impression that God was acting through Professor Lejeune: that moved me greatly.[39]

[39] Testimony of Anne (name withheld out of discretion), recorded by the author. Today Anne and her husband have five children.

CHAPTER 15

THE WISE MAN OF MODERN TIMES

1990–1993

> The most touching thing, perhaps, is that God sends his angels to the little ones, to the non-officers, to those who have heart but do not cultivate science. To scientists, to the clever, he sends only the facts. It is up to them to understand, if only they think. That is what the Magi did, but they are the exception. No one follows them. Not only does no one see what they see, but nobody even tries to see it.[1]

Jérôme stopped writing for a moment. He raised his head and peacefully, in the silence of the house where everyone else had gone to sleep, continued his meditation on the contribution of the Wise Men to the revelation of the birth of the Incarnate Word. Desire and humility. These are the two dispositions essential for "finding God". The desire of the Magi. The only ones to have looked for the star, they were the only ones to see it rise over the world. The humility of the shepherds. Having no instruction, they received the visit of the angels directly to announce to them the Good News. Thus magi and shepherds, following their own paths, can discover the Infant and adore him.

"Pascal was quite right when he said: 'What men had been able to know by their greatest lights, this religion taught to its children' ", Jérôme reflected. But humility is not the prerogative of shepherds. Jérôme observed, too, that the Magi, those wise men, had the humility to consult the theologians in order to discover what science had not been able to reveal to them: the exact place of the Infant's birth. And they did not doubt what they saw. Jérôme again bent over his page and wrote:

[1] J. Lejeune, *Histoires saines pour les enfants de Coeur*, personal reflections, no date.

> The Magi did not doubt for a moment the competence of the doctors of the Law; they decided to go and see. But the most touching thing, perhaps, is that the learned men themselves, for their part, did not even take their noses out of their books. Of course, I was not there, and this detail may seem to be invented. However, knowing Matthew, who is such a good storyteller, I think that he would not have failed to portray for us Herod and his whole court going out with the Masoretes [Jewish scholars] and craning their necks to try to see what the Magi were admiring. Believe me: they did nothing of the sort. A lot of good it would have done them, anyway; they probably would not have seen what the wise men discerned. It takes a lot of patience to decipher nature. Thus, each conscientiously did his duty, listening to the other without balking, but also without removing anything from his own assured knowledge, and this joint effort led some men of good will to the highest truth. As for the political authority, duly enlightened by faith and warned by science, it acted as usual, invoked the reason of State, and massacred the innocents. Our era knows something about that.[2]

At those words, Jérôme's heart clenched. "Fortunately," he said to himself, "the Magi, having guessed the ruler's bad intentions with regard to the Infant, did not return to inform him of the exact place of the birth. They took another route."

This story, in a few lines, gives the key to man's good relations with science: humility. The humility necessary for the scientist to recognize the limits of his science, so as not to serve schemes contrary to God's plan. The humility of the scientist that Jérôme calls for in many of his conferences:

> The only dignity of scientists is to have the audacity to say: "Really, I do not know that, I am not competent."... Scientists are absolutely not supposed to set up barriers. The thing that tells us what is good or evil is not science, but morality. And if science does not submit to morality, science goes mad.... It belongs to science to say that a human being is a human being, and then morality tells you: therefore, it is necessary to respect the human being.[3]

[2] J. Lejeune, "Foi et science", working document, no date.

[3] J. Lejeune, "De l'avortement aux manipulations génétiques", *La Nef* 11 (November 1991).

This humility of the scientist, in Jérôme's view, is expressed by the fear of offending God, not a servile fear, but loving respect for the Creator:

> [The fear we are talking about] is by no means fear of novelty or being terrified of technology; subjected to correct guidance, they are the keys to effectiveness. In order to prevent genetics from becoming inhuman, it is absolutely necessary to maintain respect for every creature, and nothing can better dispose us to this than reverence for the Creator. As people used to say in another era: "Timete Dominum et nihil aliud." That is the true liberty of the Spirit. "Fear the Lord and nothing else": all science will then remain the honest servant of mankind.[4]

This pious fear was for Jérôme the best bulwark against human folly, because someone who fears God knows that attacking human life is a grave offense against the Creator, and he uses his knowledge only for the good of humanity. Of all humanity. Jérôme was convinced that:

> beyond the intellect, there is another law of life, which commands reason as well. This law is affection for our fellowman, protection of the destitute, compassion for those who suffer, and unconditional respect, even for those who are distant, foreigners, different, and even for the unknown who will follow us on this earth.[5]

Like the Magi, Jérôme observed in nature the physical signs that proclaim the presence of God. He was not afraid to let himself be guided by their discreet but indisputable light. In observing them, he advanced on the path of knowledge. Then, like the Magi, who consulted the theologians in order to seek the Truth Incarnate that the star did not point out, when science ran out of breath, Jérôme referred to the Eternal Wisdom who led him to Truth in its entirety.

A new Wise Man, with his immense knowledge, he followed the path of Truth and soon prostrated himself at the feet of the tiny, frail

[4] J. Lejeune, conference in Aix-en-Provence, February 10, 1993.

[5] J. Lejeune, "La Biologie dénaturée", in *Idées et doctrine: Apocalypse de l'an 2000* (Paris: Hachette, 1976), 63–75.

Infant. He bowed before his patients, who were created in the image of God; like the Magi, he refused to serve the malevolent schemes of the temporal authorities with regard to them. By caring for his patients, he became a servant of the Incarnate Word, who was the object of all his attentive care. But unlike Gaspard, Melchior, and Balthasar, Jérôme could not avoid the powerful and their court and return home by another route. He was led before the greatest authorities of this world to proclaim to them the Good News of incipient life and to exhort them not to repeat the error of Herod, whose name is forever associated with the massacre of the Innocents.

The attacks against human embryos started again in the United Kingdom. After the first battle in 1985, during which Jérôme testified before the British Parliament, and the victory of the vote in favor of the Unborn Children Protection Bill, a second battle had begun. Jérôme was again deposed at a hearing, and the Duke of Norfolk courageously presented to the Chamber of Lords a second Unborn Children Protection Bill to close the door on the whims of human embryo research. Unfortunately, despite their efforts, the language was rejected, and in 1990 Parliament voted to authorize research on embryos less than fourteen days old. Jérôme was distressed. The Battle of England had been lost, and many children were condemned to die. Before the law was promulgated, Jérôme sought a solution that could still save these preborn children. Suddenly he had an idea. There was still a slim hope. It was a very daring plan, yet he did not hesitate. If there was the slightest chance to save these children, he wanted to seize the opportunity. After conferring with the Duke of Norfolk, Jérôme chose his most beautiful pen to write to the Queen of England, Elizabeth II. He wanted to submit to her "very respectfully the object of a terrible anxiety". On September 12, 1990, he wrote to her:

> May Your Majesty's kindness allow a foreign member of the Royal Society of Medicine to submit a formidable question to her. The Embryo Bill presently being debated denies the humanity of an embryo that is not yet fourteen days old. Some very young subjects of Your Majesty could therefore be handed over to experimental vivisection as long as they have not reached one stage or another determined by law. All genetic foundations for habeas corpus would be legally abolished ... and if the United Kingdom, God forbid, stopped protecting

> its weakest nationals, what might other States not do? "Est Regis tueri cives." [It is the King's duty to protect the citizens.] Would Your Majesty illustrate once more this ancient maxim by refusing royal consent to this decision that would deprive the weakest human beings of all dignity? Your Majesty's moral protection would extend, then, not only to very young British, but to all future children! In this hope, I dare to ask Your Majesty to be so kind as to forgive the great liberty of this petition and to be assured of the expression of my highest esteem and of my deepest respect.[6]

Alas, it was not enough. To all appearances, the Queen did not intervene. The law was promulgated.

Jérôme hoped all the more for the moral protection of the Queen because a few months earlier, on April 3, 1990, another regent, Baudouin of Belgium, had commanded the admiration of the entire world by refusing to sign the law legalizing abortion and by choosing to abdicate rather than to be responsible for the death of a single one of his innocent subjects. On March 19, Jérôme had written to the sovereign, citing an earlier private meeting with him in 1985, to implore him:

> I dare to beg Your Majesty to place the full weight of your immense moral prestige at the service of preborn children. May Heaven grant that there might still be at least one continental state whose head has not abandoned the lives of his youngest subjects.... May Your Majesty be so kind as to forgive this great liberty, a cry from the heart of a physician of unfortunate children....[7]

After that letter, King Baudouin had received Jérôme at Laeken Palace for a private audience. Jérôme remained very discreet about the gist of their discussion, but upon his return, when Birthe peppered him with questions, he admitted that the king had made a great impression on him:

> The man had much that was supernatural. Moreover, at the end of our conversation,... he said to me, "Would you mind if we said a prayer together?" And in that great salon, two persons met, praying

[6] Lejeune, letter to the Queen of England, September 24, 1990 [translated from French].

[7] J. Lejeune, letter to King Baudouin of Belgium, March 19, 1990.

to the Lord. I got from this the very precise and very strong idea that this king is a very Christian king. The French used to bear that title. We no longer have a king in France, but there is still a Very Christian King in the world. He is Baudouin of Belgium.[8]

In the United States, since the resounding Maryville trial, Jérôme was flooded with invitations urging him to testify for judicial matters and legislative debates. In June 1990, he flew to Baton Rouge[9] for a deposition before the Louisiana legislature in favor of a law protecting preborn children. Upon his return, he finished revising the terms of a draft bill on the health of the human person[10] proposed by Senator Bernard Seillier in the French Senate; as soon as the text was published, he sent it to his friend Martin Palmer. The latter hoped to circulate this draft bill protecting human embryos in several American states and to present it to the president of the United States, George H.W. Bush [1989–1993]. Jérôme then departed again for Canada, where he testified before the Parliament in Ottawa.[11]

These requests from across the Atlantic became more frequent in 1991. Jérôme received invitations from New Jersey, Tennessee, South Carolina, Kansas, and Illinois. Since he still sought to preserve his family, his patients, and his research, Jérôme could not travel everywhere; instead, he offered to send his written testimony. But in early February, he received a proposal that would be difficult for him to resist.

That morning, in his pile of correspondence, an airmail envelope quickly caught his attention. It came from the United States. After carefully tearing open the edges, Jérôme read the letterhead: it was from John Cardinal O'Connor, archbishop of New York, who wrote:

> Dear Doctor Lejeune, recognizing the exceptional character of your expertise in the field of genetics and of your tireless support for the pro-life cause, I write to you to ask you for help in the case of Alex Loce and twelve other demonstrators who were arrested ... in front of an abortion clinic in New Jersey on September 9, 1990. This case will have a lot of influence on legislation guaranteeing the right to life

[8] J. Lejeune, interviewed by Jean Ferré, *Radio Courtoisie*, August 16, 1993.
[9] J. Lejeune, "Tables of the Law of Life", testimony before the Louisiana Legislature, 1990.
[10] Bill on the health of the human person, the "Seillier Law", 1990.
[11] J. Lejeune, testimony before the Parliament in Ottawa, 1990.

of countless children of this country. Mister Loce was the father of a child who was scheduled to be aborted in that clinic on the date of the protest. This matter will be of great importance in establishing a precedent for recognizing the father's rights to protect the threatened life of his preborn child. This is why I call on your talent and experience. Your knowledge of genetics has greatly helped to strengthen your conviction that the child in his mother's womb is a human being endowed with the right to live. Your testimony can lead many people to the same correct conclusion. I recognize that I am making your already overloaded schedule even heavier. But the pro-life cause is so central that I humbly dare to make this request of you. If you could comply with this request, I would be extremely grateful to you.[12]

Two days later, Jérôme received a letter from Doctor Nathanson containing the same urgent request. Jérôme definitely could not turn it down. He replied to the cardinal, accepting his request, and informed Doctor Nathanson of his decision:

Dear Bernard, In fact I will do everything I can to come and to testify once again with you on behalf of the Innocents. Cardinal O'Connor also wrote to me about this matter to ask me to come. How could I refuse when you two agree in telling me my duty![13]

On April 11, therefore, Jérôme flew to New Jersey and, on April 13, testified to the court in Monstown on behalf of a father who wanted to save his baby from abortion. Jérôme's deposition made such a great impression on the judge and on Cardinal O'Connor that the latter published several months later in the newspaper *Catholic New York* an article stating his admiration. The cardinal wrote these lines on February 13, 1992, from Rome, where he met Jérôme again:

This is a truly astonishing world. I am sitting in the old Synod Hall, at the heart of the Vatican, after speaking before seventy-five members and consultors of the Pontifical Council for Pastoral Assistance to Health Care Workers; they are healthcare professionals and scientists from all over the world. They listened to me politely. But now they

[12] J. Cardinal O'Connor, archbishop of New York, letter to J. Lejeune, February 5, 1991 [translated from French].

[13] J. Lejeune, letter to B. Nathanson, February 14, 1991.

are listening to someone who has another dimension, and here they are really listening. The speaker is Professor Lejeune, probably the most famous geneticist in the world....

But that is not what makes the world astonishing. It is the faith of a person like Professor Lejeune, a faith that rises like a spire far beyond the results of his meticulous research. In each one of his words, in the tone of his voice, we understand that he refuses to take for himself the power or the authority that belongs only to God. Doctor Lejeune is the one who testified in an extraordinary case in New Jersey last year. He came from Paris to do that. This case may be the most important one ever heard in an American court....

The judge said, "Thanks to the indisputable medical and scientific testimony presented before this court, I find that the eight-week-old fetus in question in this case was a living person, a human being...." At the same time, the judge considered Mister Loce guilty of a violation, because of the 1973 *Roe v. Wade* decision of the Supreme Court of the United States, which legally authorizes the execution of the human being conceived by Mister Loce and his fiancée....

This is the same Doctor Lejeune who today is fascinating his colleagues, physicians, and scientists, and all of us, in the old Synod Hall, at the heart of the Vatican. No doubt whatsoever, what impresses us is the spirit of faith that emanates from each of his thoughts and words. What a gift for the Church, for all society! We have all made a month-long spiritual retreat in a half hour![14]

The United States was not the only country where his knowledge and wisdom were called on. Jérôme also was an expert witness at a hearing by the French National Assembly on July 16, 1991, to prepare for the future bioethics law,[15] and in August the Slovak minister of research asked him to come to Bratislava to participate in an important television program on respect for human life. His round trip was scheduled for August 15. When Jérôme received this invitation, he confided to Birthe, who was already ensconced in Kerteminde:

Here I wanted to be in the procession for the Feast of the Assumption at Notre-Dame; this changes my plans. It appears that it is very

[14] J. Cardinal O'Connor, archbishop of New York, "A Judge Ruled a Fetus Was a Living Person", in *Catholic New York*, February 13, 1992 [translated from French].

[15] J. Lejeune, hearing on bioethics by the French National Assembly, July 16, 1991.

> important for the protection of the children in Czechoslovakia, and I had no reason to refuse to render this service, other than my personal comfort.... I would have liked so much to remain calm tomorrow, August 15, but the Blessed Virgin will forgive me for missing our appointment: it is for the future tiny little Slovaks![16]

On the evening of that long day of travel and meetings, Jérôme returned exhausted but glad, because, in addition to the broadcast, he had been able to have a real discussion with the minister of research, to whom he explained the intention of *Donum vitae* and delivered the text of the Seillier draft bill. Jérôme was also happy to have participated in Bratislava in a Mass celebrated in Latin and English and to have been able to stop at the convent of the Sisters of Father Foucauld, twenty kilometers [12 miles] from the border, to ask them to pray for these intentions. Two days later, Birthe read with pleasure the conclusion of her husband's letter:

> That is all the news, my little Darling. This journey on August 15 was tiring but protected by the Blessed Virgin.[17]

That same month, Jérôme had to depart again for a series of speeches in Brazil and Chile, between August 23 and 30. In Brazil, he was invited to speak to a small congress on fetology, and this time they had even sent him a ticket. But at the last moment, the Brazilian organizer called Jérôme and, quite embarrassed, told him: "Professor, I am really sorry, but a French physician, a rather influential gynecologist, is threatening to boycott the congress if you speak. But come just the same; you will not speak to the congress, but we will organize for you other conferences, particularly at the Parliament and at the Episcopal Conference."

Jérôme agreed to change his program and, therefore, flew off to Brazil, despite this hitch. As soon as he arrived, he saw that the organizer had kept his promise and had prepared a lot of meetings for him. Jérôme therefore had conferences, interviews, and discussions, one after another, especially with the Brazilian bishops and physicians. On August 26, from Brasilia, he wrote to Birthe these reassuring lines:

[16] J. Lejeune, letter to Birthe, August 13, 1991.
[17] Ibid., August 16, 1991.

> My little Darling, I have arrived here in Brasilia after a very pleasant flight. The hotel is new, like the whole city.... The people are charming. Yesterday I did not write because I had given conferences for 2.5 hours in the morning and 2.5 hours in the evening ...; I had to catch up on a lot of sleep, especially since this morning I had to be up at 7:00 to pack my trunk and give a conference (in English) to the physicians on intelligence and genetic manipulations. It went very well; you could have heard a pin drop, and the questions afterward were very pertinent. My friend Camargo is enchanted; it appears that the dean (who presided at a first conference and had confided to me that this evening had been decisive for him) took a stance officially, in the little congress to which I had been invited, then turned away when Doctor D. threatened not to come if they invited me. The dean therefore reportedly declared that he had made his decision and that he would vote against any modification of the law that would permit eugenic abortion. Since he is a leader of obstetricians, Camargo claims that this public declaration alone was the motive for the trip!... Tomorrow, it appears that the president of the Senate will come to my conference, and maybe the one from Paraguay, who is just passing through here. All this is very touching, but fatigue is an integral part of the trip![18]

Once again, when one door slammed shut against Jérôme, others opened. As though by a cause-and-effect relationship, revealing more extensive horizons. But the situation did not escape the notice of Cardinal Moreira Neves, archbishop of San Salvador de Bahia and primate of Brazil. He was surprised at the treatment reserved for Jérôme and expressed his admiration for his work and his courage in an article that appeared several days later in the columns of a Brazilian newspaper under the evocative title: "Who's Afraid of Lejeune?"[19] Jérôme, accustomed by now to boycotts of his speeches, traveled back satisfied with his trip to Brazil. Those who had tried to imprison his word had failed, and his testimony seemed to have borne fruit. Happy now, he turned his thoughts to Paris, where his family and his coworkers were waiting for him.

His family, first of all, because Thomas was getting married at the end of September to Isabelle Collet, a charming young woman whom he had introduced to them more than a year before. Jérôme

[18] Ibid., August 26, 1991.

[19] L. Moreira Neves, "Qui a peur de Lejeune?", August 1991.

rejoiced to see all his children taking on responsibilities in life and relished the affection of each one. He particularly liked those summer evenings during which his children or his sons-in-law came to keep him company in the house that had been deserted by the rest of the family, who had left for Denmark. They were beautiful, simple evenings, over a dinner prepared by one couple or another, and the good-humored conversations ranged widely from political to philosophical topics. Jérôme, who was always happy to receive these visits, was very careful not to encroach on his children's lives and benevolently respected the sometimes surprising independence and decisions of those young couples. Besides, this originality reflected, to a great extent, the independent mind of Jérôme and the Danish education given to his children by Birthe. Jérôme respected too much the freedom of individual persons to question them indiscreetly, to meddle in their private discussions, or to try to influence their decisions. With his moral authority, it would have been so easy to give advice or to judge! On the contrary, however, he tactfully abstained from all comments on the choices or the habits of one couple or the other. And he became a thoroughly spoiled grandfather, who rejoiced to see the number of his grandchildren grow year by year: Erwan, Sixtine, Théophane, Térésa, Jean-Thomas, Louis-Marie, Blandine, Philothée, Bérénice, Thaïs, and Amédée.

Next his coworkers. At the hospital, the team would soon grow with the arrival of a new technician, Catherine Maunoury, and of a young woman physician, Doctor Clotilde Mircher,[20] who had successfully defended her thesis in July. Jérôme offered her a job in his department, and she would begin working alongside him in December. She would soon be joined by another young physician, Doctor André Mégarbané.[21] Jérôme had met him in Beirut and invited him also to work in his laboratory in Paris. Thus, in a few years, he successfully rebuilt a new team of young, motivated talent, and he rejoiced to see the bright future ahead with them.

[20] Today Doctor Clotilde Mircher is a physician-geneticist at the Institut Jérôme Lejeune, where she also participates in the research programs.

[21] Professor André Mégarbané, today in private practice, was director of the medical genetics unit at Saint Joseph Hospital in Beirut and professor on the faculty of medicine of Saint Joseph University. He works also with the Institut Jérôme Lejeune. He was a member of the National Lebanese Ethics Committee [Comité consultatif national libanais d'éthique].

Research projects occupied Jérôme's mind full-time, with a new intensity connected with current events. Legislators were drafting a bioethics bill, which heralded, not increased protection for embryos and fetuses, but the creation of legal exceptions to the law that until then had protected human life. This only confirmed the urgency of curing trisomic children. If the bioethics law currently being debated were to authorize prenatal screening of trisomic children, it would be nothing short of an emergency. "Either we will cure them of their innocence, or else it will be the massacre of the innocents",[22] Jérôme thought with dread. "I have only one solution left to save them, and that is to cure them."[23]

Jérôme was also aware that time was flying. So many years of research behind him and so few to come. In 1991, he turned sixty-five, and his retirement was imminent. For the past year, he had been full-time professor of the chair of genetics and head of the consultations department at Necker Hospital. But fortunately the plan was that, when he resigned his position as department head, he could continue to see patients for three additional years. As for his research projects, he would work with the money that he received from generous donors, as he had done ever since the CNRS withdrew his funding. In a letter addressed to one of them, he wrote:

> I thank you with all my heart for your generous assistance. This check for $4,855.75 is most welcome. We are in the midst of expanding our efforts. A new medications trial is under way (the initial results are encouraging) and will expand over the course of a year. It would be a grace to arrive at something solid for my last year as a full-time professor (I will then have three years left as a "consultant"), *Deo juvante* [God willing]![24]

In 1992, Jérôme therefore handed over his department for genetic consultations at Necker Children's Hospital to Professor Arnold Munnich and continued to see patients in the small office that was assigned to him. From October 1993 on, he would have the status of consultant. He got along well enough with the new department

[22] J. Lejeune, *Journal*, December 14, 1969.
[23] *Symphonie de la Vie* (Fondation Lejeune, 2000), 23.
[24] J. Lejeune, letter to C. Vollmer, May 22, 1991.

head—even better because he was financially independent thanks to the subsidies that he received from abroad—and he continued his research with highly valued partners, such as Professor Kamoun. Jérôme had no difficulty making that professional transition, since he could receive his patients for consultations and continue his research projects in his laboratory on rue des Saints-Pères.

The time freed up by his lighter teaching load and the reorganization of the department was snapped up immediately by requests for speaking engagements, which arrived from all over the world. Particularly from the United States. In March 1992, Jérôme received another letter from John Cardinal O'Connor[25] submitting to him a case similar to that of Mister Loce, the father who had tried to save his baby from an abortion, for whom Jérôme had testified in 1991. The cardinal begged him to come again for this matter, *Blow v. Roe*, in which his testimony would be decisive. Jérôme, therefore, flew to New Jersey and made a deposition before the Court of Monmouth County.

Martin Palmer, too, called on Jérôme in the aftermath of the trial in Maryville. After the decision by Judge Dale Young to preserve the seven embryos belonging to Mary Davis, the case went to an appeals court, then to the Supreme Court of Tennessee, which reversed the Maryville decision and ruled in favor of eliminating the embryos. Since then, Martin Palmer had endeavored to bring the case before the Supreme Court of the United States, and Jérôme did not know how to help him. In his correspondence with him and the attorney, Christenberry, Jérôme showed the utmost concern for the fate of those children. Thus he wrote in December to his friend Christenberry:

> I have not forgotten the trial in Maryville. Our dear friend Martin Palmer is doing everything he can to present the case before the Supreme Court of the United States. Could you help him by collecting all the facts that you would consider important? How can we help the judges to understand? To judge or not to judge, that is the question, and it is a question of life and death, not for poor Yorick [a character in Shakespeare's *Hamlet*], but for millions of babies yet to be born. In this Christmas season, I cannot help thinking: How can I be of help to them?[26]

[25] J. Cardinal O'Connor, letter to J. Lejeune, March 23, 1992.

[26] J. Lejeune, letter to J. G. Christenberry, December 18, 1992.

Jérôme's letters to Martin, too, show the emotion that gripped him at the approach of Christmas whenever he thought of these children who might never see the light of day. These confidences are all the more moving because they are rare. Jérôme was definitely very worried about "the seven hopes of Mary". To the point where he asked hundreds of listeners to pray for them during a conference that he gave in Nantes. Alas! The Supreme Court decided in 1993, despite all their efforts, that the seven embryos should be destroyed.

After a trip to the Philippines, where he gave a conference in Manila, then a congress in Russia, at the Ministry of Social Affairs in Moscow, Jérôme was called on in France for an astonishing trial. The now-famous Doctor Bernard Nathanson was accused of faking his film that shows *The Silent Scream* of the aborted child. The film had been distributed since 1985 in the United States but had just arrived in France. Of course, those who were taking Doctor Nathanson to court wanted to ban this film, which shows the reality of an abortion. Jérôme was called on as an expert witness for the defense. Doctor Nathanson's attorney questioned Jérôme:

> The first question that I would like to ask Professor Lejeune is the one concerning what was said to us a moment ago. They told us that it would be a sort of fraud to pronounce the word "child" in matters concerning the fetus. Calling a fetus a child, as Professor Nathanson does, was a fraud, they told us. What is your opinion on that subject?

Turning toward the presiding judge, Jérôme replied:

> Monsieur le président, I truly think that we cannot speak about a fraud. It is simply the expression of a reality. A human being exists from the moment of fertilization. This is what all professors of fundamental genetics worldwide teach, without exception, and to call a little human being a child, an infant [*enfant*] cannot be a fraud since it just means using the word "infant", "one that does not yet speak". This is so true that it is in fact language that everyone can understand; anyone seeing an embryo, or more precisely a fetus, since it was no longer an embryo that was presented in the film but, rather, a little two-month-old fetus, as big as a thumb, who sums up the whole story of Tom Thumb—all children have loved this story in which a tiny little man leads an extraordinary life—the only way

the French language has to express it is to say that this is a baby, an infant, a human being [*un être*].[27]

Then, raising one hand, Jérôme presented an enlarged photo to the presiding judge and said, "I have here a photo; it is not a photo of a human being. May I respectfully ask you: What do you see?"

The judge replied, "It looks like a little elephant."

Jérôme confirmed:

> It is a stillbirth of an elephant that is almost the same age as the person whom you see in the film. No one in the world would accuse you of a scientific fraud for saying that it is a little elephant. We are in the same area when we describe a young human being, which we call an infant or a child. That is how you just expressed yourself.

Jérôme then explained that the names given to different stages of life, such as embryo, fetus, newborn, et cetera, refer only to one and the same life that develops continuously from conception to its death. The presiding judge asked him again:

"Therefore the term 'infant/child' would be a generic term?"

"This is the generic term for the human species", Jérôme replied.

> In my discussions with mothers, I have never heard a mother speak about "my embryo" or "my fetus" that is moving. She says: "My child is moving", and she is quite right. It is natural. She is not trying to fool anyone.

Then the judge asked:

> They just told us that it was unacceptable for Professor Nathanson to use the following terms in his film: "The child who is not yet born is a human being, too, like us a member of the human community possessing all the characteristics that belong to us." I remind you that we are speaking of a ten-week-old child, a fetus. Could you tell us your opinion about this phrase used by Doctor Nathanson?

[27] This questioning is taken from the deposition by Professor Lejeune during the Nathanson trial in 1992.

Jérôme replied in detail then concluded:

> Now, to imagine that Monsieur Nathanson is not telling the most precise scientific truth when he says that this being already has all the specific qualities of the human species—"specific" means belonging to the species—it is really a quibble about words, which is unacceptable. To accuse him of scientific fraud is the most serious insult that anyone can make to a university professor. It is truly and totally out of place. It has no meaning.

Jérôme was then questioned at length about the pain that a ten-week-old fetus can feel, which is seen in the film, and his movement backward at the approach of the cannula used to abort him. At the conclusion of the trial, Doctor Nathanson was judged not guilty of fraud. The plaintiffs got nothing for their legal expenses.

In December, Jérôme had a pleasant surprise. A letter in the morning mail brought him good news:

> Dear Sir, I have the pleasure of informing you that during its last meeting on October 7, 1992, the Board of Directors of the ARC [a foundation that promotes cancer research] named Professors Jérôme Lejeune and Samuel Broder winners of the Griffuel Awards for 1992 and 1993. The 1992 Griffuel Award in the amount of approximately 550,000 [old] Francs has been awarded to you in recognition for your remarkable studies on chromosomal aberrations and their role in tumor-forming processes. Allow me to send my congratulations to you and to your family. The 1993 Griffuel Prize rewards Professor Samuel Broder, director of the National Cancer Institute.... I am anxious to explain that, given the scientific quality of the studies by the two award-winners unanimously acknowledged by the members of the Board of Directors, the vote was unanimous.[28]

This prestigious Griffuel Award was a fine recognition for his studies on cancer and, in late 1992, brought a bit of enthusiasm to Jérôme and to his laboratory team.

While Jérôme continued to pile up a thousand research projects, he observed with interest the studies by his successors in the laboratory

[28] J. Crozemarie, letter to J. Lejeune, October 29, 1992.

that he had had to leave more than ten years before. The rift of the separation had long since healed over, so much so that Jérôme did not hesitate to suggest that Bernard Dutrillaux give hours of instruction within the framework of the chair on genetics.

In February 1993, Jérôme once again addressed the French National Assembly in preparation for the first law on bioethics, and in April he was an expert witness in Canada. Then his schedule for the summer of 1993 was very busy. Besides a trip to Mexico planned in July and another in Spain in August, Jérôme first had to participate also in the international congress on the Shroud of Turin that was held in Rome in June.

Jérôme started to work on the Holy Shroud of Turin in 1988, with the International Center for Studies on the Shroud of Turin (ICSS, French acronym CIELT), following the results of the carbon-14 dating of the Shroud. These results tended to prove, according to the authors of the study, that the Shroud of Turin was fabricated between 1260 and 1390. Therefore, it was not the shroud of Christ. When it was announced with great amplification by the press, the news caused a sensation, and the Church, by way of the archbishop of Turin, Cardinal Ballestrero, who was the custodian of it, was ready to accept that conclusion. By studying the protocol used by the three teams and by questioning several persons, Jérôme had discovered some anomalies in the way the protocol was followed and publicly communicated his observations on September 8, 1989, during the international scientific symposium on the Shroud of Turin that was organized in Paris. During his speech, which concluded the symposium, Jérôme explained:

> The most surprising thing is to see some of the coolest, the most theoretical men of science, who are quite detached from the vanities of this world, becoming immediately inflamed with a passion that drives them—in a way, moreover, that is altogether remarkable for the physiologist that I am, when we are talking about an extraordinary image that until now I described as admirable, but that at the end of these two days I am truly obliged to describe as mysterious.

Then he showed that the scientists involved in this carbon-14 study, who came from the British Museum and from three perfectly competent laboratories, decided at the last moment, in a manner quite unusual in a research protocol, to change the rules: they abandoned the double-blind study that had been minutely planned by all the organizers of that extraordinary investigation.

> This drove them to a methodological error of capital importance that, in my opinion, renders null and unusable this type of experiment as it was done: this is because unfortunately, having blithely abandoned the double-blind, they told these laboratories the age of the sample witnesses.... But I must say (and you will forgive me this joke; it is a jest, above all I would not want my colleagues to take it the wrong way) that if they had made this report on King Dagobert's underpants, which they had discovered by chance, and if they had changed their protocol in the middle of it, critics would have told them, "No, you wrote your article backward."

Gales of laughter from the audience. Finally, when calm was restored, Jérôme concluded more seriously: "Then I would like to say that it would seem to be quite natural to repeat the test, perhaps not the same protocol, but to think about another protocol...."

The results of the carbon-14 study were therefore to be revised. New research was necessary. Jérôme, in his way, decided to participate in it.

A twelfth-century codex would contradict the results of the carbon-14 dating. This conclusive evidence is the Pray Codex, named after the Hungarian Jesuit who discovered it in the eighteenth century. This manuscript, dated very precisely to 1192–1195, is preserved in the Budapest Library; it bears the Number 1 in that priceless collection. When Jérôme learned about the existence of this codex, he decided to go to the source. He set out in April 1993, just a few weeks before the new symposium on the Shroud organized in June by the CIELT. Thanks to an introduction by an eminent medievalist from the Hungarian Institute in Paris, he found himself entrusted, for one hour, with this unique item from the National Library in Budapest.

Jérôme carefully took photographs of it, scrutinizing each detail. He observed the admirable designs drawn with pen and ink ornamenting the four pages of a parchment folded in two. To the three Marys who arrive at the empty tomb, an angel points out a half-rolled-up shroud. Jérôme recognized the reproduction of what was supposed to be herringbone-weave[29] fabric pierced by holes arranged in the form of an L. Above all, he observed that the marks on the Pray Codex are topologically identical to the little burned spots that we observe on the Shroud of Turin.[30] Thanks to his previous studies[31] on the Shroud of Lier, dated 1516, and to the art of origami that helped him to understand how the burned spots were reproduced in the thickness of the folded panels of the Shroud, Jérôme already knew that these spots were older than the fire in Chambéry in 1532. Now he had proof that they existed as early as 1195.

In four scenes—descent from the Cross, deposition in the tomb, the empty shroud, and the glorified Christ—Jérôme noticed also that the artist accumulated an impressive number of details: the length of the shroud is twice the height of a man; Christ is bearded with long hair and has a mark on his forehead, to the right; the body is completely naked; the right hand is crossed over the left and the thumbs are not visible; finally, only three nails are depicted, and the right wrist is wounded. In his published study, Jérôme observes:

> No other image includes all these details except the shroud that is in Turin. Since the music inscribed beneath the last picture is in "neums" (a notation predating the twelfth century), this detail confirms, if need be, the date of the Pray Codex as 1192–1195. We have to admit, therefore, that before the sack of Constantinople (1204), the Master who produced the Pray Codex was able to see a shroud absolutely identical to the one we know.[32]

This observation, therefore, renders moot the range of dates given by the carbon-14 test (1260–1390). The codex is earlier than that by more than a hundred years! Jérôme rejoiced: "The next congress will make it possible to announce these results publicly." In fact, in June, during the congress in Rome, Jérôme presented these observations. At the end of his demonstration, he concluded with satisfaction:

[29] A characteristic already noted by M. Cartigny and Father Dubarle. Dubarle, O.P., *Histoire ancienne du linceul de Turin jusqu'au XIIIe siècle* (Paris: O.E.I.L, 1985).

[30] J. M. Le Méné, *Le Professeur Lejeune, fondateur de la génétique moderne* (Paris: Mame, 1997), 117–34.

[31] J. Lejeune, *Étude topologique des Suaires de Turin, de Lier et de Pray*, July 1993, and closing speech to the symposium in Paris, September 1989.

[32] J. Lejeune, "Codex de Pray et suaire de Turin", *Lettre mensuelle du CIELT*, June 1993.

> Since the amount of carbon-14 applied to the shroud that is in Turin yielded a range of 1260–1390, and since we cannot call into question the date (1195) of the Pray Codex, and since we cannot assume that a fabric could be burned before the flax had been harvested, the carbon-14 dating is what must be reconsidered now.[33]

Jérôme's demonstration was not the only major finding presented at the congress, but it did contribute to its great success. Yet Jérôme's role did not stop there. At the end of the symposium, he intervened to contradict a Frenchman, Arnaud Aaron Upinsky (whose real name is Bertrand d'Entremont), who had been appointed by the ICSS (CIELT) to organize the congress. After the concluding remarks by the president of the ICSS, André van Cauwenberghe, Arnaud Upinsky took the microphone from his hands and, while all the participants stood up to leave, took the liberty of announcing a number of motions and resolutions that he presented as having been established by the congress. Among these motions, which varied greatly in quality, he cited the appeal to UNESCO to recognize the Shroud of Turin as part of the World Heritage. Now the Holy Shroud is the property of the Holy Father, who is the sole guarantor of its protection. But what startled Jérôme most of all was when Arnaud Upinsky declared that "This assembly, which is representative of the whole international scientific community involved in the research conducted on this archeological specimen, has thus taken note of the fact that the only scientific status of this object now compatible with the current state of the research done is the status of the authentic Shroud that wrapped the cadaver of Jesus of Nazareth."[34]

Jérôme then rushed onto the dais and in turn grabbed the microphone to point out, in a loud voice, that in the absence of any discussion and of any vote by the participants, none of these texts could be presented as a motion by the scientific congress in Rome. It was obvious to Jérôme and the most serious researchers involved in the studies on the Shroud that they did not have scientific proof that it belonged to Jesus of Nazareth. Up to a certain point, they could demonstrate

[33] J. Lejeune, *Étude topologique des suaires de Turin, de Lier et de Pray*, July 1993.

[34] Quoted from the press release prepared by A. Upinsky the day after the congress in Rome, where he repeated his own statements despite the disagreement of the ICSS. This communiqué was therefore rejected by the ICSS/CIELT, which composed another one.

that many elements of the physical reality of the Shroud agree with the Gospel account, but without being able to establish proof that it is the Shroud of Christ of Nazareth. A set of clues indicates a probability but does not constitute a proof. All the more because among these clues some are debatable and because much is still unknown.

Conversely, those who claim that the Shroud is a fake have offered no conclusive proof. The hypothesis of an unidentified medieval forger, for example, presupposes that an unknown artist in the Middle Ages could have produced this image, which no one today is capable of reproducing with contemporary technological means.

Certainly we can say that there is a strong presumption that the Shroud of Turin is that of Jesus of Nazareth. Indeed, the lesions seen on the Shroud correspond so perfectly with those reported by the Gospel that it makes the hypothesis convincing. We can even say that the probability that this correspondence is not real is infinitesimal. To refuse to take this into account "would be to rule in favor of improbability".[35]

Therefore, the reason not to be convinced that the Shroud is Christ's is not because we cannot prove it but, rather, because that conviction is outside the field of empirical science.

No doubt it will never be possible to affirm empirically that the Shroud of Turin is the same shroud that Christ left in the tomb after the Resurrection, since such an affirmation would take us from the realm of empirical science, with its limits, to the realm of Gospel testimony without material signs. (A scientific proof would be a match between DNA from Christ that had been preserved and identified and the DNA on the Shroud. Now neither is available, since the latter is too fragmented and contaminated to be significant.) The Resurrection of the Son of God cannot be proved materially. Only those who believe in the Resurrection can affirm it; scientists who do not

[35] Jacques Suaudeau, in *Le Linceul de Turin face à l'investigation scientifique*, vol. 2 (Paris: L'Harmattan, June 2018), quoting remarks by the biologist and physician Yves Delage. J. Suaudeau writes: "The professor of experimental zoology Yves Delage, a biologist and physician, who was anxious to remain faithful to his 'freethinking opinions' and to reject miracles with which 'his opinions want nothing to do, at any price', was not afraid to say that refusing to take into account the concurrence of facts and circumstances that are manifested on the image of the Shroud (scourging, crown of thorns, wound on the right side, duration of burial, ancient oriental burial cloth) would be ruling in favor of improbability."

support that statement cannot, in all honesty, draw the same conclusion. Such a statement therefore is outside the field of science.[36]

These clarifications are essential, and Jérôme could not let the end of the congress be tarnished by frivolous declarations.

The participants in the congress were already standing, the hall was filled with hubbub, and the audience probably heard neither Arnaud Upinsky's remarks nor Jérôme's. But André van Cauwenberghe,[37] who witnessed the scene from very close by, understood

[36] These explanations were given to the author by two specialists on the Shroud of Turin: Monsignor Jacques Suaudeau, a priest, doctor of medicine, and surgeon, who was scientific director of the Pontifical Academy for Life for ten years and published *Le Linceul de Turin, de l'analyse historique à l'investigation scientifique*, vols. 1 and 2 (Paris: L'Harmattan, June 2018), and Mario Latendresse, a computer scientist at the Artificial Intelligence Center at SRI International in Menlo Park (Silicon Valley). His research and his contributions on the Shroud of Turin led him to start two well-documented websites: sindonology.org (in English) and linceul.org (with less documentation, in French).

[37] To provide more complete information on this subject, we publish here two letters received by Birthe Lejeune after her husband's death and a document written by Jérôme several weeks before his death. We hope that the reader will forgive us these rather long footnotes, which could be the subject of a whole book.

Van Cauwenberghe, letter to S. de Beketch, July 8, 1993. Excerpts: "Another final scandalous incident. Just as the symposium was ending, late Saturday afternoon, I gave the final address with acknowledgments and a farewell to all the participants. Quite discourteously, A. A. Upinsky then grabbed the microphone and announced the motion that the Shroud should be recognized as a World Heritage item and therefore be placed under the control of UNESCO. That remark was a scandal, an insult to the pope, who is the proprietor of the Holy Shroud. Then Lejeune, in a fit of anger, jumped onto the stage, grabbed the microphone, and denounced that motion, which was not voted on, and with good reason. A.A.U. came over, snatched the microphone from his hands and treated him like a hoodlum."

Van Cauwenberghe, "An audience at the Vatican interrupted", letter to Birthe Lejeune, 1999. Van Cauwenberghe, outraged by what he read in certain books about the 1993 congress in Rome on the Shroud of Turin, sent to Birthe Lejeune a copy of the correction that he sent to certain authors. Excerpts: "Late that afternoon, as the organizers of the congress prepared to go to dinner, a liaison officer dispatched to me by the Vatican Secretariat of State delivered to me personally an envelope containing invitations to the papal audience the next morning, Wednesday, June 9. A collective invitation for twenty participants as well as three personal invitations; it was left up to me to write on them myself the names of the three persons whom I intended to designate.... I decided then to keep one of the invitations for myself and to deliver one to Professor Jérôme Lejeune, a well-known friend of John Paul II, and to offer the other to Monsieur Upinsky, who peremptorily told me: 'Giving one to Lejeune is out of the question. He did nothing for the symposium!' Since it is not my character to yield to such orders, I went ahead, of course.... When his allocution was finished, the pope came down from his podium and walked over to us; we were introduced to him by the professor. A brief conversation. That was when the incident occurred. I was facing the Holy Father, Upinsky was on my right, Lejeune on my left. Upinsky abruptly addressed the pope with that rapid, casual, and not very courteous way he has of expressing himself. Upinsky: 'What

the situation, and that same evening he warmly thanked Jérôme for his intervention. He did not like the attitude of Arnaud Upinsky, who thus tried to force his hand. As for Jérôme, for him an absolute criterion was complete respect for the Holy Father, and in this case it was manifestly lacking here.[38]

[financial] support do you count on giving to the Shroud of Turin, and what about its custodian?' Plainly the pope did not understand the question, and he asked that it be repeated.... The pope: 'What did you say?' Upinsky: 'The custodian of the Holy Shroud, the Cardinal of Turin!' Put off by that sort of question, the pope said: 'This is not the time!' then went off, without even taking leave of us. Indeed, what audacity to pose in that way, point-blank, to the Successor of Peter, that question, which concerns the hierarchy of the Church and was inappropriate at that moment. Matters would have remained at that had I not read in early July 1993, in the periodical *Le libre journal de la France courtoise*, an interview with Monsieur Upinsky by Madame Françoise Varlet. I quote, among others, this passage verbatim: 'They say that you met the pope?' 'Yes, the day before the opening of the symposium. To the question "What support do you count on giving to the Shroud of Turin", he replied: "This is not the moment."' Monsieur Upinsky therefore is putting in the Holy Father's mouth an answer to a question that he did not understand. The pope actually answered the partially repeated question: 'The custodian of the Holy Shroud, the cardinal of Turin', whereas Upinsky has him answering the question, 'What support do you count on giving to the Shroud of Turin?' The answer of John Paul II meant, therefore, according to Upinsky, that he was not interested in the Shroud, whereas in fact this response meant, 'The matter of the custodian does not concern you.' Whether or not you agree, in this case, with the pope's pastoral position is not the question. The question lies in the distortion of the meaning of his words. That cannot be tolerated. Being a first-hand witness in Rome to what had really happened, I could not leave things the way they are."

[38] J. Lejeune, letter to A. van Cauwenberghe, December 12, 1993. Excerpts: "A serious health problem prevented me from traveling to the ICSS/CIELT, and I ask you to be so kind as to make any decision in my place and to participate in any vote during the meeting. Since I cannot participate in the debates, therefore, I would be very grateful to you to be so kind as to inform the members present about the following points. At the end of the congress in Rome, Monsieur Upinsky presented a series of motions and resolutions of very uneven quality and, for some people, in a tone that was at the very least inappropriate. The appeal to UNESCO to recognize the Holy Shroud as part of World Heritage is one example of this. This avalanche of motions would have discredited the whole congress. This is why, right at the end of your presidential closing speech, I pointed out to everyone that in the absence of any discussion and of any vote by the participants, none of these texts could be presented as motions by the congress in Rome. This obvious truth, which apparently ruined a carefully elaborated plan, provoked the ire of Monsieur Upinsky. This ire did not calm down at all. During the meeting in Paris after the congress, M. Upinsky indulged in a strange closing speech for the prosecution and even circulated a sort of written indictment [*un libellé accusatoire*] (photocopy enclosed). In order to stem the flood, I refused to enter into that polemic and declared (I think that many members who were present remember) that: 'If Monsieur Upinsky were an honest man, he would very quickly make an appointment with me, to discuss honestly just between us the basis for his recriminations.' Instead, Monsieur Upinsky engaged in them publicly. I never heard again from Monsieur Upinsky. The conclusion is clear: Monsieur Upinsky's word is not that of an honest man."

Jérôme was always very much in demand by the Holy See. Besides the Pontifical Academy of Sciences, he participated in the studies by Cardinal Angelini, who questioned him as one of his best advisors,[39] and in the congresses for the family organized by Cardinal Trujillo. He was also consulted regularly about the moral questions connected with scientific advances: the beginning or the end of life[40] (brain death, sedation, euthanasia) or emerging topics like AIDS or overpopulation. Jérôme composed several notes on these subjects.

The study of thousands of letters received by Jérôme shows the point to which his expertise and wisdom were in demand, at all levels of the Church. In twenty years, he had become the reference point and inspiration for countless Christians throughout the world. Although the first very laudatory letters arrived as early as the 1970s, the progression in the last twenty years was significant, both quantitatively and qualitatively. Sent from all countries, these letters express the writers' immense admiration and profound gratitude for the faith, the fortitude, the hope, and the joy that he transmitted. Thus, a simple woman who listened to him on the radio wrote: "You do my soul a lot of good because your whole manner of speaking radiates love and tact toward human beings and their little ones."[41] Or a Canadian listener: "If all the great scientists in the world had straightforward minds and hearts like yours, how good it would be to live on our planet Earth."[42] Or this physician from Michigan: "Your deep faith, your great humor, and the fruit of your work give us much hope and consolation."[43] The tone of the letters is on the same wavelength as Jérôme's interior development: ever more dedicated to the service of "the poorest of the poor". This attitude shone on those who drew near to him.

In order to respond to these requests, Jérôme published a growing number of articles of moral significance. Whereas he had written only eighteen such articles from 1970 to 1979, then thirty-four in the next ten years, he had published forty of them in the three years that

[39] Conversation of the author with Cardinal Angelini.

[40] J. Lejeune, *Au commencement de la vie*, collection of several of his conferences (Paris: Mame, 2014).

[41] M. A., letter to J. Lejeune, October 12, 1993.

[42] G. G., letter to J. Lejeune, May 13, 1993.

[43] D. H., letter to J. Lejeune, January 18, 1993.

had just passed (1990–1993). His writings reveal his growing concern about the evolution of medicine and encourage Christians to become involved on the side of truth. His studies on the appearance of intelligence in the world and in man, the relation between matter and spirit, the thinking network, the logos, and human nature give way to reflections on Eternal Wisdom and the gifts of the Spirit. More and more often, too, he encouraged his readers to refer openly to Jesus in this combat of life against death, conscious that He alone will win the victory. Given the blindness of intellects and the moral shipwreck of contemporary society, which he found painful to observe, he wrote: "It is no longer the time, I think, to claim to have no profession of faith; it is necessary to choose sides: Faust or Jesus."[44]

Over the course of those years, Jérôme was working also on a book project, for which he had already determined the title: *The Table of Contents*.[45] In the introduction, he humorously describes "this essay on the world", which he structures as a conversation.

> By an ingenious fiction, I constructed in this book a universe quite similar to ours yet different, since I invented it entirely. In it I demonstrated how the subtlest movements of matter, joining in that matter the subtleties of energy, gave things their appearance, endowed animals with their form, and granted spirit to human beings. Through the same careful and almost imperceptible method, finally, I discovered in it the powerful harmony that ran this immense machine. I had come that far in my work. The only thing remaining was to name by its name this First Cause that explains and unifies all ...

Then, from "Aristotle's crossed fingers" to "Galileo's song", from "Pascal's machine" to "Maxwell's demon", via "the mill of time", "the alienation of matter", or "the descent to the mine", Jérôme leads his reader from the treasures of matter to the spirit that animates everything. Through these reflections penned by Jérôme, even the reader who rebels the most against the hard sciences feels that he has the soul of a researcher and physician, then of a philosopher. In this study of the incarnate soul and of human freedom, everything seems

[44] J. Lejeune, letter to Professor Schepens, October 10, 1993.

[45] J. Lejeune, *La Table des Matières*. This book, which Jérôme started in 1977, was never finished. The incomplete and non-definitive manuscript has not been published.

so simple and yet so profound. Jérôme's purpose—"to restore the mutual understanding of the heart and reason"—is achieved. Then the epilogue declares:

> We have gone around the world, and we rediscover the essentials. The great secret is not solely in the structure of a protein or the arrangement of a system; it is in each child and in each one of us. My considerations did not mislead you. Look at innocence; is it not precisely the unity between the tenderness of loves and the rigor of efficiency? Look at that beautiful child who is going on five years old. He already speaks, he guesses, he even reasons already, but all at once. He does not distinguish between tenderness and efficiency; we say that he plays, but he lives, in a way that is quite unified but full.
>
> Follow him to the age of reason. His keener eye begins to dissect the world; separating what is dreamed from what is experienced, he cuts from reality slices that are just his size and measures their thickness. What an immense conquest, but one that already surpasses the limits of the paradise that will soon be lost. Already a disproportion emerges between the network of loves and the circuits of logic. The crack is clearly there, advancing every day. He becomes a reasoner trying to subject the world to the influence of his judgment and is annoyed at himself if the external world resists. But this influence of efficiency, the product of the privileged development of the analytical circuits, will soon be contested by a deeper revolution.
>
> At the onset of puberty—when through hormones something of life is manifested that relates the whole past to us, to the point where one might take it for the awakening of becoming—then the fault line appears, more wide open. The crisis of adolescence is summed up in the conflict between these two networks that arrive at their full potential. With equal foresight, and equally true, one of them for the species, the other for the individual subject, but from a different perspective, they collide with each other for lack of the ability to understand each other, since they can scarcely speak to one another. Everything that a young man or a young woman knows and thinks must be recast and rethought, according to the manner of the one and the tendency of the other. And when the adult emerges from the troublesome period, the two aspects of the world, far from being reconciled, settle on one side and the other of the rift that has become still wider. Certainly, there is still a narrow footbridge, but the connection by far has not grown in proportion to the two specialized networks. If all passage between them were cut off, the individual would

be, no longer a human being, but, instead, a robot of the intellect or a slave of instinct. But the difficult passage is a bottleneck that becomes blocked at the slightest occasion.

This rift ought to be filled in at all costs. All the poets have said so, as well as the scientists and even the schoolteachers. Some strike their camp on the side of the instincts, consider them the only masters, and use reason only to construct a façade masking both evil and good, tohu wa-bohu [Hebrew: primordial chaos] and pell-mell. Others will become entrenched on the side of efficiency and cold, calculating logic and just color their diktat with a hint of sociological or humanist sentiment. But the vast majority, rejecting this heartrending choice but fearing the precipice, take the footbridge but remain there as little as possible. Hence man who swings like a pendulum, denying his loves when it is necessary to succeed and losing his reason when passion stirs him. Some individuals, however, endowed with a bigger heart, try to feel the world in order to find the reason for living: artists, lovers, and mystics do this. Others, more endowed with a strong reason, try to analyze the world in order to feel life better; lovers of science and even theoreticians, if they have good will, do this. But those who do not have vertigo look at the rift directly and deliberately settle on the footbridge that ties together the two networks of such tenuous, such fragile ties, which they repair at every moment through prayer or meditation. They tell me that wise men do this, and I believe that saints do this.

In order to write these lines, Jérôme, like the lovers of science and the wise men from his epilogue, needed to extricate himself from the "pendulum movement" so as to meditate. Thus, in July 1993, upon his return from Rome, Jérôme rested in the countryside with several of his children and grandchildren, and in the evening he told Birthe humorously about his manual occupations and the resulting aches.

My little Darling, I write to you with one eye blinking. Yesterday evening, while running an electric rasp, I got a spark in my right eye. It interfered a lot with my sleep, but since it was better this morning, I had a very busy day. In my office, first of all. I had started to make a decade-rosary for Philippe (he lost his and asked whether I had saved one for him, which unfortunately was not the case), when that little object slipped out of my hands. In order to find it, I moved this very heavy bed, which has cluttered up my office for years, when, crash, the whole thing collapsed. All the uprights, suddenly unglued, lay flat on the floor. Emptied the chests, but could scarcely get the wreck back up on its feet. Hence pried the mattress from the bed frame and, given the extent of the damage, took it apart with a rubber mallet and salvaged the pieces in good condition. The mattress and the bed frame are now at the Dulits' house. This is an incredible improvement to my office! Of course, the rosary was not under the bed but under the little secretary, hence a regular cleaning such as has not been done in ages. Finally, a new desk, a rosary made on time, stained the wooden table, second coat also on the little door ... and, with Jean-Maristote, propped up the plum tree, which in several places is sagging under what I hope are *reines-claudes* [greengages, a very sweet variety], but which might prove to be simple green plums. We will see in two months. You see, a day of vacation is a day with a lot of activity.... I love you. –Jérôme.[46]

Several days later, he received a letter from the Holy See mentioning the creation of a Pontifical Academy of Medicine; it would be up to him to get it started and to direct it. This project responded to Jérôme's insight: he was very worried about the state of modern medicine and saw an urgent need to create a network of pro-life physicians and a mutual financial assistance fund for them.

The patients are the ones who alert us to the extreme urgency: medicine is sinking.[47]

The creation of this academy was an important responsibility, and Jérôme immediately and ardently got down to work on it. The stakes were so serious that he put all his efforts into it. But his ardor would soon be slowed down by the final trial.

In August, Jérôme complained to Birthe about unusual fatigue. To the point where he could not participate in the Assumption Day procession to Notre-Dame Basilica, which he loved so much. He was always out of breath and feared a heart problem. But he waited until September to schedule medical examinations. They revealed nothing serious.

[46] J. Lejeune, letter to Birthe, July 13, 1993.

[47] J. Lejeune, letter to Father Charlot: "Un appel urgent pour sauver la médecine", July 2, 1993.

During the second half of 1993, Jérôme continued working diligently on the creation of that new pontifical academy, which would become the Pontifical Academy for Life. He corresponded with Wanda Poltawska, Cardinal Angelini, and Archbishop Re, Substitute of the Secretariat of State, the architects of this foundation alongside the Holy Father. Jérôme sent an initial plan, to which he had given long thought, including the "Testimony of the Servants of Life" that each academic would have to pronounce. He weighed every word of this text, and Cardinal Angelini greatly admired it.

Testimony of the Servants of Life

Before God and before men, we, the servants of life, testify that every member of our species is a person. The devotion due to each one depends neither on his age nor on any infirmity that may burden him. From his conception to his final moment, it is the same human being who blossoms, matures, and dies.

The rights of the human person are inalienable from the start. The fertilized egg, the embryo, the fetus cannot be given away or sold. The pursuit of his continuous development within his mother's body cannot be denied him. No one can subject him to any exploitation whatsoever. No one can make an attempt on his life, neither his father, nor his mother, nor any authority. This is why vivisection, abortion, and euthanasia cannot be the act of a servant of life.

We testify likewise that the sources of life must be preserved. Since it is the patrimony of all, the human genome cannot be at the disposal of some. It cannot be the object of ideological or mercenary speculations. Its particular features cannot be patented.

Intent on continuing the Hippocratic tradition and conforming our practice to the moral precepts of the Roman Magisterium, we reject all deliberate damage to the genome, all exploitation of gametes, and all purposeful disruption of the reproductive functions.

We reaffirm that the relief of suffering and the cure of illnesses, the preservation of health and the repair of errors in heredity, are the only goal of our efforts, always safeguarding respect for the human person.[48]

In November 1993, despite his fatigue, Jérôme traveled once again to Rome. He participated in a meeting of the Association of Italian

[48] J. Lejeune, Plan for the Pontifical Academy of Life, "Attestation des serviteurs de la vie".

Catholic Physicians, which elected him an honorary foreign member in response to his being set aside by the Centre catholique des médecins français [Catholic Center for French Physicians], and in a small task force of the Pontifical Academy of Sciences. This time again, his stay in Rome gave him the opportunity to meet with the Holy Father.

When he returned, Jérôme came down with such a serious, heavy cough that he started to guess the illness that was consuming him. He consulted his personal physician again. On December 2, 1993, the diagnosis fell. There was no appeal. Jérôme had lung cancer, too far advanced to be operable. He probably had only a few months left to live.

CHAPTER 16

WE ARE IN GOD'S HANDS

1994

Jérôme, who had watched his father die of lung cancer, knew what that meant. And that was the disease which consumed him from then on. With Professor Chrétien and Professor Israël, his oncologist friend for whose recent book on euthanasia he had just written the preface, he discussed candidly the possibility of a cure and what kind of treatment could be applied: a 50 percent chance of success with heavy chemotherapy, a very heavy dose, followed by radiation treatments. X-rays clearly showed a very large cauliflower on the upper left lobe of the lung. Jérôme was looking at a minimum of six months of intensive, painful treatment, if he survived.

His voice was distorted, but with his indescribable smile, he told his wife and his children the news. The family was devastated. He reassured them: "Don't worry; nothing will happen to me before Easter."

And to one of his daughters, who was weeping, he said delicately, "I will be a good patient, and, believe me, I will fight to the finish."

And, because his humor never forsook him: "I am being cared for by Israël and Chrétien, the whole Bible of medical science. Between the Old and the New Testament, I am in good hands."[1]

A few days later, in early December, he returned to Cochin Hospital for the first chemotherapy treatment, which lasted six days. The day before that, he had the moral fortitude and tact to write to a friend who had just announced some bad news to him:

[1] Clara Lejeune-Gaymard, *Life Is a Blessing: A Biography of Jérôme Lejeune: Geneticist, Doctor, Father*, trans. Michael J. Miller (San Francisco: Ignatius Press, 2000; reprinted Philadelphia: National Catholic Bioethics Center, 2011), 129.

> Birthe and I were on a mission to Rome, and I had some severe difficulty with my health upon my return; I just got back to the laboratory today and heard about your tragic news. You have all my sympathy.[2]

Not a word about his own tragic illness. As always, other people's pain had priority over his. Just as he was more interested in his patients and the preborn children than in himself. Thus, that same week he wrote to his friend Palmer, in the United States, to tell him his worries concerning the upcoming bioethics laws on prenatal screening in France:

"This will be a decisive matter in our country, and unfortunately I have a lung problem."[3]

Nothing more about his case. This lifelong disposition was still more manifest during those last months. Like his tact and courtesy. Thus, when he announced his terrible illness to Pierre Chaunu over the telephone and heard his friend's dismay, he said to him, "Please forgive me, I get the impression that I am causing you pain."

That year, by way of exception, the family celebrated Christmas in Paris, because Jérôme was too weak to go to the countryside, where they usually met. They were forty in all, with the grandchildren, his brother Philippe, and his three daughters who celebrated Christmas with them every year. They all came. Exhausted, Jérôme was starting to lose his hair and noticed on his fingernails marks indicating interrupted growth. On December 27, he received a very beautiful letter from a monk at the Benedictine Abbey in Randol, assuring him of his prayers.

> I pray every day for all the infants in danger of being assassinated in their mother's womb and for all those who protect them.... You are one of them, right up there with John Paul II and Mother Teresa....

The monk announced to him that the community was making a novena for his treatment, which was so important for persons with trisomy and preborn children.

[2] J. Lejeune, letter to J. G. Christenberry, December 2, 1993.

[3] J. Lejeune, letter to M. Palmer, November 27, 1993.

> Therefore I invoke friendship and tell the Lord: "Our friend and Your friend Jérôme Lejeune is sick."[4]

A series of treatments at Cochin Hospital then followed. He was put into a small room. The corridors were noisy and resonant; he could not sleep. In the next room, an old gentleman listened to the television with the sound turned up and the door open.

His daughter Clara asked Jérôme, "Papa, you cannot rest with this racket. Do you want me to go ask him to close his door and lower the volume?"

Jérôme, whose suffering was unbearable at times, replied, "No, dear, the poor man is deaf, and if he leaves the door open, it must be because he feels lonely. Let him be; he, too, is fighting the only way he can."

Physically, he was very weak. Besides his treatments, a multitude of woes afflicted his body: phlebitis, a catheter that had been inserted incorrectly, a frightening hematoma on his neck as a result of procedures clumsily performed by an attendant.... Everything went wrong. He was cold in his thick jacket, but he never complained. He joked and reassured Birthe and the children. To Marie-Odile Rethoré, who came to pay him a visit, Jérôme announced, delighted:

"My little Marie-Odile, I am the happiest man on earth. I was able to prove the mathematical theorem...." In front of him, on his bed, were scattered pages covered with mathematical formulas.

On January 13, during the night, Jérôme imagined a scene. Or did he dream it? Jérôme saw himself enter an enormous room, full of a noisy, joyful crowd, where countless candles were burning, and he saw the Holy Father cutting through the crowd and approaching. The Holy Father called him by his first name. Then "he took my head in his hands and kissed my forehead."[5] The emotion awakened Jérôme, and he wrote down the dream.

Over the course of those long days of illness, Jérôme was blessed to receive the Sacrament of the Sick, to make his confession several times, and to receive Communion frequently. On January 29, a

[4] Letter by a monk from the Benedictine Abbey in Randol to Jérôme Lejeune, December 27, 1993.

[5] Dream of Jérôme Lejeune, January 13, 1994.

young novice who had accompanied the nun who used to bring him the Eucharist, wrote to him:

> I would like to tell you how much you impressed me and especially strengthened and reactivated my faith. It was the first time that I ever saw a person receive the Body of Christ with such intensity and such truth. It was for me the Real Encounter of man and God, as I had never before seen it. I want to say thank you. Thank you for your witness, which did me a tremendous amount of good. In a society where if you call yourself Catholic you are countercultural, where lukewarmness or else indifference prevails, seeing you with God dwelling so fully in you helped me to say again: Alleluia, Jesus Christ Lives, Yes, I Believe, and it is Good to Believe in Jesus Christ.[6]

That same day, Jérôme learned that he was going to receive the Mother Teresa Medal. From his bed in Cochin Hospital, he wrote to thank Mercedes Wilson, who had just announced that news to him. The award came just at the moment when he was exchanging letters and faxes with Mercedes Wilson and Cardinal O'Connor[7] to organize the arrival of Mother Teresa in the United States. A lot was at stake. They hoped that she could speak to the Supreme Court of the United States in the Loce case, for which Jérôme had testified in New Jersey. On January 29, Jérôme wrote to Cardinal O'Connor:

> I am convinced that such an appearance by Mother Teresa would be of the utmost importance for the protection of the littlest ones.[8]

On February 10, after his third round of chemotherapy had started, Jérôme received a letter from John Paul II encouraging him and assuring him of his prayers and his blessing. In early December, a letter from Monsignor Dziwisz had already informed him of the prayers "of the Holy Father, who, very noticeably, showed great sorrow"[9] at

[6] A. D., letter to J. Lejeune, January 29, 1994. [Translator's note: the first capitalized phrase is the title of a French Easter hymn, the second—the refrain of a musical setting of the Creed. In the third phrase, the novice adapts the proverbial saying, "Il est bon de croire en Dieu" (It is good to believe in God) to Jesus in the Eucharist.]

[7] J. Cardinal O'Connor, letter to J. Lejeune, February 2, 1994.

[8] J. Lejeune, letter to J. Cardinal O'Connor, January 29, 1994.

[9] S. Dziwisz, letter to Madame Lejeune, December 11, 1993.

the announcement of his hospitalization. Monsignor Carlo Caffarra also wrote to him:

> Dear Friend and Brother in Jesus. I am keeping your suffering in my poor prayers. I ask Christ, who has called you to follow Him on the Cross, to console and strengthen you with His grace. Certainly the mission that you have carried out until now, in upbuilding the whole Church, will now continue with even more profound effectiveness.[10]

Jérôme received many thank-you letters promising prayers for his recovery. Like this letter from a former female student:

> I want to tell you how grateful I am to you; many thanks for having communicated to me your respect and love for the littlest one, for having made me understand that it was necessary to speak simply and that respect and love for our fellow men play a major role in bringing parents to accept their child's handicap. I thank you also for the witness given by your unshakable faith, which has an even wider impact because of your scientific fame. I am forwarding to you also the thanks of all the patients whom I referred to you and then saw again afterward.[11]

Jérôme's response has the gravity of a medical testament.

> The sore point is still prenatal diagnosis.... We arrive at the difficult conclusion, which has led to immense difficulties for my laboratory and has put me on the Index, as you know: prenatal diagnosis is done exclusively for eugenic purposes.... What is to be done if you practice cytogenetics? Just one response: ... put technology at the service of life. It is a difficult choice, but it is the only one possible in a country that legally kills children if they do not "conform".[12]

On his bed of pain, Jérôme tirelessly continued to work, to research, and to defend the dignity of preborn and handicapped children. Birthe, brave as ever, sent the faxes that he composed wearily in his own handwriting. Exhausted, he would answer the telephone between two bouts of vomiting to discuss a therapeutic hypothesis

[10] C. Caffarra, letter to J. Lejeune, not dated but filed in February 1994.
[11] M. C., letter to J. Lejeune, January 14, 1994.
[12] J. Lejeune, letter to M. C., February 1, 1994.

with a colleague. His mind was abuzz with ideas for research and plans to be implemented. So much so that to further his reflections on cancer, he had samples taken from his own tissues and sent them to Professor Israël. He regretfully told those who were close to him: "It is crazy how much time it takes to be sick!"

So much time wasted taking care of himself instead of being able to defend his patients and the embryos who were being threatened. Jérôme was very concerned about the series of bioethics debates that were being held in the French Parliament. His son-in-law Jean-Marie Le Méné, who was following these discussions attentively, visited regularly to report on the situation, and Jérôme, in bed, annotated documents and proposed a new declaration by physicians to publish in the press. He also took advantage of his situation to help his daughter-in-law Isabelle, who was taking her competitive teacher's examination. He told her:

"Take advantage of the opportunity; I have some time", and he reviewed for her the whole section on mathematics, despite his fatigue.

To Marcel Clément he wrote:

> Until now I have tried to be the soldier to whom the centurion says Go, and he goes. At the moment, I can go neither far nor fast. Just when it is imperative to defend the embryos who will be attacked on the day of the Holy Innocents, I'm out of breath. At the moment, faithful to the Roman Legionary's motto: "Et si fellitur de genu pugnat", I write: "And if he should fall, he fights on his knees."[13]

Jérôme kept working on the statutes of the Pontifical Academy for Life and drew up a list of faithful and effective servants of life to suggest as academicians. On February 11, John Paul II appointed him first president of that academy. It was an immense joy for Jérôme, who saw in it the surest and most effective way of serving the Gospel of Life. Cardinal Angelini himself brought the Holy Father's appointment to him from Rome. When Cardinal Lustiger learned the news, he wrote to Jérôme his very hearty congratulations:

> The Holy Father could not have made a better choice.[14]

[13] J. Lejeune, letter to M. Clément, December 18, 1993. The letter was published in *L'Homme Nouveau* on April 17, 1994.

[14] J-M. Cardinal Lustiger, letter to J. Lejeune, March 8, 1994.

Between two treatments, Jérôme returned to the house on rue Galande. Birthe had set up for him, on the third floor, a bedroom-office where he could go from his bed to the desk without too much trouble. During every moment of respite, he wrote, took notes, read, and worked. When he was too weak, he dictated his letters. On March 4, he wrote to a friend:

> The first qualification of a patient is to be patient, and the first qualification of a researcher is to research. I am developing a new biochemical schema for cancer.[15]

He gladly welcomed the friends who came by to see him and his grandchildren, who played in the house and sometimes came, silently, to kiss their grandfather, who was so sick. Sometimes he came downstairs to take his meal in the dining room, but as of November, he no longer left home, except for his hospitalizations. He was too exhausted. However, he made an exception in early March. He was a shadow of himself, but he put on the elegant suit that he wore at his inaugural lecture in 1965 and rallied all his strength to go to the Academy of Medicine to support the candidacy of his most faithful collaborator, Marie-Odile Rethoré, so as to pass the torch to her. He left in an ambulance and rode through the corridors of the academy on a gurney. He presented himself to his peers in this way, in his extreme weakness. Marie-Odile Rethoré would be elected the following year, the second female member of the Academy of Medicine after Marie Curie.

On March 14, Jérôme wrote to Penny Robertson, president of the Australian Down Syndrome Association, to cancel his appearance, which had been scheduled for a few weeks later. He had no false hopes about his condition. He confided to her:

> Because of treatment for lung cancer, I have had to cancel all my obligations for 1994, including my trip to Australia and New Zealand. I am especially sorry to have to give up these visits from friends, children, and relatives. But I cannot make you run the risk of organizing everything when there is only a slight probability that I will come.[16]

[15] J. Lejeune, letter to M. Palmer, March 4, 1994.
[16] J. Lejeune, letter to P. Robertson, March 14, 1994.

On March 15, Jérôme wrote to his friend Professor Israël, because he was worried about the health of a priest who had a malignant tumor and submitted to him his latest studies on cancer. That same day, he found the strength to respond to a person asking him about contraception. He stated precisely:

> It is not possible to choose among the teachings of the Roman Magisterium what appears "normal" and to reject what the mass media try to present as contrary to the "modern norm".

It would be his last letter. Birthe posted it after his death, adding these words:

> My husband did not have the time to sign the letter that he had written to you; he died on Easter morning.[17]

Several days later, the first radiation treatments started. The lung did not withstand it, the pleura became detached, and it was necessary to operate to drain the fluid present in the lungs. Two days before Palm Sunday, he was taken to the emergency room of Val d'Or Clinic in Saint-Cloud, near Paris. Birthe and their third son-in-law, Hervé, who had arrived in time, were present at his departure from rue Galande. The last look that Jérôme gave them, before the doors of the ambulance were closed, was overwhelming. He was plainly aware that he would never return home.

At the hospital, Jérôme suffered terribly. With each breath, day and night, the pain was difficult to bear. Jean-Marie, Karin's husband, visited him on the Friday before Palm Sunday. Jérôme gave him the list that he had drawn up of the names of future members of the Academy for Life, to forward to Rome.

The next day he had a pleural operation performed by Professor Chrétien. On Palm Sunday, he was very tired and suffering a lot. After his operation, he was unable to eat, but the nurses did not notice that of all the cumbersome tubes, not one was feeding him. Birthe was the one who realized it after several days.

On Wednesday of Holy Week, he was exhausted, his tongue was one large sore, but he welcomed his daughters Anouk and Clara

[17] Letter from Jérôme Lejeune, dictated March 15, 1994.

with a smile. Anouk suggested that he receive the Sacrament of the Sick once again. Jérôme agreed. He had moments of exhausted silence but remained completely lucid. That evening, he had a fever of 40° C [104° F] and delirium. He was transported to Des Peupliers Clinic, where there was an intensive care unit. His condition improved slightly on Thursday: his fever fell. He had an oxygen mask within reach. The mask that he had applied with so much love to his father, who was suffocating from the same disease, almost forty years before.

In the room another patient was dying. He snored horribly and called out during the night. When his family suggested that he change rooms, Jérôme answered in the negative. Because that poor man needed him. One night he had fallen from his bed, and Jérôme, although incapable of helping him alone, had been able to call the attendants to pick him up. If he had not been there, the man might have remained on the floor the whole night.

On Good Friday, Clara asked him whether he wanted to bequeath something to his little patients. Between two puffs of oxygen he replied:

"No, you see, I do not own very much. Besides, I gave them my whole life, and my life was all that I had."

Then he continued with a sigh: "What will become of them now? What must they think?"

Finally, he confided to them: "My children, if I can leave you with just one message, the most important of all, it is this: we are in the hand of God. I have had proof of this several times over the course of my life. The details are not important."

Then, after a moment of silence, he went on: "Something may happen on Easter."

To Damien, who asked him what sort of a burial he wanted, he answered: "Do as you like, my children. I have only one request: that my little patients should be allowed to come if they wish, without being intimidated, and that some places be reserved for them."[18]

At the time of his illness and final departure, his "little patients" did not forget him, either. They were there, ready to comfort the man who had so often encouraged them. For example, David, from whom he received a letter in late March:

[18] Clara Lejeune-Gaymard, *Life Is a Blessing*, 136.

Often we talk about you at home when I need a little boost! Over the years, I have come to understand how important it was that you came into our life!... So today I write you this letter to give you a little of my strength and energy. I give you a great big hug.[19]

And Cécile, who wrote this pretty prayer for him:

My God, if you please, watch over "my Friend". My family doesn't like my looks, but he thinks I'm kind of pretty, because he knows what my heart is made of.[20]

Aware that death was imminent, Jérôme, by his great serenity, impressed his family and friends who were attending him. He was ready, at peace, as a just man who knew that God, the Love who guided his footsteps, was waiting for him "on life's other side".[21] He was the one who spread joy in his family and prepared them to experience his departure in peace. They were all impressed to see his transformation: even though he was suffering terribly and was treated badly by some attendants, he had achieved complete detachment from the little everyday worries that used to irritate him so much before. They were watching his "spiritual acceleration" [before takeoff]. Knowing that death was coming, and conscious of his state, he had given and abandoned himself completely to Providence. To a friend he confided: "I have fought the fight, now I am preparing to see the Good Lord."

He celebrated his Easter by recapitulating all the work that he had accomplished for the littlest ones. His simplicity and confidence overwhelmed his friends. "He is a man of God",[22] one of his visitors thought as he left him.

On Good Friday and Holy Saturday, Jérôme asked to receive in particular visits from each of his children and from Birthe. Then he saw his brothers, Philippe and Rémy. On Saturday at 10:00, Thomas and Isabelle came back to visit him. They plainly had important news

[19] David, letter to J. Lejeune, March 20, 1994.

[20] *Symphonie de la Vie* (Fondation Lejeune, 2000), 53.

[21] Poem written by Jérôme Lejeune several days before his death.

[22] Conversation of the author with that friend of Jérôme, whose name we will withhold out of discretion.

to give him. Jérôme was very weak but listened. The evening before, his daughter-in-law had said to Thomas, "I feel something bizarre; I want to be clear in my own mind about it."

At that time, pregnancy tests had to be done fasting.... At 4:00 A.M., she woke up and did the test. They discovered that she was pregnant with their first child. Immediately they decided to go see Jérôme again so as to be the first to announce it to him. When Thomas leaned toward Jérôme and told him, "Papa, you are going to be a grandfather for the twentieth time", Jérôme was so happy that he choked for joy. To the point where Thomas and Isabelle were worried. Then his respiration stabilized, and, in a whisper, he said to them, "This is a gift from God, a buckle that is being clinched."

His youngest child had come to tell him that he would be a grandfather for the twentieth time. He was happy. When Isabelle asked him whether they could announce it to the others, without fear of it being too early, Jérôme replied, "When it is a joy like that, go ahead, don't hesitate!"[23]

With two other mothers in the family expecting, Karin and Clara, life went on. On Saturday evening, it became more and more difficult for him to breathe. Birthe wanted to stay with him, but Jérôme energetically refused. At four o'clock in the morning, his agony began. The physician attending him wanted to alert the family. Jérôme refused. He had seen his father suffocate and wanted to spare his family that. In a final whisper, before being snuffed out, he told the physician, "You see, I did right."

At 6:30 in the morning, his daughter Karin "woke up in tears, bizarre tears of joy".[24] The telephone rang ten minutes later. She said to herself, "Thank you, Lord; I'm ready!" It was Easter morning. The first bells of the Resurrection rang in the morning light. They all left for the clinic. When they arrived at the place where Jérôme was resting, they crossed paths with the priest who was bringing him Easter Communion. Birthe was the one who received the Host that was intended for him. A strong, strange peace settled over the family. His body was brought back to the house on rue Galande, and the chapel for the wake was set up in his room.

[23] Conversation of the author with Thomas and Isabelle Lejeune.

[24] Conversation of the author with Karin Le Méné.

Jean Foyer, a faithful friend, called Birthe: "What is going on? I saw the pope on television this morning. He was sad. You could see it on his face. I thought that something had happened to Jérôme."

In fact, the Holy Father, who had sent Jérôme an affectionate telegram and best wishes for recuperation the evening before, had learned of his death from his family early that morning. The next day, he sent to Cardinal Lustiger a letter expressing his extreme sorrow and his admiration for his "brother Jérôme":

> If the Father who is in heaven called him from this earth on the very day of Christ's Resurrection, it is difficult not to see in this coincidence a sign.[25]

Friends, alerted by radio or telephone, began to line up to pay their respects. Birthe was brave and welcomed them. In the afternoon, a Lebanese restaurant owner, whose tables were set out on the sidewalk fronting the house, rang the doorbell. After offering his condolences, he inquired, "Madame, do you have some way of serving dinner to everyone this evening?"

For the first time in her life, Birthe had not thought about that at all.

"Don't worry!" the visitor replied.

And a few moments later, accompanied by his servers, he came back, arms loaded with *mezze* [party platters] for the whole family and the numerous friends. They all kept Birthe company.

Three days later, on April 6, despite the belated announcement in the press, a dense, recollected crowd gathered in Notre-Dame Cathedral in Paris. An hour before the funeral, the chairs set up in the nave were no longer enough. Government officials and academics, friends and handicapped persons mingled familiarly for a final homage. Then-Auxiliary Bishop Vingt-Trois presided over the funeral ceremonies, which were concelebrated by many priests with fervent prayer. Father Guérin, superior of the Saint Martin Community, gave the homily. The apostolic nuncio read the farewell message. Two dear friends, the government minister Jean Foyer and the academician Pierre Chaunu, paid their homage to the deceased. The words pronounced by Pierre Chaunu were fraught with emotion:

[25] John Paul II, letter to Cardinal Lustiger, April 4, 1994.

> Hope, faith, and charity were inscribed on the forehead of this immensely learned scientist, the physician, the Christian doctor of the most destitute, who are also the closest to God; of this friend like few others, the friend of all the wounded beside the road from Jerusalem to Jericho, the Samaritan who meets Almighty God, begging his help for this gasping, wounded man...; of this friend, the saint who has gone before us.[26]

The crowd was suddenly overwhelmed by Bruno, a young trisomic man who, following a heartfelt impulse, made the vaults of Notre-Dame resound with these impromptu words:

> Thank you, Professor Lejeune, for what you did for my father and my mother. Your death healed me. Thanks to you, I am proud of myself.

Thank you. That was the message that so many patients, families, physicians, researchers, pro-life advocates, and friends throughout the world had in their heart. It was also the last thing that Jérôme wrote in his journal: *Deo gratias.*

In the fervor of that Mass, the faithful shared a hope stronger than their sadness. Their eyes were drawn by the striking *Pietà* set up at the foot of the immense gilded cross of the main altar. The open arms of the Mother of the Living, contemplating her Son who has been killed by men, proclaim offering and resurrection in that extraordinary sorrowful gesture. Life is stronger than death. The family gently understood that Jérôme's work went beyond them. It could not stop. "The patients are waiting." It was only beginning. *Deo juvante!* [With the help of God!]

"I am the resurrection and the life; he who believes in me, though he die, yet shall he live" (Jn 11:25).

[26] P. Chaunu, *Hommage à Jérôme Lejeune*, April 6, 1994.

EPILOGUE

When Jérôme died, many families of his patients were anxious: "Who will follow him with his competence and kindness?" "To whom shall we go?" To respond to these expectations, Birthe, her children, her son-in-law Jean-Marie Le Méné, and Marie-Odile Rethoré quickly decided to continue Jérôme's work. First, they created the Fondation Lejeune, dedicated to care, research, and the defense of the dignity of mentally handicapped persons, with Jean-Marie Le Méné as president and Birthe Lejeune as vice president, then a medical center that would become the Jérôme Lejeune Institute. Karin and Jean-Marie Le Méné personally called physicians, former coworkers of Jérôme, to ask them for assistance. Thus, in September 1997, the Institut Jérôme Lejeune opened its first medical consultation office with three of them on staff: Professor Marie-Odile Rethoré, Doctor Aimé Ravel, and Doctor Clotilde Mircher. Approved by the French Ministry of Health in 1998, the institute is today the foremost European medical center specializing in the care of patients who have trisomy 21 or other intellectual disabilities of genetic origin. It welcomes ten thousand patients for consultations.[1] The foundation, besides the support that it gives to the institute, is the leading provider of funding in France for research on trisomy 21. Since 1996, it has financed seven hundred research programs throughout the world. Finally, like Jérôme Lejeune, it pursues the courageous mission of being "the advocate of the voiceless".

The cause for the beatification and canonization of the Servant of God Jérôme Lejeune was initiated on June 28, 2007, in Paris, at the request of the local ordinary, then-Archbishop André Vingt-Trois. The archbishop thus responded to many letters from physicians,

[1] For information about the medical consultation offices, visit: www.institutlejeune.org, and concerning research and patient advocacy: www.fondationlejeune.org. [Both websites are in French. See also the website of the Jerome Lejeune Foundation USA: https://lejeune foundation.org.]

families, pro-life advocates, both in France and abroad, to obtain the canonization of Jérôme Lejeune: on the very day of his death, a petition had been signed in Latin America and sent to the Vatican making this request. Similarly, Fiorenzo Cardinal Angelini, president of the Pontifical Council for Pastoral Assistance to Health Care Workers, officially asked for this cause to be initiated, as well as Elio Cardinal Sgreccia and the International Federation of Catholic Physicians. Since then, the reputation for sanctity of the Servant of God Jérôme Lejeune has never ceased to grow throughout the world: testimonies[2] concerning private veneration and graces received are sent to the postulator in France, coming from many countries, especially the United States, Canada, Argentina, Brazil, Chile, Italy, Portugal, and Spain.

The cause of canonization is sponsored by the association of the Friends of Professor Lejeune. The diocesan inquest opened in 2007, with Father Jean-Charles Nault, abbot of the Benedictine Abbey of Saint-Wandrille as postulator, and ended at Notre-Dame Cathedral in Paris on April 11, 2012, in the presence of 1,500 persons. The study of his cause continues now in Rome, with Aude Dugast as postulator.

[2] Some of these testimonies are available [in French] at the website of the association of the Friends of Professor Jérôme Lejeune: www.amislejeune.org.

AFTERWORD

by Birthe Lejeune

So many years have passed since my husband, Jérôme, left us. So many years since we last met. The love that we shared with our five children had no equal for Jérôme except for his passion for his little patients and his devotion to their service. I have kept all these memories, these faces, these events imprinted on my memory as though they happened yesterday. But these memories are of no interest except to shed light on the present and to build the future. I do not like to turn back toward the past, and that is one reason why I do not like to read books written about my husband.

I admit, therefore, that on the day when Aude Dugast asked me to be so kind as to read over this important biography on Jérôme, I hesitated somewhat. Out of friendship for her, I did. But very quickly this duty for friendship's sake became a pleasure. One evening, I opened her manuscript, and even though I can be overtaken by sleep very easily, I devoured each page, without being able to stop, until the middle of the night. For the first time in my life, at the age of more than ninety, I read until two o'clock in the morning. I was very moved. I recognized so many events and persons that were part of our life! And I even discovered some that were unknown to me but that Aude Dugast had been able to find among the countless documents in the archives and thanks to her many meetings with those who were close to Jérôme, whether they are patients, physicians, or friends. I am thinking in particular about the journal of Jérôme's father, which I had never read; it tells us a lot about his childhood. Or the letters from his scientist correspondents, whom Jérôme welcomed to his laboratory and which I am just discovering today. Even the letters about finances that I never read over, excerpts from which the author presents tactfully. It is a masterpiece of references.

Aude Dugast was never acquainted with Jérôme, and yet I am astonished to see how faithful what she writes in his biography is to the life and spirit of my husband. Not only is her choice of the many quotations and texts by Jérôme very judicious and indicative of his work, but also the dialogues that she imagines between us are sometimes quite close to the reality. Jérôme is present in this book. These pages reveal that Aude Dugast has understood his mind, in depth. And she relates his story with heart.

Birthe Lejeune
[signature, dated February 14, 2019]

# ACKNOWLEDGMENTS

Allow me to express here my gratitude to all those who assisted me in this work.

To Madame Jérôme Lejeune, for her great confidence and the extraordinary simplicity with which she opened up to me her archives and her memory and for the friendly patience with which she answered my questions for several years.

To Philippe Lejeune, for our conversations in his studio about his dear brother. To Anouk and Jean-Marie Meyer, Damien Lejeune, Karin Le Méné, Clara and Hervé Gaymard, and Thomas and Isabelle Lejeune, for the memories that they confided to me and for their kind consideration of my works about their father and father-in-law. To Jean-Marie Le Méné, for our long discussions based on his many exchanges with his father-in-law.

To the friends, coworkers, and patients of Jérôme Lejeune who provided me with their personal memories, which were always valuable and sometimes moving. Fear of omitting some of them prevents me from making a list, but their names are cited in these pages.

To Father Jean-Charles Nault, Abbot of Saint-Wandrille, for his very reliable advice, his altogether Benedictine efficiency, and his enthusiasm. To Françoise Raguet, for her multifaceted help, her constant availability, and her multiple talents. To Bruno Galland, Lydwine Scordia, Gwendaël Poret, Anne de Nucé, Claude Harel, Françoise Chataignon, and Bénédicte Leblanc, who by their wonderful work on the archives made it possible for me to present in this book so many unpublished documents.

To Father Daniel Ols, Mayté Varaut, Geoffroy de Langalerie, Isabelle Muller, Charles-Henri d'Andigné, and Bruno Calabrese, for their sensible advice.

To my family and friends, for their kind encouragement.

To my parents, who by their example made Jérôme Lejeune so familiar to me.

BIBLIOGRAPHY

Bernet, Anne. *Jérôme Lejeune, biographie.* Paris: Presses de la Renaissance, 2004.

Colombo, Roberto. *Il messaggio della vita.* Siena: Edizioni Cantagalli, 2002.

Dugast, Aude. *Prier 15 jours avec Jérôme Lejeune.* Bruyères-le-Châtel: Nouvelle Cité, 2015.

Evrard, Gaëtan, and Dominique Bar. *Jérôme Lejeune, Serviteur de la vie* (graphic novel). Paris: Éditions du Triomphe, 2018.

Lejeune, Jérôme. *The Concentration Can: When Does Human Life Begin? An Eminent Geneticist Testifies.* San Francisco: Ignatius Press, 1990.

Lejeune-Gaymard, Clara. *La Vie est un bonheur: Jérôme Lejeune, mon père.* Criterion, 1997; English edition: *Life Is a Blessing: A Biography of Jérôme Lejeune: Geneticist, Doctor, Father.* Translated by Michael J. Miller. San Francisco: Ignatius Press, 2000; reprinted, Philadelphia: National Catholic Bioethics Center, 2011.

Le Méné, Jean-Marie. *Le Professeur Lejeune, Fondateur de la génétique moderne.* Paris: Mame, 1997.

Siorac, Céline. *Embryon mon amour, Jérôme Lejeune à Maryville.* Paris: E-dite, 2004.

Vial Correa, Juan de Dios, and Ghislaine Morizon. "El profesor Jérôme Lejeune, gran defensor y apóstol de la vida", *Educaciòn Medica,* 1994.

INDEX